ENCYCLOPEDIA OF Natural History

Consultant Editor
Joyce Pope

Foreword by
Gerald Durrell

Galley Press

Contents

8 About This Book

9 Foreword

10 The Story of the Earth

The world in space – Earth structure – igneous, sedimentary and metamorphic rocks – erosion and deposition – dating the Earth – fossils – early life – the evolution of man

40 The Pattern of Life

Living things – genetics – classifying plants and animals – famous biologists – Darwin and Wallace and the theory of evolution – ecology – parasites – plant and animal populations – habitats

84 **The World of Plants**

Bacteria – algae – mosses and liverworts – lichens – fungi – ferns – cone-bearing plants – flowering plants – plant structure – monocotyledons – dicotyledons – carnivorous plants – poisonous plants – specialised plants – plant communities

132 **The World of Animals**

Protozoa – simple water animals – worms – moss animals – molluscs – starfishes – arthropods – crustaceans – arachnids – insects – fish – amphibians – reptiles – birds – mammals

230 **Living Things and Man**

Domestication of animals – cultivation of plants – folklore and religion – rare plants and animals – conservation

242 **Glossary**

244 **Index**

About This Book

This book presents a comprehensive view of the Earth and all its living things, the subject generally known by the title of 'natural history'. Here, the whole of the natural world is brought together, because it is only by understanding all the parts that we can appreciate how and why each one fits into the total scheme.

Written and designed to be used by readers of all ages and interests, this book can be enjoyed read as a whole or, as most people will probably want to, as a book in which you can look up a specific point when the information is required. For this reason, it presents each subject spread by spread, so that wherever you open it you will find the information on any two facing pages complete in itself. Some details, therefore, are repeated from time to time, so that each two-page feature is self-explanatory. For ease of reading and comprehension, many of the technical terms are defined where they occur, as well as in the glossary which you will find at the back of the book.

Younger readers will probably find it most entertaining to begin with the pages describing the various habitats of plants and animals (pages 58–83), while others requiring more details about specific plants and animals will naturally turn to the sections on those subjects.

The scientific names for a great many of the subjects are described throughout the encyclopedia, in order to identify many of them precisely and, indeed some have no popular names. However, for some of the most familiar animals, particularly the mammals, the compilers have not felt it necessary to include this information. All the most interesting and important plants and animals are described and feature among the hundreds of magnificent colour illustrations and photographs for additional identification and enjoyment.

Contributors
Philip Burton   Robert Burton
Jean Cooke   Dr Paul Cornelius
Dr Colin Curds   Joy Etherington
Dr Anthony Fincham   Howard Ginn
Ray Ingle   David Irvine
Ellis Owen   Joyce Pope   Robert Pope
John Rostron   Theodore Rowland-Entwistle
John Stidworthy   Christopher Stringer
Kathie Way   Alwyn Wheeler

First published in Great Britain in 1978 by The Octopus Publishing Group under the title *St Michael Encyclopedia of Natural History*

Published in 1988 by Galley Press, an imprint of W H Smith Limited
Registered No 237811 England
Trading as W H Smith Distributors
St John's House,
East Street,
Leicester
LE1 6NE

ISBN 0 86136 038 9

Printed in Czechoslovakia

50419/3

Foreword

When I was young, I was brought up on the Greek island of Corfu, where I was lucky enough to be surrounded by people who shared and encouraged my interest in natural history. This meant I could keep a whole range of animals as pets and study them – animals ranging from scorpions to sea horses, from eagle owls to earwigs.

However, my great problem was that I did not have a good, easy reference work which told me about the habits of these creatures that interested me. This is why it gives me such pleasure to introduce this invaluable encyclopedia which is just the book that I dreamed of having when I was a boy, but never possessed.

I think most people are interested in animals and it is most important to know about the other living things that inhabit this planet with us and on whom we rely directly or indirectly. To me, the world we live in is such a fascinating place that I feel it would require a dozen lifetimes to even begin to understand and appreciate it. Recently I was on the island of Mauritius in the Indian Ocean and there they are fortunate in having a fabulous coral reef on which I went snorkeling every day. Within a twenty-foot radius, I saw so many forms of life that I became bewildered. The number of fish and other creatures were prodigious and you realised that, without a reference book, you were lost. That is why I think this encyclopedia is of great importance for it opens up the world of nature to us, helps us to be more aware of the fascinating and beautiful world that we share with plants and other animals and, by stimulating our interest, helps us to realise the necessity of saving and protecting the world we live in.

This, then, is a very worthwhile book and I hope that through it more people will learn about the entrancing and intricate world that we are lucky enough to live in.

The Story of the Earth

All life as we know it comes from the Earth, and has adapted over many millions of years to the changing conditions found on our planet.

For this reason, it is necessary to understand the structure of the Earth and the way it has changed during its 4,600 million years of existence before we can fully comprehend why the plants and animals of today are as they are.

It is only in this way that we can find out – for example – why Alaska, a land of snow and ice, has deposits of coal formed from tropical forests, or why some mountains are steep and craggy, while others are comparatively smooth and rounded.

This, the first section of the book, describes the Earth and its relationship to the rest of the Solar System, the rocks of which it is made, and the many processes such as erosion which have shaped its present surface. We then consider how life came into existence, and the fossils in the rocks which have preserved for us a record of plants and animals of the past. Finally, we see how life evolved, through the age of the amazing giant reptiles, the dinosaurs, to the present age of mammals and the evolution of man.

Today life is everywhere – grasses can grow even among the cinders on the rim of a volcano.

The World in Space

When we gaze into the sky on a dark cloudless night, most of us do so with a certain amount of awe or wonderment.

Suspended within this vast area, which we call space, are thousands of millions of stars, planets and other tiny solid particles grouped together in countless numbers. These massive collections are called *galaxies*, from the Greek word for milk.

Within most galaxies are systems of planets revolving around a central star to which they are attracted by gravitational pull. Our own Earth is one of nine planets within such a system revolving around a central star, the mass of blazing gases we call the Sun. The system is named the Solar System, from *Sol*, Latin for the Sun.

Some astronomers believe that the numerous galaxies within the universe were at one time part of a more concentrated mass which exploded about ten thousand million years ago, and that all we are now seeing are the particles of this enormous explosion moving further away from us into outer space.

With the latest radio telescopic equipment, they have been able to record just the faintest whisper of the echo of this Big Bang which has been travelling through space for all that long time.

What of the origin of the planets in our own Solar System? Many theories have been advanced. It is possible that the planets were part of the 'Big Bang' and that they remained a mass of hot gases until they cooled enough to solidify.

Another theory is perhaps more acceptable. Many particles which float around in space are inorganic mineral substances which have a molecular attraction for one another. Gradually, in this way, a whole mass of such particles built up into globes the size of Earth and other planets. When the collective mass of warm molecules cooled, crystallisation of the minerals occurred and the basic rock structure of the planets was formed.

What is known for certain is that Earth was at one time a molten mass of rock, and that many millions of years elapsed during which a gradual cooling-down of the mineralised rock resulted in some of the heavier masses sinking into the centre of the Earth, while the lighter ones remained on the surface, forming a crust.

Surrounding the planets in space are

Above: *Our planet Earth is 148·6 million kilometres (92·9 million miles) from the sun. It travels round the sun in an elliptical orbit which takes $365\frac{1}{4}$ days to complete the 960 million-kilometre (600 million-mile) journey. The centre of the Moon is on average 384,400 kilometres (about 238,900 miles) from the centre of the Earth; the Moon circles the Earth once in $27\frac{1}{3}$ days, which means that during each year-long orbit of the Earth round the Sun the Moon circles the Earth 13 times. The Moon is only $\frac{1}{80}$ the mass of the Earth, but it influences the Earth's orbit round the Sun, making it wobble by about 9,600 kilometres (6,000 miles).*

layers of gases. Earth's own layers are composed largely of a mixture of nitrogen, oxygen, argon and carbon dioxide, with some hydrogen and other rarer gases. These gases remain close to the Earth's surface, providing a sort of capsule in space with the planet in the middle. The heavier gases tend to concentrate in the lower layers, while the lighter gases are in the top layers. The capsule is called the atmosphere of the planet.

During the long cooling-down process of the Earth, hydrogen and oxygen were given off into the atmosphere in the form of water-vapour. In time this vapour cooled and condensed to water, eventually forming the oceans.

Although other planets have gaseous atmospheres surrounding them, it seems certain that no other planet within the Solar System has the same sort of atmosphere as our own. We also think that the planet Earth is the only planet with oceans of water, although other planets may have some water-vapour around them, and possibly ice-caps at the polar regions. Mars certainly has both ice and water-vapour.

Today when we hear of satellites we immediately think of man-made objects rocketed into space. Many of the planets within our Solar System, however, have their own satellites, which are smaller planets revolving round them and keeping within the gravitational field of the mother planet.

We call these satellites moons because Moon is the name we have given our own satellite. Some planets have more than one moon; Jupiter, the largest has 14.

Although we know very little about the moons of other planets, we are fortunate these days in knowing quite a lot about our own. One of the greatest achievements of this century was the act of sending men to the Moon. The footsteps of the first man to land on the surface of the Moon are still preserved in the light, dusty, windless surface of the satellite.

From samples of that very same dust, and other rock samples brought back subsequently, scientists have been able to learn a great deal. We now know, for instance, that the lunar rocks, though igneous in origin like many of those of Earth, contain different proportions of minerals. The very high proportion of titanium alone suggests that the Moon has never been part of our own planet, as some scientists had previously believed, but was formed separately and has been trapped in Earth's gravitational field.

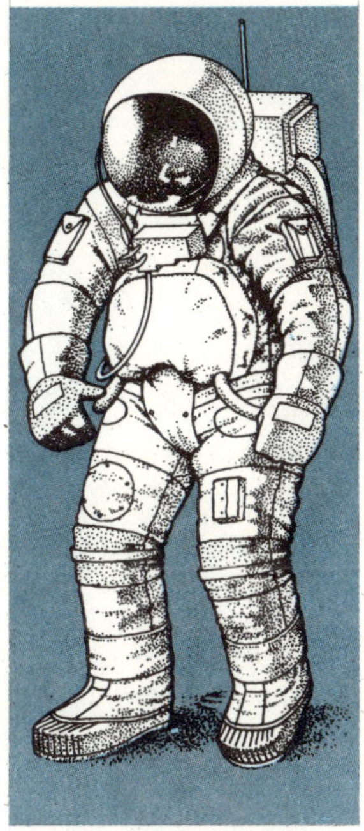

Above: *After thousands of years of mystery, and hundreds of years of careful observation from the Earth, man set foot on the moon on 21 July 1969.*

We also know for certain that the gases which surround the Moon could not support the sort of life that has evolved on Earth, and there is no evidence that any form of life, either in the form of germs or other organic matter, ever existed on the Moon.

The Moon takes about twenty-seven days to complete its orbit or pathway around Earth. We can see part of it as it comes towards our part of the world, and correspondingly less of its surface as it moves away from us. We can see it during the hours of darkness because the rays of the Sun are reflected from its surface, but in daylight the sky is too bright for the Moon to be more than faintly visible at best.

Above: *Our solar system is only a small component of a vast system of stars which rotate in a lens-shaped mass called a galaxy. We are about 20,000 light years from the centre of our own galaxy. The Universe is thought to contain more than 1,000 million galaxies, one of which, the Great Nebula, or Andromeda Galaxy, can be seen in this photograph taken by satellite. The gravitational attraction of the dense central mass exactly counters the tendency of the outer suns to leave the galaxy. There has recently been much debate about the origin of the Universe, based on the apparent movement apart of galaxies.*

The Moon performs one very important function which affects life on Earth. It causes the tides, because the Moon's gravitational pull draws the seas towards it at whatever point it is opposite.

In the time that the Earth has completed its own journey round the Sun – a year – the Moon has made 13 such journeys round the Earth. The Moon's journeys provided a very convenient and obvious way for the early classical observers to divide the year. We call these divisions lunar months.

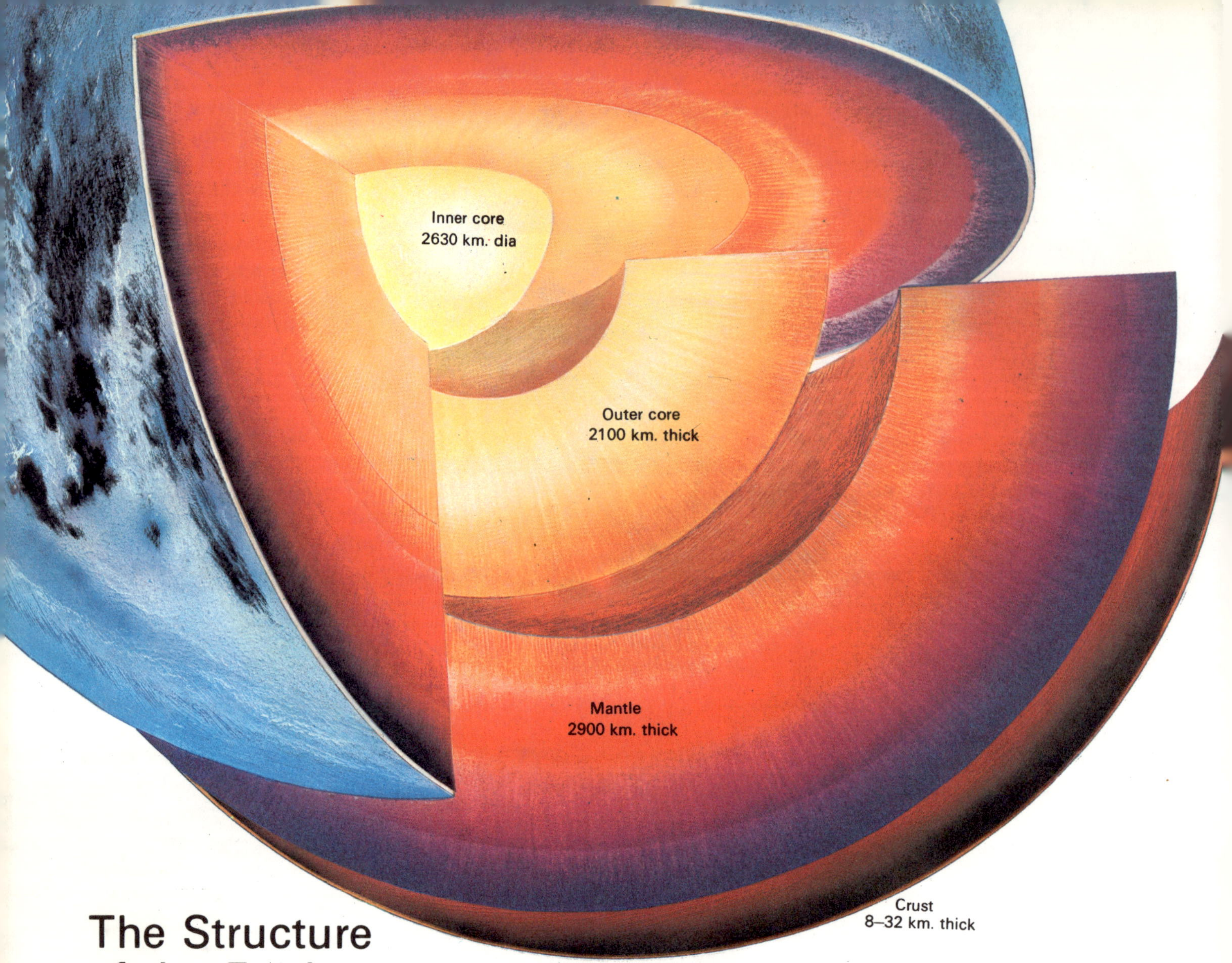

The Structure of the Earth

Experiments show that the Earth has a dense *inner core* some 2,630 kilometres (1,630 miles) in diameter, surrounded by an *outer core* estimated at 2,100 kilometres (1,300 miles) in thickness. This is enclosed within the 2,900 kilometre (1,800 mile) thick *mantle*, consisting of four distinct layers of hard basaltic rock.

The inner core, to judge by the way it transmits earthquake waves, is in a solid state, the result of the enormous pressures which crush together the very structure of the atoms of which it is composed. It is also very hot – possibly as much as 5,000°C (9,000°F). The outer core is molten, and becomes gradually less hot until at the junction with the mantle it is about 2,200°C (4,000°F). The mantle, which is solid rock, also becomes gradually less hot until it reaches a temperature of about 870°C (1,600°F) where it meets the *crust*, the Earth's thin outer layer.

The crust of the Earth, which is between 8 kilometres (5 miles) and 32 kilometres (20 miles) thick, is composed largely of granitic rock that is less dense, or of a lighter consistency, than the basaltic mantle on which it rests. This allows the lighter crust to, so to speak, 'float' or have some degree of mobility.

The mobility of the Earth's crust has been the subject of a great deal of discussion in the past. It occurred to some early geologists that the present shape of the continents suggested that they might, at one time, have fitted closer together as one central land mass.

It was not until the German meteorologist Alfred Wegener published his theory of continental drift – that is,

Above: *The crust of the Earth is a comparatively thin skin of hardened rock on the surface of a very hot ball. The centre is hottest (inner core), and is surrounded by an area of molten rock (outer core) which gradually gives way to the cooler area of the mantle. The mantle is red hot under the crust. If we imagine the Earth taken apart like an onion, it might look like this. The inner core probably solid and very dense; the outer core is thought to be molten, while the mantle is more or less solid. Geophysicists have deduced all this from the way in which earthquake waves pass through the different layers; by using very sensitive equipment they can compare the wave patterns in the mantle with those passing through the core.*

Left: *The Earth from space. It reflects sunlight just as the moon does; a man standing on the Earth side of the moon would be able to see by Earthlight during the moon's night. The white swirling masses that can be seen are cloud patterns; meteorologists study these patterns by using satellites in orbit round the Earth.*

that the continents have changed position – in 1912 that any real scientific controversy was stimulated. Almost immediately two distinct camps of opinion emerged; the 'Drifters' and the 'Non-Drifters'. Wegener suggested there was originally just one land mass, which he called Pangaea (Greek for 'all Earth'), which broke up at the end of the Permian times about 200 million years ago. Its fragments drifted into the positions which they now occupy. Although opinions still differ as to how and when this splitting occurred, most geologists now agree with a modified version of Wegener's ideas.

As it happens, there is much to be found on the bottom of the great oceans of the world which supports Wegener's ideas. Extensive submarine mountain ranges have been discovered. These mid-oceanic ridges are accompanied by trenches, some of which run along the crests of the ridges. From time to time massive volcanic activity occurs along these trenches and the huge lava flows which are formed gradually push the sides of the trenches further apart, causing the ocean floor to spread.

Below: *Volcanic activity is one of the many ways in which the surface of the Earth can change shape. Where there is a thin spot or a crack or fault in the crust, molten rock may be forced upwards through the crust from the hotter layers beneath. As well as molten rock (called lava), a volcano may eject gases and large amounts of very fine dust. The type of volcano shown here is fairly simple. Dykes and sills may wind their way through layers of rock without ever erupting at all, or may erupt a long way from the original fault.*

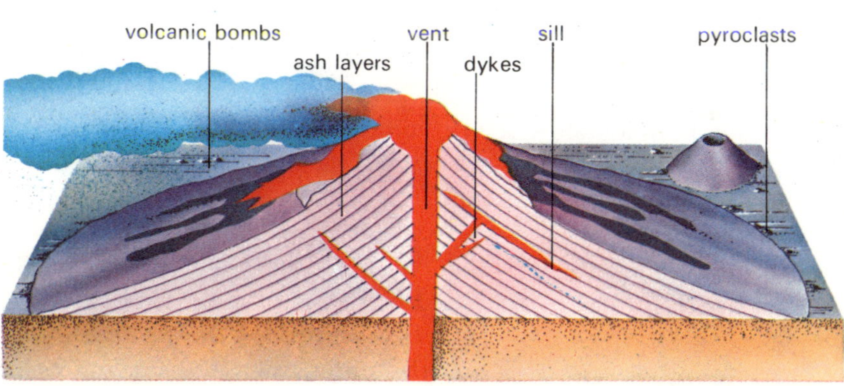

Obviously, as the floor of the ocean spreads, the continents must also move.

There are six major areas where these activities can be traced. It appears that there are gigantic rafts or plates upon which the continents are situated and which are moved by submarine volcanic and other deep crust activity. In a similar way, the plates slide under one another and are absorbed back into the crust.

This movement of the continental plates also has a continuous effect upon the shape and geography of the continents. When these vast plates move very slowly towards each other they may compress areas of softer rocks into folds which form as mountain ranges.

Although many of the great mountain ranges of the world, such as the Alps, the Harz Mountains and the Scottish Highlands in Europe, the Andes in South America, and part of the Rocky Mountains in North America, were built in this way, it is by no means the only way in which mountains are formed. The forces of erosion – wind, rain rivers and glaciers – can produce major differences in the balance of land areas.

Block-faulting can result from such erosional action and is said, in many cases, to indicate a change in *isostatic equilibrium*. This simply means that some areas of either ocean floor or continent become loaded with the sediment which is forever being deposited by rivers in their valleys or on the sea bed. Under the weight these areas tend to sink very gradually. At the same time, a corresponding area of land or sea bed rises. The massive wedges of rock which are thrown up are eventually eroded into mountain peaks. Typical examples of block-fault mountains occurring in North America are the Sierra Nevada and the Teton Range.

Another way in which mountains are formed is by volcanic action. When a volcano erupts on land it very often produces quantities of lava and ash, which build up around the centre of eruption into a gigantic cone.

Whole groups of islands have been produced by underwater volcanic action. The Virgin Islands in the West Indies have been formed in this way.

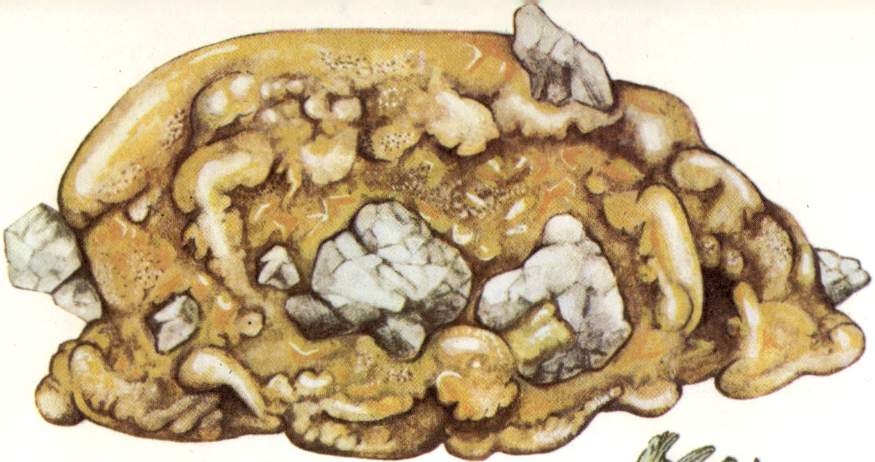

Below left: *Silver sometimes occurs in the leaf-like (arborescent) form shown here. It is used for making both ornamental and useful articles. Sterling silver is an alloy of silver and copper, harder and stronger than pure silver.*
Below: *Copper itself is a very soft metal, also found naturally in its metallic state, and is an excellent conductor of heat and electricity. It is also used in making the alloys brass and bronze.*

Top: *Gold is found throughout the world in association with quartz; this is a rounded mass of gold with quartz crystals. It is soft and easy to work, and has been used since ancient times to make precious ornaments.*
Above: *An Aztec knife which would have been for ritual use only, because gold is too soft to keep a cutting edge.*

Igneous rocks

All rocks are made up of minerals or basic elements, such as iron, copper, sulphur and oxygen. Some of these rocks may have been part of the original crust of the Earth, or may have been produced by subsequent volcanic action.

We call the rocks that have been formed from *magna* (molten liquids and gases inside the Earth) *igneous*, which comes from the Latin word for fire. They form both the oldest and the youngest of Earth's rock formations, and vary considerably in their composition. Some, such as basalt, are heavy and dense, forming massive blocks, or hexagonal columns or pillars like those of the Giant's Causeway in Northern Ireland. Others are lighter in weight, containing numerous bubbles of air, such as the pumice stone we use in our baths. However hard or soft these are, all igneous rocks are formed of crystals which have hardened in a higgledy-piggledy fashion like a three-dimensional jigsaw.

The most familiar igneous rocks are those which are produced by active volcanoes. In many parts of the world there are areas of more or less continuous volcanic eruption where, from time to time, volcanoes pour out their lava and belch forth their ash in clouds of smoke and steam. One of the best known areas is in the Pacific island of Hawaii, where the crater of Kilauea is a popular sight for tourists.

Not all volcanoes are as well behaved as Kilauea and many have caused terrible havoc. Occasionally the interior of the cone collapses, sealing the underground source of the lava which is called the 'magma chamber' of the volcano. Highly explosive gases build up under pressure in the magma chamber until they suddenly ignite, ripping the entire mountain apart.

Such an explosion did occur in 1902 on the Dominican island of Martinique in the West Indies where, in one terrifying minute, all but one out of the 28,000 people of the small port of Saint Pierre were killed by the explosion of Mont Pelée, situated just above the town.

A similar explosion occurred in 1883 when the entire uninhabited island of

Krakatoa, between Java and Sumatra in Indonesia blew its top in very much the same way as Mont Pelée, causing a tidal wave which killed 36,000 people on the shores of Java and Sumatra.

When molten rock cools slowly, some of the material of which it is made forms crystals, small amounts of hard rock which have a regular shape, with six, eight, twelve or more sides. Many crystals are valued for their beauty and hardness, as gemstones. The most valuable gemstones are diamond – the hardest natural substance – sapphire, emerald, and ruby. Fourteen other stones are commonly used as gems – beryl, chrysoberyl, feldspar, garnet, jade, lazurite, olivine, opal, quartz, spinel, topaz, tourmaline, turquoise, and zircon.

Each of these minerals has a characteristic crystal structure, as well as a distinctive colour by which it can be identified. It is through studying the varying amounts of these minerals within certain rocks and allowing for their different proportions that you can eventually recognise the rock type as a granite or an aplite, or a syenite, gabbro, pegmatite or diorite. You can distinguish these from rocks which have cooled in a different way, perhaps as lavas above ground. Rocks of this kind include the basalts, pumice, rhyolites and obsidian.

In addition to the many beautiful minerals within the rock itself, an igneous rock may also contain the metallic ores of rare and useful substances, such as gold, silver, copper, tin and zinc. Many ores are either a combination of minerals, or the oxides of the metals, which also show a series of characteristic shapes of crystallisation and form. Some, like malachite, one of the ores of copper, are renowned for their brilliant colours.

A knowledge of all these features will allow you to get some part of the way towards identifying a rock, but there is another important stage. You may know the colour of the particles you see and may even recognise their crystal structure but, as yet, you do not know whether they are hard or soft minerals. It is important to know this because their position on the scale of hardness, from 10 to 1, which was worked out in the early 1800s by the German mineralogist Friedrich Mohs, will allow you to place the rock sample into a category straight away. For instance, on Mohs' scale, diamond has a hardness of 10, corundum has a hardness of 9, topaz 8, and quartz 7. At the lower end of the scale calcite has a hardness of 3, gypsum 2, and talc 1.

By far the most important of the group of minerals which make up the igneous rocks is quartz. It is often abundant in rocks but may be difficult to recognise. It is usually almost clear and glassy, but may form the basic matrix of a rock specimen when it may be less easy to identify. Granite contains a large proportion of quartz with feldspar, biotite and mica which are fairly easy to recognise when the characteristics of each individual mineral have been studied.

Volcanic rocks are sometimes found within sedimentary or stratified layers some distance away from any known site of volcanic activity. When in their molten state, igneous or *plutonic* rocks (rocks formed deep beneath the Earth's surface) sometimes intrude or force their way along the bedding plane of already existing strata. These structures are known as *sills*. If similar intrusive spurs cross the horizontal layers and force their way to the surface, they are called *dykes*.

It may happen that a vast amount of intrusive rock is collected at one spot in the strata, forming a dome and forcing the overlying strata upwards. This phenomenon is known as a *laccolith*.

Top: *Malachite is a copper mineral found in veins, or as irregular lumps.* Above centre: *Garnet is a very hard mineral found frequently in igneous rocks.* Above: *Opal is a form of silica occurring in igneous rocks.*
Below: *The Scilly Isles are a series of granite hills, an outcrop from the sea bed, most of which is permanently submerged. The inhabited islands are the larger peaks of this outcrop. Here at Signal Rock, on St. Martin's Island, the raw granite of this igneous area can be seen.*

Secondary rocks

The two kinds of rocks which are not igneous may be termed secondary rocks, because they are formed by secondary processes. The two kinds are sedimentary and metamorphic rocks.

As the name implies, sedimentary rocks are made of *sediments* – that is, deposits of material which was at one time suspended in water or carried by ice or by wind. Unlike igneous rocks, sedimentary rocks were formed extremely slowly. They are the result of millions of years' work by the forces of erosion and the agency of rivers, lakes and oceans. A continuous cycle of breaking down pre-existing rock surfaces and redepositing the products of this action on the floors of lakes, in river beds and on the ocean bottom has produced hardened or cemented strata (layers), in which the particles are all sorted according to size.

The particles which make up sedimentary rocks vary considerably in nature, shape and size. Some deposits are coarse, sandy or gritty, containing large pebbles or large fragments of rock, while others are composed of minute dust-like particles or fine-grained crystals. Some sediments contain the fossilised remains of animals and plants.

One of the most important members of this group of rocks is sandstone, which constitutes more than 20 per cent. of all sedimentary rocks. If you take a close look at some of these deposits, you will see there are considerable differences between one sandstone and another. These differences include the sizes of the quartz grains which form the basis of the rock, the shape of the grains – those worn by wind are quite different in appearance from those worn by water – and also the way the grains are cemented together.

Some sandstones contain a mixture of large rounded pebbles set in a matrix or background of smaller grains. These sandstones are known as *conglomerates*.

Sedimentary rocks can be classified roughly into two main groups. Those which are very largely composed of fragments of other rocks are called *clastic*, and include the *arenaceous* or sandy deposits as well as the coarser conglomerates. Some *argillaceous* (clayey) rocks, such as mudstones and shales, are also included in this group.

The second group is the *non-clastic rocks* – the limestones, siliceous deposits, such as flint and chert, and carbonaceous rocks, such as peat, coal and asphalt. It also covers the sedimentary iron ores, residual deposits such as laterite, and *evaporites* which are represented by beds of gypsum and deposits of rock salt.

Perhaps the most interesting of the group is limestone. This can be deposited as a result of chemical precipitation of calcium carbonate which may, in some cases, be due to the secretion of calcareous material by aquatic animals and plants. Some limestones are composed almost entirely of the fragmentary remains of numerous shellfish, and are called shelly limestones. Similarly, chalk, which is a very pure limestone, consists partly of coccoliths, the calcareous skeletons of algal plants which were abundant in the Upper Cretaceous seas at the time

Below: *We are able to draw this diagram which represents the Grand Canyon, in North America, because weathering and the rapid Colorado River have, over 10 million years, gouged out this mile-deep scar in the Earth's crust. The successive layers of sandstone, limestone and shale were laid down over a period of 600 million years, during which warm seas receded and advanced over what was then a flat area. Some violent geological upheaval then raised the deep layers of sedimentary rock high above sea level. The Colorado River is now slowly wearing its way into the pre-Cambrian rocks at the bottom of the canyon. This is still some 800 metres (2600 feet) above sea level.*

when the chalk was deposited.

One of the finest-grained deposits is clay. This is usually a deep-water sediment and is composed of fine particles of crushed quartz, feldspar, and aluminium silicates (clay minerals). They have often been made from weathered and eroded granite, which is redeposited in this form.

Both sedimentary and igneous rocks may change in character as a result of some geological influence. This influence may be vast pressure, due to movement of the Earth's crust, or contact with hot volcanic rocks or other igneous material. When such influences occur, the original rock loses its former identity and emerges as a completely different type of rock with perhaps the same chemical composition. It is then known as a *metamorphic* rock, from a Greek word meaning a change of shape.

A very good example of the way in which pressure can change the character of sedimentary rock is shown by slate. Sometimes, as a result of regional uplift of underlying and overlying strata, sediments of the clay group are subjected to very high pressure by the bending and stretching of these beds. As a result, the clay layers are squeezed and consolidated, and become slate. Basically, the rock has not changed a great deal in its chemical composition. It still contains the mica and quartz of the original clay, and possibly other minerals as well.

Above: *The diagram on the opposite page is a cool interpretation of this breathtaking sight. This photograph of the Grand Canyon from the South Rim shows buttresses descending to the Colorado River below. The strata of the rocks show up clearly, each layer representing millions of years of sediment slowly settling on the bed of an ocean. The seas receded from time to time, returning again with a different composition of minerals and life forms to deposit a different sediment. This great slice out of the crust of the Earth reveals more than 500 million years of sedimentation. These do not necessarily represent a continuous sequence of deposition.*

Quartzites are metamorphosed forms of sandstones. Some are pure and white in colour, with a high proportion of quartz; others contain varying amounts of impurities or other minerals, which make them streaked or mottled.

Marble, which in some cases looks similar to quartzite, is formed when limestones come into contact with hot igneous rocks. When the original limestone is particularly pure or without additional minerals, then the change is by recrystallisation and as a result a highly interlocked mosaic of calcite crystals is formed. These rocks are found in large areas in Italy and are quarried for use in sculpture or as tombstones. The less pure marbles often have large veins of colourful and variegated patterns which, when polished, are extremely decorative; they are often used for ornamental objects, and for facing stones on buildings.

Until comparatively recently, all geologists thought that granites were igneous rocks which had cooled slowly to form the familiar grey and white and pinkish hard rocks that you often see polished as building stone. Now, some geologists believe that granite is a metamorphic rock, being the recrystallisation of an already existing mass.

Erosion and Deposition

The processes of erosion and deposition go together. The sedimentary rocks that have been so slowly built up over thousands of millions of years are themselves merely part of a gigantic cycle of building up, breaking down and consolidation.

The processes of erosion are as varied as the rocks they affect. Destruction may be mechanical, by the action of rivers, sea, wind or rain; or it may be by chemical action, involving the decomposition of rock by oxidation, hydration, carbonation and solution. Whatever the process may be, it affects igneous, sedimentary and metamorphic rocks.

The variety of rocks in both composition and hardness has already been discussed. Some, such as clays and shales, wear away fairly rapidly, while the basalts, gabbro and hard igneous and metamorphosed rocks take longer to destroy. Sometimes there are alternate layers of hard and softer rocks, and the softer layers are eroded, leaving the harder rocks exposed like steps or ledges.

One of the chief agents of mechanical erosion is the sea. The continuous restless movements of the oceans are constantly wearing away the coastlines. The pounding of storm waves undermines cliffs, which are broken up on the shore by a succession of tides. The products of such destruction may be transported then deposited further along the coast. Shingle spits and extensive beaches are the outcome of this type of erosion. An example of this process is seen in eastern England: in the northern parts of Norfolk and Suffolk the cliffs are fast disappearing, while further south huge sand and shingle banks have accumulated as a result of the southerly drift of the tides.

Above: *This granite arch at Quiberon in Brittany has been shaped by the action of wind and sea. The softer rocks were worn away first, and the ceaseless movement of the waves has continued to erode the hard granite. Erosion is, of course, a continuous process; it will continue as long as the Earth exists. A similar arch, in chalk, can be seen at Lulworth Cove in Dorset.*

The wind is also highly destructive. The abrasive power of loose particles of dust and sand, whipped up by strong air currents and storms, etches the surfaces of mountains, cliffs and hillsides, sometimes reducing them to sculptured pinnacles. The great columns of Bryce Canyon in Utah stand as monuments to a gigantic plateau carved and dissected by the winds and dissolved by the rains of millions of years.

Rivers are both constructive and destructive elements in this cycle of events. Over a period of many thousands of years, a river cuts through the rock surfaces of a plateau like a mechanical saw. In time it may meet a surface which is more resistant than the others, and the progress of erosion is slowed down. It may be that somewhere along the length of the river a geological fault has reduced one land level, causing a step which immediately becomes a waterfall. The resistant rock above may be overlying

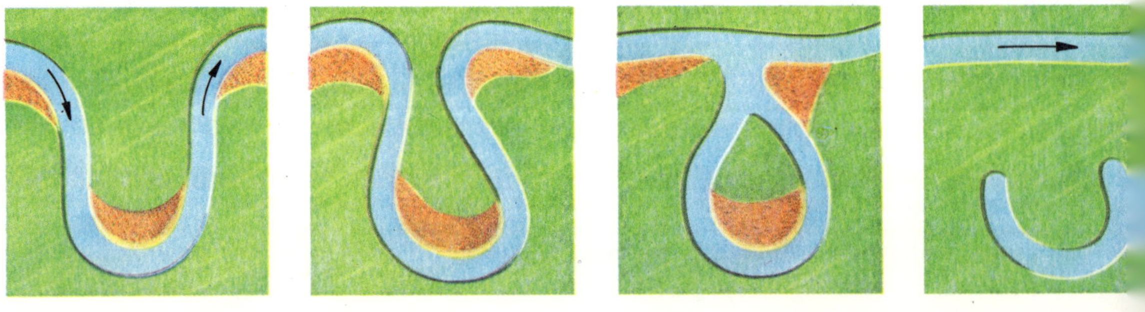

Right: *A river carries solid particles which tend to be deposited on the inside of bends. The stronger current on the outside of the bends wears away the banks. The bend thus becomes sharper. As the two sharp bends come together, the current will gradually break through between them, leaving an ox-bow lake.*

softer sediments, such as shales or clay. When this is the case, the thunderous volume of water cascading downwards dissolves the softer sediments and wears them away.

This undercutting occurs in a great many waterfalls but the most remarkable example must surely be the Niagara Falls, between Canada and the United States. This waterfall is one which, if left to its own devices, would eventually cut back upstream for some distance. Because of its beauty and sheer grandeur, man has not allowed Niagara to do this. Approximately one fifth of the water which would normally cascade down the falls has been diverted to another river, so that the progress of natural erosion has been halted, or at any rate retarded.

Rivers can also build land surfaces. The ever-increasing amount of silt and sand which accumulates at the mouth of a river may gradually build up large flat alluvial plains or delta country. The Mississippi River delta and the silty estuary of the Matanuska River in Alaska must be among the finest examples of this sort of river-building in existence.

When a river reaches old age or maturity, it sometimes develops *meanders*, semicircular curves along its course. As it gets steadily older it may even undercut its banks on the outside of each of the curves and, at the same time, deposit sand and silt along the inside of the curves. Two excellent examples are the Yellowstone River in Wyoming, and the River Gilpin in Cumbria, England.

Glaciers are also builders of land, as well as tools for destruction. The melt water from a glacier may cut down into a valley floor and carry away tons of eroded material, depositing it some considerable distance from the glacier itself. The melt water behaves in the same way as a fairly mature river. Sometimes these streams or temporary rivers find their way between the jointing planes of a massive limestone and, through continuous percolation, may hollow out vast caves stretching for miles. The potholes and caves of Derbyshire and Cheddar in England were created in this way, as were the celebrated grottoes of the Pyrenees in France.

The moraine, or débris which a glacier collects as it gouges its way across the land, is deposited at the sides of the glacial valley and in the centre of the glacier's path. A deposit at the end of a glacier is called a terminal moraine.

Ice, too, is an agent of erosion, but in a different way. When water enters the fine cracks and crevices on the surface of rocks it can penetrate some way into the rock itself. If this water freezes, it increases its volume by nine per cent. and consequently expands. The expansion prises up the edge of a cracked surface, or widens an already existing crack so that the rock splits into smaller fragments. Alternately freezing and thawing in this way can reduce large rocks to tiny particles.

The chemistry of rocks can bring about their own destruction. The natural weathering of a mineral may reduce it to a corrosive substance, such as acid, which then acts upon the surrounding rock, possibly dissolving part so that it is carried away in solution in rainwater.

Above: *Spectacular shapes can be created by dry erosion. As this rock's base continues to be worn by wind-blown sand, it will eventually topple.*

Below: *Glaciers are great levellers. During the Ice Age, when glaciers covered great areas of the Earth, sharp rocks were smoothed and mountains reduced to gentle hills under the current of slow-flowing ice. The ice also carried enormous pieces of loose rock along, which sometimes gouged long scars in the landscape before they were dropped great distances from their origin. Glaciers continue the process of erosion and deposition in mountainous areas, for these tremendously heavy sheets of solid water are constantly moving. To a geologist, every feature of a glacier has its name: 1 bed-rock; 2 transverse crevasse; 3 medial moraine; 4 ground moraine; 5 lateral moraine; 6 corrie; 7 tributary glacier; 8 corrie basin; 9 arête.*

Dating the Earth

It is extremely difficult to estimate the actual number of years which have passed since the Earth's crust cooled down. Even today, with all the resources of modern scientific methods, attempts to place a definite date on the origin of the Earth remain speculative.

For hundreds of years, and indeed through most of the 19th century, many people were firmly convinced that the views expressed in the Old Testament of the Bible were to be taken literally; therefore they found it impossible to accept scientific theories about the age of the Earth given by leading geologists.

Literal-minded followers of the Bible found it easier to believe the chronology devised – from Biblical evidence – by the Irish scholar James Ussher, Archbishop of Armagh (1581–1656). This chronology, still to be found in some Bibles, gave the date of creation as 4004 BC. Dr. John Lightfoot (1602–1675), another Biblical scholar, who became vice-chancellor of Cambridge University, actually determined that the Earth came into being '. . . on October 26th, 4004 BC, at 9 o'clock in the morning'.

Fortunately modern technology has provided more precise methods of dating rocks, the science of *geochronology*. These methods are based on calculating the amount of radioactivity emitted by certain elements contained within rocks. These elements emit radiation at a constant and measurable rate, changing gradually into other elements. The unit used for calculation is the half-life, that is, the time in which half the atoms of a radioactive substance decay and are transformed into atoms of other elements.

Below: *Radioactive dating is a useful technique which has been developed quite recently. It is based on the fact that a radioactive substance has a decaying rate which is precisely known. By measuring the amount of radioactivity in a fossil or rock, its age can be calculated. Uranium, which has a very long half-life, is used in dating the oldest rocks. In this diagram, the dark spots show the amount of uranium in three levels of rock, the oldest rock is at the bottom. The light spots are lead, which is what is left when uranium decays.*

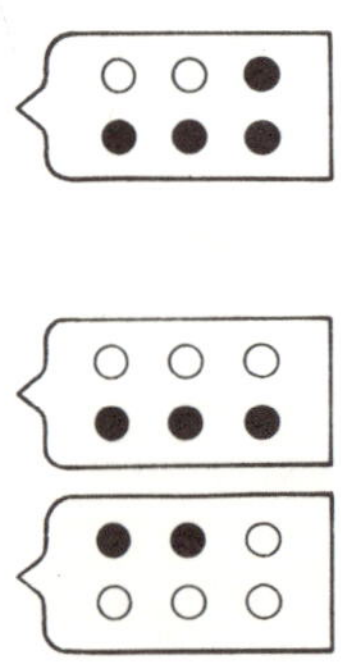

For example, uranium^{238} changes into lead^{206} with an estimated half-life of 4,500 million years. (The superscript numbers indicate particular isotopes of these two elements, isotopes being atoms of the same element which differ in atomic weight, or mass). Working with uranium^{238}, geophysicists have discovered that the oldest rocks found occur in West Greenland, and are probably 3,800 million years old. From this information, they have estimated the Earth's lifetime at something in excess of 4,600 million years.

Other methods are used for dating the Earth. It is obvious that in the Earth's crust, rocks found at lower layers are older than those nearer the surface. In many instances, each layer of rock contains characteristic fossils, which are found nowhere else. A study of strata has led to the science of stratigraphy, which allows comparative dating. A system has been worked out, based on assemblages of fossils, enabling geologists to know the age of any fossil as older than X, because it is found with species occurring only in strata

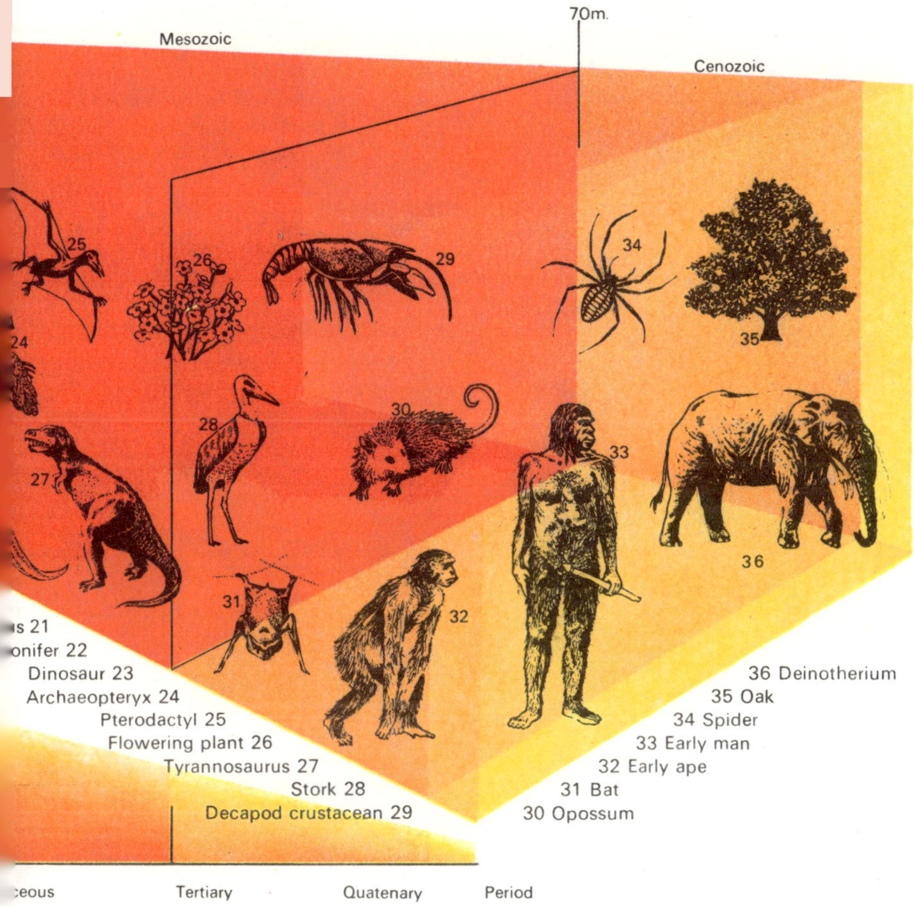

below those containing X, but younger than Y because it is found with species which only occur in strata above those containing Y. This is called 'comparative dating' and is the chief dating method used for sedimentary rocks.

The scale which most geologists are concerned with is one which starts some 600 million years ago in Cambrian rocks and ranges from that point in the geological column to present times. We call this the Phanerozoic scale, from the Greek *phaneros*, visible, and *zoos*, life. It includes all those rocks in the geological column which provide fossil evidence of life in the past.

The geological column starts much further back in time than 600 million years. It is divided into five major divisions or eras. The first era, from about 3,500 million years ago, is the Azoic, or era without life, for in these rocks no fossils are found. The second is called the Proterozoic era, or era of first life, which started about 3,000 million years ago. This is followed by the Palaeozoic, or era of ancient life, (the start of the Phanerozoic scale), the Mesozoic, the era of middle life, (225 million years ago), and the Cenozoic or era of new life (from 70 million years ago). The eras are defined by major changes in plant and animal life, perhaps caused largely by periods of great mountain-building activity, which caused considerable changes in habitats throughout the world.

Each era is broken down into periods, characterised by smaller groups of plants and animals, and the periods are usually named after the place where rocks of that age were first definitely studied – the Cambrian in Wales, for example.

In addition to the basic age of the rocks studied, the nature of each succeeding layer tells us a great deal more about the actual conditions in which they were laid down. For instance, in one part of a large continent there may be desert conditions, and in another a vast lake. Although the two deposits are registered as the same geological age, the life which existed within each environmental unit may be very different.

The differences are shown in the sort of deposits which go to make up the strata. Lake deposits probably contain fresh water fish remains and rounded silty deposits of fine sand. The desert sands are more angular, because they have been subjected to erosion from wind. They may even show signs of frost pitting, since some deserts alternate from very hot to very cold. A whole picture of conditions in geological times can be seen in this way.

Above: *This time-scale shows a succession of plants and animals from the Pre-Cambrian period 4,600 million years ago to the present. One thing that is immediately obvious is that the species with which we are now familiar have only existed during recent geological times.*
Below: *Beachy Head, Sussex, a chalk cliff which yields many flinty fossils.*

The Origin of Life

In the previous chapters we have been able to explain something about the origin of the Earth. We have discussed how the latest dating techniques can estimate the age of the planet. What we cannot do is to give any firm indication as to when life, in even the simplest form, began to develop. Nor can we tell in just what form life on Earth first appeared. The oldest fossils we have are those of comparatively well-developed animals.

Given all the facts regarding the fundamental ingredients of life, it is tempting to try to emulate nature and synthetise the beginning for ourselves.

In 1953 Dr. Stanley Miller of the University of Chicago, Illinois, conducted a series of experiments which were designed to illustrate that life could have started on this planet quite spontaneously.

Dr. Miller selected four gases which almost exactly matched the Earth's early atmosphere. He passed water vapour through a mixture of methane, ammonia and hydrogen, and then passed an electric charge through the mixture of vapour and gases, which caused it to *condense* (turn to liquid). He continued this process for several days. The liquids drained into a reservoir flask in the apparatus. After a week Dr. Miller examined the contents of the flask, and found it contained compounds of carbon, hydrogen, oxygen and nitrogen together with the basic elements of life itself, *aminoacids,* the units of which protein molecules are built.

Dr. Miller had proved that, chemically, these fundamental proteins could have been formed in an atmosphere of methane (CH_4), ammonia (NH_3), water vapour (H_2O) and hydrogen (H_2).

Previously other scientists had proved that proteins could exist without free oxygen, the gas normally considered essential to life – in other words, the primitive proteins which we have just discussed would be preserved in an atmosphere which contained no free oxygen. They would accumulate within the oceans.

There are, of course, many arguments against this idea, but it may be that the young Earth did contain an atmosphere which had no free oxygen. The oxygen could have been added to the atmosphere when plant life evolved.

If this theory holds true, the oceans

Below: *Water condensed out of the atmosphere of the cooling Earth to form the oceans. In the oceans, simple carbon-hydrogen and nitrogen-hydrogen compounds reacted to form larger molecules. Life began here.*

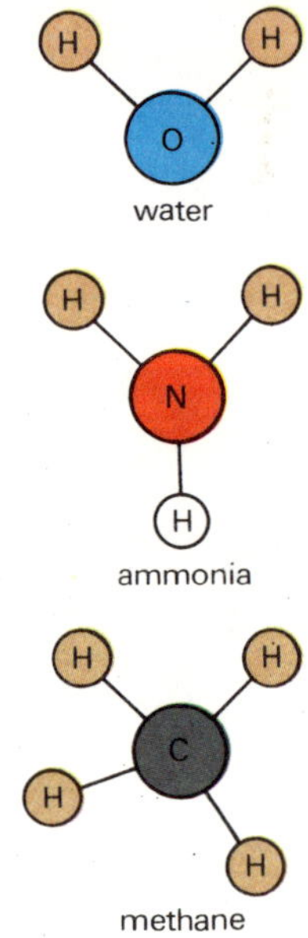

would have become a gigantic soup of aminoacid molecules. In time molecules of proteins of different sorts would touch one another and become entangled, so that a jelly-like network of protoplasm would evolve into a primitive cell.

Such a cell would have split into several parts, producing more cells. Some of these cells might have been very early sulphur bacteria, which probably have given rise to green plants with chlorophyll.

This is only a very simplified version of what might have happened. Many scientists believe that certain meteorites, originating from outer space, came into the Earth's atmosphere and landed on the surface of the planet. They brought with them tiny cellular structures of primitive single-celled plant life, and these contaminated or infected the surface of the Earth. The plants eventually turned into multicellular organisms which provided the basis for early forms of life.

In support of this theory, there are examples of meteorites containing what some scientists believe to be remains of very primitive fossilised plant life. A plant-like sponge sphere was found deeply embedded in a meteoritic particle which fell in Tanzania in 1936. Under high magnification it was seen as an almost spherical object with a band around its middle, and covered with short spines, rather like some species of algae today.

So at least we have alternative views as to the origin of life on Earth.

One thing is absolutely certain: life began in a very simple way, and it took thousands of millions of years to evolve into a form which we can recognise as an organised animal.

Below: *Thousands of years ago, the earth may have looked something like this. The land consisted of bare rock, weathered only by rain and heat. The seas were much less salty than they are today, but probably contained many dissolved organic compounds such as amino-acids. This stage in the evolution of the seas is described as a 'primeval soup'. We think the tides were much higher and more frequent then; thus pools of thin 'soup' must have been left out to dry in the hot primeval sun and became concentrated. This would have greatly increased the chances of molecules interacting to form more complex molecules – the precursors of the proteins.*

Fossils

The record of past animal and plant life is preserved in the rocks in the form of fossils, the mineralised or petrified remains of animal life.

When we find fossils, we do not always know just how much of the original animal or plant has been left behind, because the soft or fleshy parts have decomposed and vanished. In some very rare cases whole animals have been preserved more or less in the state that they were just before they died. In Siberia and northern Alaska fossil mammoth remains have been discovered in frozen ground where they have been preserved in a state of 'deep-freeze' for some 25,000 years.

Another example of preservation in almost natural state occurs when insects are engulfed by resin from trees. In time the resin hardens to amber, with the insect neatly enclosed.

Such examples are exceptionally rare. Most animal fossils found are either impressions of the hard parts of the animal, such as the shell of a mollusc, or the bones of a skeleton. Even these are very often changed from their original state by chemical replacement or mineralisation.

Sometimes the teeth of a shark or large reptile are preserved in their natural state; usually percolating water which filters through sedimentary rocks carries with it particles of dissolved chemicals, such as silica, iron, phosphate and lime compounds, which are deposited in the cellular structure of animal and plant tissue. In most cases, this cell replacement produces a perfect replica of the original structure.

Sometimes this process works in reverse. A mollusc or brachiopod shell, when the animal dies, may become filled with sand or sediment from the ocean floor. The whole shell is then buried under successive layers of younger deposits on the sea bed. In time the sand or sediment within the shell solidifies to the same degree of hardness as the surrounding rock. Percolating acidified water then removes the original shell substance by dissolving it and, at the same time, leaves the infilling sediment as a complete internal cast of the original shell.

The state of preservation of any fossilised animal depends very much upon

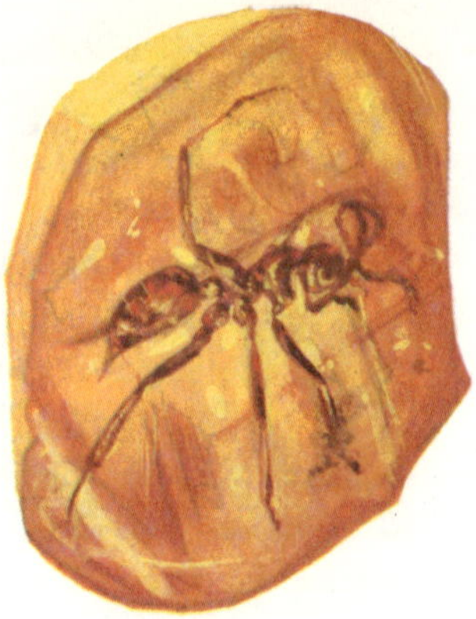

Evidence of past life is found in many media. Above: *An ant beautifully preserved in amber.* Below: *A crinoid which has left its cast form in limestone.*

Left: *Mammoths, like this one, from the northern steppes, have been found in permanently frozen soils where they have been since they died over a million years ago. Biologists have been able to dissect them – a rare privilege when handling extinct animals. It has even been possible to study their last meal.*

the nature of the surrounding material. In peat bogs, particularly those in Ireland, skeletons of terrestrial mammals have been discovered in a very fine state of preservation. It seems that the peat itself contains substances which prevent or delay normal decomposition, and many a skeleton of a deer or other animal has been retrieved almost as fresh as when it went in.

The asphalt pits at La Brea, Los Angeles, are celebrated for their deposits of animal remains. Skeletons of *Smilodon* – the sabre-toothed tiger – and mammoth and rodent remains have been collected by the ton from these rich localities.

In British Columbia, Canada, a bed of compacted shale of the Middle Cambrian age (about 550 million years ago) was studied near the town of Burgess. It revealed something which has never been equalled before or since. Within the shale were numerous fossil trilobites (prehistoric water-living arthropods) and worm-like animals so well preserved that all their legs and hairy projections from their bodies were present.

Life in the past has not only left its bodily remains but also its tracks and markings. Wherever animals tread or move about on soft ground they leave a trace or footprint by which they may be identified. This is also true of fossil animals. Turtles, dinosaurs, snakes, deer and many other animals, including invertebrates such as molluscs, have left trails which have become fossilised.

Fossils occur mainly in sedimentary rock (see pages 18–19) although there are a few examples of fossils being found in igneous rocks, having been engulfed by lava or covered by volcanic ash. Limestones are the chief source of fossils, some forms such as chalk consisting almost entirely of fossil shells of molluscs or brachiopods.

The presence of certain fossils may indicate the type of climate which prevailed during some stage in geological history. Corals are evidence of warm water conditions, while some algae or seaweeds are known to have flourished in cool conditions.

Abovc all, fossils arc still the chief means by which we can correlate strata. They form a link between rocks of similar age but from different areas. They also provide some of our natural resources. Coal is made of compacted tree and plant remains; oil is formed from shellfish and other animal remains, and diatomite, a substance used as an abrasive and for filtration, is the remains of myriads of diatoms, single-celled plants.

Right: *Fossil plants are not as common as animal fossils, since plant tissues tend to rot down before the fossilisation process can begin. Millions of years of photosynthesis have given us coal, which might be described as fossilised energy. However, unusual conditions have produced some truly fossilised plants, like this tree trunk in the Arizona National Park.*

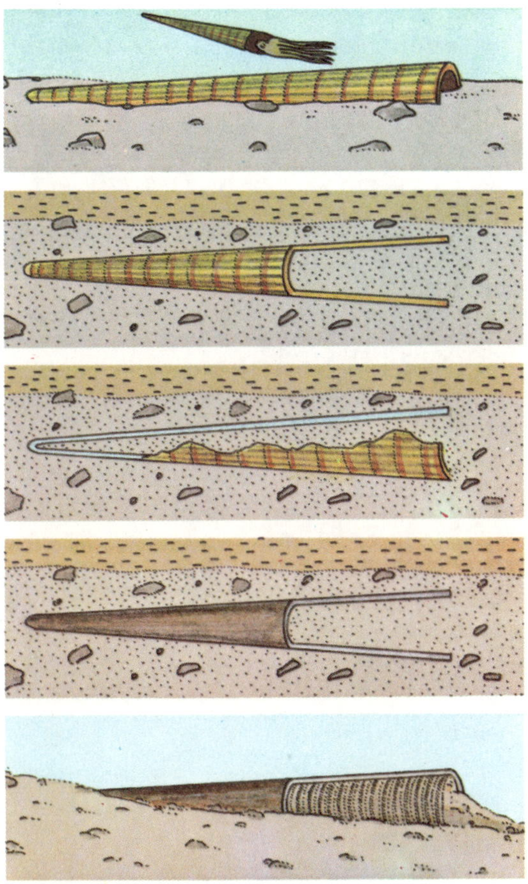

Below left: *This diagram illustrates how the shell of a primitive cephalopod became a fossil. When the animal died, its shell fell to the seabed where it slowly sank into the mud and was overlaid with yet more detritus. As the layer on top of it grew heavier, the mud in which the shell was buried became denser and harder. In this hardened layer of chalk, sandstone or shale, the original shell slowly decayed, leaving a mould of itself which slowly filled with a mineral leached from the surrounding rock, making a cast of the original shell. The cast is the fossil which is exposed perhaps millions of years later.*

Above: *Ammonites are among the fossils most commonly found in Jurassic shales. They are the fossils of shells of soft-bodied molluscs related to squids and can be found made of many minerals, including agate. They occur in an enormous range of sizes.*

Life in the Past

You cannot obtain a very clear picture of life in the past by merely looking at a group of fossils in a museum. In order to reconstruct the conditions in which animals and plants lived in prehistoric times you need a great deal more background knowledge. It is not even sufficient to accept that this or that fossil animal lived in fresh water or marine conditions, on land or in the air.

To derive the maximum information from these fascinating objects, you must first make careful notes about the rocks from which the fossils were collected. You need to know what sort of sediment they were found in: not just that it was clay or limestone, but what sort of clay, for example – whether it is mottled, streaked or dark blue in colour, or whether it contains particles of sand or grit. You must know whether a limestone is hard, compacted or crystalline, whether it also contains pebbles or sand, and even what shape these sand grains and pebbles are.

All this information matters greatly to the *palaeoecologist* (person who studies the nature of past environments) for, without it, he cannot be certain that fossil specimens were either shore dwellers or from deep waters or whether they walked on their hind legs, swam part of the time, flew or made burrows.

It is also important to collect or make notes about the many associated forms of fossil life. If you restrict collecting to one group of animals or plants, you cannot always piece together a very accurate vision of community life. Just as you depend upon the lives of other people and animals in your own environment or community today, so animals of the past had to rely upon other forms of life nearby. They had to obtain a steady flow of food which, for carnivorous prehistoric animals, was supplied by other animals.

The amount of energy or movement created by waves dashing upon a sea shore is also an important and measurable factor in the determination of an environment. An active environment might provide just the sort of habitat that would suit some molluscs or crustacea, whereas others might prefer less energetic surroundings in slightly deeper water.

You can add together all the information that you have gathered about each individual group of animals that lived in Cambrian times, for example, and from it determine just when the group came into existence, how it changed or adapted itself to new conditions, whether it increased in number and diversity of species, and when it declined or became extinct.

Cambrian seas, in general, were fairly quiet wâters, with many simple, soft-bodied animals which had begun their evolutionary existence in Precambrian seas (those before 600 million years ago). As time progressed, the number of different forms of life increased and such groups as graptolites – twig-like marine animals – were represented.

This was also the age when trilobites – early shellfish – abounded and many new genera and species of these segmented arthropods were created. They were so numerous and diverse that they became the dominant form of life at that time. Some species were tiny, fragile forms with delicate limbs, while others grew to enormous proportions. One of the largest species of trilobites was *Paradoxides*, which attained a length of 450 millimetres (18 inches). The mode of life of these creatures varied a little, but it was mainly as scavengers of the muddy sea-bed, where they crawled or slithered over the surface.

Molluscs, though very simple during this time, were quite well represented by several species of bivalves and gastropods

Above: *It is very hard, on a lonely site miles away from home, to discover that a perfect fossil just cannot be extracted without a missing tool. These rather ordinary-looking objects should together provide a basic fossil-collecting kit. It is preferable to remove a fossil whole, and for this a cold chisel with a 15-millimetre (½-inch) blade is best; the chisel can be used to break out the portion of rock in which a fossil is embedded. The geological hammer is used both for chiselling and, with discretion, breaking rock. In softer rocks a penknife or trowel may suffice. The next important step is to record the find. For this, one needs a geological map and a label. The location of the find and notes about other points of interest in the locality can then be attached to the fossil immediately. Some fossils are very delicate, especially those in shales, and it is wise to wrap each individually to prevent harder specimens spoiling soft ones. A haversack to carry tools and specimens and provisions completes the basic equipment.*

(sea-snails). Very primitive cephalopods, related to the squids or octopuses, were also present.

Brachiopods, another group of simple marine shellfish, were beginning to develop. The chief genera during the early Palaeozoic (600 million – 400 million years ago) belonged to the *inarticulata,* those species which had two separate valves (shells) which were not hinged together.

With a few exceptions, marine life continued much in this style all through the Ordovician and Silurian periods (from 500 million years ago to 400 million). The exceptions were the introduction of new sponges, corals and echinoderms, and minute crustacea called ostracods, which thrived towards the end of the Silurian period. Brachiopods, many now with hinged valves, were never more numerous than they were in the Silurian period, and vast numbers of diverse species were evolved.

It was also at the end of the Silurian period that one of the most primitive fossil vertebrates occurred. The remains of a fish-like creature known as *Jamoytius* were found in estuarine shales of the Upper Silurian series in Strathclyde, Scotland. A simple tube-like animal with lateral and dorsal fins, somewhat like the living *Amphioxus,* started what was to become one of the most fascinating and involved evolutionary trends. With this fossil came the dawn of vertebrate life.

A vast evolutionary 'explosion' occurred within the fishes which began and lasted throughout the entire Devonian period (400 million – 350 million years ago). Many new genera and species were evolved which quickly adapted themselves to rapidly changing conditions in both the sea and fresh water.

Above: *Sea cliffs are often a rich source of fossils. In soft cliffs such as chalk and limestone the sea constantly erodes away the cliff face, exposing fresh surfaces. Many important finds have been uncovered in this way, as well as by rock falls on the coast and inland. Great care must be taken when investigating crumbling cliffs.*

Below: *Some common fossils. The lamp shell (1) is a brachiopod which has two valves, one larger than the other. Trilobites (3), the dominant fossils of the Paleozoic era, are early arthropods. Sea urchins (4) came later, in the Silurian period. The molar tooth of a cave bear (2) is the actual tooth and, unlike most fossils, has not been mineralised.*

Some larger scaly fishes developed a rudimentary lung and strong muscular fin-bases which, during the increasing drying-up of lakes and rivers at this time, allowed them to adapt themselves to a partial out-of-water existence. Their muscular fins enabled these fishes to haul themselves from one muddy pool to another. These fishes were the *osteolepids* and must have included the ancestors of the amphibia. At the same time, the lung-fishes evolved. These, like the osteolepids, had lungs, but unlike them, showed no tendency to come out onto the land. Instead, when their pools dried out, they buried themselves in the mud in a mucous cocoon, breathing air. Many lungfish fossils have been found in this state. With the rise of amphibians in the swampy freshwater pools, and the ray-finned fishes (see page 175) in the sea, rivers and lakes, the osteolepids went into a decline.

It is quite noticeable that throughout the history of evolution one group of animals was very often replaced within its own environment by another almost completely unrelated group. This faunal replacement may be regarded as a sort of 'take-over' by a stronger, more dominant class of animal from another successful, but possibly weaker, group.

Early Life on Land

As we have seen on pages 28–29, life on Earth began in the sea. Fossilised remains of the simplest single-celled organisms have been found in rocks that are almost 3,500 million years old. Life presumably evolved before then, but there are no older rocks so far discovered. Modern life is almost entirely dependent on oxygen in the atmosphere or dissolved in water. It is almost certain that in the primitive earth there was no free oxygen. There is evidence from rocks older than 2,000 million years that they were laid down in an oxygen-free environment, whereas younger rocks show evidence of oxygenation. The origin of this oxygen is uncertain (see page 24).

Although life is so old, its early development was apparently slow, and many millions of years passed before complex, many-celled animals evolved. A number of these animals are known from fossils in very ancient rocks, but it is not until the Cambrian period that life apparently became abundant.

There seem to be two reasons for this: one is that many creatures at that time developed hard shells, which made it more likely that they would become fossilised after death; and the other is that by that time, almost all of the main types of animal organisation which survive to the present day had evolved. From Cambrian rocks the remains of most of the major phyla of the present day have been found.

The first land plants of which we have certain knowledge through fossils were flourishing during the Devonian period, which began about 395 million years ago. Among the earliest of these plants was a spore-bearing plant – related to ferns and mosses – called *Rhynia,* because its fossilised remains were found at Rhynie, in the middle of Scotland's Grampian district. *Rhynia* had no roots or leaves, but consisted of a creeping underground stem, off which sprouted slender shoots. The shoots ended in *sporangia* – spore-producing organs. Other plants of the middle Devonian period have been found, and they resemble mosses. But by the late Devonian some plants had evolved with large, fern-like leaves.

The first amphibians appeared a few million years after *Rhynia.* It seems possible that they evolved in swamp lands which dried out from time to time. Those animals which were able to venture into the air and move across dry or semi-dry land to fresh pools were the ones which survived. Large footprints – some of them

about 150 millimetres (6 inches) long – have been found in Devonian rocks in Europe. These early amphibians, the ichthyostegalians, had many characters similar to those of their fish ancestors.

The Carboniferous period, which began 345 million years ago, was the time when life on land really exploded. This period gets its name from the fact that it was then the great coal beds which provide us with so much of our present-day fuel were laid down. Coal is largely carbon, the pressed and decomposed remains of vast forests. The trees in them were giant ferns and club-mosses.

When these plants died, fresh trees grew on top of their remains, layer on layer for millions of years. As the plants rotted they formed peat; the peat became coal when it was overlaid with sand and rock, and squeezed in the many upheavals of the Earth's crust.

Land-living invertebrates lived in the forests of the Carboniferous period. They included spiders and early insects. Some of these insects were like dragonflies, but had a wingspan of up to 750 millimetres (30 inches). These flying insects cannot, however, have been the first of all insects to have existed, for more primitive, wingless forms – such as silverfish – survive to the present day, and these forms must have preceded the flying kinds.

These insects, swarming in the primeval forests, provided a source of food for land animals, thus encouraging amphibians to spend more time ashore. At this time many new species of amphibians appeared. Some had massive bodies and thick bony skulls, somewhat like present-day crocodiles.

From the armoured amphibians evolved pioneer forms of salamander-like creatures, with smooth, powerful bodies and long tails. Other forms became burrowers, or sought refuge in streams and caves. Gradually the evolution of the first reptiles came about. Reptiles developed from amphibians, almost certainly from a type known as seymouriamorphs.

The main step in evolution was that the first reptiles were also the first animals capable of living completely away from water. This involved the development of a horny skin which was capable of protecting the animals against drying out. Amphibians still do not possess such a skin (and have also lost the hard armour of early types), and so they are forced to live always in moist environments, or in water.

Plants were developing right through the Carboniferous and Permian periods, and at this time the first seed-bearing plants evolved.

These trees are all types of primitive ferns, club-mosses and horsetails. The two tall ones on the right are cordaits and those at the extreme left are club-mosses. This marshy habitat of the Carboniferous period was the result of geological upheavals which created folded mountain ranges in areas that had previously been under the sea. Some aquatic animals were stranded in this new half-and-half habitat. The fish in the picture is a crossopterygian, similar to the ancestors of land quadrupeds. The amphibian is shown enlarged for the sake of clarity. Invertebrates were already in possession of the land; the giant dragonfly had a wingspan of 70 centimetres (27½ inches), and ants also lived in the forests.

The Age of Reptiles

Left: Pteranodon *had a wingspan of over 7½ metres (24½ feet). It probably did not fly in the way that modern birds do, but was capable of using the claws on its wings and feet to climb up cliffs or trees, from which it could take off and glide.*

During the Permian period, which began 260 million years ago, reptiles of many kinds developed. Most were heavily-built, lumbering creatures, but as time went on they became more varied and some were quite agile. By the early Triassic period, 35 million years later, the main branches of the reptile family tree had begun to develop, and we can see the principal ways in which reptiles were to occupy the land and waters of the earth for the next 200 million years.

If you look at the diagram on these pages you will see that some reptiles seem to have changed very little since early times. The tortoises and turtles of today are very much like those of the past. There were also many others not in the least like modern reptiles. Some returned to the sea; these were the ichthyosaurs, or 'fish-lizards', which must have looked and behaved very like the dolphins of the present day. Perfectly adapted for an aquatic life, these streamlined creatures swam by movements of their tails, had limbs transformed into flippers for steering and a back fin for maintaining stability in the water. They breathed air through nostrils near the top of the head and produced living young, born tail-first into the sea – all characters we can see in dolphins.

Today's large toothed whales were matched by the pliosaurs, while the plesiosaurs and placodonts led the same sort of life as seals and walruses respectively. On land, just as today, some animals were plant-eaters, while some fed on flesh, either as hunters or as scavengers. An important group of hunting animals were the ancestors of the mammals.

Perhaps the most important of all the reptile groups were the archosaurs. These animals were not only the ancestors of the present-day birds and crocodiles, but included the flying reptiles of the past and, most dramatic of all, the dinosaurs.

The archosaurs are defined scientifically by the shape of certain bones of their skulls. Early archosaurs included a group called the thecodonts, small animals, up to 2 metres (6½ feet long). Much of this length was taken up by the tail. The head had fairly long jaws, armed with sharp pointed teeth which grew in sockets. If a tooth broke or became worn, it was pushed up by another which grew from the socket. The thecodonts were four-legged animals, but the hind limbs were much longer and stronger than the forelegs. Probably, if they had to run fast, they went up on their hind legs, rather like the Australian frilled lizard (*Chlamydosaurus kingi*) of today. Perhaps to protect them against larger flesheaters, the thecodonts had small plates of bone, called *scutes*, set along their backs.

The earliest dinosaurs were very much like thecodonts. Somewhat larger in size, their hind legs were stronger and they were much more truly bipedal (two-footed). They had no bony armour on their bodies, but probably escaped from enemies by their ability to run fast, at least for short distances. Throughout the whole history of the dinosaurs, some species remained small and active, and it is from among creatures very much like these that we must look for the ancestors of the birds. Some of these little dinosaurs were undoubtedly the equivalent of present-day hunting mammals.

Some dinosaurs developed to a greater size. Perhaps this occurred (as it has to some extent with other animals) because

Above: *Plesiosaurs were marine reptiles. They were about 3 metres (9¾ feet) long and had inflexible bodies with short tails. This led naturally to the development of flippers for swimming, and long agile necks for catching fish.*

size is, in itself, a protection. Few creatures will attack a really big animal, even if it has little obvious armour. Most of the dinosaurs were very large and probably few other animals would have attacked them. Like the thecodonts, some of these large dinosaurs were carnivores, but it is likely that they were mainly scavengers, finding dead, or killing sick or injured animals. They were probably not capable of the sustained output of energy required for active hunting.

Tyrannosaurus, one of the most famous of dinosaurs, was of this kind. If it killed its prey, it would have been with tremendous blows of its taloned feet, and its daggerlike teeth would only have been used to tear the flesh from the carcass. *Tyrannosaurus* would have been able to deal easily with a small reptile. It is possible that if it had killed really large prey it would, like a present-day crocodile, have guarded it, driving off other scavengers until the feast was finished. This would perhaps have taken many days.

Some of the large dinosaurs seem to have increased in size so much that they were forced to return to a four-legged stance. In many respects they were like the flesh-eaters, but really huge land animals are nearly always plant eaters, and these monsters developed into herbivores which eventually became the largest animals ever to walk the earth. One of the biggest was *Brachiosaurus,* which is estimated to have weighed about 70 tonnes. Single bones have been found which indicate that some of these animals were even larger. There is much evidence to suggest that at least some of these animals spent much of their time in shallow water, which would have supported the weight of their vast bodies. They had enormously long necks, which probably lay out over the surface of the water and allowed them to gather food from a wide area.

As a rule, water plants have soft leaves and the teeth of these giant reptiles were adapted to deal with such a diet. Placed entirely in the front of the mouth, where they would have been at a great mechanical disadvantage if it came to dealing with tough foliage, the teeth of *Diplodocus* were like the blunt teeth of a rake.

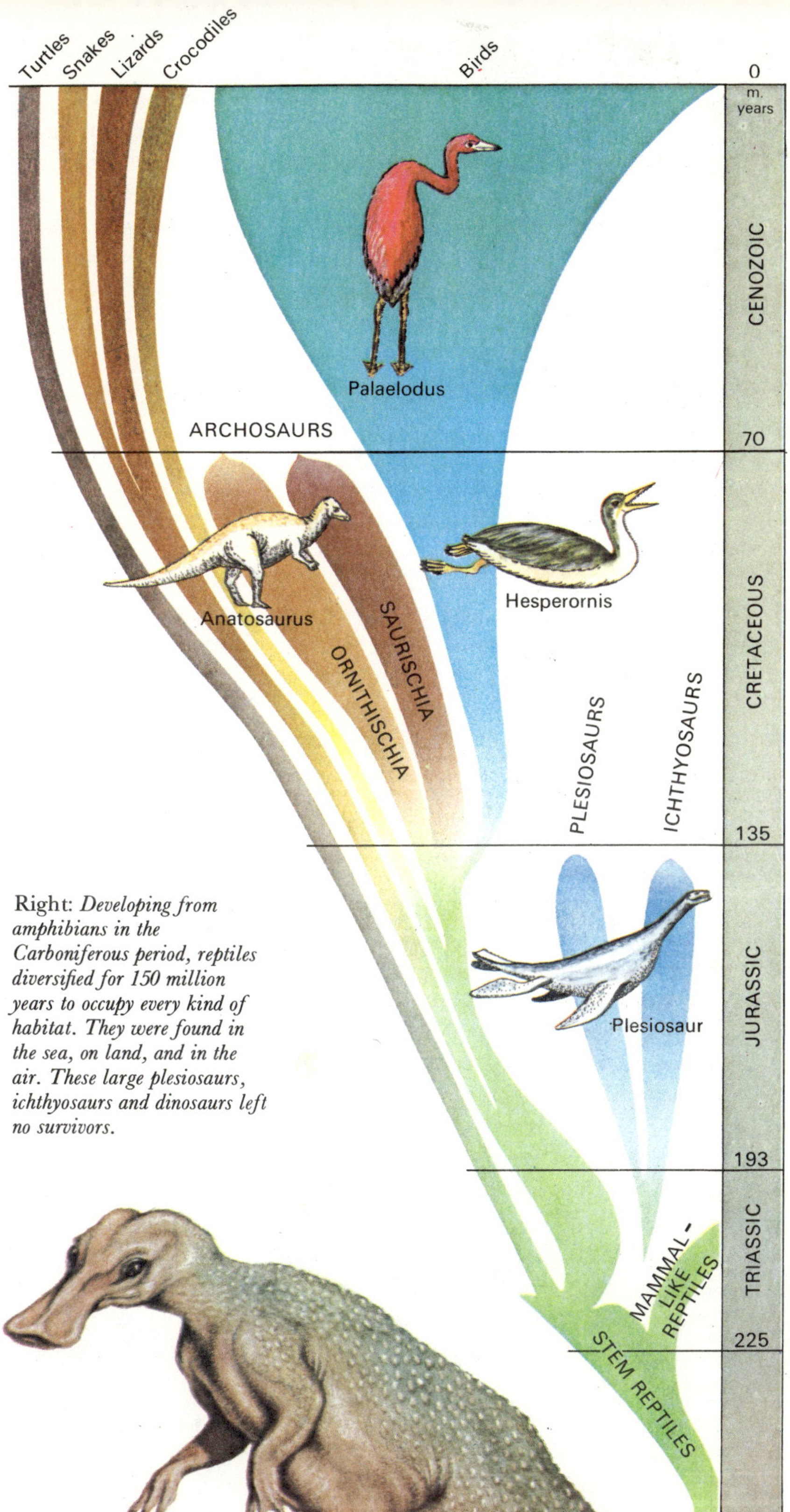

Right: *Developing from amphibians in the Carboniferous period, reptiles diversified for 150 million years to occupy every kind of habitat. They were found in the sea, on land, and in the air. These large plesiosaurs, ichthyosaurs and dinosaurs left no survivors.*

Right: Trachodon *is an example of the strange shapes achieved by herbivorous dinosaurs. It is known to have lived in marshy places, and the striking resemblance of its 'bill' to that of a duck makes it thought that it probably fed like ducks do today.*

Discovering the Dinosaurs

If you look at the dinosaur family tree, you will see that there are two main branches. On one side are the saurischians, which included all of the flesh-eaters and the heavyweight, four-legged plant-eaters. On the other side are the ornithischians, which included a large number of two-legged forms as well as the four-legged armoured types. The words 'saurischia' and 'ornithischia' refer to the shape of the bones of the hips, which were different in the two types.

There were other differences, too. The saurischians all had their teeth in the front of the mouth, which means that they were not well adapted to feeding on tough food which would require much chewing. The ornithischians, with very few exceptions, had horny plates – in some rather like the bill of a duck, in others curved like a parrot's beak – in front of the mouth and their teeth were all placed far back in the jaws. All the ornithischians were plant feeders. The teeth in their upper and lower jaws could move against each other with a grinding action, which meant that they could eat harsh vegetation, which required a lot of chewing. One species had about 3,000 teeth in its mouth at any one time. Each tooth was small, but together they made a millstone for grinding the toughest plant food.

In spite of the size and variety of the dinosaurs, they all died out at the end of the Mesozoic era, 70 million years ago.

How, then, do we know so much about these vanished monsters? We know when they lived, because we find their fossils only in rocks of the Mesozoic era. From the fossils it is easy to tell the size of the animals and their general shape, for all land animals with backbones are built to a similar pattern, and it is possible to compare the bones of dinosaurs with those of known animals and to estimate their function. In a few places, the mummified skin of dinosaurs has been found. This tells us of the texture, if not the colour of the creatures.

The story of the discovery of the dinosaurs is one full of romance. Although in some parts of the world dinosaur remains had been known to man since ancient times, they were not recognised as the remains of animals of the ancient past. Some were thought to be the bones of giants. So far as we know, the first person to record the finding of a dinosaur bone was an English clergyman, Robert Plott, who in 1677 published a description and

Top: *The swamp-dwelling* Corythosaurus *was a vegetarian. It is thought that the crest was present only in males, and may have been used in feeding underwater.* Above: *The carnivorous* Ceratosaurus *had a formidable array of sharp teeth, well suited to grasping and tearing its prey. These were both bird-hipped (ornithischian) dinosaurs, and walked on two legs with the help of a tail.*

Left: Brachiosaurus *was a four-footed giant that lived in water. Its legs could not have supported its 50-tonne body on land. The tiny sensory brain in its skull was supplemented by a much larger motor brain in its pelvis that probably controlled body movement.*

picture of a bone found in Oxfordshire. The bone itself is now lost, but the picture shows it to be part of the femur (thigh-bone) of a dinosaur.

It was not until the 1800s, when the need for stone to build more houses and roads meant that many new quarries were opened up, that more dinosaurs were discovered. The first recognition of the fact that gigantic reptiles existed in the past goes to another Englishman, Dr. Gideon Mantell (1790–1852) whose wife discovered a worn tooth by a roadside at Cuckfield, in Sussex, in 1822. Mantell puzzled over it and some giant bones, also found in southern England, until a chance encounter with an acquaintance who was studying the American lizard iguana led to the similarity of the shape of the teeth of the two animals being noted. *Iguanodon*, the 'iguana tooth' got its name because of this.

While Mantell was pondering, Dr. William Buckland, a leading geologist at Oxford University, described some giant bones which had been found in that area. He named them *Megalosaurus*, which was, therefore, the first dinosaur to be scientifically recognised. The name 'dinosaur' was not coined until 1841, by which time numerous big bones had been found in many places.

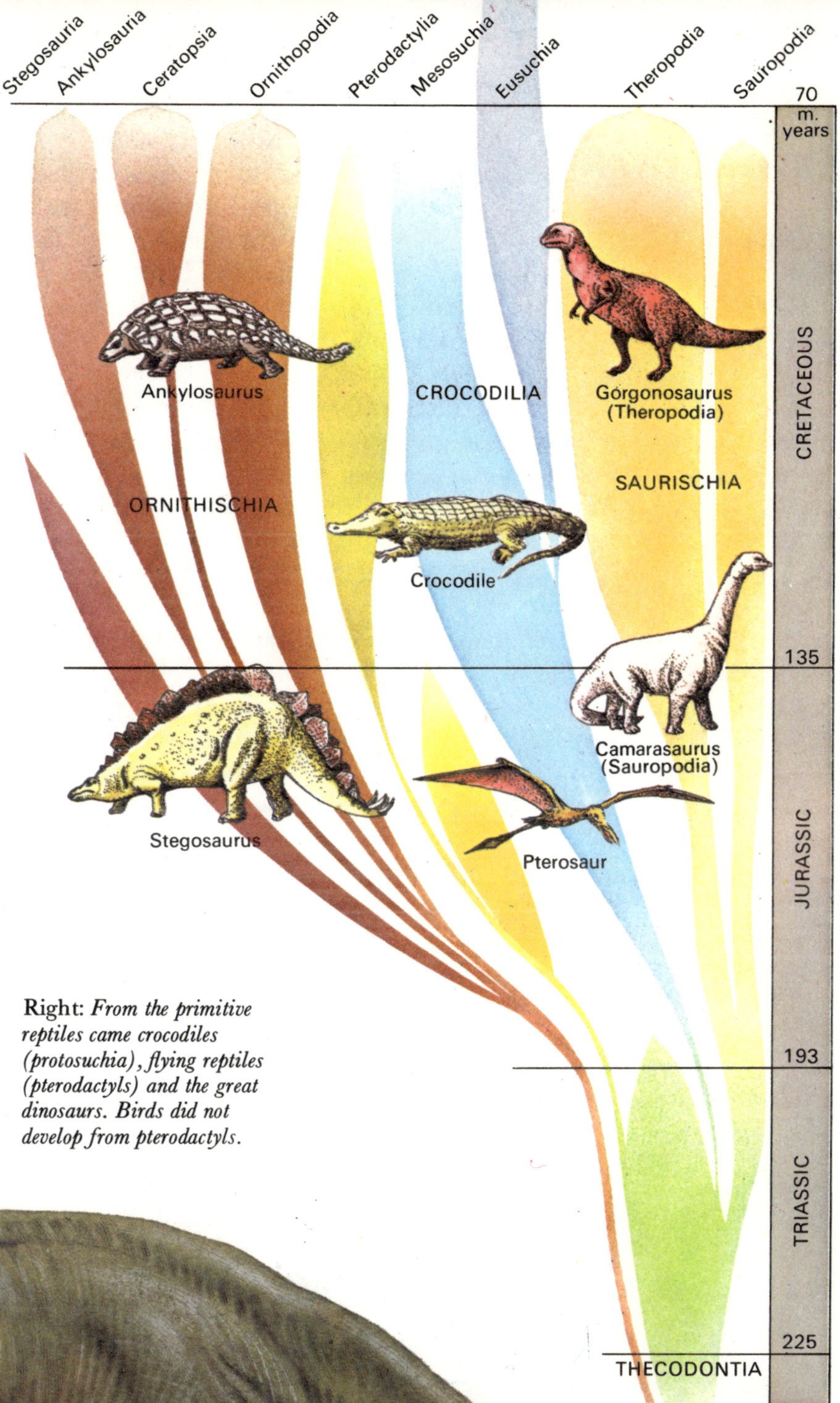

Right: *From the primitive reptiles came crocodiles (protosuchia), flying reptiles (pterodactyls) and the great dinosaurs. Birds did not develop from pterodactyls.*

Right: Tyrannosaurus rex, *the largest carnivore that has ever lived, stood about 5½ metres (18 feet) high. It looks as if it was a horribly effective predator. The herbivorous* Triceratops *needed the protection of both a bony shield to cover its vulnerable neck and of its long horns against a frontal attack.*

The Age of Mammals

Looking back over the long history of evolution of all animal groups, we can see that, in many cases, a dominant group may have one or more 'understudy' groups waiting to take over if there should be a decline in the main stock. The group making the 'take over' need not necessarily be in any way related to the main group, but may fill what is known as an *ecological niche.* It replaces the position in the environment originally held by the dominant group.

When the dominant dinosaurs and other specialised reptiles declined during the later part of the Cretaceous Period – more than 70 million years ago – there was a well-established, but not particularly variable, group of mammals which had originated about 150 million years earlier.

There were many differences between dinosaurs and mammals. Mammals are warm-blooded animals, needing coarse hair or fur for body protection, while reptiles have much cooler blood and no hair. Mammals reproduce themselves by giving birth to live offspring which they suckle, unlike reptiles which lay eggs and take little or no care of their young.

Mammals developed steadily for thousands of years. By Cretaceous times they had divided into two main branches. One of these consists of the marsupial mammals (see pages 208–209).

By the end of the Cretaceous period marsupials were widespread throughout both the northern and southern hemispheres of the world. Later they became more isolated and remained almost exclusively within the southern hemisphere, where most of them are found today. They developed principally in Australia, where isolation from the rest of the world ensured they were free from competition from the second branch of the class, the normal placental mammals. See pages 206–207 for more information about placental mammals.

During the early Cenozoic times – from 70 million years ago onwards – a great many new kinds of mammals evolved, and some became isolated, developing within their own continent or geographical area. There were large and small *ungulates,* hoofed plant-eating mammals such as *Uintatherium,* a six-horned rhinoceros-like animal with modified teeth. Even-toed

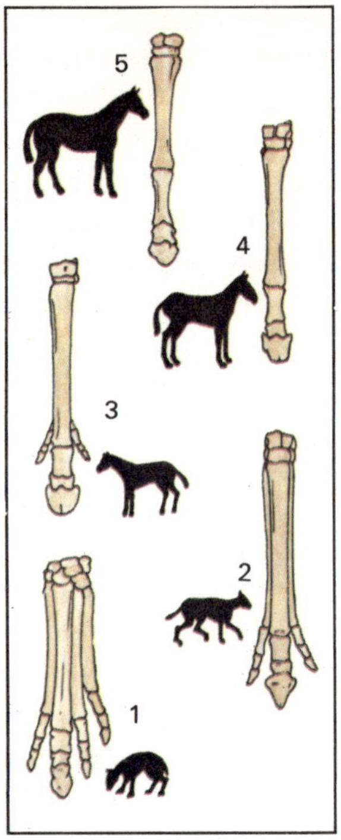

Above: *Tracing the evolution of the horse's front foot, the toes of the Eocene* Hyracotherium *(Eohippus) (1) already showed one larger than the other three. In the Oligocene* Miohippus *(2) another small toe has disappeared. By the late Miocene,* Merychippus *(3) has a well-formed hoof and two very small lateral toes, which have vanished from the foot of the relatively recent* Equus *(4, 5).*

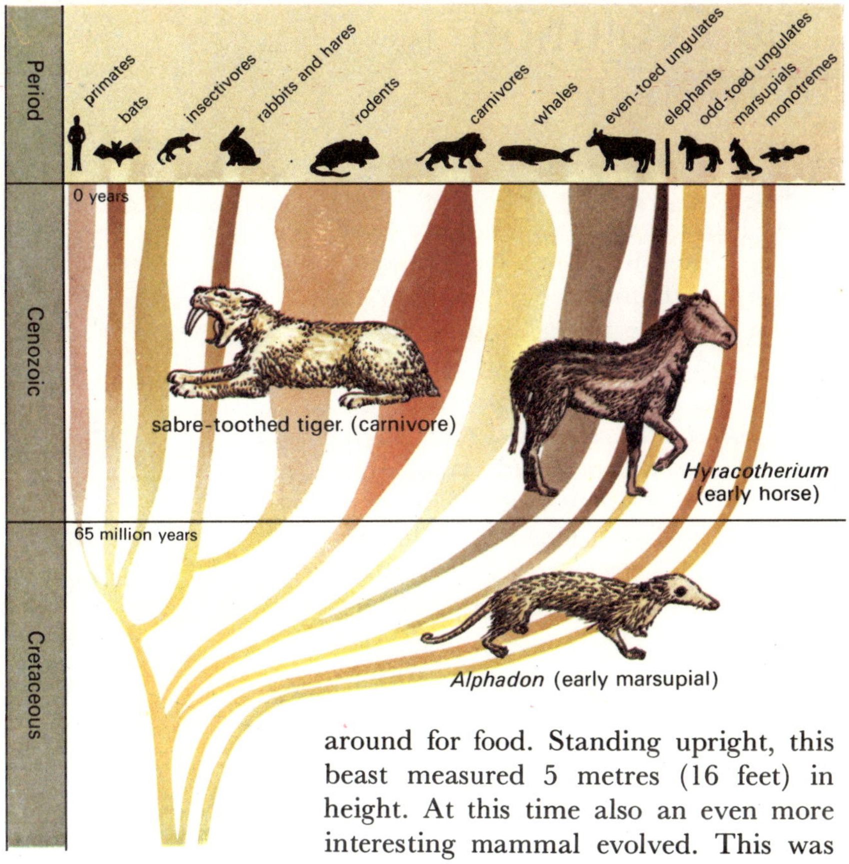

Above: *Mammals arose from reptiles in the Triassic/ Jurassic period, but did not assume importance until the Tertiary period more than 50 million years later. A great expansion then took place among all mammal groups – only the main orders are shown – which produced the species of mammals alive today. Some types have changed very little from their Tertiary ancestors; others are still evolving to produce more advanced species.*

ungulates – those with two or four toes, such as deer, camels and pigs – became dominant, eventually replacing many of the odd-toed ungulates – those with three or five toes. At the beginning of the Cenozoic era a number of different ungulates had developed in northeast Africa, in the Fayyum region south of Cairo, near the River Nile.

Also developing about this time in the same area near Lake Moeris – now known as Birkit Qarun – was *Moeritherium,* an early ancestor of the elephant, at that time no bigger than a sheep. It was pig-like in appearance, with an elongated jaw.

In the continents of North and South America, many different kinds of mammal were beginning to evolve. In the Eocene epoch, beginning about 55 million years ago, *Hyracotherium,* the early ancestor of the horse, hid among the leafy glades. It was a small, almost dog-like animal, having four toes on its front feet and three on the hind, and was probably a swift runner. This feature of its toes is one which we can use to illustrate the evolutionary process. By Oligocene times, about 38 million years ago, a further development of the forefoot had reduced the number of toes to three. This fleet-footed mammal eventually developed the middle toe of the three, reducing the two side toes to mere swellings on the foot. This led to the evolution of the hoof of the modern horse.

About 14 million years later a llama-like camel, *Alticamelus,* about 3 metres (10 feet) high, appeared on the central plains of South America. It is probably from this that the present-day llama developed.

A million or so years ago in the pampas of Argentina a giant ground-sloth, *Megatherium,* was busy stripping the leaves and bark from the trees and rooting around for food. Standing upright, this beast measured 5 metres (16 feet) in height. At this time also an even more interesting mammal evolved. This was *Glyptodon.* a giant armadillo. Protected by a huge carapace of bony plates, this animal has had a long fossil history.

At this stage in the history of North and South America, there was apparently no land bridge (the Isthmus of Panama) between them as there is today. Therefore, the very different mammal communities of these two continents remained isolated until much later.

However, many of the mammal species which occurred between 70 million and one million years ago in North America also existed in Europe. Mammoths, rhinoceros, deer, antelopes, bisons and wolves were common to both areas, as were bears, squirrels, hares and lynxes. This means that there was almost certainly a land bridge further north, between Alaska and Asia, or perhaps a massive frozen sea area.

By the end of the Cenozoic era, about 25,000 years ago, mammals appeared to be in decline. There are today far fewer genera and species in many groups than there were 12 million years ago. But the survivors have established themselves all over the world as the dominant form of life on Earth.

Left: *The rhinoceros-like* Uintatherium *(2) of North America and* Arsinotherium *(5) of Africa lived about 40 million years ago.* Moeritherium *(6) was an early relative of the elephants and* Hyracotherium *(7) an early horse.* Macrauchenia *(4),* Glyptodon *(3) and* Megatherium *(1) were part of the unique, recently extinct South American fauna.*

The Evolution of Man

All people alive today are classified by zoologists as members of the genus *Homo* ('man') and species *sapiens* ('wise'). We and our closest living relatives, the apes – the gorilla, chimpanzee, orang-utan and gibbon – are grouped with monkeys, lemurs and lorises in the order Primates.

Primates show certain characteristics which originally evolved for life in the trees. These features include hands which are used for grasping and hanging from branches, well-developed eyesight, and eyes which face forwards to help judge distances accurately; a shorter snout – because smell is less important than sight to Primates – which also helps forward vision; unspecialised teeth so Primates can eat various kinds of food; well-developed care of infants and a social system; and a well-developed brain.

Man shows each of these characteristics and has a particularly great development of the brain. Man has teeth suitable for an *omnivorous* diet, (one consisting of both meat and plant materials); a skeleton adapted for *bipedalism,* (walking upright on the hind legs); and has cultural features, including language, tool-making and tool use, and a complex society consisting of families and tribes.

Primates are known as fossils from the Palaeocene epoch, 65 million years ago, and had probably already evolved several million years earlier.

By about 15 million years ago there were apes inhabiting not only Africa (various species of *Proconsul*) but also Europe and Asia (various species of *Dryopithecus*). Among the fossil remains of these Miocene apes are fragments of jaws and teeth which seem more similar to those of man. These we call *Ramapithecus.*

The details of this evolution are not well recorded by fossils until the end of the Miocene epoch and the beginning of the Pliocene epoch, about 5 million years ago. But by then the more advanced hominid genus *Australopithecus* had evolved and probably inhabited much of southern and eastern Africa. The Australopithecines

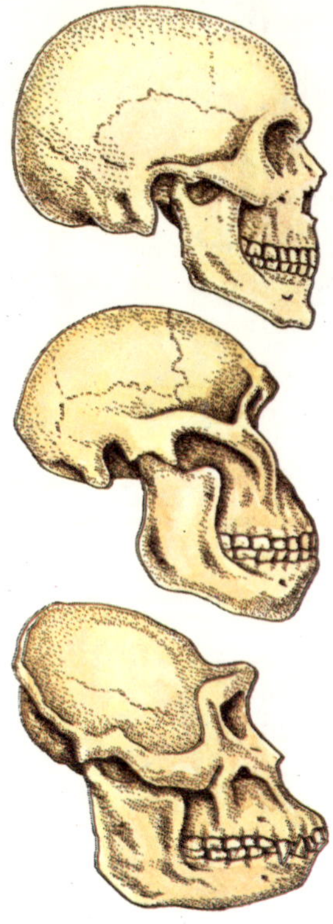

Above: *The centre skull (above) is a primitive man,* Australopithecus. *The top skull is that of a modern man, while the one at the bottom is an ape skull.* Below: *Early man-made tools. The pebble-tools come from early Pleistocene deposits. Hand axes like the ones at the top right are from Acheulean deposits (Lower Palaeolithic). The centre row are Upper Palaeolithic gravers or burins. The axe head and harpoons are more recent artefacts.*

were adapted to walk upright, although they did not walk in exactly the same way as does modern man. Their teeth were similar in pattern to our own, but were much larger, and so their jaws and faces were also large. But the brain of *Australopithecus* was only about the same size as that of modern apes.

So the Australopithecines were not yet 'man' and some forms of *Australopithecus* were clearly not our ancestors. These were the robust Australopithecines, classified as the species *Australopithecus robustus* and *Australopithecus boisei*.

In contrast to the large robust forms, the other species of *Australopithecus, Australopithecus africanus,* was lightly-built and had a more varied diet, probably including meat obtained by scavenging. It was this form, or something closely related to it, which gave rise perhaps 2 million years ago to the first true men. At that date there were hominids (humans) in eastern and southern Africa which were well adapted for walking upright, and were using various kinds of pebble-tools. These very early members of the genus *Homo* are sometimes classified as *Homo habilis*.

By 1·5 million years ago, in the early Pleistocene epoch, the form of man known as *Homo erectus* was inhabiting parts of Africa and Asia. His skeleton was still robust, but in most respects was like our own. The size of the brain had grown to

about 800–1,200 cubic centimetres (48–73 cubic inches), while the face and teeth had become smaller. However, the bones of the skull were thick and there was a bar of bone, called a *supraorbital torus*, above the eye-sockets. *Homo erectus* was the discoverer of fire.

Remains of *Homo erectus* are known from many places including Europe, China, Java, North Africa and Kenya. During a period of at least one million years these people developed human culture well beyond the simple Australopithecine level, and by 300,000 years ago our own species *Homo sapiens* was evolving from *Homo erectus*. Fossils showing the early stages of the evolution of *Homo sapiens* have been found at several European sites, and although the fossils are still primitive in certain respects, the brain and teeth are essentially modern.

During the Pleistocene epoch the Earth's climate fluctuated at times, leading to the spread of ice-caps over the northern continents. Cultural advances allowed a specialised kind of *Homo sapiens*, Neanderthal Man, to survive in areas of Europe and Asia south of the ice-sheets 50,000 years ago.

Modern man, *Homo sapiens sapiens*, appeared at least 40,000 years ago and reached Europe over 30,000 years ago, in the form of the *Cro-Magnons* who produced the beautiful cave paintings discovered in France and Spain.

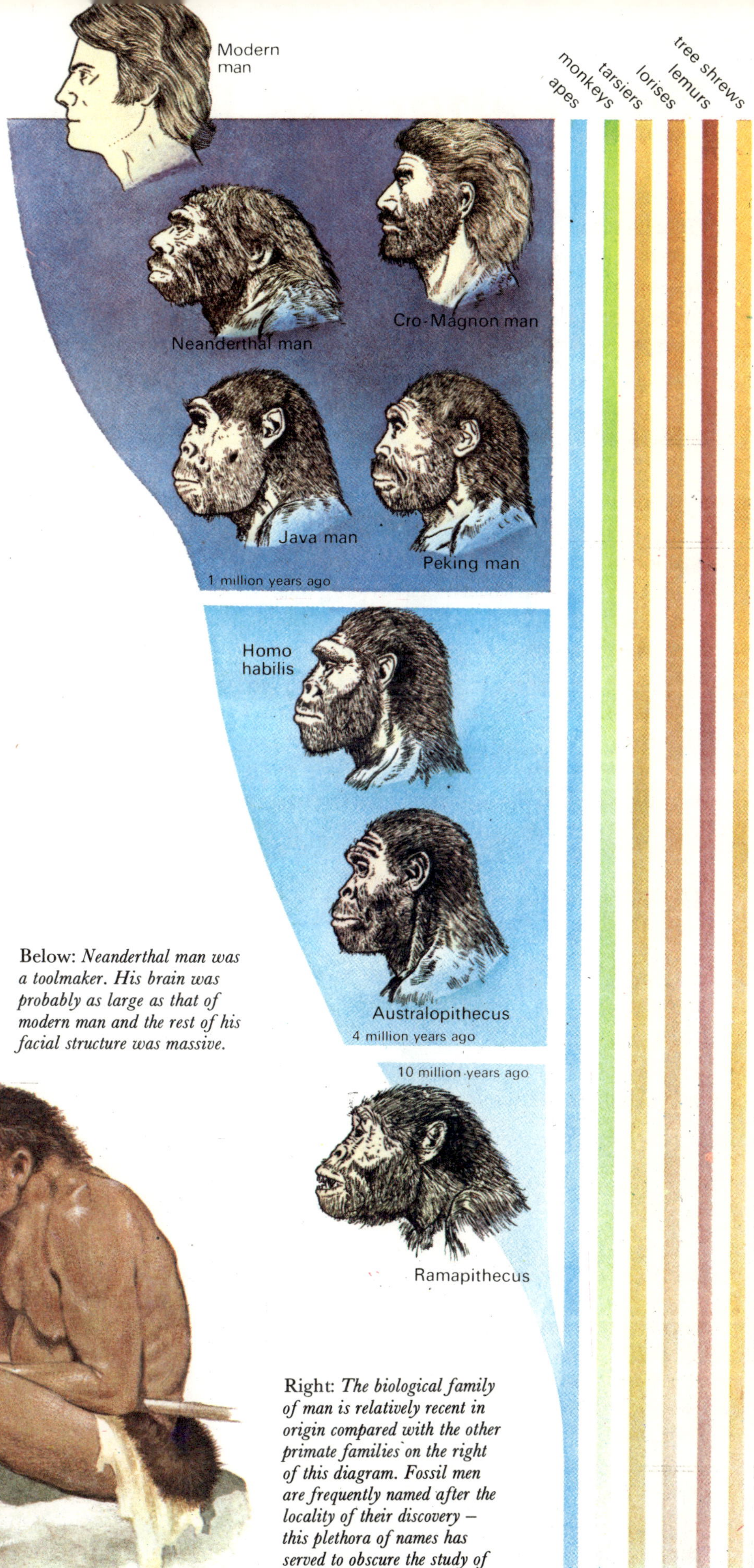

Below: *Neanderthal man was a toolmaker. His brain was probably as large as that of modern man and the rest of his facial structure was massive.*

Right: *The biological family of man is relatively recent in origin compared with the other primate families on the right of this diagram. Fossil men are frequently named after the locality of their discovery – this plethora of names has served to obscure the study of man's origins.*

The Pattern of Life

Living things today are the descendants of the prehistoric plants and animals described in the previous section of this book. Although life is constantly changing and adapting to varying circumstances, the basic ways of surviving on this planet have altered little since the Palaeozoic era which ended about 270 million years ago.

Plants and animals as we know them have either adapted to the environments in which they live, or have sought habitats which provide them with the surroundings which they need in order to flourish. In this section we shall consider the various kinds of habitats in the world, and the species of plants and animals which are commonly found there. The kinds of habitats are formed partly by the physical nature of the environment – sea, mountains, plains, sheltered, exposed – and partly by the climate, which ranges from very hot to bitterly cold, and from dry to wet.

The section also covers some of the ways in which living things are studied and classified, and the great naturalists who have led the way in such studies. We can see, too, some of the ways in which plants and animals evolve and change, and gain some idea of the vast numbers of living things that exist on this planet.

Each feather on a pheasant is intricately and subtly coloured to form a part of the whole pattern.

What are Living Things?

Living things fall naturally into five main groups – animals, plants, fungi, bacteria and viruses. They have in common the fact that all are capable of growth; that is to say, all living things absorb food substances into their tissues in an organised way. (This differs, for example, from the simple soaking up of water by a porous rock.) Living things are also capable of reproducing their own kind. Thus growth and reproduction are the main characteristics of living as compared with inanimate objects. The study of life and of living things is called biology, which is grouped with other studies – such as chemistry and physics – under the general heading of science.

All living things consist of one or more units of living substance called protoplasm. In most organisms the protoplasm is divided into one or more cells. A cell is the smallest identifiable unit of life, any part of a cell being unable to live on its own. Each cell has, among other things, a nucleus which governs the life-processes within the cell. Many organisms consist of numerous cells joined together and dependent on one another in the way that ants in a colony depend on one another.

Aggregations of cells often form tissues such as muscle, bone, cartilage or wood of which higher organisms are built. Three of the main groups of living things – animals, plants and fungi – form tissues, but the other two – bacteria and viruses – do not form tissues, and remain as separate, single-celled individuals.

Animals – the study of which is called zoology – are the most highly advanced of living things. They are distinguished in most cases by being able to move very fast when compared with plants, which have only slow growing movements as a rule. However, the most important difference from the biologist's point of view is in the method of feeding. Animals feed on the tissues of other living things, such as plants, other animals and bacteria.

Plants, on the other hand, manufacture their own food substances from simple

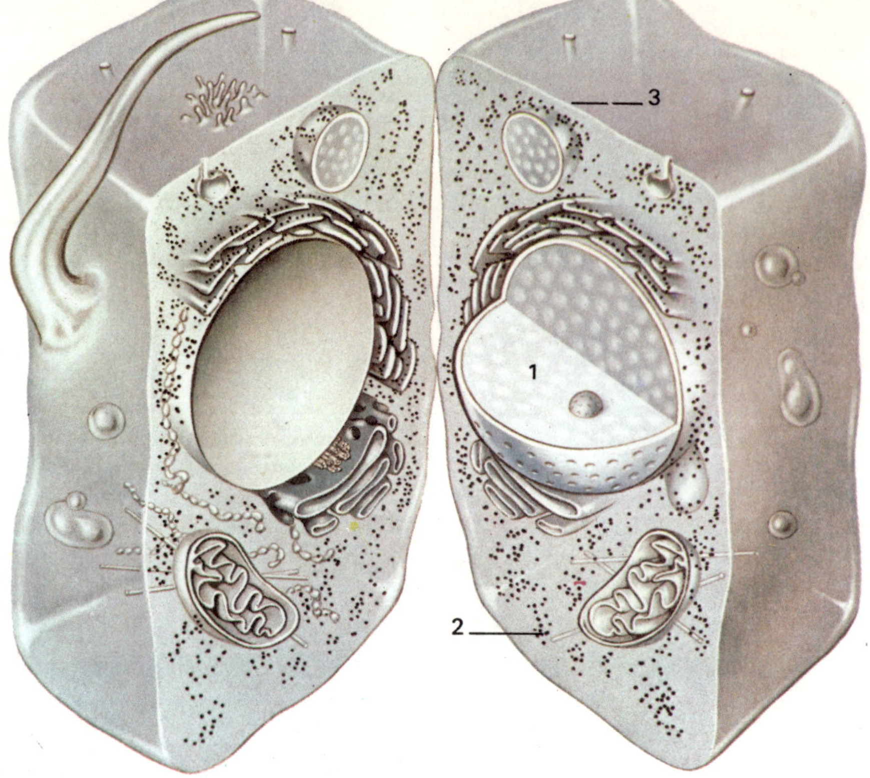

Above: *The animal cell is made up of two main areas, the nucleus (1) and the cytoplasm (2). The nuclear chromosomes control the cell organisation and heredity. The many organelles in the cytoplasm are vital to the metabolism of this complicated living factory; the plasma membrane itself (3) is a complex structure selectively controlling intake and output.*

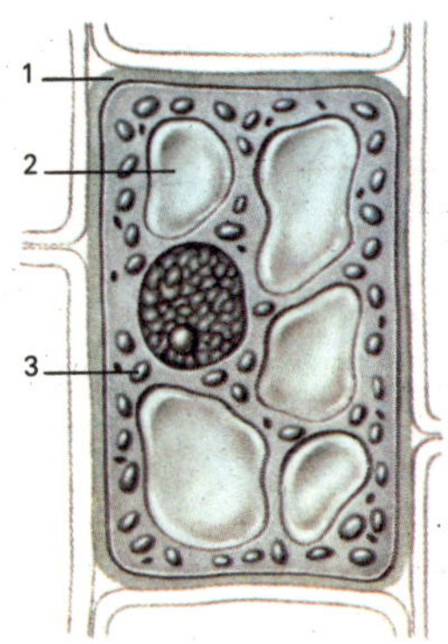

Above: *There are two important differences between this plant cell and the animal cell (above). Plant cells have rigid cellulose walls (1), and normally contain vacuoles (2) filled with cell sap. Secondly, plants have chlorophyll for photosynthesis, contained in chloroplasts (3).*

chemicals dissolved in water (pond water, soil water and sea-water, for example) using an important process called *photosynthesis*. In this process a plant converts water and carbon dioxide into sugar, using energy derived from sunlight. Oxygen is given off as a by-product into the air. Photosynthesis requires one of the activating chemicals in the plant tissues before it can occur. These chemicals are coloured, the commonest in land plants being the green-coloured chlorophyll and in brown sea-weeds the brown-coloured fucoxanthin. The chemicals give the plants their overall colour, and are called plant pigments.

Other important ways in which plants differ from animals are that the cell walls of plants are composed of cellulose – which those of animals are not – and that plants on the whole are stationary.

Animals which eat plants only are called *herbivores*. Those which live on animal tissue are called *carnivores*. *Omnivores* eat both plants and animals. This food, when digested, is broken down by the animal, with the release of carbon dioxide and water among other things.

A very simple summary of the relationship that exists between plants and animals is that plants build up sugar and related substances, and animals consume them and break them down. The breaking-down process, called *respiration,* (the same word is used for breathing in higher vertebrates) is thus the reverse of photosynthesis. It is fair to say that as fast as the plants consume water and carbon dioxide and manufacture sugar with the release of oxygen, animals break down the sugar (after eating the plant material), using the oxygen in the process and producing carbon dioxide and water.

Animals and plants are characteristically made up of cells (or consist of one cell) each with a nucleus. Bacteria are unicellular. They are unlike both unicellular plants and animals because they have a different kind of nucleus, they do not photosynthetise, and do not consume solid food. Some bacteria are parasites, living inside other organisms and causing diseases, while others are free-living, absorbing nutrients from their surroundings. All are microscopic in size.

Above: *A simple food chain. Plants provide food for vegetarians like the aphid here, which is in turn eaten by the larvae of the lacewing fly. Flies are in turn eaten by other predators, represented here by a flycatcher, which is itself preyed on by others like the cat. Thus the cat depends ultimately on plants for food, through a chain of other consumers.*

Left: *Plants make carbohydrates out of simple substances. These are used by all the other creatures that depend on them for nourishment. Carbon dioxide and water provide the raw materials and the energy for photosynthesis is obtained directly from sunlight trapped by chlorophyll in the plant cells. Oxygen – another vital requirement of nearly all living things – is released at the same time. The arrows show the passage of materials within the plant when photosynthesis – the process of making sugar – takes place.*

Fungi – particularly the toadstools – resemble plants superficially but lack the pigments of plants and do not photosynthetise. They rely for their food-source on dead or living animal and plant matter. Fungi differ from plants and animals in that their cells often have numerous nuclei (not just one), or to put it another way cell walls occur between the nuclei only at long intervals. Those cell-walls that exist consist in most cases of a substance unlike the cellulose of plant cells, although chemically related to it.

Viruses, which are the smallest living things and are too small to be seen with an ordinary microscope, cause a variety of diseases. They differ from other living things in not having a nucleus. Viruses occur only in the tissues of other living things, being found alike in animals, plants, fungi and bacteria.

Although growth and reproduction are the two features possessed by all living things, most also have other characteristics which distinguish organisms from inanimate objects. Many have some awareness of what is going on around them, and this is called sensitivity.

Another characteristic of living things is that, following the consumption and incorporation of nutrients or food, there is waste to be disposed of.

Genetics

If you look closely at a population of living things, animals or plants, you will usually find that no two individuals are alike in every way. There is variation in appearance from one to another. Some of this variation results from the surroundings in which the individual animal or plant has grown – for example plants grown in shady places are often taller and more straggly than plants of the same species grown in the open. Other variation between individuals is not caused by environment but results from the unique make-up of each individual, and is termed *genetic variation.* In most cases the appearance of an individual organism is determined partly by the animal's environment and partly by genetic variation.

The tissues of all living things are made up of cells. The growth of each cell is controlled by its nucleus or central part, so the growth, extent and nature of each tissue is under the control of myriads of nuclei in its component cells. The activity of each nucleus is controlled by long, thread-shaped bodies called *chromosomes.* These chromosomes make up most of the nucleus. Each has along its length numerous chemical complexes, each of which is called a *gene.* The chemical construction of the genes controls the activities of the chromosomes, and hence those of the nuclei and of the cells, so that ultimately the growth and construction of the whole organism is controlled by the genes.

Since an organism acquires its gene complement during the fertilisation of the egg from which it develops, it inherits its genes jointly from its two parents. The passing-on of genes and of the effects they produce (the characters) in the whole organism is called *heredity,* and the study of the variation due to the genes is known as *genetics.*

The rôle of genes in the passing-on of characters has not always been understood. The first person to show how some of the characters of a parent could be transmitted to its offspring was probably a monk, Gregor Mendel (1822–1884; see pages 48–49). He studied mathematics and biology at the University of Vienna before entering the Augustine monastery at Brno, now in Czechoslovakia. In the 1850s and 1860s, Mendel conducted simple experiments using pea-plants, which showed several important facts.

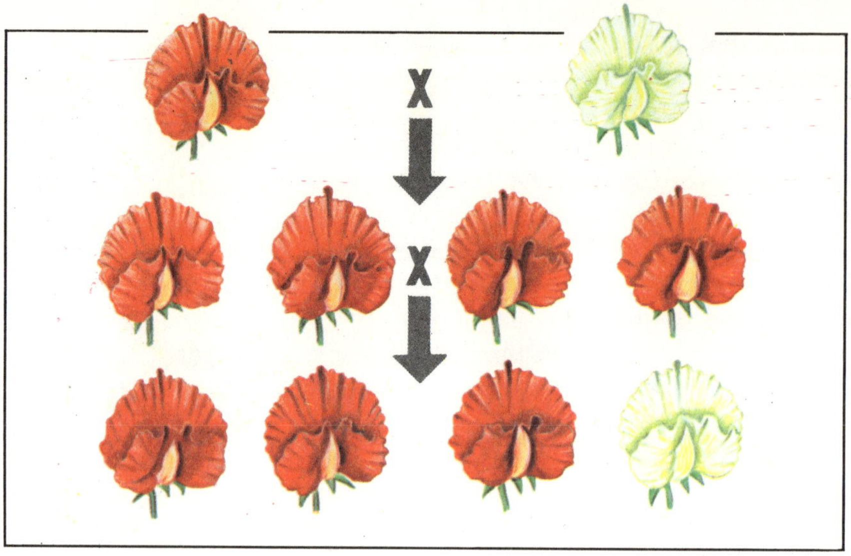

Above: *A red-flowered sweet pea is crossed with a yellow-flowered one. Their offspring are all red, but the next generation shows about three red offspring to each yellow.*

Firstly, Mendel found that there were some 22 pure-breeding *strains* (varieties) among his plants. Secondly he found that if he crossed certain of the varieties, say those having green seeds and those with yellow seeds, all the offspring were plants producing yellow seeds. Breeding from these seeds, to produce a second generation, resulted in some plants having yellow seeds and others having green seeds. The two kinds were almost exactly in the proportion of three yellow to one green.

Mendel repeated this experiment for many of the characters by which he identified his strains, and always got an answer close to three to one. By clear and ingenious reasoning he deduced that one kind tended to appear in preference to the other if both were present in the make-up (one would now say *gene-complement*) of the parent plant – in other words one character was 'dominant' over the other, which was 'recessive' and disappeared in the first generation to reappear in the second.

Mendel could not explain his intriguing results and they were not understood until around 1900, when the following explanation gradually dawned on the biological world. Whenever a cell divides to form two new cells its nucleus divides into two as well. Prior to cell division each chromosome has divided *along its length* to form two identical half-chromosomes, or

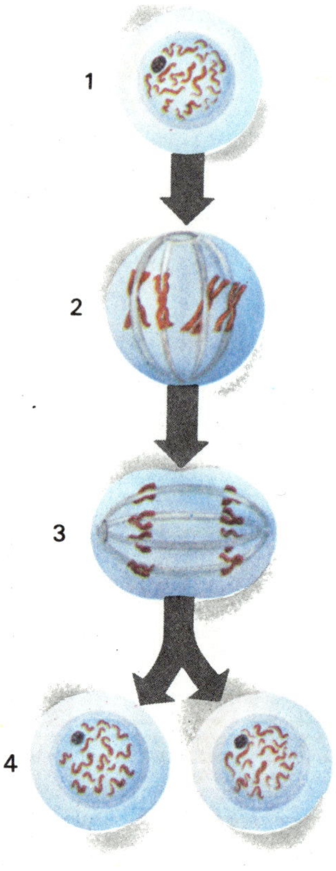

Above: *Mitosis. The chromosomes become visible in the nucleus (1). Each chromosome has split lengthwise so that there are two of each (2). A complete set then passes to each end of the cell (3) which divides (4). Each daughter cell now has a full chromosome complement.*

Far right: *Crosses between different species, like this zebra-horse cross (mid-left), are usually sterile.*
Below: *Meiosis. Chromosomes appear (1), similar pairs align (2) and one of each pair moves to each end of the cell(3) which divides (4). Each chromosome doubles lengthways and then undergoes mitosis (5, 6). Each of the four daughter cells is haploid (has half a chromosome complement). Fertilization restores a full set.*

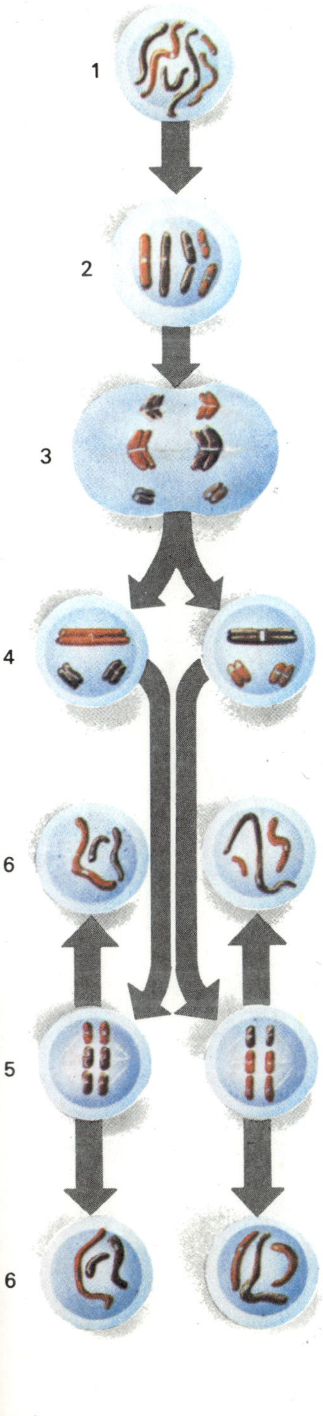

chromatids. Each half-chromosome forms, with half-chromosomes from the other chromosomes, one of the new nuclei, the other half-chromosomes forming the other new nucleus. New cells form around each of the two nuclei. This process of nuclear division is called *mitosis*.

After cell-division each half-chromosome begins to manufacture a new half-chromosome along its length, restoring the chromosomes to full size.

Each half-chromosome manufactures a new half-chromosome along its length, restoring the chromosomes to full size.

When eggs and sperm (or the corresponding structures in plants) are produced, however, this manufacture of the new half-chromosomes does not occur. This type of nucleus division is càlled *meiosis*. During fertilisation the corresponding half-chromosomes from sperm and egg fuse together to form full chromosomes. In this way the chromosomes of the fertilised egg, and hence those of the resulting embryo, carry genes derived jointly from the two parents.

Every cell in the body of an animal or plant (reproductive tissue and special tissues such as blood excepted) contains a particular number of chromosomes, which is constant for its species. For example, man has 46 chromosomes, the fruit-fly 8, the garden pea on which Mendel worked 14, the bullfrog 26, the potato 48, and a species of crayfish 200. The numbers are all even, and we find that they represent pairs of *similar* chromosomes (not to be confused with the identical half-chromosomes).

In many species the control of whether an individual is male or female rests with one pair of chromosomes, the sex chromosomes. In man, for example, one of the chromosomes consists of a pair of similar chromosomes which may or may not be alike. If they are alike (each chromosome being called 'X') the individual will be female, but if one of these chromosomes is of a slightly different ('Y') variety the individual will be male. These two kinds of chromosomes of the male separate during the manufacture of sperms, so that half of the sperm contains 'Y' chromosomes which will cause male offspring to

develop, and half contains 'X' chromosomes which result in female offspring.

Thus the sex of a human baby – though not of the offspring in all animals – is determined by the kind of sperm which fertilises the egg. The human female plays no rôle in sex-determination.

Some genes appear only in the male, others only in the female. These genes are located on the sex-chromosomes and are called *sex-linked genes*, producing sex-linked characters. Because of this the mode of inheritance differs in the two sexes. Colour blindness in the man is an example.

Oc̀casionally, a gene changes apparently spontaneously, perhaps in response to X-ray bombardment from space; that is, it *mutates*, and subsequently has a slightly different influence on the structure or working of the species from that which the gene had in its original form. By this means an offspring might differ from its parents – usually only very, very slightly – although breeding true itself.

Most mutations are not beneficial, but occasionally one occurs which enables its bearers to survive slightly better than those without it, and the new gene may eventually spread through the population, replacing the old one. In such a case the whole population will have changed its character, and an evolutionary advance will have occurred.

Classifying Plants and Animals

Most people talking about a particular kind of plant or animal refer to it by a familiar or popular name. The use of that name at once conjures up in the mind of a listener not only that they are hearing about – for example – a tiger, but also a mental picture of the animal: that it is a member of the cat family, has four legs, is furry, has stripes, and is dangerous. In this way we can recognise not only that the animal under discussion is a tiger, but also that it is related to domestic cats, and has a particular place in nature's scheme of things – in other words, we unconsciously classify it.

Today, more than 1,250,000 different species (kinds) of animals have been recorded and described, with more than 300,000 species of plants. With so many living things to classify, popular names are just not enough. And, in addition, people have many different popular names for the same things, at least as many as there are different languages, and often use the same popular name to describe different things: for example, 'robin' is used to describe two completely different species of birds on opposite sides of the Atlantic Ocean. But over the past 300 years a sound system of classification has been evolved. The science of classification is known as *taxonomy*.

The earliest naturalists were concerned mainly with finding out how many kinds of animals and plants there were. Plants were easier to study, because they did not run or fly away when approached, and as a bonus to those who studied them they often provided herbal remedies and cures. Frequently the study, classification and naming of plants went hand in hand with the apothecary's trade. A folklore grew up surrounding plants which had a medical use, were good to eat or poisonous, or were useful for their timber.

An English botanist, John Ray (1627–1705), was the first person to make an organised classification of living things into species, and to group similar species together into larger groups (genera and families).

Even today living things have still to be completely catalogued, and new species of the smaller animals, particularly insects, are being discovered every year. Classification is largely undertaken by professional biologists in national museums.

The scheme of classification of plants and animals used today is based on the logical process perfected by the Swedish naturalist Carolus Linnaeus (Carl von Linné, 1707–1778). It is designed so that the relationship of each species to all other living and fossil species can be seen at a glance.

A species is defined as a group or population in which the individuals can interbreed successfully. Usually it is very time-consuming to determine whether a particular form, thought to be a new species, can or cannot interbreed with an already recognised species, so for practi-

Below: *Horses and zebras form a small family of closely related species. Their exact classification has been difficult because it is not known whether all the races of the domestic horse, represented here by the Dartmoor pony,* Equus caballus, *evolved from Przewalski's horse,* Equus przewalskii, *or from its subspecies the tarpan,* Equus przewalskii gmelini. *Tarpans are now extinct – the last one in captivity died in 1919 – but originally lived wild on the Eurasian steppes. Przewalski's horse now only lives wild in the Altai Mountains and western Mongolia, where it has to compete with domestic cattle, but it breeds successfully in zoos. Asses,* Equus asinus, *are another type of horse. Two species of wild ass still live in Asia and Africa; the domestic donkey is descended from the African species. The zebra,* Equus zebra hartmannae, *is closely related to horses, so closely that they can interbreed, which is why all these species are assigned to the genus* Equus, *but exact species are difficult to define.*

cal purposes species are recognised by biologists from their overall appearance (shape, size, colour, or habits).

Problems of identifying species vary. In some butterflies the females of several species resemble each other, and their coloration bears little relation to that of the males, which similarly resemble each other. At first glance it seems that there are only two species – one being the colour-form of the females, the other that of the males – but a close examination shows differently.

In some groups of animals there are many species, in others only a few. For example, there are about 30,000 species of fishes, but only 750 species of ribbonworms. The most numerous group is that of the insects, with more than 1,000,000 species.

Each species (or group of individuals thought to represent a species) is given a special scientific name of two parts – the genus and species. For example, the scientific name of one of the seagulls common

in Europe, the herring gull, is *Larus argentatus*. The name has a Latin ring about it, and it is written in *italics* to show that it is a scientific name and not part of everyday language. The genus name has a capital letter; the second, descriptive name has a lower-case letter. It does not have to be perfect Latin, merely to sound latinised. Scientists of all countries understand which species is meant when this name is used; whereas the name 'herring-gull', translated literally by, say, a Japanese scientist, might be taken to mean a gull which ate herrings, which it is doubtful the herring-gull ever manages to catch!

Right: *Carl von Linné, called Linnaeus because the language of scholars was Latin, was a Swedish naturalist. He published the definitive edition of his* Systema Naturae, *the basis of modern classification, in 1758. The use of latinised names in the international system of naming plants and animals continues to this day.*

The birds, together with the fish groups, the Amphibia and the classes Mammalia and Reptilia (mammals and reptiles), form the vertebrates. The vertebrates and three other obscure groups form the phylum Chordata – all the members of which have a backbone or other kind of stiffening rod.

The chordates, together with 22 other phyla including Mollusca (molluscs, pages 144–147), Annelida (true worms, pages 140–141) and Echinodermata (starfish and their allies, pages 148–149) make up the kingdom Animalia, the animal kingdom. This is contrasted with the two other kingdoms of living things, the plants and the bacteria and viruses.

Famous Names in Biology

Many of our present advances in science are possible only because of the work of biologists of the past. The discoveries of a few of the most famous of them are described here.

Aristotle (384–322 BC), probably the best known of the ancient biologists, was also a widely respected authority in other fields, including politics, art and astronomy. Among his contributions to biology was the idea – still accepted today – that living things are as much a part of the natural universe as the stars, the Sun, the Earth, water and rocks.

Pliny (Gaius Plinius Secundus, AD 23–79), known as Pliny the Elder, was a noted Roman student of natural things who perished while studying an eruption of the volcano Vesuvius at close hand. The 37-volume encyclopaedia which he compiled from over 2,000 ancient books remained the most widely-used text book of natural history for 1,500 years.

Right: *Pliny the Elder was not really a naturalist. His most famous work, the 37-volume encyclopedia of natural history, was compiled from existing publications and hearsay. It was considered such an authoritative text that, in days when scholarship was valued more highly than original work, it held back the progress of science for hundreds of years. It is a superb historical record of scientific thinking in 50* AD. *Many editions of this encyclopedia were published; this one dates from 1476, nearly 1,400 years after the death of its author.*

William Harvey (1578–1657) was an English physician who gained a reputation for his medicine in London hospitals, eventually becoming court physician to King James I and, later, King Charles I. In 1628 he published his discovery that blood flows round the body in veins and arteries, pumped by the heart.

Anton van Leeuwenhoek (1632–1723) was a Dutchman who invented a simple microscope. Among his discoveries were the blood capillaries linking the arteries to the veins; the fine structure of muscle, teeth and eye-lenses; and the role of sperm in fertilising eggs. He was the first person to see protozoans, red blood cells and rotifers.

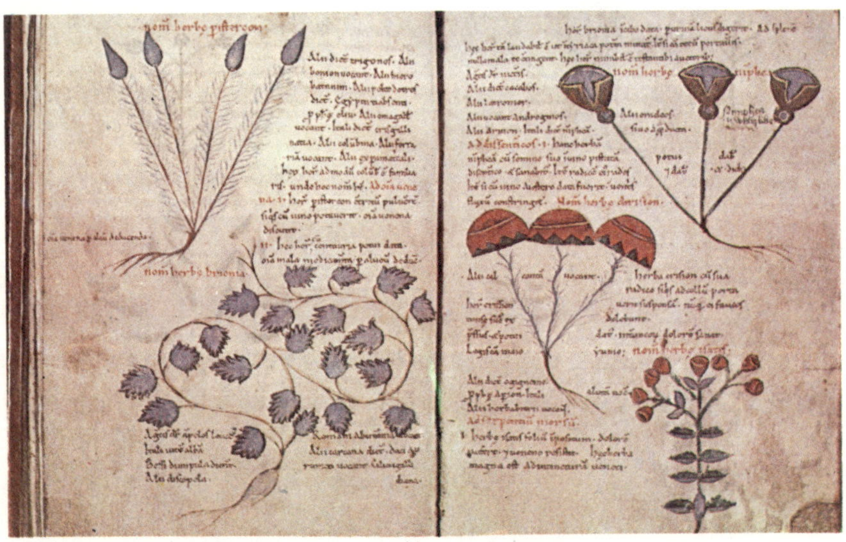

Below: *The medicinal use of plants is an extremely old practice. The use of herbal medicines has been based on many different principles through the ages, from trial-and-error to the phases of the moon, and countless books have been produced for the guidance of medical practitioners, witches and housewives. A page from a typical medieval herbal is shown here. Herbals such as these varied in the accuracy of their plant descriptions, but many of them were beautifully illustrated.*

John Ray (1627–1705) was an English botanist and zoologist, whose book *General History of Plants,* written in Latin, summarised in 2,860 pages all the botanical knowledge of the time. He made a careful study of plants and concluded firstly that 'like begat like' and secondly that they could be grouped into true-breeding populations or species.

Georges Louis Buffon (1707–1788) was a wealthy French scientist, who was probably the first person to discover eggs in the mammalian ovary; and was the first scientist to regard man as an animal.

Kaspar Friedrich Wolff (1733–1794), a German doctor who spent the last 27 years of his life lecturing on anatomy and physiology in Russia, became well known only after his death. He was the first scientist to come to the conclusion that, since animals and plants are both made up of cells aggregated to form tissues, they are essentially similar.

Carl von Linné (1707–1778), usually

referred to today by the Latin form of his name, Carolus Linnaeus, was a Swedish physician and botanist who carried on the classification of plants and animals begun by John Ray. He wrote many books on plants and animals. He gave every animal and plant he knew a two-part Latin name – a practice still followed today.

Charles Darwin (1809–1882), probably the greatest British naturalist ever, proposed biological theories which had a considerable impact on the man-in-the-street in Victorian times. While in his early twenties he joined a globe-circling expedition aboard HMS *Beagle*. His researches suggested that a species could evolve into slightly new forms when conditions changed, by a process called natural selection (sometimes called 'survival of the fittest'). Hence he concluded that man had evolved from apes, although not from modern species.

Gregor Mendel (formerly Johann Mendel) (1822–1884) was an Austrian monk who spent most of his life in a monastery in Brno, now in Czechoslovakia. He showed that some features of the pea-plants in his monastery garden, for instance red flowers, were 'dominant' over white flowers, the offspring of one of each parent all being red. Since in the next generation white flowers reappeared he concluded that the white and red 'characters' – now known to be carried by genes – had been 'segregated' in the meantime.

Louis Pasteur (1822–1895) was a French chemist famous for his work with bacteria. While a young man he decided – in opposition to the chemists of the day – that the souring of milk was caused by organisms. Since other processes (now called fermentations) involving the decay of food had other results, he concluded that many species of micro-organisms (today called bacteria) existed. He showed that the micro-organisms were carried through the air on dust, hence their presence everywhere, and that they could be eliminated by boiling and keeping things airtight. This process, now modified, is today called pasteurising in Pasteur's memory.

Thomas Hunt Morgan (1866–1945), an American geneticist, studied the inheritance of characters in the fruit-fly. His results linked together the evolution theory of Darwin and the heredity theory of Mendel, and gave a deeper understanding of how the theories might operate in nature. He thus laid the foundations of modern genetics.

James Dewey Watson (born 1928), an American biochemist, and Francis Crick (born 1916), a British biologist, together worked out the structure of the substance DNA (short for Deoxyribonucleic acid). DNA is a complex chemical of which chromosomes and genes, in the nucleus of all animal and plant cells, are made. It controls the form of all living things.

Sir Peter Medawar (born 1915), a British biologist, in 1953 successfully made tissue grafts from one mouse to another. Previously such grafts were rejected by the recipient's body and failed. Medawar's superb work paved the way for organ transplants between humans.

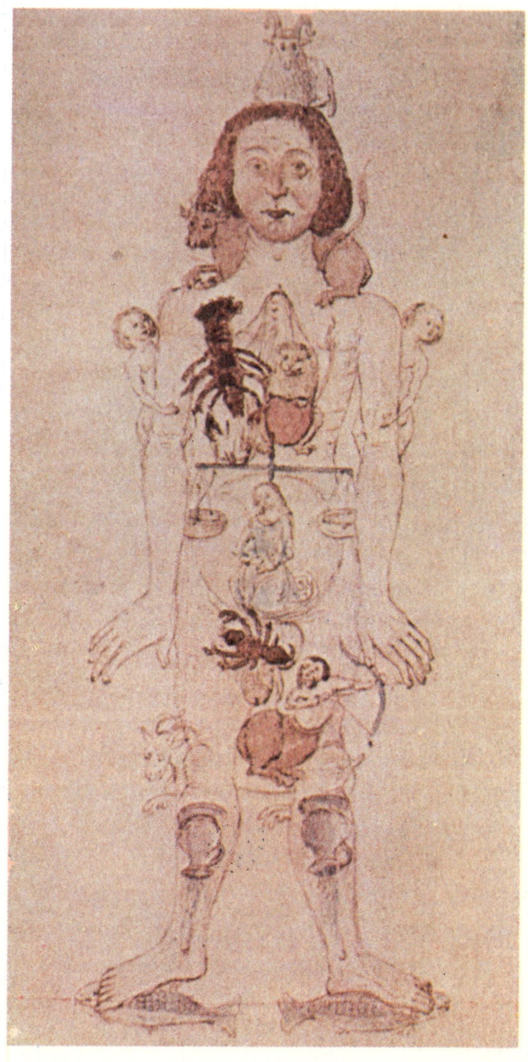

Above: *The top diagram of DNA is taken from the paper published by Watson and Crick in* Nature *in 1953. The two ribbons represent two chains of molecules, held together by 'rods' which are pairs of ring-like molecules. The lower diagram shows the same structure as a solid.*
Right: *In astrology, each sign of the zodiac controls a part of the body. The head is dominated by Aries, neck by Taurus, Gemini for the arms, Cancer the breast and Leo the heart; Virgo rules the belly and Libra the hips; Sagittarius between the thighs, Aquarius the legs and Pisces controls the feet; Capricorn guards the rear whilst Scorpio is associated with the sexual organs.*

Evolution

It is generally accepted that present-day animals and plants differ from those of the past, having changed by a general process called evolution. But this theory has been widely accepted for little more than a hundred years.

The first scientists to realise that changes must have taken place were a French naturalist, the Comte de Buffon, and an English physician, Erasmus Darwin, both working in the mid-1700s. In 1809 another French naturalist, the Chevalier de Lamarck, wrote a book, *Philosophie zoologique,* in which he developed the theory of evolution still further. He took the view that species could change by tiny modifications, generation by generation; but he also thought that changes taking place in an animal's lifetime could be passed on to its descendants.

The present theory of evolution was evolved by two British naturalists, Charles Darwin – grandson of Erasmus Darwin – and Alfred Russel Wallace, working independently.

When he was a young man of 22, Darwin went as naturalist on a round-the-world map-making cruise aboard a British naval survey ship, HMS *Beagle*. The cruise lasted from 1831 to 1836. In the Galápagos Islands, some 970 kilometres (600 miles) off the coast of Ecuador, Darwin came across a group of birds, later to become known as 'Darwin's finches'. They were similar to each other in colour, song, nests, and eggs, and were clearly descended from the same finch stock, but each had a different kind of beak, and each was adapted to a different way of life. There were seed-eaters, a fly-catcher, a 'woodpecker', and other types. Darwin assumed that the ancestors of all these types had been blown to the islands in freak weather, survived, and changed somehow into the various forms.

In the years after the voyage Darwin gradually came to the conclusion that individuals better adapted to their environment would tend to leave more offspring, while those kinds less suited would gradually die out.

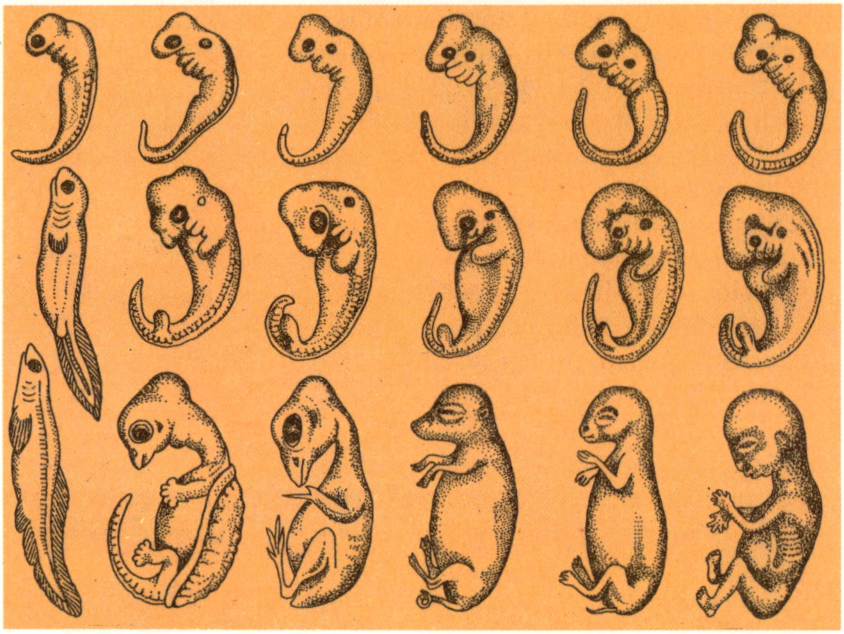

Above: *The development of embryos of different species. From left to right: fish, tortoise, hen, pig, rabbit, man. The young embryos in the top row are remarkably similar but the fish remains much the same while the others change.*

In his search for an illustration of the process of evolution nearer to home than the Galápagos Islands, Darwin studied several domestic animals and plants. Domestic pigeons, for example, had been bred from the wild rock dove into a variety of forms such as the white fantails, tumblers, pouters and racing pigeons. Similarly, horses had been bred into forms as different as slim, fast racehorses and heavy, powerful shire horses. In each case man had decided which animals to keep for the breeding stock, and had imposed what Darwin aptly called 'artificial selection'; that is, survival of those most fitted to man's purpose.

Meanwhile Alfred Russel Wallace had reached similar conclusions by working along different lines, during travels in the Amazon River area and the Malay Archipelago. Wallace noticed that there are big differences in the mammals of Australia and islands close to it, and those of other nearby islands which are linked, zoologically speaking, to mainland Asia. He also noticed that nearly-related species occurred close together, while more distantly-connected relatives were more widely spread. Finally, he noticed that while large groups, such as fish and sea-urchins, existed for long periods in the fossil record, individual species in these groups died out and never reappeared, being replaced by others.

Wallace sent an essay on his theory to

Above: *The peppered moth, showing both light and dark forms. In areas where dark moths used to have an advantage because the trees were darkened by industrial pollution, they are now becoming rarer where pollution is controlled and the trees are becoming cleaner.*

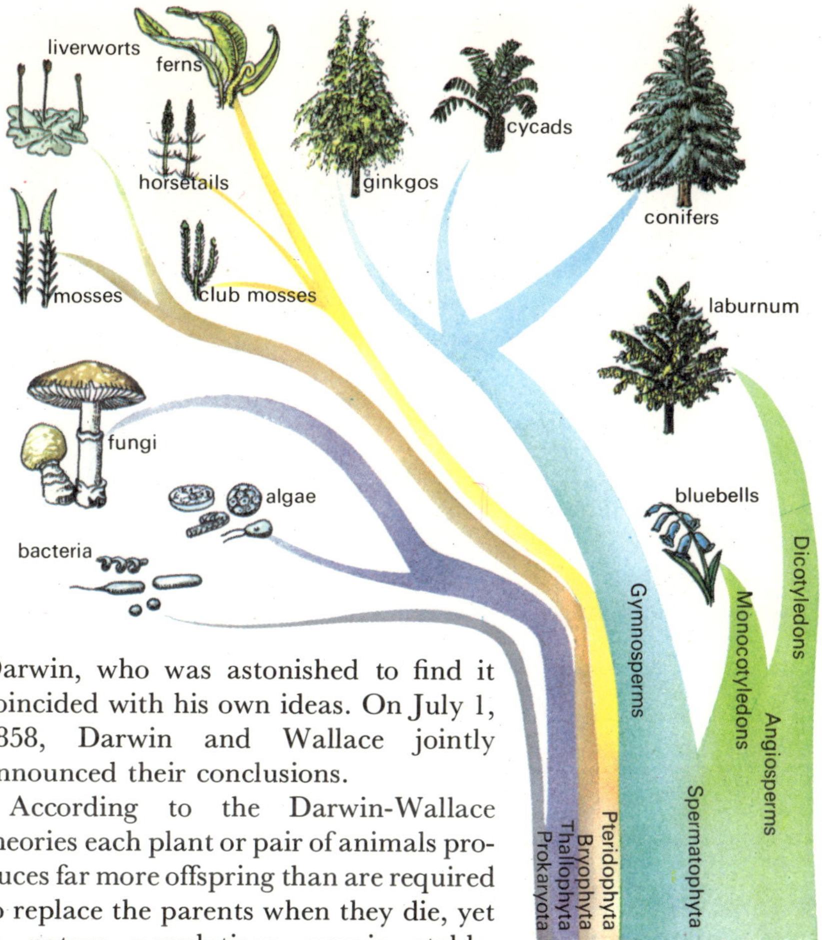

Above: *The evolution of plants. The variety of plant families on the Earth today have developed through the ages from less diverse groups by a process of adaptive radiation and specialisation. The same ancestral stock has produced trees and toadstools.*

Darwin, who was astonished to find it coincided with his own ideas. On July 1, 1858, Darwin and Wallace jointly announced their conclusions.

According to the Darwin-Wallace theories each plant or pair of animals produces far more offspring than are required to replace the parents when they die, yet in nature populations remain stable. Darwin and Wallace saw that among the young born only few could hope to survive, and because all living things vary those that did survive would be the ones best adapted to their environment. These would in turn produce young which would, because 'like produces like', resemble their parents. Advantageous change would therefore spread through the population, and in the course of many generations, would change the species. This process of survival of the fittest is known as natural selection.

A modern example of the process of evolution by natural selection in action is provided by the peppered moth. The moth is normally pale in colour, a mottled grey which enables the moth to settle, wings outstretched, on the bark of a lichen-covered tree and be unnoticed by predatory birds. Many years ago British naturalists found a second variety of this moth, with dark, sooty wings.

Research has since established that the two kinds of moths are, in fact, of the same species, but the dark moths live in urban surroundings, where the trunks of the trees on which they live are dark with industrial grime. The only difference between the two moths is in one *gene* – part of the cell which controls inherited characteristics. This particular gene regulates the amount of the black pigment, melanin, in the moth's body. Gene changes of this sort are called *mutations,* but the mechanism that controls them is not yet fully understood.

Since the time of Darwin and Wallace no shred of reliable evidence has been produced to cast doubt on their evolutionary ideas, although they have been adjusted slightly to take new findings into account. Biologists have now had time to make a more detailed comparison of related animals and plants and to show how they might have evolved from a common ancestor. Similarly, it is now thought that the behaviour of animals has evolved just like their structure.

Further evidence of evolution has come from a study of embryos and their development before the animals are born. It has been found that embryos pass through ancestor-like stages during their development. For example all mammals, including man, pass through a stage before birth in which they have gills. Finally, geologists have now a far wider range of fossils than was available to Darwin and Wallace, a range which on its own would be sufficient to suggest that evolution had occurred.

Left and below: *Three of the seed-eating ground-finches of the Galápagos Islands. Each eats a different type of seed.*

Ecology

Ecology is the study of the way in which plants and animals live in nature. It deals with their habits, their ways of life and their relations with their surroundings. The word ecology comes from the Greek *oikos,* meaning house, and indicates the fact that every living thing needs a place in which to live. However, a place to live is not enough on its own – it must be the right kind of place, in the right kind of 'neighbourhood', with an adequate food supply and freedom from attack.

The many different places in which living things are to be found – such as woods, ponds, streams, sea-shore, caves and mountain-tops – are called *habitats.* Each habitat can be subdivided further: for example woods can be classified by their kinds of trees, as oak woods, pine woods, beech woods, and each of these woodlands can be still further divided in other ways, for instance, tree tops, bark, leaf litter and soil.

Every habitat has its own particular kinds of animals and plants, and on the whole they stay within their usual surroundings. It follows that living things are adapted – usually very well – to the habitats in which they occur. Nevertheless life is seldom easy. There is in the natural world what is aptly referred to as a 'struggle for existence'. This fight for survival can be divided into two categories of difficulties which have to be overcome by an individual if it is to survive – physical and biological factors.

The physical factors are easy enough to appreciate. An organism needs to be in a habitat of the kind of temperature, light intensity, water supply, altitude, pressure or depth in the sea to which it is adapted, to list some of the more obvious physical features. The biological factors are less obvious. An individual must be able to locate a place of the right kind in which to live. Many organisms produce numerous young, and it is not always easy for a young individual to find somewhere to grow where one of its own kind does not already exist. Even if it finds a suitable place, it must then face competition for food from members of its own species and other species. The organisms of its own and other species together form the *community* in which it lives.

Communities have an organisation which seems to be the same in any habitat. You can think of a community in the form of a pyramid. At the bottom are the plants. In a grassland community, for example, plants absorb nutrients from the soil and in the presence of sunlight manufacture sugars and other carbohydrates. The next layer in the pyramid consists of the herbivores (plant-eating animals) which by their activities convert the plant material into animal protein. The herbivores are preyed upon by the next layer, the carnivores (meat-eating animals), most of which cannot eat plants directly.

Below: *This pyramid represents the amount of energy stored in each link of the food chain. All energy in living systems derives originally from the sun. Green plants are the only organisms which can directly utilise the sun's energy (light), and convert it into chemical energy. They are thus called* primary producers *and they form the base of the pyramid. Herbivorous animals form the next layer. They are termed the* primary consumers, *and the energy stored in this layer is only 10 to 20 per-cent of that in the bottom layer. The higher layers, the secondary and higher consumers (carnivores), store less and less energy, hence the pyramidal shape.*

The top layer consists of further carnivores which prey upon the previous ones.

Thus energy from the sunlight, trapped by the plants and incorporated in their sugars, becomes available to all the animals in the community. The result is what is called a food chain. A simple food chain might run grass – mice – foxes – bears, but generally there are so many alternative sources of food that the food chains interlace to form food webs.

You might imagine that within each food level there would be strong competition between species attempting to consume the same source of food. Among large animals and some predators this may be partly true, but in general there is such specialisation in food requirements and feeding habits that no two species living in the same habitat make precisely the same demands on it, and in times of hardship each species can turn to its own specialisation for survival.

Not all relations between species involve a struggle. *Symbiosis* (living together) may take the form of *parasitism,* in which one partner benefits at the expense of the other (see pages 54–55). There are many partnerships which involve a close and beautiful harmony. For example the common hermit crab has a soft body and inhabits the discarded shells of whelks and other marine snails. On the outside of the shell is often found a particular kind of sea-anemone, while inside, alongside the crab, lives a polychaete worm. The anemone and the worm feed on tiny scraps from the crab's meals, while providing in return some disguise and protection from predators; thus both the crab's partners benefit. Living together in this way is called *mutualism.*

Some kinds of protozoans are found only in the guts of certain species of termites. The termites eat wood, the cellulose or raw material of which they can digest only with the assistance of these protozoans. The protozoans in return receive from the termites a supply of food and a place to live.

Association for mutual benefit exists between certain kinds of ants and the large blue butterfly. The eggs of the butterfly are tended by the ants. When the caterpillars hatch from these eggs they develop 'milk glands' along each side which exude a food substance which is collected and eaten by the ants.

In some partnerships the two organisms live together in harmony; only one partner benefits positively but the second partner comes to no harm through the association. The remora is a fish that sticks itself to sharks by means of a sucker on top of its head. It hitches a lift on its host and feeds on morsels from the shark's meal, but apparently provides no service in return. This type of symbiosis is called *commensalism.*

Above: *Hermit crabs live in empty whelk shells, and a so-called parasitic anemone,* Calliactis parasitica, *is nearly always borne on the shell. The relationship is by no means one-sided as this name suggests. Both crab and anemone benefit – an example of mutualism.*

Below: *Food chains in the sea. The tiny, single-celled diatoms are called the 'grass of the sea' since they are the primary producers. The primary consumers are the animals of the plankton. Fish, from sprats to sharks, form the secondary and other consumers.*

Parasites

Very few living things survive in complete isolation and most live in complex communities among large numbers of plant and animal species. Each alters the habitat slightly by being part of it. Plants take minerals from the soil or water, reducing the availability of these essentials for other plants. Animals eat plants, or each other, clearly altering the environment as they do so. Plants by photosynthesis and animals by breathing both change the balance of oxygen and carbon dioxide in the air, thus altering the general conditions for life.

Perhaps because of the way that organisms affect each other, they are, in nature, usually spaced out. The trees in a wood cannot grow successfully if they are too close, and among animals even creatures of the same species normally keep a certain distance away from each other, unless they are joining in a specific social activity. Watch a herd of cows feeding – they move as a group as they eat, so that none will be closer than a certain distance from her nearest neighbour.

This individual distance is a very real thing. It accounts for the fantastic precision with which great flocks of birds can fly, or big schools of fishes swim. As soon as one of the leading birds or fishes moves, it enters the territory of one or more neighbours, and these animals move in turn, the action being transmitted very rapidly through the whole group. It is only during times of abnormal stress or panic that animals allow the close approach of others.

Above: *The relationship between the buffalo and the red-billed oxpecker sitting on its nose is mutually beneficial: there are enough external parasites on cattle to support oxpeckers completely.*

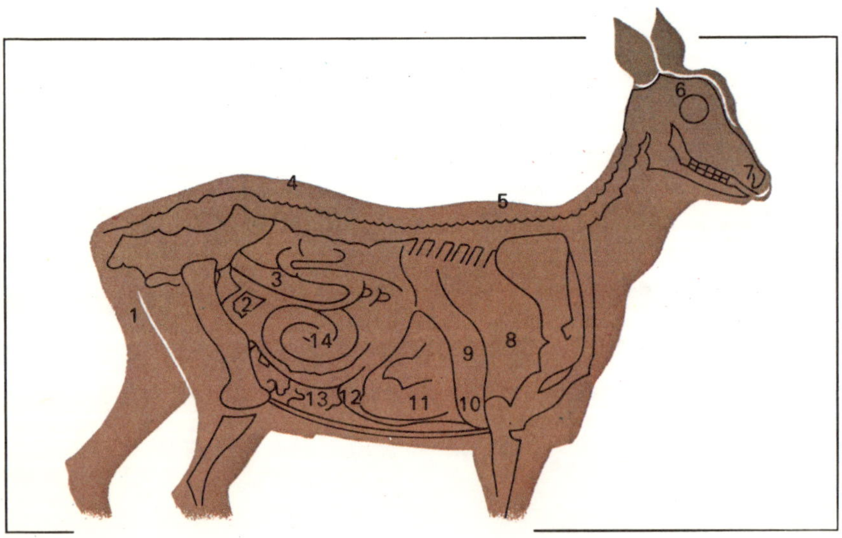

Below: *Some of the sites in which a deer may be parasitised. It may have ticks in the groin (1), louse maggots or parasitic fly grubs under the skin of the back (4, 5), gad-fly larvae in the nose (7) and lungworms in the lungs (8). Gut parasites include round-worms in the stomach (11), duodenum (12, 13), small intestine (14) and large intestine (3). Tapeworms also live in the intestine (14), but their cysts live in the brain (6). Flukes live in the liver (9), bile ducts (10) and plexus (2). An animal so heavily infested in all these places would be unlikely to survive.*

Even so, animals sometimes allow others, usually of a different species, to associate with them. At first it may be because both benefit slightly from the partnership, as a sheep that allows a jackdaw to sit on its back. The bird is getting an easy meal from the ticks on the sheep's fleece while the sheep is relieved of these annoying parasites. Some kinds of animals have developed this kind of mutually helpful relationship much further.

In other cases, one partner takes while the other gains nothing. This situation, found among both plants and animals, we call *parasitism.* Parasites are found among all the major groups of animals in the world, and there are few species which are free from them – there are even parasites of parasites (hyperparasites).

Some parasites live on the outside of the host's body (*ectoparasites*); others which live internally are known as *endoparasites.* In general, parasites are much smaller than their hosts, although there are exceptions such as the cuckoo, which is larger than most of the birds whose nests it inhabits.

The reason for this disparity in size is that it is in the parasite's interests to keep its host alive so that the host can continue to provide the parasite with living space and food. If the parasite made demands upon its host that were too great, then both would probably die, for most parasites are poorly equipped to live outside the bodies of their hosts. Some invertebrates have insect parasites which kill them after they reach a certain stage of development, but the parasites of vertebrates normally do no more than weaken their hosts. As most parasites have no need to move far their limbs are reduced, and since they have no need to search for food their sense organs are minimal.

Nearly every parasite is 'host specific'; in other words, it can normally inhabit only the one species. It seems as if the parasite finds a chink in the structure or behaviour of the host which allows it to attack at that point. For instance, a cuckoo can only be successful because the little birds whose nest it takes over do not, apparently, recognise their eggs or chicks if they are removed from the nest. Once the cuckoo chick has thrown out the host's eggs or young, they become alien objects, to be ignored, even if they could easily be retrieved. The foster parents lavish their attentions on the usurper instead.

In general, however closely the parasite may adapt itself to the host's way of life, and however little it may take, the host still wishes to be rid of its uninvited guest which must, therefore, make strenuous efforts not to be removed. A dog scratches to remove the fleas, which grip its coat with their clawed feet to avoid being dislodged. Internally, the powerful digestive juices of the same dog may be constantly attempting to dissolve a tapeworm, but failing because of the 'anti-enzyme' the parasite is thought to produce to protect itself.

In a long-lived host, the parasites are likely to be long-lived also, but a large population must not be allowed to build up, for too heavy a demand on the host might kill it and all would die. The young of internal parasites are voided from the host's body, usually as eggs. The eggs hatch into larvae, usually very different from the parent. They often have a complex life history, passing through the bodies of one or more intermediate hosts before being ready to live in the same species as their parent. These intermediate hosts are frequently invertebrates and play an essential part in the distribution of the parasite species. Even so it is a hazardous way of life, and most parasites produce far more young than do other species. Some very small parasites may be injected directly into their hosts' bodies by bloodsucking insects which are known as *vectors* or carriers.

The abundance of parasites leads us to wonder why they are there. They can be regarded as specialised predators, but since they do not kill their prey directly, they must play a different part from the large carnivores which control the numbers of herbivores and weed out the weak and sickly from among them. Much work needs to be done before we can understand in full the part parasites play in the general economy of nature.

Right: *Mites and ticks are spider-like parasites, some of which trouble man. Ticks penetrate the skin with their sharp mouthparts to gorge themselves on blood. Smaller mites cause problems among poultry, pigs, bees and many other domestic creatures. Here a water scorpion is carrying its load of parasitic mites.*

Below: *European cuckoos do not build nests or take any part in rearing their young; they simply make use of the parental instincts of other birds. A female cuckoo lays her eggs singly in nests already containing eggs; the eggs may be coloured to resemble those of the species that the female prefers to parasitise. The young cuckoo ensures its own survival by pushing out other eggs and baby birds from the nest as soon as it hatches, and the parasitised parents expend the whole of their feeding power on the intruder. Here a whitethroat is the chosen foster-parent.*

Plant and Animal Populations

Some kinds of animals and plants are quite rare, many are very common, and between the two extremes other kinds are more or less abundant.

In an oak woodland in western Europe, for example, the number of resident badgers might be a few dozen, the earthworms would almost certainly number hundreds of thousands, and some kinds of insects would quite possibly number millions. This much perhaps is obvious, but what is quite remarkable is that, although all the animals and plants in a forest (and in many other habitats) occupy much of their time busily eating each other, nevertheless from year to year their numbers remain more or less constant. We would be surprised to find thousands of badgers in a wood where previously there had been only a few dozen, and equally surprised to find only a handful of worms and hardly any flies.

In a well-balanced community of plants and animals there is a comfortable number of each species which can be accommodated in any particular area. In other words, the density (number per unit area) remains roughly steady. There are exceptions, and two of these, the lemmings and the locusts, will be discussed later.

A group of individuals (plants or animals) living in a particular area (field, island, county, country, or any other area that one might choose) is called a population. The word comes from the Latin *populus,* meaning people. In general terms, populations are controlled in their size by two kinds of influences – those which increase them, and those which decrease them.

If nothing controlled the number of badgers in a wood, they would increase in numbers until the wood was overflowing with them. If a pair of animals produced a mixed litter of four offspring, that would be two pairs in the place of one. The next generation would be four pairs, the next eight pairs, and so on, so that after only 16 generations there would be 131,072 badgers, that is roughly one for every word in this book! And that is assuming that in each generation the parents died at the end of each year – a most unlikely state of affairs. Such population increases never occur in badgers, and indeed rarely occur in nature, but the number of offspring produced in a healthy, stable population is nevertheless usually slightly greater than the number of offspring required to maintain the numbers. This leads to the 'survival of the fittest' (or, equally, a 'death of the least fit'), an important part of the theory of evolution (pages 50–51).

Many features of the environment (surroundings) of animals and plants have the effect of limiting their numbers. The most obvious perhaps is predation. As animals and plants increase in numbers so their predators eat more of them, and as a result of the better feeding conditions produce more offspring themselves. For a time the predators may increase in numbers, but sooner or later the population of the food-organism diminishes and the numbers of the prey animal similarly decline as its food runs out. However, such simple examples are met with in the living world only in communities having relatively few species. These communities include those in Arctic and desert regions.

In communities where there are a great many species, as in woodlands, each prey organism usually has several predators, and each predator several prey-sources, so that although the simple predator-prey relationship tends to operate, it is obscured. When one food starts to run out,

Above: *An English countryside scene. All the creatures are going about their business – perhaps not all at the same time as the picture suggests – but their lives are finely tuned together. The worms pulling down leaves are helping to enrich and turn the soil in which plants grow; they also provide food for moles and other animals and birds. Grasses are eaten by rabbits, which in turn support carnivores like stoats and foxes. Rabbits also help to control the growth of plants, eating some grasses and herbs in preference to others. The wood mouse here is feeding on beech mast from the tree*

overhead, an important source of winter food for rodents; it is in turn eaten by owls. Birds feed on a wide variety of foods; the insect-eaters like blackbirds, thrushes, tits and robins hunt in different ways so that they are able to occupy roughly the same area, though blackbirds seem to be increasing while thrushes are declining in many places, which may be due to competition between them. They nest in different situations, too, again managing to avoid competition by keeping apart. Chaffinches are seed-eaters, like other finches, and also utilise the beech mast.

another is eaten instead, or as well, and the first food does not become exhausted.

Another regulating factor is the availability of space in which to live, and this is particularly important for animals with strong territorial instincts. Thus each European robin in a wood has a territory which it maintains at a certain size. If, at the end of a breeding season, there are so many robins that the territories will not all fit into the wood, then the weaklings are chased out. These weaker birds may have to move into unfavourable areas.

The robins still in the wood do not put up with smaller territories to accommodate the new recruits to the population. If they did so, they might lack enough food for the winter, or for feeding their young the following summer, and by the following year the species might reach very low numbers. Territorial behaviour thus prevents overcrowding and preserves the food supply.

Features of the environment which affect individual animals also affect the population of which they form part. Non-biological aspects of the environment important to the survival of organisms include temperature, light, water availability, nutrients, currents, pressure and soil type.

Sometimes it seems that the natural population checks do not work normally, since great increases in the numbers, or 'population explosions', occur. So-called plagues of greenfly, ladybirds and other insects are at least partly due to the weather, but other plagues (or high densities) result from a number of causes. Well-known examples are the eruptions in the populations of locusts and lemmings.

The migratory locust (*Locusta migratoria*) of Europe and Asia lives in desert or semi-arid country and in most years remains there, eating only the local vegetation. When the population builds up, rather different individuals, more active and with longer wings, develop within the population and massive migrations start.

Plants in the path of the locust swarms are totally stripped of leaves and stalks, and the impact on the local human population, deprived of food crops, is appalling. Such outbreaks have been recorded since antiquity. Since about 1700 there has been at least one locust plague recorded every 40 years or so.

Lemmings are mouse-like voles which live in Northern Europe and northern North America. Every three or four years the lemmings increase in numbers, and so do the Arctic foxes and owls which prey on them. Soon the lemmings eat all the available herbage and die in vast numbers – and with them the owls and foxes. In such simple communities, with few species, alternative food sources are not available.

Many lemmings – and owls – disperse southwards in plague years, but few if any return.

Life in the Sea

The vast expanses of the ocean form more than just a thin skin of water over the Earth's crust – the average depth is more than 3,660 metres (12,000 feet). When we remember that skin divers rarely work at more than 60 metres (200 feet), we can see that most of this vast volume of water remains unvisited by man. How then do we know about the oceans and their life?

Most of our knowledge of the oceans is gained through the work of survey vessels. The crews of ships discover the depth of the ocean bed by echo-sounding; the type of sediment on the bed by the use of dredges; and the temperature and characteristics of the sea water by the use of Nansen jars, which bring up water samples from different depths for laboratory analysis. Trawls, traps and nets of various kinds are used to investigate life of the oceans. Film and television cameras, triggered by the action of animals taking a bait, also help to gain an idea of life in the depths.

The picture which emerges is of an area of great richness of life. Yet this is strange, for much of the ocean is cold and devoid of light. A poor place to live you might think. And so it looks from the surface where, apart from the occasional fishes or dolphins leaping, there is no sign of the life below the surface.

All animal life depends on plants, for even the carnivores (meat eaters) feed on creatures which have fed on plants. The seaweeds which grow on the shore disappear as the water deepens, but the open ocean is not without plants – however they are all microscopically small. Imagine a forest, broken down not into leaves and branches but into individual cells. The plants of the sea are all single cells, each one capable of using the Sun's energy to power its foodmaking factory.

This need for light means that the plant life is concentrated near to the surface of the water, and the largest numbers of animals are found there too. Many of these animals are tiny floating scraps of life, and like the plants are too small to be seen with a naked eye. Some of these small animals are the *larvae* (young stages) of larger sea creatures; others are just very small animals. These tiny animals and plants together form a mass of minute life we call *plankton*. Plankton is the basis of the life of the sea, for it is the food of slightly larger creatures, which are, in turn, fed on by bigger ones still. This 'eat and be eaten' relationship forms what is sometimes known as a food chain; but the term food web describes it better, for many kinds of animals and plants are involved, predators becoming prey at different stages of the pattern.

Crustaceans and other floating or planktonic animals such as sea butterflies (pteropods) abound in these upper layers

Below: *A profile of the sea bed. The land mass of the continent continues as the continental shelf, not usually more than 200 metres (600 feet) deep. At the edge of the shelf the seabed begins to slope down more rapidly – though still quite gently – the slope shown in the drawing is much exaggerated. The sea floor varies in depth between about 1 and 10 kilometres (½ to 6 miles), but the bulk of the sea floor is between 3 and 6 kilometres (2 and 4 miles). These great depths beyond the continental slope are called the abyss, and occasionally they may be gouged with deep trenches: the deepest of these is well over 10 kilometres (6 miles deep). Animals on the sea floor form the* benthos, *but the majority will live swimming freely in the water. These form the* nekton. *They may be divided into those of the continental shelf and those of the open sea. The latter are termed* pelagic. *The pelagic nekton is zoned vertically. The upper waters of the oceans are illuminated and the plants can utilise the sun's energy directly. They are the main source of nourishment for those living below. Here we find most of the plankton.*

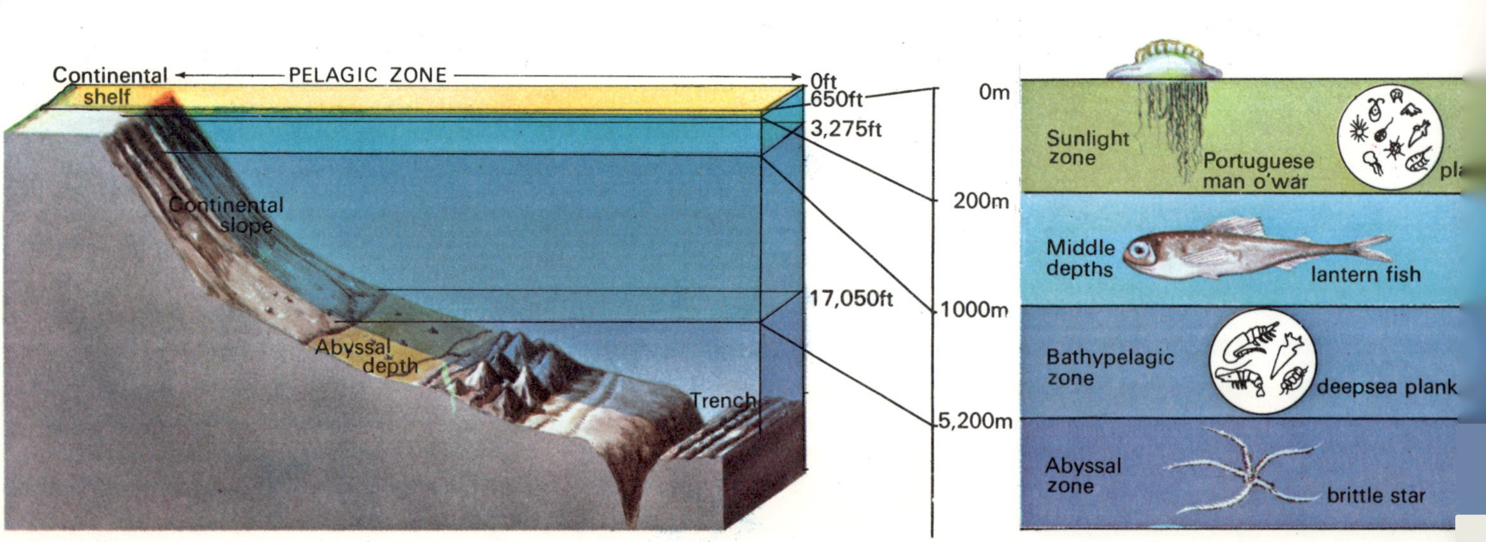

Animals feeding directly or indirectly on the plankton include the tunny, flying fish, turtles and dolphins. The portuguese man o' war floats on the surface, catching small fish with its trailing tentacles. Below this sunlit zone lie the middle depths. Here daylight just filters through. Many fish such as the lantern fish, hatchet fish and some stomatoids live here during the day, rising nearer the surface at night to feed on the denser plankton nearer the surface. The sperm whale will dive to these depths in search of squid. Lower down, where light does not penetrate the bathypelagic fauna lives. Deep sea plankton is specialised to feed on the gently falling detritus from above. This plankton forms the diet of Gulper eels and other fish which in turn are preyed upon by deep sea squid. The curious octopus-like vampire squid also lives here. At these depths, but on the sea bottom of the continental slope the rat tail fishes are found. Even the abyss is populated particularly by deep sea angler fishes bearing illuminated lures. Tripod fish and brittle stars are found on the sea floor and deep sea cucumbers burrow in the ooze.

of the sea. Great schools of fishes move in seasonal migrations from feeding to breeding grounds. Some of these fishes, such as herring or mackerel, are small. Others, such as tunny, grow to a length of 2 metres (6½ feet) or more. Most open-water fishes are streamlined, fast-swimming creatures, blue or grey backed and silvery below. Sharing this upper water environment are many species of squids, which vie with the fishes for speed and grace and voraciousness.

Whales are also animals of the surface of the sea. Some large whales feed entirely on plankton; the toothed whales, which include the porpoises and dolphins as well as the large sperm whales, eat fishes and squids.

Below about 200 metres (660 feet) the sea bed slopes away towards the abyssal depths. Here the water is dark and cold. Slow-moving currents are present, but the effect of waves, which occur only in the topmost waters of the ocean, is quite absent. The only life here is derived from the surface. The dead bodies of surface animals sink slowly through the water, attacked by scavengers. The scavengers are themselves food for a host of carnivorous squids and fishes, which include the strangest of living creatures. Most are small and dark coloured; many have huge, very sensitive eyes which make use of any light. Most of the light there is comes from the animals themselves, many of which have light-producing organs on their bellies and sides and round their eyes.

Food is scarce in the deep sea, and the animals that live there must be certain to hold what they can catch, and avoid becoming somebody else's meal. Deep-sea fishes in particular are armed with huge curved teeth which prevent the escape of any prey. Some have mouths which open to admit a meal larger than themselves, and they can push their delicate gills out of the way to prevent their being damaged by larger, struggling prey.

Finding a mate may be difficult, although light signals may be used to attract one. In some species a male, when he finds a female, attaches himself to her, becoming parasitically dependent on her. The oceanic squids are, if anything, even more bizarre than the fishes, with fragile bodies and huge eyes.

On the floor of the deep sea, sediments accumulate, often composed largely of the minute skeletons of tiny plants and animals. Few creatures live on this soft mud. Those that do are often blind, but with sensitive spines or spots on their bodies which can detect water pressure changes, and so tell of the presence of possible food or enemies. They never venture into the warm, sunlit fertile waters of the upper ocean, for they are perfectly adapted to their way of life, and they die if they are taken from it.

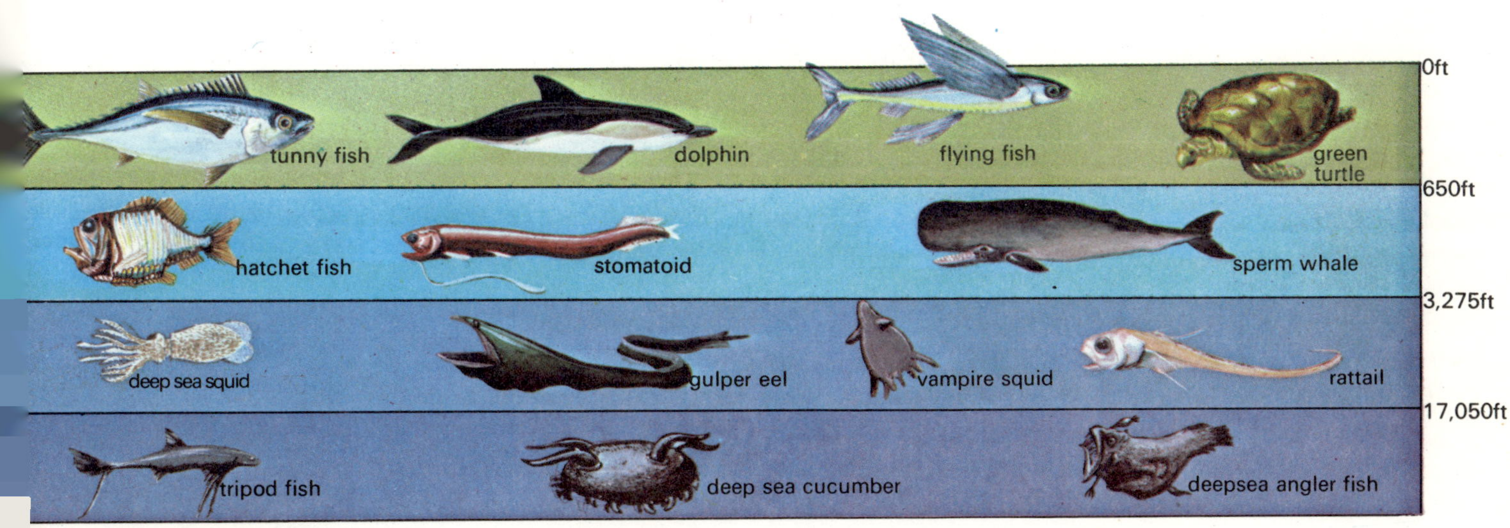

Life on the Shore

Where the land and the open sea meet, the water creeps twice daily down the shore to uncover the beach, then returns to drown it once more. We can see at once from this that the plants and animals of the seashore have to be able to withstand far greater changes in conditions than either those of the land or of the open oceans. Yet the seashore is rich in life of many kinds, with animals and plants adapted to the variations within the habitat.

These variations are greatest at the top of the beach, where a rock pool may be left as the tide retreats. If the weather is hot, the pool warms up quite quickly; some of the water evaporates so the salinity (proportion of salt in it) increases. If the weather is wet, the pool becomes diluted with rainwater and the salinity decreases.

Organisms living near the lower edge of the shore have to suffer great light variations. At high tide, when they are covered with up to several metres of water, most of the light may be filtered out so they have to exist in near darkness.

Apart from all these disadvantages, the plants and animals of the seashore have to stand the ever-present danger of battering by the waves. In times of storm the waves come crashing on to the beach with unbelievable force, carrying rocks and sand which tear and shred anything not firmly anchored or armoured.

Because of the different conditions at the top and bottom of the beach we find zonation, or change in the types of plants and animals, as we progress from the land towards the sea. This can be seen most clearly in the plants. Seaweeds found high on the shore can withstand long periods out of water; those less well equipped to survive exposure are found progressively lower down the shore. Each zone characteristically has a single dominant species of brown seaweed.

Seaweeds are very different from large land plants. They have no roots, stems, leaves, flowers or fruit. They are attached with 'holdfasts' to rocks or other solid objects on the beach, and they reproduce mainly by means of spores which float into the sea to found a new generation. Few animals can eat seaweeds, but the plants provide shelter against the dryness of low tide and the pounding waves of high tide for many creatures.

Representatives of almost all the major groups of animals are found on the seashore. Some are herbivores, such as the limpets which graze on young seaweed growth from the rocks and return exactly to their home spots as the tide begins to fall. Some plant eaters are specialists, like the beautiful blue-rayed limpet, which eats a protective notch for itself in the stipe (stalk) of an oarweed. Other herbivores, such as the sea slug *Aplysia,* eat a wide range of plants.

Many seashore animals are carnivores. Some, such as the plant-like sea anemones, catch and hold any small creature unfortunate enough to brush against their tentacles, which are armed with paralysing poisonous sting cells. Others, such as the dog whelk and the necklace shell, feed on bivalve shells, whose armour they pierce with their file-like tongues.

Carnivorous creatures, such as some fishes, lie in wait for their prey and dart out for the kill when they see it. Yet others, such as the starfishes, are slow-motion hunters, almost never failing to get a meal, for their tube feet enable them to hold on to their prey until it weakens. Some animals are active hunters, like the octopuses which search, usually at night, for crabs which they take back to their lairs to devour.

Many seashore creatures are filter feeders. Filter feeders draw large quantities of sea water into their bodies, where there is some mechanism for straining out the minute particles of life which abound in it. Sponges, bivalve molluscs and sea squirts all feed in this way.

Finally, there are the scavengers. These include many sorts of crabs and other arthropods, as well as some of the birds to be seen on the seashore. Scavengers have a most important job in the seashore community for they feed on dead and decaying plants and animals, and so keep the beaches clean. By their activity they return the complex materials of once-living things to the ocean, where they can be taken up again by plants.

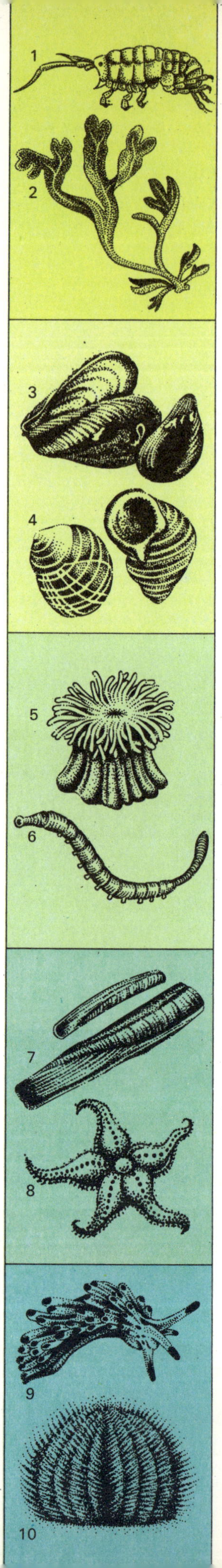

Above: *Seagulls are cliff-top dwellers. Their nests are made of vegetation, including seaweed, in which four eggs are usually laid. They are scavengers, clearing the beach of dead creatures when the tide goes out as well as actively fishing. Their droppings help to fertilise the cliff face.*

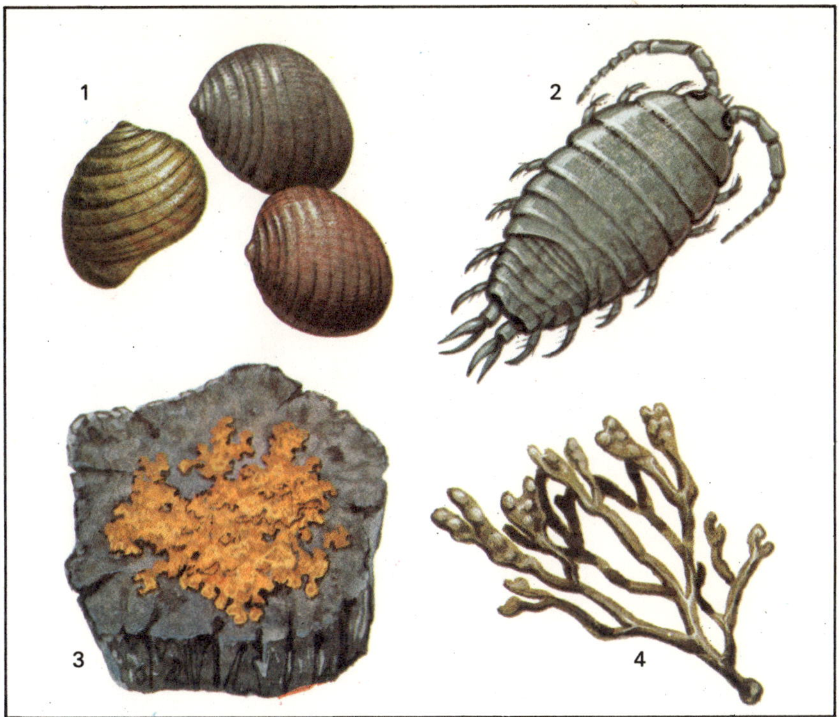

Above: *High up the beach, barely touched by the sea, lichens (3) encrust the rocks. Slightly lower, where they are moistened by the high tide, are tough seaweeds like channelled wrack (4). Living amongst these water-retaining seaweeds, molluscs such as these periwinkles (1) can be found. Arthropods are represented in the damp weed by such species as the sea slater (2).*

Left: *Some animals and plants of the shore in the order in which they live, from top to bottom, from high tide mark to below low tide. 1 sandhopper; 2 flat wrack* Fucus spiralis; *3 mussels; 4 periwinkles; 5 sea anemone; 6 lugworm; 7 razor shells; 8 starfish; 9 sea slug; 10 sea urchin.*

Below: *Between high and low tide marks, sandy shores are occupied by small scavenging crabs and worms which retreat into burrows at low tide.*

Below: *Prawns and more delicate seaweeds are found in the larger and deeper rock pools lower down the shore.*

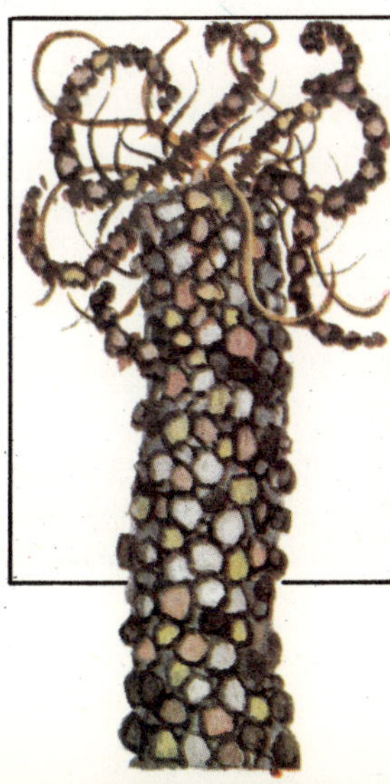

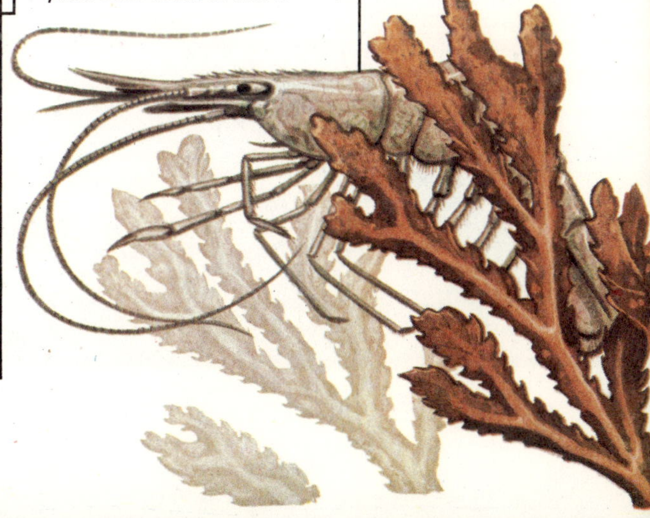

Life on Coral Reefs

Coral reefs – formed by the limy skeletons of tiny animals called polyps – are perhaps the most brilliant and most densely populated of all the living places in the world. They are found only in the tropics, for reef-building corals cannot survive for long in cool water. They are found near land, because they can thrive only in shallow water.

Those living reefs which seem to be growing out of the middle of the oceans are almost always on top of volcanic cones. The top of the volcano usually lies a little way beneath the surface of the sea. The reef grows in a ring, following the shape of the cone, and shelters the calmer waters of the shallow lagoon that is formed inside the ring.

Sometimes the reefs grow on a huge depth of dead coral rock. This is evidence that the sea bed has been sinking slowly, while the coral has been growing upward at the same rate.

The reason that reefs need such conditions to develop is that the reef-building corals all contain minute plants in their tissues. These plants require light in order to thrive, and since even the clearest sea water filters out the light, the corals cannot survive in water more than about 50 metres (160 feet) deep. You may ask why the corals need the plants. This question is not easy to answer completely, but the plants probably act to some extent as garbage recycling systems. The corals produce waste products, some of which the plants remove for their own growth. In making their own food from this, the plants produce oxygen as a by-product, which can be taken up by the corals.

Above: *In this photograph of Raiatea, a volcanic island in French Polynesia, the growing coral reefs can be seen clearly as light-coloured patches. The coral has grown round the island on the underwater slopes, where it will eventually reach the surface and die, leaving a limestone harbour wall round the island with deep water on either side of it.*

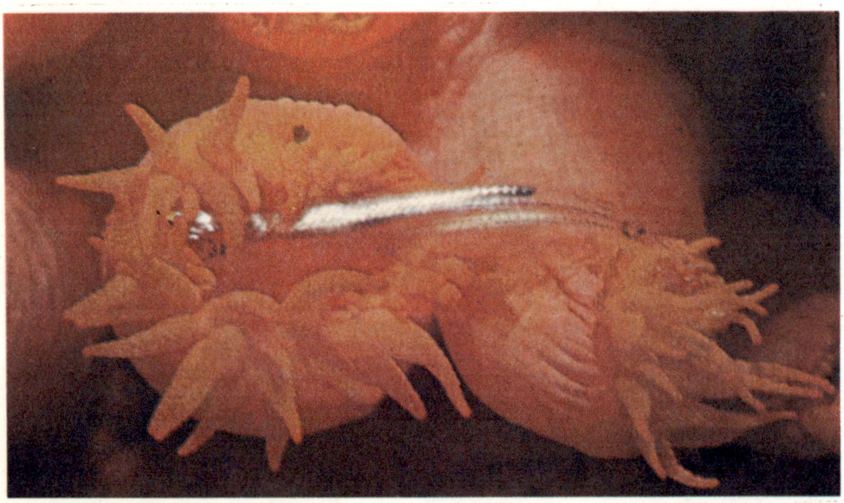

Below: *This reef-forming coral is a colony of anemone-like individuals called polyps. Two polyps, photographed during their nocturnal feeding period, have captured a fish in their tentacles. Under the polyps is a limestone skeleton continually secreted by the coral, raising it higher and creating a growing mound of limestone which will reach the surface as a reef.*

It is also possible that the plants help the corals to get the minerals with which they build their limy skeletons. The exact relationship is not understood, but if a coral is shaded, so that the plants cannot photosynthetise, it will probably die.

Reef-building corals are almost all colonial. That is to say that, although a reef may start as a single polyp which settles on a rock or some other hard object at the end of its larval life, it soon buds off another individual which, however, remains attached. Before long, many thousands of polyps are present, each a separate animal, but all connected by their hard limy skeletons, which together form a rampart in the sea. This coral wall often drops steeply away to the ocean depths on the seaward side of the reef.

The most active reef growth is found where there is a strong current carrying countless planktonic animals to the corals' mouths. On the outer edge of the reef rough water may break the more delicate growths. On the sheltered, inner edge, silting may prevent healthy growth, but growth is often vigorous, especially in the channels which cut through the reef.

Many corals are brilliantly coloured. The soft tissue covering the chalky support may be green or yellow or pink or purple, and even when the polyps are not

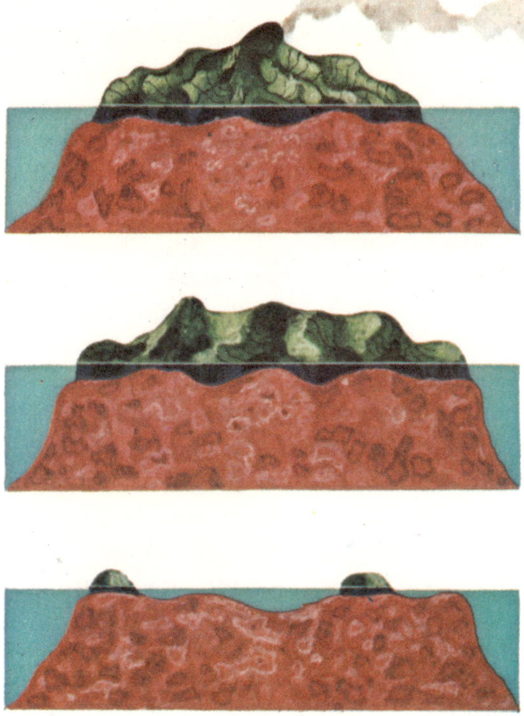

Left: *Volcanoes are unstable structures; they throw out molten rock and gases and often collapse into the hollow space that is left inside. This hollow is called a* caldera, *and such calderas are frequently found in the Pacific Ocean. When a volcano has been colonised by coral, the limestone reef remains even when the volcano collapses. The result is a coral atoll – a ring of coral surrounding a peaceful lagoon. Lagoons are sometimes completely enclosed, their living inhabitants without contact with the sea except in stormy weather. More often, however, they have one or more gaps into the open sea, since coral reefs are rarely complete rings.*

feeding the reef is a bewildering maze of hues. The flower-like polyps expand as they feed, and waves of movement may pass across the reef surface as they sway in unison to the passing water currents.

The vivid reef is populated with equally brilliant inhabitants. Gorgeous coloured parrot fishes, butterfly fishes and wrasse wear the brightest colours to be seen on the reef. Each of these species has its own way of life. The butterfly fishes have protruding snouts, with small, fine teeth, with which they nip the coral polyps from their stony homes.

Parrot fishes have strong teeth in the front of the mouth, with which they chew the coral branches, extracting the living material in their digestive systems. The broken-down coral which they excrete sifts down to fill in the holes in the dead coral reef. Parrot fishes are among the most important consolidators of the reef, providing conditions on which further growth can take place.

Many of the fishes of the reefs swim in large schools, but some, such as the predatory trumpet fish, are solitary, hiding round the blocks of coral and waiting for an unwary small fish to swim within reach. On the edge of the reef sharks may have their territories, but sharks rarely come into the shallow water of the lagoon, for they are creatures of the open sea.

Many relatives of the corals help to make up the reef. They include soft corals, sea fans and sea whips, which all form colourful plant-like growths across areas where currents bring them plenty of food morsels. Large sea anemones spread their tentacles. Massive sponges make growths which rival the corals in places.

As well as these sedentary creatures, there are many capable of active movement on the reef. Some of the most noticeable are the sea urchins. Often dark green or purple in colour, they occupy every crevice in the coral.

Related to the starfishes are the sea cucumbers. These static-looking animals are partly protected by their rough skin and partly by their ability to eject portions of their body. Some of them throw out sticky threads which entangle an aggressor, while other kinds can jettison practically all of their soft internal organs. These are eaten by the attacker, and the sea cucumber renews what it has lost in the space of a few weeks.

Starfishes are not as a rule very common on coral reefs, but in some areas recently one species, known as the crown of thorns, has increased greatly and is killing the reef by feeding on the coral polyps.

Many other animals are abundant on the reef, but some of the most beautiful are the sea snails, which vary from tiny cowries to huge conches and triton shells. The largest of all bivalve shells, that of the giant clam, often grows surrounded by coral, while the biggest of all the sea snails, the bailer shell, crawls over the reefs looking for food.

Below: *Corals grow in many different ways, resulting in characteristic shapes for different species. Some types form rounded boulders, others are tree-like. This staghorn coral is usually found on the sheltered side of a reef or lagoon. At low tide and in bright light the polyps retreat into their coral cups, emerging to feed underwater at night.*

Life in the Soil

In some places we can see the rocks of which the Earth is made. They stand out, bare and stark, in mountain tops and some stony deserts. We can see them in cliffs at the seaside and in places where stone or minerals are quarried, but in general the rocks are masked by soil.

As we walk across a muddy field or park, we may imagine that the soil is almost endlessly deep beneath our feet, but this is not so. In a very few places in the tropics the soil may reach a depth of 15 metres (50 feet), but in most of the cooler regions of the world it is very much less than this and may be no more than a few centimetres thick.

Yet this thin blanket is the source of almost all living things on land. Very few plants can live without soil. The exceptions are some lichens and a small number of mountain plants which can push their roots deep into cracks to obtain the water and minerals that they need. Even these plants contribute to the formation of soil where they live.

The first step in the making of soil is the breakup of the parent rock. The chief agents in this are the forces of water, ice and wind, but they alone cannot make soil. Soil is the result of complex chemical, physical and biological processes.

One of the ways of classifying soils is by neasuring the size of the rock particles which they contain. Coarsest is a gravel soil, which contains particles up to the size of small pebbles. Sand is slightly finer, loams have smaller particles still, while in a clay soil, the particles are less than 0·0125 millimetre (1/2000 inch) across.

Water is an important part of the soil for it surrounds each particle with a jacket of moisture. Minerals from the broken rock are dissolved in the water and are then used by plants, whose roots drink in the nourishment. If there is a great deal of water moving through the soil, minerals may be leached, or carried away by it.

If you dig a hole in the ground you can see that the soil varies at different depths. There is a layer, usually only a few millimetres thick, which is often dark in colour with *humus*, the remains of plants which have not yet been completely broken down. This is called the A horizon. Below this is the B horizon which is usually much thicker. There is no free humus here, but the soil feels crumbly to the touch, and there are plenty of dissolved minerals, so plants can take up the nutrients that they need. Below this is the C

Above: *Three common inhabitants of leaf litter: a springtail (top), a mite (centre), and a pseudoscorpion (bottom).*

Below: Some of the living things which can be found on and under the ground at the edge of a wood. The wood ant (1) excavates its nest (2) under a fallen tree trunk where a bracket fungus (12) has established itself. The shaggy ink-caps (13) are slightly out of place, being more commonly found in grassy meadows – sometimes even in ploughed fields. Boletus toadstools (14) are found in many different kinds of woods. The vegetarians represented here are the millipede (3), slug (8) and snail (9); field mice (7) eat all kinds of seeds. Worms (11) live under the ground, dragging down rotting leaves into their burrows by night to feed on them in privacy. Sexton beetles (5) also thrive on decay, excavating a pit under a dead animal and then feeding and laying their eggs on the buried carcase. Centipedes (4) are carnivorous, hunting under bark and in the ground for their invertebrate prey. The tiny shrew (10) is constantly hungry, burrowing among the surface layers of the soil and among grass roots in search of worms and similar prey. The other beetle illustrated (6) is Tetratoma fungorum. *These are only a tiny sample of the creatures which live in earthy places; digging up a small area of soil – especially in woodland – will reveal a surprisingly large number of species.*

horizon, or subsoil, penetrated only by the deep roots of plants which are the pioneers of soilmaking.

The soil is always being renewed. Fallen leaves and other dead organic material enrich it each year, but a certain amount is removed by erosion. In a normal soil this erosion is held in check by the new resources trapped by the deeper-rooted plants, but it is a delicate balance which can easily be upset. Destruction of vegetation or wrong farming methods may cause soil erosion. Once the soil has gone it may take thousands of years to build up again, and nothing much can live there until this happens.

The amount of living material in the soil is far greater than most people imagine. A tree needs as much root system underground as it has branches and leaves in the air. Besides the great tap roots and other visible roots there are the microscopically tiny root hairs, which have the job of taking up water and minerals.

As well as the roots, seeds and spores are abundant in the soil and form the food of many soil-living animals. Smaller still than these are the hosts of bacteria and their predators which swarm in the soil.

Although some ant and termite colonies may delve many metres deep in the soil, most animal life is confined to the topmost layers. Perhaps the most important creatures are the earthworms which act as natural ploughs, turning and aerating the soil and bringing down into it leaves from the surface litter layer.

The most numerous of soil animals are almost certainly the nematodes or eelworms. These tiny creatures, many of them microscopically small, occur in staggering numbers – a square metre (1 1/5 square yards) of grassland sometimes contains more than twenty million of them. Many feed on other nematodes or on other tiny organisms, but some species attack plants and can be serious pests of crops. In the darkness of the soil, a fierce warfare goes on, in which the nematodes are attacked by a variety of predators. Perhaps their strangest predators are minute fungi, which act either as living flypapers, or as lassos which trap and strangle the nematodes.

Most humus occurs in the topmost layers of the soil and it is here that we find the largest variety of animals. Most of them are tiny, but all have a part to play in the complex balance of life in the soil. The smaller forms include mites, springtails and false scorpions, and among the more easily visible species are centipedes, many sorts of insects and their larvae, and spiders. These form the food of many small vertebrates, from amphibians to birds and mammals.

Life in the Polar Regions and the Tundra

The polar regions are, strictly speaking, limited by the Arctic and Antarctic circles. These circles mark the limits of the regions where, for some time each year, the Sun does not go below the horizon, giving the long light days of summer. This advantage is balanced by the continuous dark of winter, when the Sun does not appear in the sky.

The low temperatures found in polar regions means that the land is snow- or ice-covered for most of the year, and survival is difficult or impossible for most plants and animals. Most of the north polar area is sea; the appearance of land is given by the ice covering it, although this ice is in fact moving.

The South Pole is in the middle of a continent, but most of this is covered with an ice sheet which is up to 3,000 metres (10,000 feet) thick. In some places great mountain ranges rise through the ice, but their slopes are barren of all life. Only near to the coast can any life exist. Here a few primitive plants and insects are resident, able to grow briefly during the Antarctic summer and then go into a resting phase in the long cold winter.

In the lands bordering the Arctic Ocean, there are similar primitive plants and animals which can stand such harsh conditions, but since the area is backed by a temperate continent, more species have found their way into the harsh Arctic habitat.

Below: *The Tundra does not support many species of large animals; those which live there tend to be great travellers since vegetation is scarce in these vast chilly areas. The mammals shown here are vegetarians of the North American tundra. The caribou (left) is wholly adapted to the seasonal movement of the frost. In winter its dense coat fades to a dull white colour, and even its hooves become sharper so that they can grip the icy ground. Caribou feed on grasses in the summer and lichen in the winter. Musk oxen (centre) also eat lichen, as well as bark, in the winter; their summer food is a tundra dwarf willow. They have thick, shaggy coats, and wide-splayed feet which enable them to walk on snow. Musk oxen congregate into herds in winter, but split into smaller groups in summer. Lemmings (right) also depend on the lichen of the tundra for food. They themselves are the staple diet of arctic foxes and snowy owls. Lemming populations are known to be unstable; every three or four years they become too big for the scanty food supply. European lemmings migrate at such times, but the collared lemmings of North America just die of starvation.*

Fishes are abundant in northern and southern polar waters. They are food for sea birds and seals, some of which migrate into the northern polar area to produce their young. Most of the birds remain on the sea cliffs, where they nest for the shortest possible time, returning to sea in some cases before the young are fledged.

Some species of seals remain in polar waters throughout the year; they gnaw breathing holes in the ice, which they must keep open to survive. Whales migrate into the polar waters, following the food supply of summer plankton and fish.

One large predator, the polar bear, survives in the far north. Although technically a land mammal, the polar bear spends most of its time by or in the sea, for it is a powerful swimmer.

In the south polar area there are no land-based mammals, although seals are abundant. Penguins are perhaps the best-known creatures of the south polar area, where some species nest in immense colonies.

Bordering the wastes of the Arctic are areas where the climate is so cold that the ground is frozen throughout the year, except for the top half metre (18 inches) or so which thaws in the summer months. This allows a great variety of living things to thrive, but their activity is packed into a few months and they are dormant for the rest of the year.

This zone of the Earth's surface is called the tundra. In winter it is snow covered and apparently lifeless. In summer time the rolling plains are covered with dense, low-growing vegetation. There are many small pools and meandering streams, because the frozen subsoil prevents the

Above: *The arctic fox, shown in its summer coat (above) and its thick white winter coat (below), is a carnivore whose main diet is lemmings, but it will also eat birds, fish and seal pups. Its thick tail is used as a muff while it sleeps, curled up in a snow burrow, in sub-zero temperatures.*

water from escaping into deeper layers. The water remains on the surface to make a boggy quagmire of vast tracts of land.

The knee-high vegetation is largely composed of woody plants – miniature trees, such as dwarf willows and birches. These can withstand the gales which howl over the land, and in winter are buried and protected by the heavy snowfall which would break and destroy larger plants. Summer comes late in the tundra, but when the warmer weather arrives it brings an amazing flush of life.

Some insects which may be incredibly abundant in the tundra are biting flies; these torment human beings and other animals alike. Dragonflies and other aquatic insects are found in the pools, but so brief is their period of development in each year, that they may take several years to complete their growth.

In the summer many birds migrate to the tundra. Some, such as ducks and geese and waders, find the moorlands with plenty of water just right for nesting places. Other birds are insect-feeders.

Some mammals also migrate. Chief among these are the reindeer of Europe and Asia and the caribou of North America. They browse on the low-growing vegetation, eating not only the flowering plants, but others as well. One lichen, which may be an important part of their diet, is the tough, shrubby *Cladonia rangiferina,* mistakenly called reindeer moss.

Enemies which the reindeer have to face include the wolves, social animals hunting in packs. Smaller than the wolves and less social is the Arctic fox. This little creature feeds on anything that offers, even vegetable food.

Most numerous of the mammals are the voles and lemmings. These little creatures live among the bases of the stems of the plants, remaining awake there under the snow during the winter. Sometimes they make burrows in the surface soil.

Like almost all rodents, the lemming populations fluctuate in numbers, but in the tundra, which is a relatively simple environment, the checks and balances of the complex habitats of warmer climates barely exist. It is easy for population buildup to occur, until there are huge numbers of the little animals in some seasons. These plagues end as suddenly as they begin, and in a short time the numbers are back to normal once more.

Right: *Vegetation is scarce in the North American tundra. In winter virtually all that can be found are species of* Cladonia, *lichens known as reindeer mosses. In summer, grasses and some flowers, like the arctic poppy, grow for a short season. These few plants support the musk ox and reindeer as well as the lemmings which the snowy owl preys on. In years when lemmings are abundant, the snowy owl lays up to 13 eggs – nearly twice the usual number.*

Life in Coniferous Forests

South of the tundra is a broad belt of land with higher rainfall and temperatures than are found in the tundra. The climate is suitable for the growth of trees, but it is still a harsh environment, and the trees have to be able to withstand heavy snowfall and prolonged, very cold winters.

The boundary between the two climatic and vegetational regions is not a clean-cut line. In the north the growth of trees is sparse, but further south the trees grow taller and closer together. First comes a zone of birch trees, like those found on mountain slopes. These soon give way to a broad belt of coniferous (cone-bearing) trees – pines, spruces and firs.

Left: *Of all the species of squirrel in the world, more than a third of them are flying squirrels like this. There may be some advantage for an arboreal animal to be able to move in this way. A wide flap of skin from elbow to knee can be stretched by extending the legs, allowing the squirrel to glide through the air to a lower branch of a different tree. The tail can be used like a rudder to change direction slightly, and the squirrel lands by stalling and hanging on with its sharp claws. It can climb in the usual way, and generally moves about by climbing.*

The endless sea of dark green trees is broken only by browner patches of bog, for most of the great northern forest area, or *taiga*, as it is called, lay under glaciers during the last Ice Age. Much of the low land is now covered with *moraines* (piles of débris carried by glaciers) which dam little pools and force the streams to meander aimlessly across the countryside.

The coniferous trees are well adapted to the severe climate. The heavy, waxy covering of the needle-shaped leaves repels snow and ice. If there should be a blizzard, the flexible, whippy branches bend downwards so the snow slides off them.

At first sight there is little life in the taiga, but the evergreen trees give dense, year-long cover and protection to many sorts of creatures. Some of these are rare; the Siberian tiger, largest of all the tigers, survives in small numbers in the great northern forests. Other animals are more abundant; the elk (known as the moose in North America) is the largest species of deer. This giant animal, which may be up to 2·28 metres (7½ feet) at the shoulder and weigh 820 kilogrammes (1,800 pounds) is found particularly in the swampy areas. It often wades into the water, partly to escape from tormenting insects and partly to feed, for it is specially fond of the stems and roots of water lilies and other aquatic plants. This creature seems to be increasing in numbers.

Other smaller deer, such as the roe deer in the Old World and the black-tailed deer of North America find shelter and food among the evergreen forests.

Members of the weasel tribe are abundant. Agile pine martens inhabit the branches of the trees, where they hunt squirrels and birds. On the ground true weasels and stoats stalk small game, while the wolverine (also aptly called the glutton in places) is mainly a carrion feeder. Its habit of removing animals from traps has brought it into conflict with man, for most of the human inhabitants of the taiga are trappers. To a glutton, mink or beaver in a trap is just as acceptable a meal as one that has died naturally.

Smaller animals include the jumping

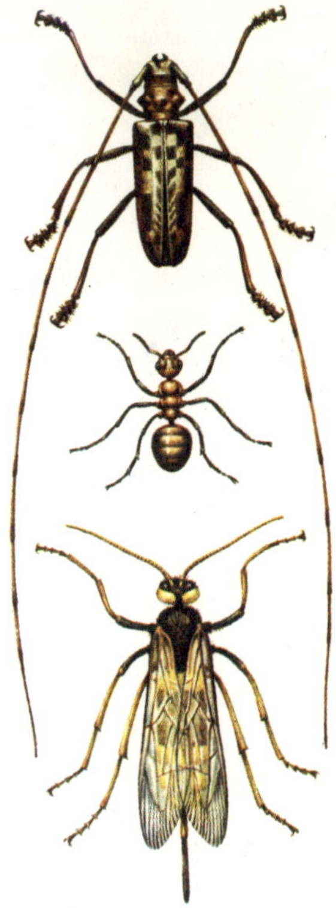

Top: *A longhorn beetle the southern pine sawyer,* Monochammus titillator. Above: *The giant wood wasp* Sirex gigas: *both of these have larvae that damage timber by boring into trees.* Sirex *grubs eat into heart wood.* Above centre: *The red wood ant* Formica *is well known to picnickers.*

Above: *Crossbills are finches with beaks adapted for breaking open pine cones to reach the seeds inside. They live in pine forests in the colder parts of the Northern Hemisphere. They climb in a rather parrot-like fashion to the end of branches where they balance precariously while feeding.*

mice, and the flying squirrels which inhabit the trees, leaping and gliding by means of a flap of skin stretched between fore and hind legs.

Birds also abound in the northern forests. Many species of game birds are among them, from the solitary turkey-sized capercaillie, which feeds on the shoots of the conifers, to smaller species such as the hazel hen. This gregarious bird prefers places where there is dense ground cover beneath the trees.

In North America the now rare spruce grouse augments its voice in the breeding season by drumming with its wings on a hollow log. Other drummers include the woodpeckers, which tap their beaks against hollow branches, producing an extremely loud sound which carries through the woods.

Many creatures feed on pine cones, but few do so more neatly than the crossbill, whose curved beak can twist back the woody scales so that it can reach the sweet seeds inside with a minimum of effort.

Brilliantly-coloured jays, cardinals and grosbeaks compete for vegetable food while acrobatic small birds such as siskins, titmice and chickadees feed on the seeds of alders and birches, and on tiny insects found in the foliage.

Insects are very abundant. Some, such as the caterpillars of the pine hawk moth, feed on the foliage, among which they are wonderfully camouflaged. Others, such as the grubs of the giant woodwasps, spend the whole of their larval lives burrowing into the wood of living trees and are protected, in effect, by their food supply.

On the ground many ants are found. The red wood ant makes anthills of pine needles and twigs. This creature is a voracious hunter of tree-living species of insects, and its tracks can often be traced many metres from the nest. The worker-ants search all the trees and destroy so many forest pests that in some parts of the world they are protected by law against damage by humans. The law cannot, however, be applied to bears, which sometimes claw out winter dens from the ants' huge heaps of vegetation – the ants themselves having retreated to the underground parts of their 'palaces' for the cold season.

In the cold forests of the north, fallen pine needles decay slowly, so the soil tends to be acid, with few worms or other small animals. Even so, there is enough food to support a rich fauna of insectivores such as shrews. These voracious creatures remain active throughout the year, feeding on huge numbers of insects, grubs, spiders and harvestmen. Shrews are often the food of birds of prey, including owls. There is no doubt that many of the stories of ghosts found among the peoples of the far north started with the weird cries of the hunting owls.

Right: *Like the tundra, coniferous forests stretch in broad belts across North America and Eurasia. Since the dominant plants are evergreen trees, there is constant shade in these forests, which means that shrub and herb growth is scarce. The moose is the largest animal living here. It is the largest living deer, and feeds by browsing on trees and bushes. In summer it ventures onto wetter ground to find aquatic plants, especially water lilies. Moose may weigh more than half a tonne, and have splayed feet which help to carry their great weight safely over swampland and across snow. They live in small groups in summer but congregate into herds in the winter, possibly for protection against wolves and pumas.*

Life in Deciduous Forests

Coniferous trees are found mainly in the cold northern lands. Further south, where the weather is warmer, they are replaced by forests of trees of a very different kind. These great woodlands, which form a belt of trees across much of Europe, Asia and America, wherever the land is not too high and bleak for their survival, are made up of *deciduous* trees.

Deciduous trees have pale green leaves, usually broad and blade-like in shape, for which reason they are often called broad-leafed trees. The woods, however, are green-coloured only in the summer months, for as winter approaches, the leaves are shed and during the colder parts of the year the trees stand resting. This loss of leaves is very important to the life of the forest, because the fallen leaves break down easily in the soil. Deciduous forest soil tends to be rich and fertile, with many kinds of tiny plants and animals living in it.

The loss of leaves by the trees affects other plants as well, for it lets light through to the ground. In deciduous woods many sorts of spring flowers, such as primroses, wood anemones and bluebells, flourish. These plants have a brief period of growth and flowering which ends when the trees develop their leaves in the late spring. At the height of summer not enough light reaches ground level for the small plants to grow.

A big tree may have a host of other plants growing on it, and can give support to climbers, such as honeysuckle and ivy. The roughness of its bark offers a home to tiny plants such as the algae, lichens and mosses commonly found there.

An old tree may trap fallen leaves in the broad crotch of its branches, and in the humus, which the rotted leaves form, rooted plants such as ferns or even some flowering plants may grow. Semi-parasites like mistletoe may flourish on the branches.

It is not surprising that with so rich a growth of plants, many kinds of animals thrive in broad-leafed forests, although

Left: *The gall-wasp's larva secretes a substance which causes a leaf to form a protective covering for the larva. This is called a gall.*

Left: *This male stag beetle has large mandibles. They are probably somehow connected with courtship. Other species may have such large 'horns' that it is hard to imagine what possible advantage they may have.*

Right: *Nearly every wooded area of the world has its woodpeckers; there are over 200 species. Apart from digging out prey from tree trunks and drilling holes to nest in, the great spotted woodpecker is known to 'ring' trees to obtain sap, like the closely related North American sapsuckers.* Below: *The badger is a well-known inhabitant of deciduous woodland, living fastidiously in an extensive underground system of burrows – called a sett – and emerging at night to eat a wide variety of food, from berries to beetles.*

some of them go into hibernation or long periods of inactivity during the winter.

The insects of the forest are particularly abundant and varied – however, they are mostly so beautifully camouflaged that they are very difficult to see. Some important ones include those caterpillars which appear in early summer to feed on the new green foliage of the trees. Sometimes there are so many of them that they almost completely strip the leaves from the trees.

The caterpillars known as 'loopers' or 'inchworms' because of their way of walking are particularly destructive. They look like twigs of their food plants, and are very difficult to see, but in spite of this they are an important food for many birds, such as titmice, when these are feeding young.

More important, probably, are the insect predators. These include the beautiful caterpillar-hunting beetle *Calosoma* and many sorts of small relatives of the wasps which are parasitic upon the caterpillars and eventually kill them.

Deciduous woodlands are rich in birds. These range from tiny insect-eaters, such as wrens, titmice and warblers, to medium sized seed-eaters, such as pheasants. Many woodland birds change their food according to the season, feeding on insects in the spring and summer, berries and fruit in the autumn, and worms and grubs in the winter time.

Some of the most specialised of the grub-feeders are the woodpeckers. These birds are excellent tree-climbers, with toes which in most species grip the bark in four different directions, and a stiff tail which acts as a support. Woodpeckers have strong beaks with which they can drill into the tunnels made by beetle and woodwasp grubs, and long tongues with which they winkle the insects from their hideouts.

Mammals are abundant in broadleafed forests. The rich fauna and flora of the woodland floor support shrews and mice of many kinds. These little animals make their burrows among the fallen leaves and surface roots.

Other small mammals include the woodmice in the Old World and the similar deer mice of North America. These agile and elegant little animals feed on nuts, berries and insects and may venture from their original woodland homes into cultivated lands and gardens.

Above: *Of all the woods in the world, this peaceful bluebell wood represents the sort most familiar to us. Because of its temperate and pleasant nature, man has made more inroads into this kind of wood than any other, and it is here that the balance of nature is in most danger of being upset. The contrast between winter and summer is marked by leaf fall, allowing light to penetrate to ground level and encouraging the growth of small leafy plants beneath the trees. Many deciduous trees produce fruit or nuts and there is a great deal of food available for a diversity of herbivores both large and small. The large ones have been reduced in number by hunters throughout man's history, but small ones are abundant, providing food for many carnivores such as stoats, weasels, polecats, foxes, owls and still, in some American forests, bears. Temperate deciduous woodland once covered all of Europe, as well as eastern North America and parts of Japan, Australia and the southern tip of South America. It is here that man has turned the fertile soil to his advantage and much of the woodland has been lost as a result.*

In the Old World dormice inhabit the more southerly woodlands. Squirrels are common tree canopy inhabitants, and carnivores include a wide variety of flesh eaters from the tiny weasels to the heavyweight badgers.

Martens may hunt the squirrels in the trees; in North America the raccoon, which is an expert climber, may steal birds' eggs, but is more likely to live near streams and feed on crayfish and other such water-living delicacies. Larger ground-living animals include wild pigs, bears and deer.

In the southern hemisphere broad-leafed trees occur in the southernmost parts of South America, New Zealand, and parts of Australia. In general, these forests have fewer species of animals than their northern counterparts. New Zealand, for example, has no native mammals apart from some bats, although woodland creatures such as red deer introduced from Europe live very successfully there.

Australia has many mammals living in the forests. These are all *marsupials* (see pages 208–9), and lead similar lives, as hunters or hunted, to their counterparts in the north. In South America the southern beech forests, although extensive, contain few mammals and birds.

Life in Grasslands

Where there is insufficient moisture for trees to thrive, grasslands cover the Earth's surface. Some grasslands are in temperate areas, as, for example, the vast steppes of northern Asia and the prairies of North America.

Grasslands may also be found in tropical areas. The great grasslands of Australia, Africa and South America are different from those in temperate areas in many ways because of their higher temperatures. They share, even so, the feature that grasses are the dominant plants, except in places where there is plentiful water. By a river, for instance, trees replace the grasses.

Many other kinds of plants flourish in the same area as the grasses. Most of these have underground food storage systems such as bulbs or tubers, and they blossom early in the year, covering the plains with a blaze of vivid colours. These plants soon die down as they are overtaken in growth by the grasses, which produce their flowers later in the year.

Compared with the trees of the forest-land, grasses are all small plants with long, narrow leaves. Their flowers are unobtrusive, with no bright petals, sweet scent or nectar to attract insects, for the task of pollination is performed by the winds which sweep across the open plains.

Above: *One of the most familiar of cage birds, the budgerigar* Melopsittacus undulatus, *is a native parakeet of Australia. In the wild, budgerigars travel in large flocks across the savannah, feeding on grass seeds.*

Below: *Grasslands are found in every climate. There are grasses that grow on salt marshes; others live high up on mountains, and some kinds of grass can survive in extremely dry near-desert conditions. Grasses stabilise the soils they grow in, for their roots make a firm mesh on top of loose soils and enable slower-growing plants to get a hold.*

Grasses provide food for many kinds of creatures. The chief of these are the grazing animals, which feed on the highly nourishing leaves of the grasses. The plants survive the animals' browsing because of their curious method of growth. The point of growth is low on the plant, so the leaves cut by the animals' teeth merely continue to grow upwards. The grazing animals are mostly large and live in vast herds, which move round the plains in regular migrations. They never overgraze and destroy the grass completely. Their droppings fertilise the ground, so that minerals for new growth are constantly being supplied to the grasses.

In Africa the savannahs and veld were once populated by great herds of antelopes and zebras, which are mainly grass feeders, and giraffes, which feed on the leaves of trees. These herds have now been largely destroyed by man.

In North America the vast herds of bison and pronghorn antelopes which once roamed the prairies have been almost entirely destroyed by man, and in Australia the same fate has overtaken the grazing kangaroos. In parts of South America man has replaced the deer, foxes and hares of the pampas with his cattle and sheep. In Asia the wild horses have all but disappeared, but in recent years strict conservation in the southern part of the Soviet Union has meant the return of the saiga, a kind of antelope, to its former haunts.

The great herds were hunted not only by man, but by other predators. In Africa, these predators included lions, leopards, cheetahs and hyaenas. Wolves hunted

over much of Asia and in the colder parts of the world, and in Australia the thylacine or Tasmanian wolf fed on the kangaroos. In the steppes of eastern Europe little ground squirrels (genus *Citellus*) live in vast underground colonies, which are matched by the 'townships' of the prairie dogs in North America – more than a million of them may make their burrows in a huge underground labyrinth. Both these kinds of animals are regarded as agricultural pests.

Not only mammals but large numbers of birds inhabit the grassy plains. In the warm grasslands of the southern continents, large, flightless grazing birds are found; the ostrich in Africa, the rhea in South America and the emu in Australia. All these long-necked birds have sharp eyes for detecting predators, and escape by running at speeds said to be up to 48 kph (30 mph). In the cooler grasslands of the Old World great bustards take the place of the ostriches; they are large, long-necked birds, swift runners, capable of flight, but taking to the air reluctantly. They normally get protection from their camouflage colouring, which blends perfectly with their surroundings.

Perhaps the most familiar of all grassland birds is the budgerigar. This little green parakeet used to exist in countless millions in the grasslands of Australia. Nearly as many probably now live as pets in all parts of the world. Under domestication colour varieties have been produced, so budgerigars now exist in all shades from white through blues and greens to yellows.

Insects also abound in grasslands. Some, such as grasshoppers and locusts, compete directly with the large animals for food. Members of the cockchafer family feed in the grub stage on the roots of the grasses, and they themselves are food for many birds and small mammals. Others, such as the dung beetles, are indispensable to the health of the grasslands, for many of them carry the droppings of the larger creatures down into the soil as food for their larvae. The plants benefit from this activity, for they take the minerals they need from these buried resources.

Below: *The prairies of North America once supported enormous herds of bison. At the beginning of the 19th century, there were more than 60 million bison, but by 1889 these had been reduced by hunters to just 541. Bison are now only found in parks and reserves. They feed entirely on prairie grasses.*

Left: *When a dung beetle finds a pile of fairly fresh dung, it shapes some into a ball, and then rolls the ball away by pushing it backwards with its hind legs.*

Life in Deserts

Deserts are generally defined as places where there is an average of less than 125 millimetres (5 inches) of rainfall in a year. This may mean several years with no rain at all, and then a downpour which brings many millimetres of water in a night.

Some deserts appear to be nothing but a barren stony or sandy wasteland. Most, however, have some plants growing, although they are unlike the plants of other areas in many ways. To begin with they have to guard against losing any water which they have managed to find, especially in the hot deserts, where day-time temperatures may rise to over 54°C (130°F). They do this chiefly by having very tiny leaves – sometimes these are no more than thin spines, through which water cannot be lost – and by having a heavy cuticle over the plant which acts as a waterproof coat, retaining moisture.

Desert plants reach their water supplies in several ways; some, such as the mesquite bush of the American deserts, have roots which may stretch down more than 30 metres (100 feet) into the ground to tap the water supply. Others may have roots which spread widely through the soil.

A feature which is noticeable in deserts is the way that the plants are spaced out. The cause of this is that the plant roots produce minute amounts of chemicals called *inhibitors,* which poison the ground for any other plants that grow too near. Many desert plant seeds also have inhibitors on their outer coats. This prevents them from germinating if there is a heavy dew, which may moisten the seeds, but not dampen the ground properly.

These seeds can lie dormant in the soil for years until there is one of the rare rainstorms which really soaks the soil, and this also washes the inhibitors off the seeds' coats, so that they can grow. Following rain, the desert suddenly changes colour with a brief flush of green replaced by the brilliance of the short-lived flowers.

There are surprisingly large numbers of kinds of animals in deserts, although because of the lack of food and water they are generally far more widely spaced out than similar creatures might be in lusher habitats. In the Sahara, a single desert mouse may need 2 hectares (5 acres) of territory to survive; in a wetter climate,

Below: *The two main difficulties of desert life are drought and temperature. Although there may be a seasonal rainfall in a desert area, water is always almost absent, and the lack of humidity means that daytime temperatures are extremely high while at night it becomes extremely cold. Not all deserts are hot places though, the Gobi desert of Central Asia has a cold climate. The desert scene depicted below shows a variety of species found in the North American deserts, which have a more diverse flora and fauna than those of the Old World. The plants are: 1 giant cactus; 2 opuntia cactus; 3 Joshua tree. They are all equipped to store water, losing*

as little as possible by evaporation. These plants form a source of water and food for many desert insects which are, in turn, the food of larger animals. Amphibians, reptiles, mammals and birds alike tend to cope with the temperature problems by adopting burrowing habits. They have different ways of conserving water; some of them do not even drink. 4 kangaroo rat; 5 burrowing owl; 6 kit fox; 7 desert tortoise; 8 sidewinder; 9 mule-deer; 10 antelope squirrel; 11 cottontail rabbit; 12 chuckawalla; 13 couch spade-foot toad; 14 horned lizard; 15 western rock-skink; 16 Gila monster; 17 pocket mouse; 18 prairie falcon.

such as that of Central Europe, a related species may live at a density of several individuals to 0·4 hectare (1 acre).

Animals which spring to mind immediately as desert creatures are the camels, the single-humped Arabian species being found from North Africa to northern India, while the two-humped Bactrian camel occurs in the colder deserts of central Asia. These animals can go for long distances without food or water, and a camel can lose up to one-third of its body weight without harm when it has to go without drinking for a long period. After this, however, the animal has to make up the deficiency as quickly as possible and a thirsty camel can drink over 135 litres (30 gallons) of water at one time.

It is among the small desert mammals, however, that we find the most extraordinary ability to survive without water. Little rodents live in some of the driest hot areas of the world. These animals remain during the heat of the day in burrows tunnelled well beneath the burning surface of the ground so they keep cool. At night, the rodents – jerboas in the Old World and kangaroo rats in the deserts of western North America – emerge to search for the seeds on which they feed. These little creatures can live their whole lives without drinking, for their bodies manufacture a little water in the process of digestion.

There are few true desert birds, but one which is often found nesting near the edge of a desert is the sand grouse. This bird may fly long distances to an oasis to collect water, which it carries back in its crop for its nestlings.

Reptiles thrive in hot desert areas. They lie hidden under stones or in burrows in the heat of the day, and are active during the cool of evening and early morning. The 'sidewinding' snakes have developed a way of moving which allows them to pass easily over loose and shifting sand. Many of the snakes are venomous, and the only poisonous lizards are found in the deserts of North America.

Insects also are found in deserts. A few, such as some of the long-legged spiny black tenebrionid beetle species, are found only in hot deserts. Others, such as the desert locust, develop in semi-desert conditions, and as they feed may well spread, at least for that season, to the limits of the desert.

Life in Tropical Forests

The tropical rain forests of the world stretch across the continents on either side of the Equator. At one time these great carpets of trees were broken only by the oceans and high mountain ranges, for tropical forests do not occur higher than about 700 metres (2,300 feet) above sea-level. They are limited to the north and south by the decrease in rainfall, for the type of vegetation in these forests needs at least 1,250 millimetres (50 inches) of rainfall in a year.

No tropical forest has been glaciated in recent times. One result of this is that a very large number of kinds of plants and animals can be found there. These organisms live in a pattern of species which have evolved together over a very long period of time. As a result, great specialisations have tended to develop and of all the land areas, tropical forests are the richest in life.

The most obvious plant inhabitants of the forest are the trees themselves. Many of them are huge, with slender trunks, strengthened by buttresses at the base, but stretching upwards for perhaps 50 metres (160 feet) before the first branch appears. The crown of each tree is fairly small for such a tall trunk, but the trees crowd together to form a continuous canopy, which shadows the lower regions of the forest. There may be a layer of lower-growing, shade-tolerant trees, but there is little ground cover. Those plants which can survive in such deep shade have large, fragile leaves, unlike the tall trees which have tough leaves.

It is only when a tree falls or is felled that sufficient light penetrates to the forest floor for much growth to occur at ground level. This secondary growth of saplings and other competing plants is in nature short-lived. Only where man brings light to the forest does the tangle referred to as the jungle persist.

One of the remarkable features of a tropical forest is the large number of different kinds of trees, which all compete in the same area.

If you could climb to the top of the trees, you might be disappointed in the flowers, for most of them are rather small, although there are many species of orchids and other plants which use the trees for support and these often have large and gorgeous flowers. In the canopy of the forest you would find the tops of the scrambling lianas (climbing woody-stemmed plants), which look, at lower levels, like great ropes hanging down from the tall branches.

At whatever time of year you were to climb to the treetops, you would always

Below: *The lush growth of a tropical forest needs plenty of moisture. Many such forest areas have regular periods of heavy rainfall, but this Peruvian cloud forest is kept damp by being in the zone of mist on a mountainside.*

Left: *This flying snake* (Chrysopela) *is one of the tree-dwellers of the tropics. The keeled belly-plates that help it to climb can be seen.*

Right: *Life in tropical rain forests is arranged in horizontal layers. The tallest tree tops form the sunny upper layer, and so on down to ground level where light is scarce. Each level contains a different selection of species; even mosquitoes can be distinguished according to which 'floor' they live on; they breed in pools held by leaves.*

find the forest was green, for although individual trees may shed their leaves, they do not all do so at the same time. Neither do they all flower at the same time, and fruit of different sorts may be found throughout the year.

Because of the year-long food supply, there is always plenty to eat for the many species of forest animals, although the fruit-eaters may have to travel widely to find enough. Several species of animals may be feeding from trees of the same kind, some taking the fruit before it is properly ripe.

Because there is so little growth on the ground, there are few large animals in tropical forests, and these never form big herds like their plains-dwelling relatives.

It is beside rivers, and where light can penetrate to allow denser growth, that other creatures can flourish in the forests. Many tiny creatures live in the leaf litter on the ground, and feed on the fallen leaves, among them ants.

The forest canopy is where life is really abundant and insects, birds and mammals of many kinds flourish. Gaudy butterflies, many protected from predators by their nasty taste, flutter slowly about. The birds are also brilliantly coloured, although in the bright light of the forest these colours merge into the background, and so the birds may be very difficult to see. Among them are the sunbirds of the Old World and the hummingbirds of the New World, which take nectar from the flowers and pollinate them.

Parrots fly in noisy flocks from one fruiting tree to another. They are wasteful feeders, but in the forest the damage that they do often provides food for other creatures, less well able to tear open tough skins of fruit or crack the shells of nuts and seeds. Parrots nest in holes in the trees, and many never come to the ground at all. Birds are also the major predators of the tree tops, with such large birds of prey as the harpy eagle taking a toll of the other tree dwellers.

There are also a great many mammals in the forest summit. Monkeys are perhaps the most obvious, as they are mostly social and noisy animals.

In South America the sloths are among the most curious of the arboreal inhabitants. Sloths lead a slow, upside-down life. camouflaged by the hanging mats of their coat, in which each hair is grooved to form a furrow where algae grow. There are even several insects which feed on these plants and are found nowhere else than in company with the sloth.

Besides these animals which are found nowhere but the forests, rodents and bats are both abundant there. The bats include some of the most grotesque and – also in South America – the most feared, the blood-feeding vampires, which may transmit many diseases, including rabies.

Most forest rodents are harmless to man and include various climbing mice and squirrels. Flying squirrels are found in tropical forests throughout the world, with the exception of the forests of Australia and New Guinea, where they have their marsupial counterparts in the flying phalangers.

Other Australia-New Guinea marsupial counterparts for forest animals of Africa and America are cuscuses and tree kangaroos, which have a similar ecological niche to lemurs, and various small possums which are herbivores and insect-eaters.

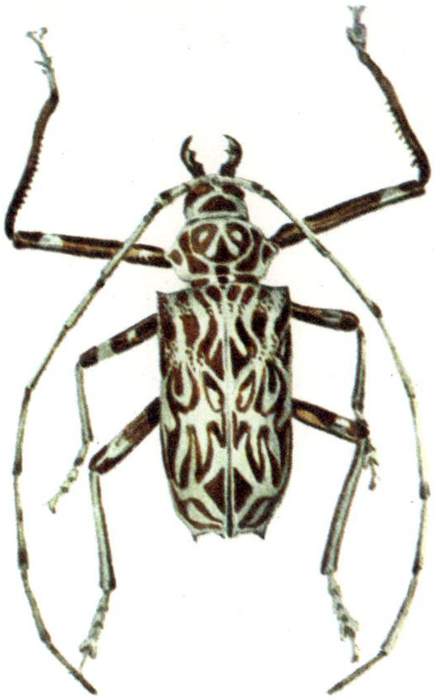

Above: *The harlequin beetle is a long-horned (longicorn) beetle. Temperate zone beetles of this family are often drab, but this tropical species is brightly coloured. Longicorns are nearly all wood-borers.*

Below: *Birds are found at all levels of the tropical forest. Macaws and toucans live in the upper arboreal layers, nesting in tree holes. Tanagers and sharpbills occupy various levels. Hummingbirds are interesting because different species are found at each level. Cock-o'-the-rocks are ground-living birds, nesting in caves and performing fantastic communal dances on the ground in forest glades. The birds shown here are (clockwise) paradise tanager (top), scarlet macaw, Cuvier's toucan, ruby topaz hummingbird, cock-o'-the-rock, and crested sharpbill.*

Life on Mountains

Mountains are, in general, inhospitable places where few animals and plants can survive. There are many reasons for this, but an important one is that most mountains are cold places, for as you rise above sea-level, the temperature drops. For every 300 metres (1,000 feet) up the air temperature becomes 1·9°C (3·4°F) colder. At the top of the world's highest mountain, Everest (8,847·7 metres; 29,028 feet above sea level), the temperature is 55°C (100°F) cooler than at sea-level. As a consequence all the world's high mountains, even those on the Equator, are snow-covered.

If you go up a mountain in the Alps, you find that the vegetation changes, from the lush woodlands of the valley, through coniferous forests on the lower slopes, through high grasslands with tough shrubs, to an area where mosses and lichens are practically the only growing things. In tropical mountain ranges there may be a zone of tall bamboo, which has no exact equivalent in temperate regions. At the very top of a mountain there is generally nothing but rock, snow and ice.

While the lower slopes provide homes for many creatures, the upper zones are almost devoid of life. Conditions on a bare rock face may change dramatically, for the heat of the Sun warms it to a high temperature in the middle of the day, but the temperature falls rapidly if it is shaded by a nearby peak. In times of storm, the slope is washed by rain or lashed by hail and, especially towards the winter's end, may be swept by avalanches.

In spite of these disadvantages, plants and animals do thrive in mountains, wherever there is sufficient shelter. In the protective lee of a boulder, or in a crack in a rock face, deep-rooted plants may be found. Some, such as the filmy ferns, need a very high level of humidity to survive and so are well suited to such a place. Tiny spiders, and insects such as springtails, are also found in such places, while in the summer months others are briefly present, feeding on the nectar of the flowers.

There are few reptiles in high mountains, but many species of birds, such as wall creepers, make their living in areas of rock and lichens. The alpine chough is a scavenger and general feeder, which has discovered that human visitors to mountains can mean rich pickings. Choughs are often found round climbers' huts in the Alps, and one accompanied an Everest expedition to a height of 7,925 metres (26,000 feet).

Mammals of the mountains include

Below: *A large animal living in a mountainous area must be agile and sure-footed as well as able to keep itself warm. The mouflon (left) is a sheep of Sardinian and Corsican mountains. Ibex goats live near the snowline in Europe and western Asia. The camel-like vicuña, found high in the Andes of South America, has a fine, warm coat which is highly prized in the manufacture of textiles.*

Right: *Alpine flowers include the blue gentian and the edelweiss. They have a short season in which to display their conspicuous flowers to attract insects, so that their seeds can ripen early enough to survive the hard winter. Flowering time must be synchronised with the appearance of pollinators.*

Above: *Among the pollinators of the alpine flowers above is the Apollo butterfly* Parnassius apollo. *It is a member of the swallowtail family and its caterpillars feed on low-growing mountain stonecrops.*

some small rodents which live beyond the limit of the grasslands. Many kinds of marmots are to be found in such surroundings. They survive the presence of birds of prey by being among the most alert of all animals, diving into their deep burrows at the first sign of danger. It is in these burrows, stopped up with a plug of rock and earth, that they hibernate throughout the winter months. It is estimated that some species spend more than seven months of each year in the coma-like state of hibernation.

Pikas, which are related to rabbits, live in North American upland regions. These little animals gather and dry grass to carry into their underground stores for winter. Chinchillas also are mountain animals, although very few of them survive in the wild. The reason is that they have been hunted almost to extinction for their beautiful fur coats. They keep warm by having fur different from that of all other animals, for each hair divides into about twenty finer hairs. In this way, more air is trapped to make a warm blanket round the chinchillas' bodies.

The large mammals of mountain areas, like the birds of prey, have to some extent been driven there by human persecution. Many mountain animals, such as the chamois, formerly lived at much lower levels of the Alps than they occupy today. Most of the large mammals of high mountains are members of the goat or cow families, stocky, short-legged animals, protected, at least in winter, with dense woolly coats.

In Europe the chamois and the ibex or mountain goat, are found in the high Alps and Pyrenees. In the wilderness of the high mountains of Asia, yaks, gaurs and several types of mountain sheep and goats such as tahrs exist, while in North America the bighorn sheep and Rocky Mountain goat are found at high altitudes.

All these animals are astonishingly agile on steep rock faces, where their hooves give them an almost suction-cup grip. They live in small herds, and move in the summertime to the highest levels of vegetation to feed on the plants growing on almost inaccessible ledges and slopes. In the winter they are forced to retreat to a lower level, perhaps even down to the coniferous forests.

Left: *Here is one way of visualising the horizontal zones of a mountain: the bottom level is called the colline; the next is montane; above this is the sub-alpine zone, with the alpine above it, and at the top is the perpetual snow. Although these animals have been placed in particular zones, there is much vertical movement between levels according to season.*

Life in Fresh Water

Compared with the vast volume of the sea, the amount of fresh water on Earth is small, yet it forms an important living place for many species of plants and animals. Fresh water occurs in rivers, lakes, ponds and swamps, and because each of these habitats provides different conditions for life, the variety of freshwater organisms is very great.

A river alone may offer many niches for life. In the mountains, where it rises, tiny streams rush down the steep slopes, often tumbling as waterfalls over rocky barriers. This is known as the *torrent reach*. Few things live in this water, because of the speed and variability of the flow. As the torrents join up, they form bigger streams, still fast-running, with the clean, cold water containing lots of oxygen. This part of the course is called the *trout reach*.

As the river approaches the plains its course begins to curve. It is still running fairly fast and contains a good deal of oxygen, but it is burdened with a load of small stones and silt which it has scoured from its earlier course, and these may be dropped as the river swings across the plain. Deep, clear pools may be formed. This part of the river's course is known as the *barbel reach*, for this fish is specially well suited to such conditions.

When the river approaches the sea, its flow becomes slower as it meanders in great loops across the plains. The water is warm, and murky with the silt that it carries, but there is little oxygen compared to the higher reaches. Life of many kinds thrives here, and this part of the river is called the *bream reach*, after one of the slow-moving fishes found there.

Finally, as the river meets the sea, we find the *estuarine reach*, which is influenced by the salt water brought in by the tides.

Lakes differ from ponds in that they are

Far right: *The otter (18) feeds mainly on eels and other coarse fish. It is nocturnal and rests in a burrow or holt in the river bank during the daytime.*

Below and right: *Plants which root at the bottom but emerge include the water lilies (9) and arrowhead (16). Common coarse fish are the eel (14) and roach (12). The pike (10) feeds on these and also on young coot and duck, such as the mallard (6). These feed by up-ending. The heron (8) feeds on fish whereas the dipper (11) and reed warbler (5) feed on insects; the dipper walks along the bottom to find its prey; the reed warbler feeds on flying insects as does the dragonfly (7).*

Below and right: *A coot (1) sits at the pond's edge by some water forget-me-not (3). On the grass are a stonefly (2) and a mayfly (4).*

Left: *Common waterside plants include the lesser reedmace (15), the water dock (17) and yellow flag (13).*

deeper and usually much larger. Light cannot penetrate to the bottom of a lake so, like the deep sea, most of a lake's water is cold and dark and contains little life. The edge of a lake may be pond-like, for here light can reach through the water, which is shallow enough for plants to be rooted in the bed of the lake. In swamps there is shallow water, which often contains very little oxygen and may dry up altogether in times of drought.

As in the sea, some of the plants of fresh water are formed of single cells. These are most commonly found in still waters and are the most important plant life of lakes. Where the water is shallow and not fast-flowing, rooted plants grow from the stream or pond bed. Near the edge of ponds or streams these plants may form clumps of vegetation, such as bulrushes and papyrus grass. In deeper water long stems may carry leaves which float on the surface of the water.

A few kinds of larger plants float on the water surface, not rooted in the mud below. These are, however, mostly found in ponds, lake edges or very slow-flowing rivers, for winds may spring up over lakes, and these would drive floating plants across the water to pile up and die on the shore.

The small animals of fresh water are in many cases like those which survive in damp soil. You may say that something is 'as dull as ditchwater', but a drop of water from a ditch can be seen under a microscope to contain a huge number of minute living things. They include single-celled plants, such as diatoms and desmids, protozoans such as paramecium, and other fascinating scraps of life such as the rotifers or 'wheel animals' which with their whirling bands of *cilia* (fine thread-like organs) feed on the smaller creatures about them, and are themselves trapped by the writhing arms of hydras which live among the water weeds.

Paper-thin flatworms glide over the mud, which sometimes looks red with the massed bodies of tubifex worms. Water fleas and cyclopes dart among the foliage, and are food for larger predators such as the dragonfly nymphs or the larvae of beetles. Amphibians and little fishes may feed on these immature insects, and themselves may be the food of water birds, such as ducks and grebes. The birds must beware the biggest of the fishes – a large pike can snap up ducklings or even adult birds as they swim – while mammals such as otters may tackle large fishes.

Most water mammals of cold areas are protected by heavy coats of fur. Beavers, minks and muskrats are examples of animals which keep warm in this way. The outer layer of the fur is formed of long and fairly coarse 'guard hairs' which clamp down, making a waterproof overcoat over the soft inner hairs. The fur traps lots of air, which means that the animal's body stays warm and dry.

In the tropics water-living mammals do not need heavy fur. The hippopotamus, which spends all day in the shallow water of lakes and rivers, has practically no hair. On land, when it comes out to feed, the hippo looks clumsy; under water it is buoyant and graceful. The capybara of South America is another creature with only thin fur.

Life on Remote Islands

The islands of the world can be classified into two main types. Many, such as the islands of the British Isles and Japan, are continental islands. They are part of a nearby continental land mass, which they resemble in their geology, climate and the plants and animals found there.

Others are called oceanic islands. Many, such as the islands of Hawaii and the Galápagos, are the tops of volcanoes which have erupted from the ocean bed. Their underwater cones have finally grown tall enough to stand out above the sea. Coral islands have been built up from the limy skeletons of innumerable tiny animals, called polyps. Some coral islands are built on submerged volcanoes; others may be evidence of a change of level of the sea bed.

Most oceanic islands are small but all are isolated by great stretches of water which separate them from the nearest continent, from which they differ in geology, climate and the living things found there.

You may ask how living things get to oceanic islands. If you were to visit an oceanic island, you might well see quite a lot of familiar living things. They were probably taken there by man, because he thought they would be useful to him, such as crop plants; or because he thought they would be beautiful, such as some brightly coloured birds; or sometimes by accident, such as rats and mice.

But what were the islands like before man arrived? Often they contained many strange plants and animals which were later not able to compete successfully with those brought by humans and are now very rare or even extinct. How these origi-

Below: *Birds are well equipped for travel. The magnificent frigate bird,* Fregata magnificens, *has a 2-metre (7-foot) wing span. It nests in the New World tropics. Tropic birds like* Phaethon aethereus *also travel widely. The Indian flycatcher,* Tersiphone paradisi, *a small mainland species, is sometimes found on small islands vast distances from its mainland home. One of the honeycreepers of Hawaii, the iiwi,* Vestiaria coccinea, *feeds on nectar. Other closely related species have different beaks.*

Left: *The Pacific Ocean contains many coral archipelagos. These arise as volcanoes which are then colonised by corals. Larger islands are found along a ridge of the seabed which extends from Taiwan, through the Philippines and New Guinea, to Fiji. One of these islands is New Britain, east of New Guinea. The peak shown here is a volcano called Mount Bagum.*

Below: *Nothing can live on an island where there is no vegetation, and colonising plants are most important in establishing a community. They might begin with those with wind-blown seeds. The plant family Compositae has members with flying seeds and is well represented on isolated islands. Hawaiian composites illustrated here are* Argyroxiphium sandwicense *(centre), which lives at high altitudes in volcanic ash and cinders,* Argyroxiphium virescens *(left) and* Dubautea plantaginea *(right).*

Above: *The Hawaiian lacewing,* Nesomicromus drepanoides, *has adapted to island life by becoming flightless. Its heavy wings act as weights to prevent it from being blown out to sea.*

nal inhabitants reached the islands is sometimes a mystery, but there seem to be four main ways in which they could have settled there.

Sea reptiles, mammals and birds may arrive by their normal methods of travel, swimming or flying. These animals find the islands in the course of their wanderings, and use them as resting or breeding places. Many oceanic islands have (or used to have) colonies of seals, sea birds and turtles similar to those found in other parts of the world.

The rest of the inhabitants of the islands usually relied less on their own energy to get there. Many arrived in the first place because they had been blown there during a storm. Birds and large insects such as butterflies can be driven many miles out to sea by a freak wind. Most become exhausted and drown, but a few from time to time make a landfall on a remote island.

The constant winds of the upper air carry small organisms. These organisms are often lifted high into the atmosphere, and can be carried vast distances before a break in the wind allows them to fall. Usually they land in the sea, or on some place where they cannot survive, but occasionally one falls on land.

A fourth way of getting to an oceanic island is to be carried by the sea. Every year, rivers in spate tear through forests, undercutting their banks, so that trees fall into the water. A mat of vegetation may be formed which is large and stable enough to survive many weeks at sea. As a rule, these floating islands become waterlogged and sink, but sometimes a part of one is cast on to a distant island. Most of the animals which may have been clinging to the trees when they fell into the river – squirrels or monkeys for instance – die, but a few survive. In tropical areas these animal passengers include reptiles, especially little tortoises which can often float long distances as their original raft becomes waterlogged. Animals living in timber, such as the grubs of wood-boring beetles, may also survive.

From this we can see that certain sorts of plants and animals may be found on oceanic islands: birds and large insects which may be blown by the wind; tiny insects and spiders; minute seeds such as those of orchids, or the spores of mosses and ferns, or seeds with parachute hairs like the dandelion; and reptiles and other creatures which can stand rafting. But no large mammals or plants with big and heavy seeds are likely to reach the islands.

Once a plant or animal has reached an oceanic island it usually finds itself in a place with few competitors. Here its descendants are able to thrive, and often grow bigger than their original mainland forms. Many island races of birds are large, and tropical island reptiles are often giants of their kind.

Islands are usually windy places, and birds and insects which fly strongly may be blown away again, this time probably not lucky enough to survive another long sea journey. Birds which prefer walking to flying tend to be the ones to survive. They have less need for flight because on oceanic islands there are few predators, so the animals have no fear of each other, nor of man when he arrives there.

This lack of fear has in many cases been disastrous for them, and animals too tame to realise their danger were killed in huge numbers for food by visiting sailors. In the 1900s, however, the importance of oceanic islands has been realised: it is seen that they are natural laboratories, where species of plants and animals can be observed in the process of evolving from the original mainland forms to new types adapted to their island home. Many oceanic islands have now been made into nature reserves.

The World of Plants

Plants are among the most successful of living things. They can live in places where animals cannot survive, and though many plants live for only a few months, others, such as the giant redwood trees of North America, live longer than any animal.

In most instances it is easy to tell plants from animals: nearly all plants are green and cannot move about, while animals can usually move freely. But there are exceptions to this simple rule, since some animals spend part of their lives in one fixed place, and plants such as fungi are not green.

True plants have bodies formed of cells, each cell being enclosed in a more or less rigid wall made of cellulose – a substance not usually found in animal cells. Most plants get their energy from the Sun, using this energy to manufacture their own food from carbon dioxide in the air and mineral salts in the soil.

The plant kingdom can be divided into several broad divisions: the Thallophyta, which comprises the algae and fungi; the Bryophyta (the mosses and liverworts); the Pteridophyta (ferns, horsetails and club-mosses) and the Spermatophyta (seed-bearing plants). The Spermatophyta are divided into the gymnosperms, plants with exposed seeds, and the angiosperms, with seeds enclosed in fruits. The bacteria and blue-green algae were once included in the plant kingdom, but are now regarded as a separate kingdom – the Prokaryota.

Fly agaric toadstools push through the soil among pine needles in an evergreen wood.

The Simplest Organisms

The Prokaryotes are the simplest living organisms of the present day, if we do not count viruses as living organisms. They differ from other organisms in having no well-defined *organelles* in the cell – no true nucleus, with its special surrounding membrane, no plastids such as those which carry the photosynthetic pigments of higher plants, no flagella of the elaborate type common in both the plant and animal kingdoms.

There are two groups of prokaryotes, the bacteria and the blue-green algae. Bacteria are so small that they were not discovered until the 1600s and the invention of microscopes, but they are very important organisms indeed. They can be minute spheres (known as *cocci*), sometimes less than 1μ (1/25,000 of an inch) in diameter, or straight or curved rods, mostly simple but sometimes branched. Bacteria are unicellular, multiplying typically by simple division of the cell, but daughter cells may stay united in chains, plates, packets or clusters.

When conditions are good each division occurs after only a very short time, so that a single bacterium dividing every half hour could produce a population of 281½ million million in only 24 hours. It is not surprising, therefore, that bacteria can be very numerous indeed. They are widespread, from high in the atmosphere to deep in the soil, in almost boiling hot springs and in the great ocean deeps, and both on and in plants and animals.

The bacterial wall has a firm inner layer surrounded by a slimy sheath. Many bacteria can move, either by wriggling or through the movement of whiplike strands called *flagella* (though much simpler than the flagella of true plants and animals). Many bacteria can form special long-lived resting stages with thick walls, and these *endospores* may remain alive even after boiling, drying, freezing or storing for centuries. Such spores are not reproductive bodies – they are an insurance against unfavourable conditions.

Bacteria take in nutrients by absorbing them through the cell wall. Some bacteria have photosynthetic pigments similar to, though not identical with, those of higher plants, and can thus get energy from sunlight. Most bacteria get their vital energy in other ways, for example by oxidising ammonia to nitrous acid (as in *Nitrosomonas*), hydrogen sulphide to sulphur (*Beggiatoa*), or sulphur to sulphuric acid (*Thiobacillus*).

Other bacteria get their energy by breaking down organic materials into simple inorganic molecules. This process of bacterial decay is very important in recycling essential elements which might otherwise remain locked up in stable compounds such as cellulose and lignin, which form the hard parts of higher plants. Such bacteria play an important part in sewage disposal.

Bacterial decomposition is directly useful to man in diverse processes such as flax retting (soaking), vinegar production, and the making of butter, cheese and yoghourt. Along with other microorganisms, bacteria perform very important digestive functions in the gut of higher

Above: *Nostoc, a filamentous blue-green alga, is generally seen as the large mass shown here. It can take up nitrogen from the air and use it to manufacture organic compounds that the more complex plants cannot make for themselves. When life was just beginning on Earth, this ability would have been extremely important.* Below: *The enlarged drawing of an individual colony of nostoc shows the strings of nitrogen-fixing globules.*

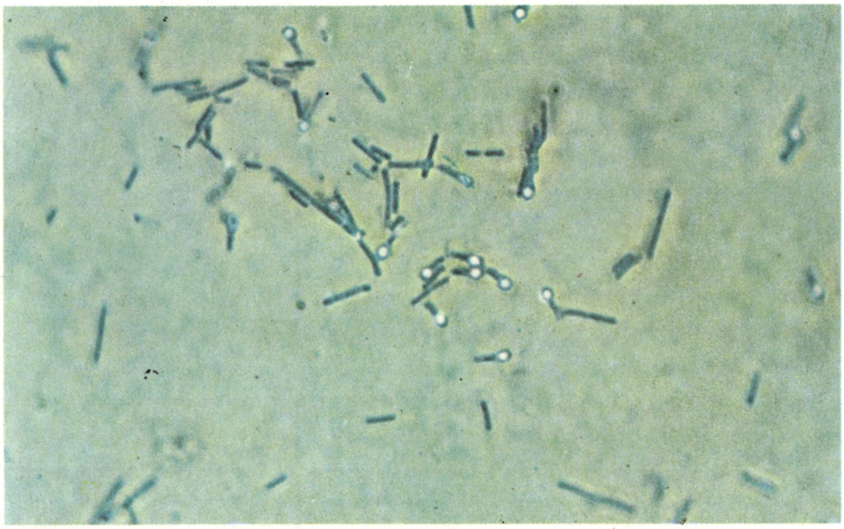

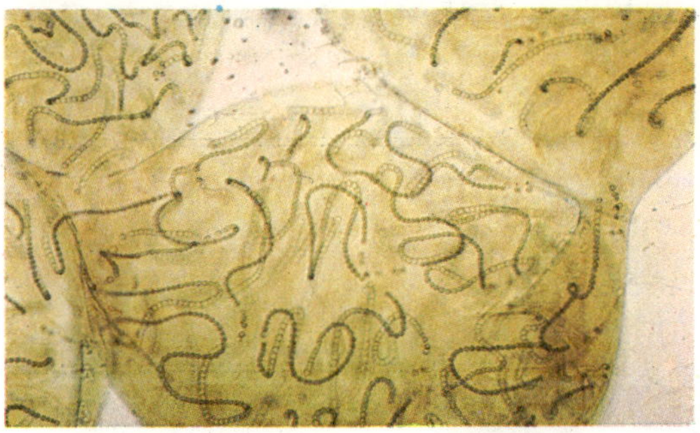

Above: *One of the comparatively small number of disease-causing bacteria is* Clostridium tetani. *It can live in the absence of oxygen and causes the disease called lockjaw, or tetanus, if it gets into a deep wound. It lives in soil where farm animals have been, and may remain dormant for many years.* Left: *Nostoc seen through the microscope.*

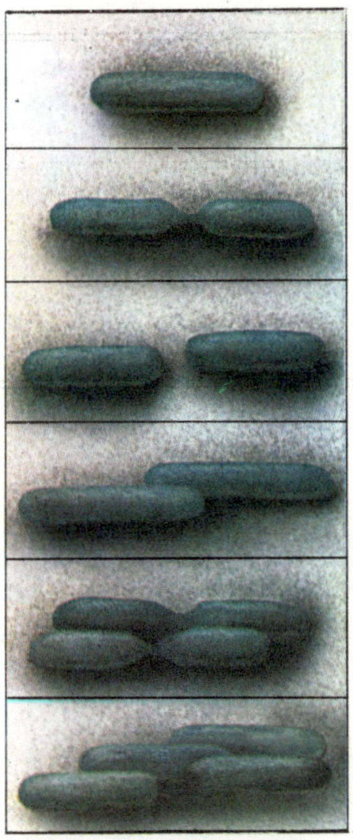

Above: *A single bacillus grows and then divides into two cells by simple cell division. One cell, under favourable conditions, doubles itself in under half an hour; the next half hour will see four cells produced. Large numbers can thus be rapidly attained.*

organisms, assisting ruminants to digest grass, providing man with vitamin K, and helping to keep populations of potentially harmful micro-organisms from growing seriously large. By selecting suitable strains of bacteria, man can use them commercially, producing valuable chemicals such as acetone and butanol.

Another important service performed by bacteria – and also by some of the blue-green algae – is the conversion of atmospheric nitrogen into compounds such as nitrites and nitrates, which can then be taken up by other plants. These processes require a great deal of energy, but without such 'nitrogen fixation' other organisms, unable to fix nitrogen for themselves, would soon be suffering from a shortage of this essential element, which is needed for growth.

Nitrogen-fixing bacteria and blue-green algae may be free-living in soil or water, such as the bacteria *Azotobacter* and *Clostridium*, and the blue-green algae of the genus *Nostoc*, or may be associated symbiotically with other organisms, such as bacteria of the genus *Rhizobium* in the root nodules of flowering plants of the bean family.

Unfortunately not all bacteria are so beneficial. Many cause very serious diseases, such as bubonic plague, cholera, typhoid fever, anthrax and tetanus. The most virulent known natural poison is produced by the bacterium *Clostridium botulinum* – the fatal dose for an adult human is about 0·0000001 gramme!

Fortunately many bacterial diseases can now be checked by antibiotics, and those such as scarlet fever now rarely cause virulent epidemics. Bacterial diseases such as leptospirosis of cattle and bacterial soft rot of plants can cause great losses to farmers, and decay of stored food and other materials through bacterial action can also be very serious. However, we should certainly be much worse off without the various activities of these tiny organisms than we are with them.

Blue-green algae are generally much larger organisms than bacteria, and although many are unicellular, others form colonies or simple and even branched filaments. Their photosynthetic pigments include phycocyanin (blue) and phycoerythrin (red), and despite their name they are by no means always blue-green, but may be black, brown, red, blue, green, yellow, or intermediate shades. Like the bacteria they reproduce by simple cell division, and can form thick-walled resting spores (*endospores*). They do not have flagella, but some can move by gliding or twisting, (for example, *Oscillatoria* species).

Blue-green algae may live on land, in fresh water or in the sea, and like bacteria some can flourish in apparently very hostile environments, such as hot springs of 85°C (185°F) or more. They are very abundant at times, producing sometimes toxic water blooms, and *Trichodesmium*, a reddish marine planktonic species, probably gave the Red Sea its name. The fixation of nitrogen by blue-green algae in rice paddies enables large crops of rice to be harvested successively with no addition of extra fertilisers. Blue-green algae may form symbiotic relationships with other organisms, as for instance with fungi to form some types of lichens.

The Smaller Algae

Algae are plants of relatively simple structure. Their bodies are not clearly separable into stems, roots and leaves, but unlike the fungi most of them can trap light energy by photosynthesis. They do not, however, have the special reproductive structures known as *archegonia* which the liverworts possess. The blue-green algae, which lack a cell nucleus with its own special membrane, are now generally placed in the Prokaryota kingdom along with the bacteria.

There are many other kinds of algae, ranging from minute cells too small to be studied in detail by ordinary light microscopes to giant seaweeds 50 metres (164 feet) or more in length. They occur in both fresh water and in the sea, in brine so strong that the salt is crystallising out, on snow and ice fields, in soil and on rocks, and on and in other organisms. They may be motile (capable of movement), in which case it is sometimes hard to decide if they are plants or animals, drifting in open waters or firmly attached to a substrate (base). Features important in their classification include the nature of the photosynthetic pigments, the form and structure of the cell wall (if present at all), the kinds of reserve foods they store, and the form and position (or absence) of *flagella* (long whiplike structures by which their owners can propel themselves through the water).

Green algae (the group Chlorophyta) include many unicellular species (and larger kinds dealt with on the next pages). The *Chlamydomonas* type is fairly representative of species or stages which are able to move. It has a cellulose wall, a large cup-shaped *chloroplast* (an organelle containing the photosynthetic pigments), a starch-forming centre (*pyrenoid*) towards the rear end, two whiplike flagella at the front end, and a small red eye-spot which makes the organism sensitive to direction and strength of light.

In some cases, groups of such cells remain banded together into motile colonies, which may include many hundreds of individuals, as in species of *Volvox*. One species with reddish pigments, *Haematococcus pluvialis*, is sometimes so abundant in tiny pools and puddles as to colour them red – probably the origin of stories about red rain. Species of *Chlorella* have small globular cells without flagella. They have been widely used in experiments to discover the nature of the photosynthetic process, and also for mass culture.

Microscopic green algae are often associated with other organisms in special relationships for their mutual benefit, a relationship known as *symbiosis*. Symbiosis of an alga and a fungus produces the compound organism known as a lichen (see pages 94–95). Similar relationships have been established between algae and flatworms, coelenterates, sponges and shellfish, and are perhaps responsible for the rapid growth of coral polyps and the great size of the giant clam.

Diatoms are a group of algae with a cell wall in two parts bound together by bands. The wall is composed of silica, often finely sculptured into intricate pat-

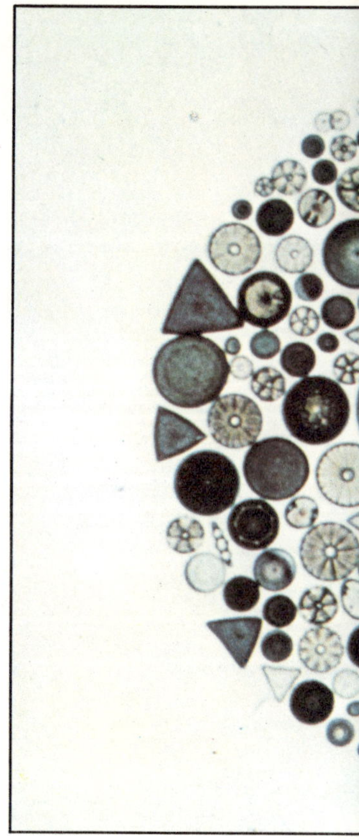

Left: Noctiluca, *a large dinoflagellate that feeds on diatoms. It uses its flagellum for catching food rather than for swimming, which makes it hard to say whether it is a plant, like its nearest relatives, or a simple animal. It is also known for the bluish light it emits.* Below: *A mass of* Noctiluca *in the plankton can give a glow to the entire surface of the sea at night, with brighter flashes on disturbed water.*

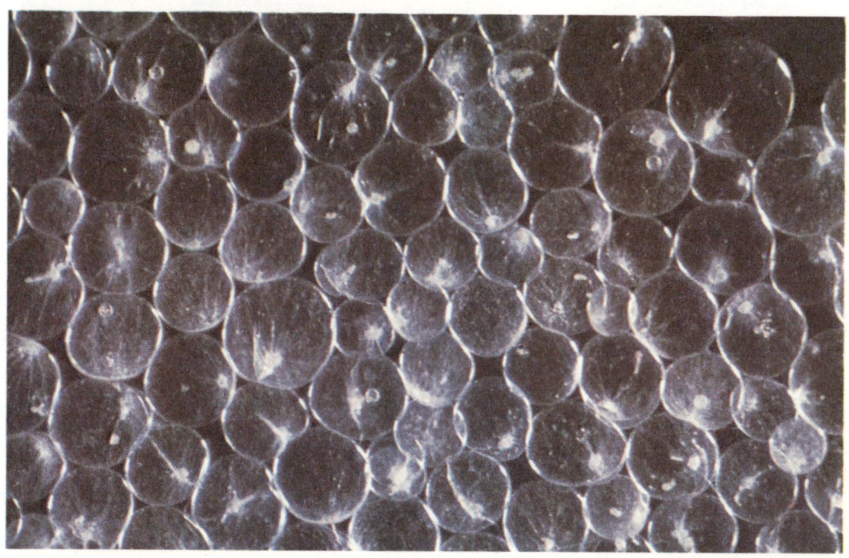

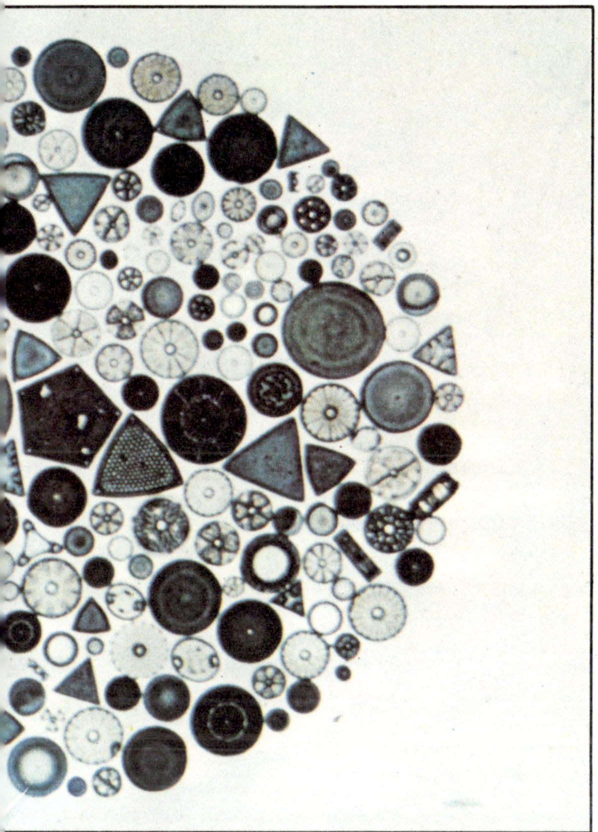

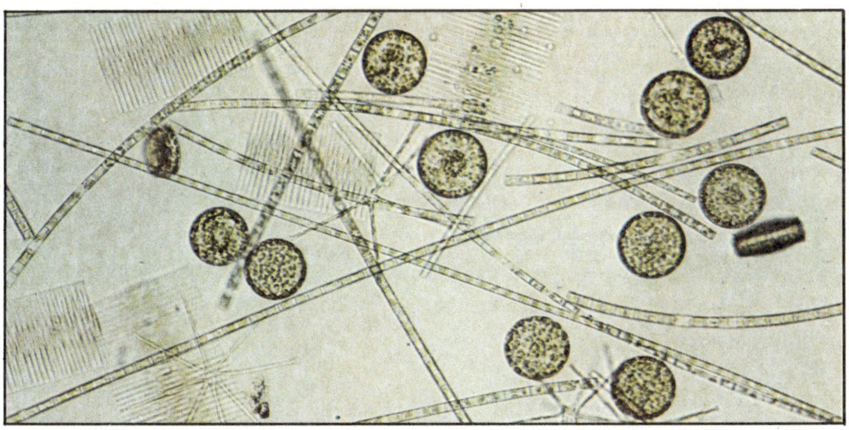

Left and below: *Diatoms make up most of the plant plankton (phytoplankton). They exist in a great variety of shapes, ranging in size from 1/200 to 1 millimetre (1/1250 to 1/25 inch). Marine diatoms live in the surface (euphotic) waters, and their silica skeleton is intricately shaped to help them to float. Some kinds contain a little drop of oil which also helps buoyancy. They reproduce rapidly, mostly by simple cell division, when the water in which they live is rich in nitrates and phosphates. Each diatom 'shell' is made up of two halves and when the cell divides the new cells each take half of the original shell and make another to complete the skeleton. Sexual reproduction is also thought to occur. It has recently been discovered that diatoms are not only present as floating plankton in fresh and salt water, but also live in wet places like soft muddy and sandy shores. They may be extremely abundant in such places, providing food for the browsing and filter-feeding animals which live there. All life depends basically on plant photosynthesis and, small as they are, these tiny plants exist in such abundance throughout the oceans of the world that they can be said to support the whole marine foodchain.*

terns. There are two main forms, the *centric* diatoms, with walls like little circular boxes, and the *pennate* diatoms which are elongated into boat-shapes or needle-shapes.

Free-floating diatoms are often an important first link in food chains of open waters, both freshwater and marine. They can form enormous populations, and their almost insoluble cell walls can accumulate in vast deposits, forming *diatomite*. Diatomite is used extensively as an insulating material, for fine polishing (in toothpaste, for instance), and in dynamite to stabilise the very unstable explosive nitroglycerine.

Coccolithophorids are small free-floating organisms with calcareous (chalky) plates on their outer surface, often present in vast numbers in the sea. Their scales form an important part of the oozes which accumulate on ocean floors.

Dinoflagellates are another group of mainly marine, free-floating micro-organisms. Their outer walls consist of plates, often drawn out into long spine-like processes, with two furrows, one around the middle, the other from the middle to the rear end, and they have two flagella, one in each furrow. Some (*Noctiluca*) produce a brief flash of light when disturbed, so that oars dipped into water in which they abound seem bathed in cold fire.

Large populations of reddish coloured species of dinoflagellates can colour the waters in which they occur, forming water blooms known as 'red tides'. They produce very powerful poisons, causing widespread death of other organisms, particularly fish. They may be absorbed by shellfish such as mussels, which can then be highly poisonous to humans or birds which eat them.

Euglenoids are a group of flagellate organisms which are often considered to be animals rather than plants. They have a thick outer skin (*pellicle*) but no cell wall, though some are surrounded by a *theca*, a rigid outer casing open at the top. Some, such as *Euglena* species, have green photosynthetic pigments, others are colourless. Some of the colourless species absorb their food as particles in a truly animal way. Most euglenoids are fresh-water organisms, often abounding in very polluted ponds and puddles.

Although most algae are aquatic, some are common in damp soils and on shady surfaces where they are not too likely to dry out, and algae such as *Pleurococcus* often cover the bark on the shady side of trees with a green film. However, the free-floating aquatic populations of microscopic algae (*phytoplankton*) are much more important. They provide the food for minute animals which in turn are eaten by larger ones, thus forming the basis for food chains which may ultimately feed man.

The Larger Algae

Nearly all the larger species of algae belong to the *green algae* (Chlorophyta), *brown algae* (Phaeophyta) or *red algae* (Rhodophyta). The green algae occur in fresh water, salt water and on land. As well as the unicellular types described on pages 88–89, they include types forming simple filaments (such as *Spirogyra*), branched filaments (such as *Cladophora*), flat sheets (such as *Ulva*) and complex fronds (such as many *Codium* species). Their photosynthetic pigments are the same as those of higher plants.

Spirogyra species live in slow-flowing streams or in ponds. Each plant consists of a series of cylindrical cells, each cell containing one or more ribbon-like *chloroplasts* (bodies containing chlorophyll) twisted into spirals, studded with *pyrenoids* (small starch-forming centres). *Cladophora* species may be freshwater or marine. *Cladophora rupestris* is a dark bluish-green seaweed growing commonly on shady rocks and in pools around many coasts. The sea lettuce (*Ulva lactuca*) is also found on tidal shores, often in brackish water. It grows particularly well in water polluted by sewage, so although it can be eaten it is as well to check first where it grew. *Codium* species may form mats, balls or large branched fronds of interlaced tubes, giving them a spongy texture.

The biggest of the green algae is about 2 metres (6½ feet) long, but brown algae can be much bigger. They are almost all marine. The photosynthetic pigments in brown algae include fucoxanthin, which gives the characteristic brown colour to the plants.

In sheltered bays and channels the slimy unbranched cords of *Chorda filum* may grow to 10 metres (33 feet) long, forming a dangerous trap for unwary and inexperienced swimmers. Rocky shores where the waves do not beat too fiercely are characteristically draped with brown seaweeds in a series of horizontal bands, each species growing at its own particular level. The wracks dominate the intertidal shore, giving way to the even larger oarweeds at low water level.

Oarweeds have stout branched finger-like processes which cling tightly to the rocks, flexible but tough stems and flat blades, often deeply divided into ribbons. They form underwater forests up to 6 metres (20 feet) high in shallow coastal waters where the bottom is rocky, and are an important source of *alginates* – chemicals which are widely used in a variety of industries, such as printing, textiles, food processing and pharmaceuticals.

The giant kelp (*Macrocystis pyrifera*), which can be 60 metres (200 feet) or more long, is harvested in California, South Africa, the Falkland Islands and elsewhere for the alginate industry. Its fronds,

Above: *The mass of filamentous alga seen festooned around stems and floating in the water, above, is a type like* Spirogyra *(right). This grows so rapidly in summer that it can almost choke a slow-moving river. It passes the winter as resistant spores and is transmitted like this from one body of water to another by wind or animals.*

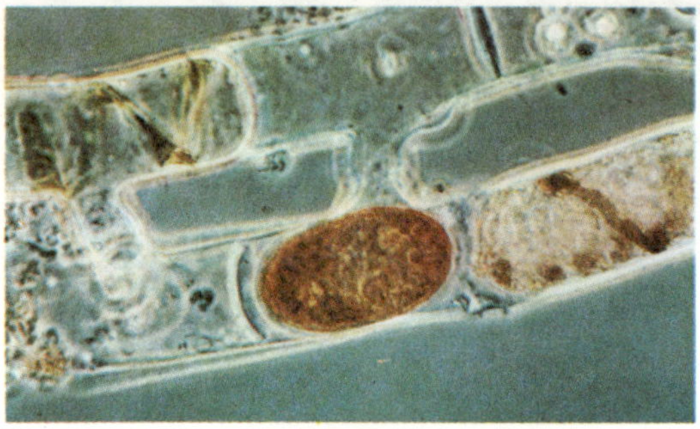

Above: *Spore formation by sexual reproduction in* Spirogyra. *Two filaments of* Spirogyra *have come to lie parallel for a few cells of their length, and extensions of the cell walls have grown out and joined to form conjugation tubes. The entire contents of one cell (top) have passed through the tube and fused with the other cell to give a thick-celled spore. The cell on the left is about to do the same. A normal active* Spirogyra *cell can be seen on the right of the picture. Spores like this are formed in the autumn and in dry conditions.*

Above: *The green seaweed (right and bottom) is* Enteromorpha. *This can tolerate some freshwater and often marks small streams running down the shore. The two brown algae are channelled wrack* Pelvetia canaliculata *(top left) and flat wrack* Fucus spiralis. *These both occupy positions high on the shore.*

Left: *Kelp,* Laminaria, *is a seaweed which usually grows under water, anchored to the sea bed, sometimes reaching up to 50 metres (160 feet) in length like this mass from a beach in the Falkland Islands. Most kelps are smaller than this, however. Their leaves are rich in a glutinous water-retaining substance called alginate, which is extracted commercially for use in many industries; in dressing textiles and in making styptic wound dressings, for example. Kelps and other seaweeds are also a valuable source of fertilisers.*

supported by gas-filled vesicles, float on the surface of the sea, often forming very effective shelter belts on wave-exposed coasts. *Sargassum natans,* a relative of the wracks, forms large free-floating masses in the Sargasso Sea.

The red algae are also almost all marine. Their red colour is due to the pigment phycoerythrin, which bleaches rapidly when exposed to bright sunlight. Red algae may also contain a blue pigment, phycocyanin.

Many of the most brightly coloured and delicate species of red algae grow in shady crevices or in deep water, while many of the species which grow on open rocks between the tides do not look red at all but olive-green or purple. Purple laver (*Porphyra* species) has thin, flat purplish fronds which are collected and used for food in many parts of the world. In Japan it is cultivated on nets supported on frames, forming a large and important industry.

Other red seaweeds, particularly species of *Gracilaria,* form the source of agar-agar, a jelly-like substance used for culturing micro-organisms and in food processing as a packing material. A similar product, carrageenin, is derived from Irish moss (*Chrondrus crispus* or *Gigartina stellata*), species which grow abundantly on many British shores.

One group of red seaweeds, the corallines, encrust themselves in lime (calcium carbonate). Some form flat growths over rock surfaces, cementing the rocks together and protecting them from erosion; some are important elements of coral reefs, protecting the more delicate animal corals from the full force of pounding waves.

Some of the green seaweeds (e.g. *Halimeda* species) can also encrust themselves with lime in similar fashion, and the stoneworts, or charophytes, which grow in freshwater ponds and ditches, are likewise impregnated.

Many algae have a life cycle which includes two free-living stages, one (the *gametophyte*) producing sex cells (*gametes*) which fuse and then give rise to the other stage (the *sporophyte*). This in turn produces spores which develop into the first-stage plants, completing the life cycle. In some, such as *Cladophora,* the sporophyte and gametophyte look alike, but in others they are very different. The *Porphyra* frond, for instance, is the gametophyte, and the sporophyte is a minute pink filament burrowing in shells.

The great oarweeds are sporophytes, while their gametophyte stages are microscopic branched filaments, rarely if ever seen except in laboratory cultures. The wracks have only one free-living stage in their life-cycles. Male gametes and egg cells are produced in special structures formed in cavities (*conceptacles*) in the swollen ends (*receptacles*) of branches. These structures are extruded, gametes and eggs are released, and fertilised eggs grow into new wrack plants.

Most red algae have an even more complicated life-cycle. The small male gametes have no flagella, so have to be carried passively to the female plants, where they lodge on the *trichogyne,* a long hairlike process. The male nucleus enters and fuses with the female nucleus, but then a structure, the *carposporophyte,* is formed, producing spores (*carpospores,*) which are released and grow into the sporophyte plants.

Mosses and Liverworts

Midway between algae and ferns comes a phylum of plants known as the Bryophyta, from two Greek words meaning 'moss plants'. The bryophytes are the mosses and liverworts, lowly plants which are particularly common in damp, shady places, where they often crowd together to form mats or cushions.

Bryophytes mostly have simple structures, without roots and with only small leaves or none at all. They absorb water and nutrients through hairlike cells called *rhizoids*. About 23,000 different kinds of bryophytes are known, widely distributed around the world, from seashore to mountain tops, from the polar circles to the Equator, on land and in fresh water, but never in a marine habitat. However, not all plants named as mosses belong here – for instance Iceland moss is a lichen, Irish moss is a seaweed and Spanish moss is a flowering plant.

Bryophytes have a life-cycle with two stages, one producing spores, the other producing *gametes* (the male and female reproductive cells). The spore-producing stage remains attached to the gamete-producing stage, never becoming completely independent of it. A spore germinates to produce a *protonema* – a green thread – on which one or more special growing points appear. From these the bryophyte plants develop. Leaves may develop as outgrowths from the stem.

Left: *The leaf-like thallus of* Lophocoela heterophylla, *a leafy liverwort, has no roots. It scatters its reproductive spores by means of bursting capsules which can be seen here.* Above: *Bog moss,* Sphagnum, *forms large wet patches on boggy ground. It also has no roots; the lower parts of the plant die away as the plant grows.*

Below: Polytrichum auranticum, *a large hair moss, can be distinguished by the stalked male organs (antheridia). It is growing beside a cushion moss,* Leucobryum glaucum, *in the acid moorland soil favoured by both species. Cushion mosses show how rootless they are by the way in which they will continue to grow even if dislodged.*

Male gametes are formed in structures called *antheridia*. Each antheridium consists of a mass of very small cubical cells inside a jacket of larger flatter cells, on a stalk. The female reproductive organ, the *archegonium,* is vase-shaped, with a single egg cell in the lower part of the vase. Each of the small cubical cells of the antheridium produces a single male gamete, a tiny wormlike structure with two long whiplike processes, called *flagella,* emerging from the front end. Mucilage in the cells absorbs water, the cells swell and split, and the little gametes swim off by lashing their flagella.

In the meantime the cells in the neck and upper part of the archegonium have broken down, producing a gummy fluid which contains a substance attractive to the male gametes. With luck one of these finally reaches the neck, swims down it and fuses with the egg cell. This fertilised cell then grows into a structure which typically consists of a foot, sunk into the parent plant and drawing nourishment from it, a stalk and a capsule. Within the cap-

Above: *Common cord moss,* Funaria hygrometrica, *is frequently found on burnt or limed soil. Here it is growing on a burnt tree trunk. Its liking for burnt places can mean that there has been a fire where it is found, even though this may not be immediately obvious.* Funaria *has antheridia (male organs) and archegonia (female organs) on separate plants.*

sule are formed the spores, in most bryophytes each one being a small, thick-walled cell. These are eventually released and dispersed to germinate and grow into new bryophyte plants.

Liverworts and mosses differ in several important ways. Liverworts are generally simpler in structure than mosses. They usually grow flat on the soil or decaying wood, with an upper surface which is clearly different from the lower side. Some kinds have no leaves at all, just a flattened, often forked body which can be quite bulky. Leafy liverworts typically have the leaves in three distinct rows, two towards the upper side and one, usually of much smaller leaves, on the underside. Moss leaves are rarely in distinct rows.

The capsules also show a number of differences. Those of many liverworts open by four splits in the walls, which then peel back like the petals of a flower. The spores in many species are dispersed by movements of *elaters* (special sterile cells) among them, which twist and straighten in response to changes in dampness of the air. Mosses do not have elaters, but do usually have much more elaborate capsules, often with a central column of sterile cells and outer layers of green pigmented cells which can carry out photosynthesis,

Above: *This picture of the liverwort,* Lunularia cruciata, *clearly shows the gemmae – asexual buds – growing from the thallus. These gemmae are formed on both male and female plants, and germinate to produce new plants.*

so that the capsule can trap some of the Sun's energy for itself.

The opening of the capsule is a generally much more elaborate business in mosses than in liverworts. Typically a *calyptra* (small conical cap) of parental tissue is first shed. The capsule then begins to dry out, and the wall ruptures along a line of weakness which separates off an *operculum* (small circular cap). Beneath this cap lies a double row of teeth which can fit together to close the opening, or can stand erect to let the spores out. Like the elaters, they are very sensitive to changes in moistness of the air, so the capsule remains closed in damp weather. In dry weather the spores are shaken out like pepper from a pepperpot and carried away by the wind.

Because the male gamete has to have a surface film of water through which to swim to the archegonium, the bryophyte life-cycle does not seem very well adapted for life on land. To compensate for this, bryophytes have very efficient methods for vegetative reproduction. If separated off, almost any living cell from any part of a plant can grow into an entire new plant, and as old stems die the branches can become independent plants.

Although individual bryophyte plants are generally small and inconspicuous, their ability to multiply rapidly enables them to become quite important parts of vegetation. Species of *Sphagnum,* which are capable of absorbing and holding enormous quantities of water, often form the main vegetation of bogs in cool, wet climates, their remains gradually changing into peat. *Rhacomitrium lanuginosum* forms grey-green mats on exposed mountain tops and upland moors, often where little else will grow. On burnt ground the small pale green rosettes of *Funaria hygrometrica* are often abundant. The leafless liverwort *Lunularia cruciata* is a frequent pest of gardens and greenhouses.

Although bryophytes can be important parts of many types of plant community, they are of little economic importance. The highly absorbent *Sphagnum* is used as a packing material, particularly by horticulturists, and also as substitute nappies for Lapland babies.

Lichens

Lichens are flowerless plants which grow on bare rocks, the trunks of trees, and similar places, often giving a characteristic greenish colour to a 'weathered' surface. But though they are plants, lichens are not single organisms. Each lichen is an intimate association (symbiosis) between a fungus and an alga, which forms a compound organism with unique and special features of its own. There are more than 16,000 different kinds of lichens known, and they have successfully colonised unpromising habitats from seashore to mountain top, flourishing in the Arctic tundra and tropical forest alike.

On rocky seashores they often form distinctive horizontal bands, with black lichens (*Verrucaria* and *Lichina* species) below high tide level, yellow and orange lichens (*Caloplaca* and *Xanthoria* species) just above and grey lichens (such as *Ramalina* and *Parmelia* species) becoming more abundant as exposure to salt spray decreases. However, like mosses, lichens are most luxuriant in moist, warm conditions, when they grow freely over both ground and vegetation, with large lichens such as *Usnea* species hanging in festoons from the trees.

The lichen is mainly composed of a much-branched network of fungal strands, with the algae usually confined to a narrow zone just below the surface (*heteromerous* lichens) but sometimes scattered more or less uniformly throughout the plant body (*homoiomerous* lichens).

Left: *The beard lichen,* Usnea *sp., is one of the fruticose lichens.* Above: Xanthoria *is a 'leafy' lichen, found on rocks, walls and roofs. They are more tolerant of air pollution than many other lichens; one species,* X. parietina, *thrives on asbestos roofs in cities.*

Below: *One of the largest of British lichens, tree lungwort,* Lobaria pulmonaria, *forms characteristically square-cut patches on old forest trees. The lichen here is wet; when dry it is yellowish-brown. It is still common in Scotland, but is found only in woodlands sheltered from pollution in the south.*

The fungi of heteromerous lichens usually have green algal partners, which may be unicellular, such as *Chlorella, Palmella, Protococcus* and especially *Trebouxia;* or filamentous, such as *Trentepohlia.* The homoiomerous lichens typically contain blue-green algae, such as the unicellular *Gloiocapsa* and the filamentous *Nostoc.* The same alga may be concerned in very different lichens, and sometimes there may be different algae in different parts of the same lichen.

In some lichens the association is a very loose one, a weft of fungal cells spreading round small groups of algal cells. These *leprose* lichens are especially frequent in warm moist climates, and may be considered very primitive. *Crustose* lichens have a more highly organised structure. A distinct upper surface layer of *hyphae* (fungus threads) tightly cemented together with mucilage, can often be seen. Below this in heteromerous lichens lies the algal zone, small groups of algal cells being surrounded by thin-walled and relatively loosely interwoven fungal hyphae. The fungal layer below this may be embedded in the substrate – the rock or other substance on which the lichen is growing.

Squamulose lichens have the upper surface compacted into scales, while *foliose* lichens, although still pressed closely against the substrate, have a distinct underside layer, often like the surface one. They are sometimes bound to the substrate by thread-like attachment strands called *rhizinae,* but the margins are always free.

Fruticose lichens have the structurally most advanced form. Rhizinae hold them to the substrate, but the main frond, which may be erect, prostrate or hanging down, has a central zone of loosely interwoven fungal hyphae (sometimes with a hollow in the middle), surrounded by an algal zone. This in turn is surrounded by a well-defined outer layer of fungal hyphae, tightly cemented together. The frond may be simple, but more usually is much branched, and may be as much as 5 metres (16 feet) long.

The algae reproduce by simple division of cells or sometimes by spore production, but are not dispersed independently of their fungal partners except perhaps accidentally. The fungal partner can reproduce by spore production in most cases, with fruiting bodies similar to those of independent fungi, and the often brightly-coloured spore cups of many species can be easily seen.

Most lichens are *asco-lichens,* with an ascomycete as the fungal partner. These produce typically eight spores in a sporangium, either in an open cup lined by sporangia or in a flask-shaped pit with a narrow mouth. There are a few *basidiolichens,* in which the fungal partner is a basidiomycete, with typically four spores produced on stalks from each sporangium. Presumably when these spores germinate they must 'capture' a free-growing alga of suitable type in order to reconstitute a lichen, but little is known of their fate.

Lichens can also reproduce vegetatively in various ways. The frond may become fragmented, and wind-scattered bits may eventually grow into new lichen plants – the only known method of reproduction for species of *Coriscium,* for instance. Other lichens may produce structures known as *soredia,* consisting of a few algal cells surrounded by a ball of fungal hyphae. The soredia are released through cracks in the surface layer, and are dispersed by wind, insects or mites. Another type of reproductive body is the *isidium,* an outgrowth from the upper surface of the frond which readily breaks off at the base and is then likewise wind-distributed.

The partnership is undoubtedly a very successful one, for many lichens can flourish in habitats where no other kind of plant can survive. The fungus protects the alga from excess heat, light and drying out, while the alga carries out photosynthesis, and in some cases nitrogen fixation also. The fungus absorbs materials from the algal cells by processes called *haustoria,* which may be flattened against the cell wall of the algae or may even enter the algal cells.

Although lichens are most common in warm moist conditions, some species can survive and grow where conditions are very dry, very hot or very cold. Under such unfavourable conditions growth may be very slow – perhaps less than 0·5 millimetre (1/50 inch) a year – but such lichens may live a long time, possibly for centuries.

Above: *Dog lichen,* Peltigera canina, *was named by Linnaeus in 1753. The name probably refers to its common use at that time in treating rabies. It has a downy surface and is classed as a broad-lobed 'leafy' form. The specimen shown here has clearly visible brown terminal fruit bodies.*

Above: *This specimen of* Roccella *was found in St. Finan's Bay, County Kerry; it is also found in the extreme south-west of the British Isles. The genus is mainly Mediterranean; one species,* R. tinctoria, *was once an important source of a purple dye called orchil or orseille.*

The Smaller Fungi

Fungi are plants which have no *chlorophyll*, the green pigment which enables other kinds of plants to make their own food using sunlight as a source of energy. There are probably as many as 100,000 different species of fungi making up this large group. They grow in all parts of the world, from the tropics to the frozen polar regions, and they grow in almost every conceivable kind of habitat – even such unlikely ones as acid vats and bottles of disinfectant! They are of immense importance to man, both as friends and foes.

The simplest fungus consists of just one cell, but more typically fungi have plant bodies formed from slender, long, much-branched tubes called *hyphae*, interwoven to form a *mycelium* (network). In some fungi the hyphae are divided by cross-walls; in others there are no cross-walls except where reproductive bodies or damaged parts are being shut off. Fungi reproduce mainly by spores, produced in immense numbers and often widely dispersed in air and water.

Because fungi must get their vital energy by breaking down materials containing energy made by other organisms, they are all either *saprophytes* (living on dead or waste organic matter), *parasites* (drawing their nourishment from living hosts but contributing little or nothing in return), or *symbionts* (sharing their lives with quite different types of organisms to their mutual advantage, as in the lichens – see pages 94–95). But they do not always stick to just one of these categories.

Like bacteria, fungi can be *decomposers*, breaking down often complex organic materials to simpler inorganic molecules which can then be recycled. From man's point of view this ability can be useful when the materials are dead leaves, fallen trees or drowned flies, but upsetting when they are stored foodstuffs, cloth, books, or structural timber. In the same way fungi may be helpful when they attack insect pests or weed plants, but troublesome when they destroy crop plants, or cause the illness of domestic animals or even of man himself. Fungi can provide food for man, but many species are very poisonous, as we shall see. Fungi can also be used industrially to provide important chemicals such as antibiotics, citric acid, carbon dioxide and ethyl alcohol.

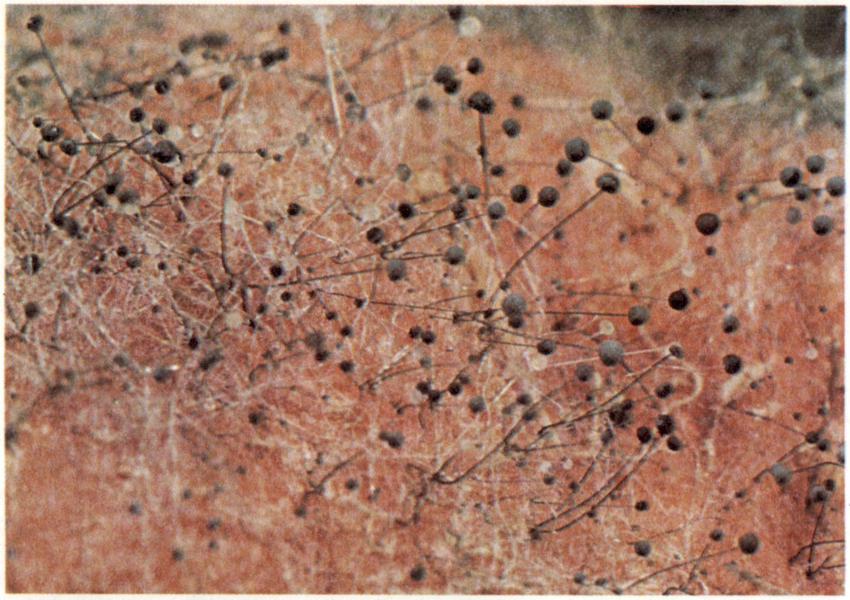

Above: *Pin mould,* Mucor, *growing on a carrot. The pinheads from which it gets its name are the reproductive sporangia; when ripe they burst to release a black dust of spores. These are asexual reproductive organs, but* Mucor *also reproduces sexually in a different way to form resistant spores.*

Above: *This orange growth is a slime mould,* Reticularia lycoperdon. *Slime moulds do not form the thread-like mycelium characteristic of most fungi, but appear to be masses of protoplasm without even cell walls. However, cell walls are formed round reproductive cells.*

For convenience fungi may be divided into two groups, the smaller fungi such as moulds, and the larger fungi, which include the familiar mushrooms and toadstools (see page 98–99).

Some of the simplest fungi are on the borderline between plants and animals. Such are the slime moulds (Myxomycetes or Mycetozoa), which have no true cell walls and move around like amœbae, swallowing bacteria and other small particles. Some slime moulds grow into large sheets of protoplasm almost 1 metre (3¼ feet) in diameter, and sometimes brightly coloured. Slime moulds produce spores which do have cell walls. Most are free-living in habitats such as woodland litter and compost heaps, but some invade other plants as parasites, notably *Plasmodiophora brassicae,* which produces the clubroot disease of cabbages and turnips.

The main groups of true fungi are based

Left: *This buttercup plant has been affected by a type of fungus known as smut,* Urocystis anemones. *The effect of this parasitic mould is clearly seen. Smuts also attack crops and can cause much damage to horticulture.*

Above: *An apple infected with brown rot, caused by the fungus,* Sclerotina fructigena. *It has in fact reached the stage known as Black Apple, where the fungus is producing spores in rings round the completely rotten fruit. This apple also has a patch of* Botrytis *on it.*

on the kinds of *sporangia* (spore cases) formed in the basic life cycle. Many fungi, however, are known to reproduce only from spores borne directly on hyphae (*conidia*). These are provisionally lumped together as *imperfect fungi.*

Phycomycetes (the algae-like fungi) have few or no cross-walls and produce spores in large numbers inside sporangia. The simpler kinds include the downy mildews, which live inside higher plants, sending out their stalked sporangia through the plant pores, also the fungi (*Pythium* species) which cause damping-off disease where seedlings are grown closely packed together and over-watered.

The late blight of potatoes, which ravaged potato crops in Europe in the 'Hungry Forties' of the 19th century, was caused by one of these fungi (*Phytophthora infestans*). More than a million people died of starvation in Ireland alone.

Ascomycetes (sac fungi) normally have only four or eight spores, produced inside a special sporangium called an *ascus,* though they may also produce conidia, often in enormous numbers. They include the yeasts, fungi reduced to single cells, which are used by the brewer to make alchohol and by the baker to make carbon dioxide, which causes his bread to rise. The blue-green moulds are in this group; they are found all too often on bread, fruit and other foodstuffs. But they include *Penicillium notatum,* from which the antibiotic penicillin was first extracted.

The powdery mildews, which grow on the outside of plants such as roses, are also Ascomycetes; so too is the very poisonous ergot fungus (*Claviceps purpurea*), which attacks the developing grains of grasses, particularly rye. Eating bread made from infected rye causes the terrible affliction, widespread in medieval Europe, known as St. Anthony's Fire (not to be confused with erysipelas, also called St. Anthony's Fire). The Dutch elm disease which has destroyed so many elm trees both in Europe and in North America is also caused by an ascomycete (*Ceratomella ulmi*), the spores of which are carried from tree to tree by bark beetles.

Above: *The rust on this meadowsweet leaf is another destructive basidiomycete, like the smut. Both cause danger to crops.*

Basidiomycetes (club fungi) have four spores budded off on the outside of a sporangium called a *basidium.* Among the smaller ones are the rusts and smuts, which can be destructive to economically important crop plants. The smuts produce masses of black, powdery spores – hence their name – while some of the rusts produce rust-coloured spores in spots or streaks on the host.

The Larger Fungi

The larger fungi are those which produce fruiting bodies of clearly visible size – in the case of the giant puffball as big as, or even bigger than, a football. They are all members of the Ascomycetes and the Basidiomycetes.

The larger Ascomycetes can be divided into cup fungi, in which the *asci* (see pages 96–97) are grouped in a surface layer which is often shaped like a shallow cup, and flask fungi, in which the asci are sunk in little flask-shaped cavities in the fruiting body, as for instance the ergot fungus. The orange-peel fungus (*Peziza aurantia*) is a fairly common species of cup fungus with a rather flattened fruit-body up to 100 millimetres (4 inches) around.

The common morel (*Morchella esculenta*) is a stalked cup fungus fruiting in spring which is very good to eat, but the most highly prized edible fungi are the truffles (*Tuber* species). Truffles produce their fruiting bodies underground. The spores are spread by animals, which are attracted to the truffles by their enticing smell, dig them out and eat them. The spores pass unharmed through the animals' digestive systems. Truffles, which are considered great delicacies, are hunted for in some parts of the world by pigs and dogs trained to sniff them out in the oak and beech woods where they grow.

The larger Basidiomycetes include many varied fungi. The Jew's ear fungus (*Auricularia auricula*) grows on elder bushes, and the fruiting bodies do indeed look like rather shrivelled brownish ears. The name is a corruption of 'Judas's ear', from the legend that Judas hanged himself from an elder tree. Although not very appetising-looking, it is edible.

Most of the larger Basidiomycetes have their basidia (spore-carrying cells) directly exposed to the air when mature. Many fungi grow on living or dead timber, and can cause great damage. One of the most destructive is the dry rot fungus (*Merulius lachrymans*), which attacks timber, reducing it ultimately to powder. There are also many kinds of wet rot fungi, which attack only very wet wood and can be serious pests, such as when they attack pit props in mines.

Typical gill fungi have the gills on the lower side of a cap supported by a central stalk, which may have a ring (*annulus*) round its upper end and a small cup (*volva*) round the base – useful features in identification. Gill fungi include the cultivated mushroom (*Agaricus hortensis*) – which has an annulus but no volva – and its many wild relatives such as the field

Right: *The destroying angel fungus is as deadly as its name. It grows in damp deciduous woodland, and is commonest in autumn. It is completely white, including the gills, with a ring (*annulus*) on the upper stem, a scaly stalk and a bulbous base with loose ring (*volva*). Similar edible mushrooms have coloured gills (pink to chocolate) and lack a volva.*

Above: *The death cap toadstool begins as a small compact body just under the soil surface. It becomes egg-shaped with a swollen base. The cap and stalk develop enclosed in a membrane which tears as the stalk lengthens and remains as a loose basal cup, exposing the greenish-white cap. The crowded white gills are exposed as the cap expands, and the torn membrane which covered them remains as an annulus. It is very poisonous.*

Left: *The fly agaric fungus is common in birch and pine woods. It has a bulbous many-ringed base, a loose well-marked annulus, and a bright red cap, usually flecked with small white patches, the remains of the outer membrane. Formerly it was mashed up with honey as a fly trap, and this explains the name of this fungus. It is poisonous.*

Above: *Jew's ear fungus fruiting bodies are often abundant all the year round on elder trees, as rather gelatinous brownish-red brackets clustered on dead branches.*

Above right: *The beefsteak fungus attacks oak trees and causes serious damage. The fruiting body forms reddish brackets, often very large, with pale pores underneath; a reddish juice is produced from damaged parts. It is edible but unappetising.*

mushroom and the large horse mushroom.

Other gill fungi are often contemptuously dismissed as mere 'toadstools', but they include many species which are good to eat, such as the parasol mushroom, the chanterelle and blewits. Another edible species, the lawyer's wig fungus, has a tall cylindrical cap: as the spores ripen the edge of the cap dissolves away, and the black spores suspended in this liquid give these fungi their general name of ink caps.

If you gather wild fungi to eat you should be very careful, for some are very poisonous – indeed, it is best always to go with a fungus expert. The most deadly fungus is the death cap (*Amanita phalloides*), a white-spored woodland fungus with a slightly greenish cap, with annulus and volva, probably responsible for 90 per cent of deaths from fungus poisoning, as eating even a small piece is almost always fatal. Some fungi produce hallucinations when eaten, and have been used in religious ceremonies in various parts of the world.

Meadowland fungi are often responsible for forming the so-called 'fairy rings'. The mycelium spreads out in the soil, producing a ring of fruit bodies around the edge, often with a bare inner ring where the tightly-packed fungal hyphae are starving the grass roots, and a luxuriant grass ring within that, where the dying hyphae restore food to the soil. The best known fairy ring fungus is *Marasmius oreades,* but many other species can produce the same effect.

The fungi known as boleti are pore fungi with caps and stalks like mushrooms. They include the cep (*Boletus edulis*), a much sought-after edible fungus.

Many Basidiomycetes release their spores inside the fruit-bodies. These include earth stars, bird's nest fungi, puffballs and stinkhorns. The earth stars have a thick outer coat which splits open and spreads out like a little star; the bird's nest fungi have a cup-shaped outer envelope that holds several little rounded spore-containing bodies like eggs in a nest. The puffballs produce enormous numbers of tiny dry spores inside a thin but tough membrane which opens at the top. The slightest pressure on this membrane releases clouds of spores, which are carried away on the lightest breeze. Several species are small, round and white, and when they grow on fairways they can be very confusing for golfers! The largest, the giant puffball (*Lycoperdon giganteum*) may have a dry weight of over 700 grammes (25 ounces) and contain over 20 million million spores.

The stinkhorn's fruiting body when young looks not unlike a rather globular hen's egg, breaking open at the top to produce a hollow spongy stem, with a cap covered by a greenish liquid containing the spores. This liquid has a most vile and far-reaching stink, which attracts carrion flies from far and near. The flies eat it up and thus carry away the spores; these can pass through the flies' digestive systems.

Ferns and their Allies

Botanists group some plants together and describe them as 'pteridophytes' – a word which means 'feather plants' – because most of them have large, feather-shaped leaves. The best-known of these feather plants are the ferns.

All the feather plants have two phases in their existence. The first is short-lived; the plant may look like a liverwort (see pages 92–93), or be so small that it can be recognised only with a microscope. This shortlived phase needs damp conditions for survival. It reproduces quickly to form a large and longer-lived phase, as in the familiar ferns which we see growing.

The larger plant has a more complicated structure, for it is made of cells of four kinds. each of which has a special part to play. One is concerned with food manufacture, another with support. The remaining two are vascular tissues which distribute water and food around the body; their position can be recognised easily in leaves, where they occur in the veins.

The outermost layer of cells in some parts of the body can make a *cuticle* or external skin; this is a waterproofing layer which helps to stop too much evaporation of water into the air, essential for land-growing plants.

Pteridophytes are larger than liverworts and mosses, with stems bearing leaves which manufacture food, and roots which act as anchors and absorb water and soil salts.

Above: *These two ferns, prickly buckler-fern* (Dryopteris lanceolatocristata) *(left) and soft prickly shield-fern* (Polystichum setiferum) *(right) have typically fern-shaped leaves. They grow in sheltered places, and differ from bracken in having short rhizomes which produce a clump of leaves in the shape of a basket.*

Below: *Hart's tongue fern* (Phyllitis scolopendrium) *(left) and common polypody* (Polipodium vulgare) *(right) are less common than the buckler or shield ferns. They can easily be distinguished from bracken-like ferns by their less feathery leaves. Polypody ferns grow in damp woodland, while the hart's tongue ferns are found in rocky places.*

The commonest pteridophytes, the ferns, are world-wide in distribution. They grow in woodlands and forests, in hedgerows, in open grassland, on mountains and sometimes even in water.

The most widely distributed and successful fern is bracken, *Pteridium aquilinum.* Bracken has a *rhizome* – a long underground stem – which is dark brown or black, with a light line on either side through which the stem is probably ventilated. The stem grows at the tip; it branches and as the older parts die away the branches separate, and so the number of plants increases. The main stem lies deep in the soil, but from it thinner branches grow up towards the soil surface, and these bear well-spaced leaves in two rows, one on each side of the rhizome.

In contrast to bracken, which often grows in open ground, there are many ferns which prefer more sheltered positions, such as banks and woods. These ferns have short rhizomes, which do not spread rapidly, and form leaves in groups shaped like baskets. The buckler ferns, *Dryopteris,* and the shield ferns, *Polystichum,* are like this.

The large phase in the life of ferns eventually forms reproductive organs, the *sporangia,* which are borne in groups at the edge or on the underside of the leaf. Each group is protected by a flap which shrinks and curls away when the sporangia are ripe, exposing them to the air. Each individual sporangium consists of a box containing reproductive cells, the *spores*, and is attached to the leaf by a long stalk. The sporangium has an ingenious mechanism for opening the box, which depends on a curved strip of cells on one side. When the air is dry, these cells straighten out slowly to open the box, and then recoil quickly, like a catapult, to fling the spores out into the air where they are carried away by the breeze.

Other pteridophytes are not so common as ferns and they are very different in appearance. Horsetails (*Equisetum*) really do look like the tails of horses; only the stem which comes above the ground stands upright. The branches hang out at the side loosely, so the plant is not quite so compact as the tail of a horse. The above ground stems are ridged on the surface, where there is a great deal of silica in the supporting cells. Silica makes the stem surface very hard.

The remaining pteridophytes are clubmosses, plants which are not unlike mosses in appearance, but which form upstanding, club-shaped branches when they reproduce. Clubmosses are smaller and more delicate than ferns and horsetails, and are less common. They grow mainly in tropical and subtropical regions, and few can survive colder conditions of climate.

Related to the clubmosses is a smaller and rarer plant, the quillwort, *Isoetes*. Quillwort is a water plant growing in lakes, with a short upright stem anchored in mud by roots and a group of simple upright leaves.

Horsetails and clubmosses form sporangia on special branches – the *cones* – which are held well above the rest of the plant. The sporangia have ejector mechanisms like those of ferns, which fling out the spores.

While today pteridophytes are small plants which do not form a major part of our flora, fossils show that many millions of years ago, in the Carboniferous period, they were very abundant, and the clubmosses and horsetails were big trees. It is the remains of such plants that have made much of the coal we burn today.

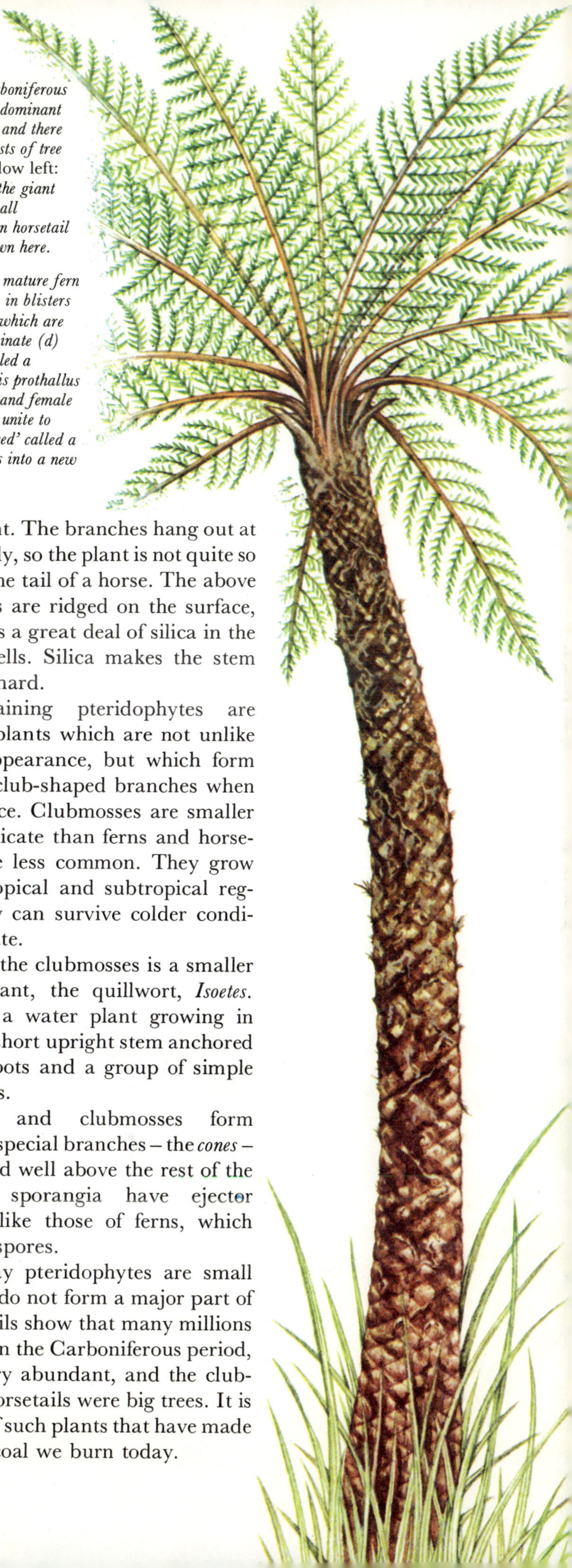

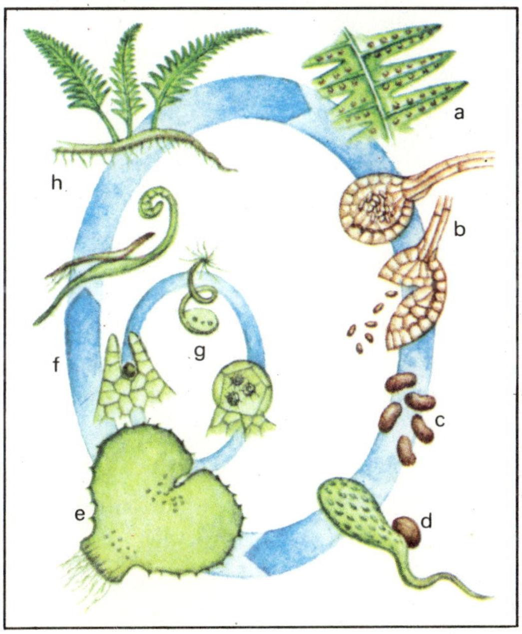

Right: *In the Carboniferous age ferns were the dominant form of plant life, and there were extensive forests of tree ferns like this.* Below left: *Also present were the giant ancestors of the small present-day common horsetail and club moss shown here.*

Bottom left: *The mature fern produces spores (c) in blisters under the leaf (a) which are ejected (b) to germinate (d) into a tiny leaf called a prothallus (e). This prothallus produces male (g) and female (f) gametes which unite to give a fertilised 'seed' called a zygote. This grows into a new fern plant (h).*

Plants bearing Seeds in Cones

Gymnosperms are plants which form seeds in cones, but not flowers or fruits; they are mainly evergreen trees. The term *gymnosperm* comes from two Greek words meaning 'naked seeds'. Gymnosperms first appeared in plant history a little later than the pteridophytes (see pages 100–101). Early gymnosperms had fern-like leaves and elaborate *sporangia* (spore-forming organs).

While ferns have sporangia which fling out the spores, gymnosperms have some sporangia which retain them. The retained spore grows eventually into a minute new plant, the embryo. The whole structure, sporangium with the embryo plant inside, is called a *seed*. However, unlike the flowering plants, gymnosperms have no carpel around the seed.

Present-day gymnosperms are not like ferns; they are always upright plants, with erect stems carrying leaves up in the air away from the ground, and one main root, bearing side roots, growing down through the soil. There are two main orders of such plants, the Cycadales and the Coniferales, and some minor orders. Cycads grow in warm regions such as Australia, South Africa, eastern Asia and tropical parts of the Americas. Cycads have the appearance of palms, with an upright unbranched stem, sometimes short, but more often tall and up to 20 metres (65 feet) in height, with large, tough leaves which form a crown at the top.

Above: *The shoot of cedar (left) has whorls of narrow spine-tipped leaves. The maidenhair shoot (right) has stalked, fan-shaped leaves.*

Below: *The Cedar of Lebanon (left) is a large hardy tree with multiple upright trunks and a domed or flat-topped crown. The maidenhair tree (right) is deciduous, with either a branched and spreading crown, as here, or one less branched, and slender.*

Left: *The cycas, native to Australia and Polynesia, is an unbranched tree with large, fern-like leaves. The stem is only slightly woody; it is supported partly by tough leaf bases, that persist after leaf fall. The crown bears a single cone.*

Conifers are tall, much-branched trees, which are often shaped like a cone, but also have reproductive branches which are called cones. Conifers are remarkable for their great size and age.

The tallest trees today grow in California, either near the coast – the Californian redwood (*Sequoia sempervirens*) – or in the mountains – the wellingtonia (*Sequoia gigantea*). The present record for height of a living tree is held by a Californian redwood at 111 metres (366 feet).

The dominant conifers of the northern hemisphere, which make forests across

North America, Europe and Asia, are spruce and pine. Spruce (*Picea*) is a tall tree with small, hard leaves often ending in a spine; when the leaves are shed the leaf stalks remain, leaving the stem with a very rough surface. The Norway spruce (*Picea abies*) is probably the most familiar species, because it is commonly used in Europe as a Christmas tree. Pine (*Pinus*) is not as tall as spruce, and has a very distinctive appearance, because the leaves are shaped like long needles, almost always in groups of 2, 3 or 5. Other conifers related to these are the firs (*Abies alba*) recognisable by small circular scars on the stem when the leaves drop away, cedar (*Cedrus*) with clusters of leaves, larch (*Larix*), one of the few conifers to shed leaves in autumn, and Chile pine or monkey puzzle (*Araucaria*) with tough broad leaves. The cypresses (*Cupressus* and *Chamaecyparis* species) have small, scaly leaves closely pressed to the stem, and shoots which are often flat.

All these plants form cones of two types. One is small and short-lived, with sporangia which release spores into the air. The other is tough, woody, and longer-lived, with more elaborate sporangia, called *ovules*. Airborne spores are carried into the ovules, a process known as pollination; it is a necessary step before ovules can change into seeds. When ripe the seeds are shaken out of the cones and are carried away by air currents. In a few conifers a soft, fleshy, brightly-coloured cone is formed, red in yew, and blue-purple in juniper. Birds are attracted by the bright colour, eat the cones, and later pass out the seed unharmed with the fæces, thus distributing the seeds.

Of the small orders the most interesting is the Ginkgoales, most of whose members are known only as fossils. The one remaining member of this order is the maidenhair tree (*Ginkgo biloba*). Over a million years ago the maidenhair was spread widely around the world, but it now survives wild only in one province in China. It is tall and slender, growing to about 35 metres (115 feet) in height, with fan-shaped leaves quite unlike those of any other tree, and so can be identified easily.

While cycads and maidenhair have a scattered distribution, conifers are forest-makers. Natural conifer woods and man-made plantations are often dark. The evergreen trees have dense branches with leaves lasting more than one year, and the shade cast may allow only scanty growth of ground vegetation. Below ground, tree roots often become enveloped by a layer of fungal *hyphae* (filaments), which seem to promote the growth of the tree. The fungus only comes above ground to form a fruiting body. This is the explanation for finding certain types of toadstools growing under certain types of trees.

Above: *Juniper is unusual among conifers in that the cones themselves become succulent. Juniper is found as a low-growing shrub over most of its range, but in favourable places it may be quite a large bush, up to 2 metres (6 feet) high. The foliage is a bluish-green colour, and the leaves are drawn out into spines.*

Far left: *The swamp cypress of Eastern North America is a medium to large deciduous tree with green leaves becoming red-brown in autumn. The trunk is wide at the base, with fibrous bark. Those growing in swamps form erect branch roots, or 'knees', believed to help aeration of underwater parts.* Left: *Common yew of the Northern Hemisphere is a bushy tree or shrub. Young trees have a conical crown with widespread branches; old trees are less regular.*

Above: *The cones of a larch. Each cone is made up of a spiral sequence of scales, which are modified leaves, around a central stem. Between each scale and the central stem lies the reproductive organ. In the smaller, male cone this bears the pollen. In the larger, female cone, it ultimately forms the seed.*

Flowering Plants

Angiosperms are plants which form flowers and produce seeds enclosed in containers – fruits. The word *angiosperm* comes from two Greek words meaning 'seed receptacles'. The flowering plants developed much later than the naked-seeded gymnosperms, probably a little more than 135 million years ago. Their origin is a mystery, but from fossil remains we learn that their numbers increased rapidly while the gymnosperms became less abundant.

Flowering plants are the dominant land plants today, with about 250,000 species. No other group approaches this number. Unlike simpler plants, where there is a clearly recognisable appearance for each group, the flowering plants are incredibly varied. It may be this variation which is the key to their success, for they are able to grow in a wide range of conditions. Variation is seen clearly in their size; they range from the small duckweed (*Lemna*), a plant which floats on fresh water and is less than 3 millimetres (1/8 inch) across, to the Australian blue gum tree (*Eucalyptus*), for which a height of over 100 metres (325 feet) has been reported.

The flowering plants can be divided into two groups, named according to the number of *cotyledons* (leaves) in the *embryo* (the young plant in the seed).

Monocotyledons have one seed leaf. This group includes plants which have shoots that are often unbranched, stems which may remain underground, long leaves with parallel veins, and many small roots. These plants on the whole are *herbaceous* (soft bodied), and only occasionally do they become woody, for example, the bamboos which can grow up to about 30 metres (100 feet) tall, and trees such as the palms which can grow up to 40 metres (130 feet).

The most important and successful family of monocotyledons is the grass family (*Gramineae*). Grasses cover about one quarter of the land surface of the Earth, forming prairies and steppes; they are vital food for many herbivorous animals; and the cereals, such as wheat, maize (corn) and rice provide food for man.

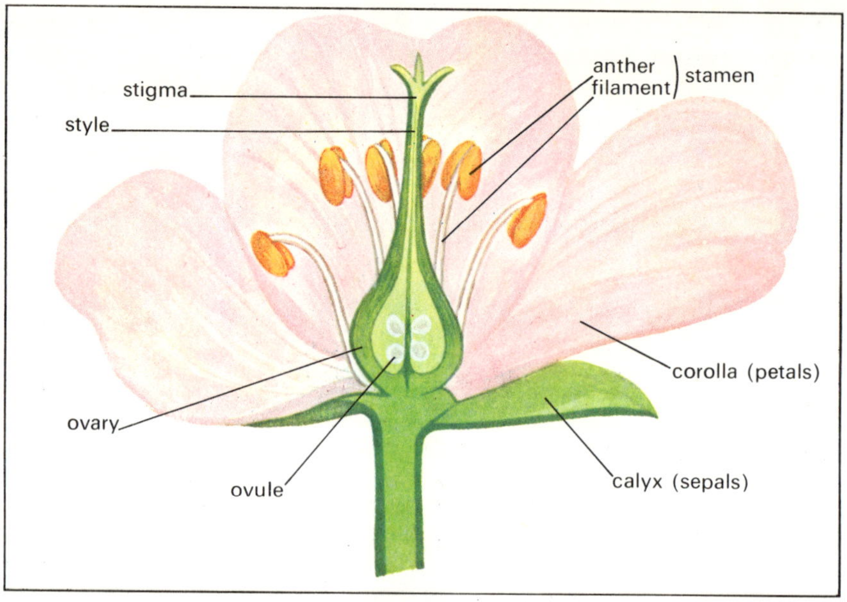

Above: *The parts of a flower.*

Dicotyledons have two seed leaves. This group includes plants which have shoots usually branched, stems which grow above ground, broad leaves with veins making a network, and one main root. These plants are sometimes herbs (that is herbaceous or non-woody), but are often woody and grow into large trees; they never reach the giant size or age attained by the conifers (see pages 102–103).

Like the conifers, the dicotyledonous trees form woodlands and forests. In the hot, wet climate of the equatorial region, tropical rain forests are formed of evergreen trees; these extend as a belt across Central and South America, central and west Africa, the Indian sub-continent, Sri Lanka and Malaysia. Many species of trees live in such tropical rain forests. In the cool climate of more northern regions

Below: *Duckweeds (1) are leafless plants with short green stems, which float on the surface of ponds and ditches. The white water-lily (2) has large, flat leaves with breathing pores on the upper surface. The water crowfoot (3) has finely divided submerged leaves and broad, kidney-shaped floating leaves. Hornwort (4) is unusual in that the whole plant, including the flowers, is always submerged. Curled pondweed (5) overwinters by producing small bulblets on its creeping stem. The amphibious bistort (6) has two different growth forms: one in water and the other on waterside ground. The familiar reed mace (bulrush) (7) and yellow flag (8) are both frequent at the edge of slow-moving rivers and dykes, whereas the watermint (9) is found in marshy ground nearby.*

Above: *The berries of the mistletoe are sought after by birds, especially the mistle thrush, and are thus dispersed.* Left: *The dodder, growing here on gorse, lacks the green pigment completely. The mature plant is red, and has neither roots nor leaves.*

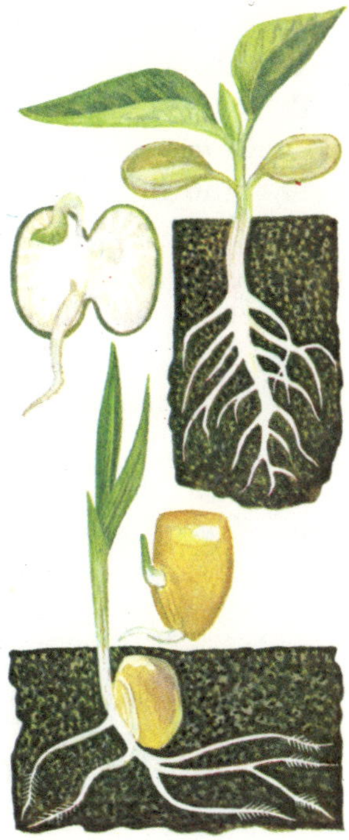

Above: *The bean seedling (above) has the two large seed-leaves typical of dicots. The germinating maize seed (below), has only one leaf.*

in Europe, Asia and North America, where winters are cold, deciduous trees which drop their leaves in autumn form temperate woodlands.

One of the features in which flowering plants show variation is their life-span. Some angiosperms are small, short-lived, form fruits and seeds and complete their whole life-cycle within a few months. They are known as *ephemerals*. Many persistent weeds such as shepherd's purse (*Capsella*) behave in this way.

Some angiosperms complete their cycle only once in a growing season, and last through the winter as seeds; these are *annuals*. Others, the *biennials*, have a two-year cycle, lasting through the first winter as a plant in which much food is stored, and then flowering and fruiting in the second year.

The rest of the flowering plants are *perennials*, lasting for many years and usually flowering each year. They may have a long life-span, but the form in which they *perennate* (survive between seasons) varies. They may be tough enough to overwinter in their normal form, as do the bamboos and the trees, but many monocotyledons and a few dicotyledons survive as underground parts which have become swollen with food material, often starch and sometimes sugar. Plants which grow in this way may form swollen underground buds called *bulbs* (such as daffodil, *Narcissus*), swollen stems called *corms* (such as *Crocus*), underground stems called *rhizomes* (such as *Iris*), swollen ends of underground stems called *tubers* (such as potato, *Solanum tuberosum*), or swollen roots (as in *Dahlia*).

After they are formed, the various vegetative parts have a period when their chemical activities are very slow; they do not grow and are said to be dormant. They stay in this state until they are activated by outside conditions of temperature and light, which start up a chain of processes. The plant is released from dormancy, and growth takes place.

Perennation underground enables plants not only to last through the winter, but to survive fire, a hazard of open grassland. Overground vegetation is burnt, but underground plant parts are often unharmed.

There is one further outstanding feature in which the flowering plants differ from most other groups; this is the variation in the way in which they obtain food. The vast majority are independent plants which manufacture all their food starting with photosynthesis, provided they can obtain carbon dioxide, water and mineral salts. A few angiosperms are not able to manufacture their own food and have to depend on some other plant as a food source. Mistletoe (*Viscum*) grows on branches of trees such as apple or lime, sending root-like projections into the wood of its host which enable it to absorb water. Because mistletoe is green it is able to make its own food once it has water.

Below: *The broad-leaved dock (12) is a common weed of gardens and roadsides, whereas the mullein or Aaron's rod (13) is found in open grassy places. Rosebay willowherb (14) is increasingly common on derelict land, but is normally a plant of woodland edges and clearings, as are brambles or blackberries (15). These spread by taking root at the tip of their arching shoots. Honeysuckle (16) is one of our few woody climbers. The flowers are most strongly scented at night.*

Below: *Silverweed (10) and the marsh yellow cress (11) are both found in damp places. Silverweed's name comes from the appearance of its leaves. The yellow cresses resemble the edible watercress.*

Roots and Stems

Roots form the underground part of a plant; they anchor it to the ground and absorb materials from the soil. Each root grows mainly at its tip, which is protected during downward passage through the soil by a 'root cap'.

Just behind the tip is the most important absorbing region, for here the root surface grows out into a very large number of fine hairs which pass between the soil particles. Each hair is an ideal absorbing cell, because it has a large surface area. Water and salts pass into the root mainly through the hairs by a process known as diffusion. The water and salts then pass into the centre of the root, where long-distance transporting or conducting cells are located.

The transporting cells are arranged in upright files, one cell on top of another; one vertical file of cells is called a *vessel*. Each cell is a hollow cylinder, so the vessel is a long pipe, which joins with similar pipes in the stem and leaf. Along these pipes water and salts flow from the root into the *shoot* (stem and leaves).

Water and salts are used by the plant in its food manufacturing processes and growth, but much of the water is eventually lost from the shoot: it evaporates into the surrounding air, which is usually dry in comparison with the water-filled cells. *Transpiration* (water loss) is partly controlled by a very thin, outside waterproofing layer, the *cuticle,* and pairs of adjustable surface cells, the *guard cells,* which regulate the size of holes in the shoot surface.

Water-conducting cells always occur in groups (*xylem*) and are accompanied by groups of food-conducting cells (*phloem*). The two together form the *vascular distributing system,* and have an additional strengthening role. The vascular system forms a central core in the root, a wide cylinder of strands in the stem, and a network in the leaf. Such a system is adequate for distribution purposes in small herbaceous plants, but for those plants which become large, and those which last for more than one growing season, additional conducting cells are demanded.

New conducting cells are formed by a ring of cells, the *cambium,* which lies between the xylem and phloem. Cambium cells multiply and form new xylem cells (wood) to the inside, and new phloem cells to the outside of the ring. The activity of the cambium is influenced by a chemical substance, *auxin,* which is formed as buds expand in the spring. So for a long-lived plant there are new vascular cells each growing season, and this is particularly clear in the wood as growth rings. Counting the rings is the most reliable way of estimating the age of a woody plant.

A plant which continues to grow in this way for many years develops into a tree with a stout trunk (woody stem). The oldest wood in the centre of the trunk may become impregnated with substances which cause it to change colour and become darker. The oldest wood also loses its conducting role, and gradually dries out, so it contains a great amount of air. This is in contrast to the younger, outer xylem, the sap wood, which still conducts water.

The cells which make up xylem vary from one tree species to another, and so,

Below left and below: *Roots and stems are the transport organs of a plant. Water and salts are taken out of the soil by the roots, and are carried upwards through root and stem to the leaves, flowers and fruits. Food manufactured in the leaves travels down the stem and root, and is thus distributed throughout the plant. Roots have a protective tip so that the delicate growing point is not damaged as it pushes through the soil. They also have thin-walled hairs through which water and dissolved substances can pass. Stems have a mechanical function in supporting the weight of the plant – or part of it – and the tissues are arranged so as to give rigidity to the stem. 1 root cap; 2 root hair; 3 xylem; 4 phloem; 5 epidermis; 6 cortex; 7 pith.*

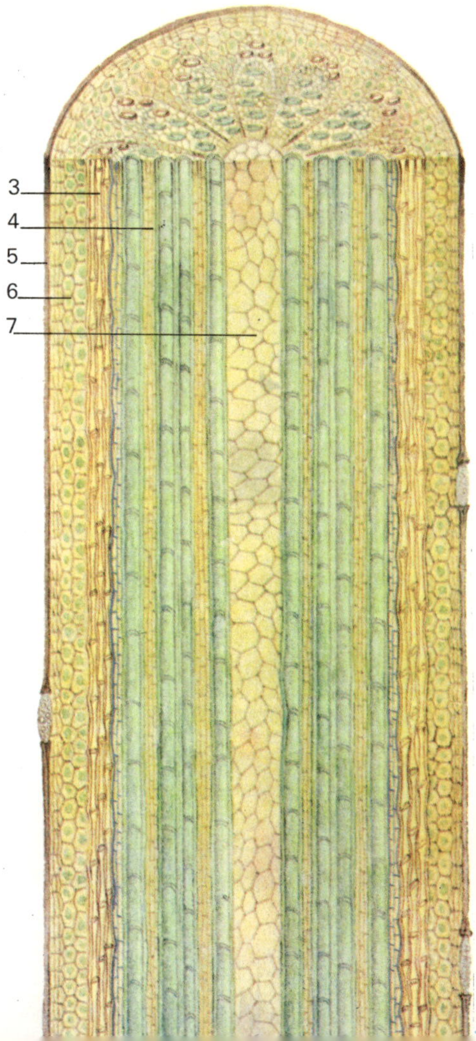

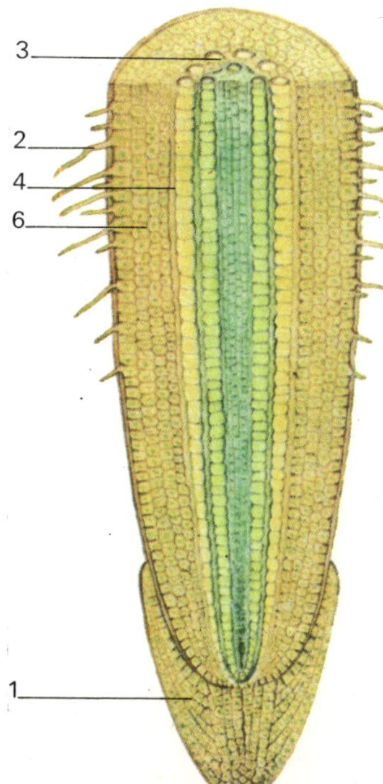

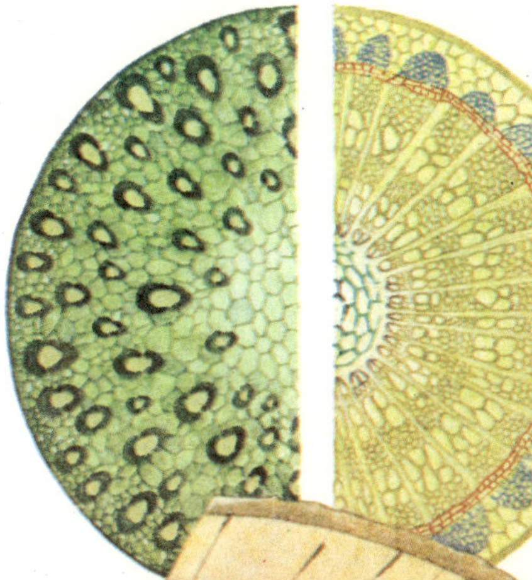

Far left: *The typical monocotyledon stem has vascular bundles scattered about a pithy core. Only in a few species is the stem woody.* Left: *Dicotyledon stems have the vascular bundles in a ring in the outer part of the stem. This arrangement is readily converted into a woody stem.*

Above: *The trunk of a tree is a stem in which the woody tissue fills almost all of the available area. Phloem is present as a layer round the outside; channels also extend into the woody trunk to give it nourishment. Every year the tree trunk grows in girth faster in spring and more slowly in winter; this growth shows in the rings. The bark on the outside is a special adaptation of woody stems; it is constantly replaced from underneath so that the widening stem always has a protective layer on its outer surface.*

Below left: *Silver birch.* Below centre: *Plane. Both these shed their bark, birch in thin, papery strips, and plane in brittle flakes.* Below right: *The oak tree develops a thick furrowed bark. Cork is obtained from an oak,* Quercus suber.

like conifers, different angiosperm woods vary in properties and are used for a number of purposes. The extensive use of oak for shipbuilding many years ago led to a serious shortage of oak.

One hazard of forming new conducting cells in older stems and roots is the resulting increase in thickness, which could strain the surface and cause it to break. Surface damage could be a disaster because it would allow uncontrolled water loss and the entry of organisms causing disease. Before any such breakage occurs a second ring of cells, the cork cambium, develops outside the conducting region and forms a layer of cork, which acts as a waterproofing and protective barrier. Cork inevitably interferes with ventilation, so ventilating pores called *lenticels* are formed; these can be seen quite clearly in young twigs as dots on the surface of the stem.

Cork formation, like that of wood, is also seasonal, and over a number of years cork layers are formed on both stem and root. On the stem the older, outer cork layer becomes increasingly stretched and dried, and develops a very characteristic appearance for each species of tree. A record of cork pattern (a bark rubbing) can be obtained simply by fixing a piece of paper on a tree-trunk and rubbing over it with charcoal. Some trees, such as beech (*Fagus*) have a smooth cork or bark pattern; others such as oak (*Quercus*) have a deeply channelled bark; and the chestnuts, particularly sweet chestnut (*Castanea*) have a twisted, channelled bark. The pattern of the bark affects to some extent the amount of damage to a tree struck by lightning. A tree is a good lightning conductor because it provides an unbroken path for the conduction of electricity from the treetop to the soil. Smooth-barked trees conduct all over the trunk surface and down to the roots and soil. Rough-barked trees have no continuous conducting surface, so lightning strikes inwards into the furrows and damages the tree.

Bark, which is strictly cork with some extra cells, is of some commercial importance as it is continually produced by a tree. At intervals of some years it can be stripped away and replaced by a new growth of bark. Corks for bottles are made from the cork oak (*Quercus suber*).

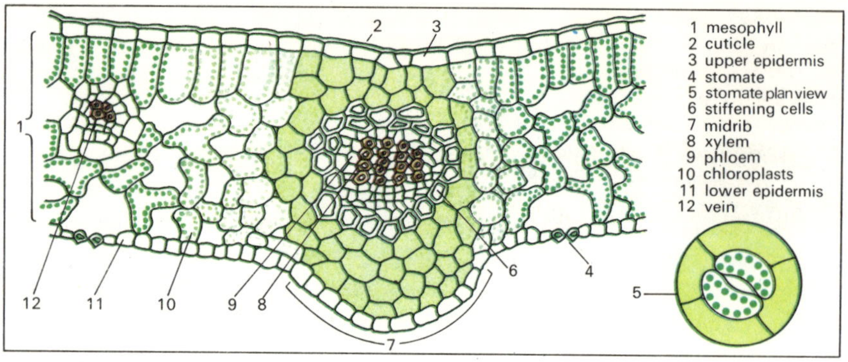

Leaves

Above: *Section of a leaf, showing the midrib composed of a core of xylem surrounded by phloem. Veins are branches from the midrib. The inset shows a plan view of a stomate.*

Below: *Leaves may be simple or compound, shiny or hairy. Each plant has leaves adapted to its particular life-style. These shown here are: 1 walnut; 2 horse chestnut; 3 sycamore; 4 lavender; 5 ivy; 6* Maranta leuconeura.

Leaves are flat outgrowths from the surface of a stem. They work according to the position and time at which they are formed. The most obvious and most abundant type of leaf, the foliage leaf, is the main site of a chemical process, *photosynthesis*. Leaves in seeds, the cotyledons, store food or absorb it from the rest of the seed; leaves in flowers, the sepals and petals, protect other flower parts and attract animals, while leaves surrounding buds during winter, the bud scales, are generally tough and protect the young shoot.

The photosynthesis of foliage leaves is the fundamental food-manufacturing process of all living organisms. Photosynthesis occurs only in coloured plants, and does not occur in colourless plants such as fungi (see pages 96–99). The nutrition of plants, and eventually the nutrition of animals which eat plants (herbivores) and animals which eat other animals (carnivores), depends upon it.

Most foliage leaves are thin and have a large surface area to absorb light and carbon dioxide from the air. Much of the light falling on a leaf-surface passes through the leaf, and only a small part is absorbed. An even smaller part is passed into the *chloroplasts*, those cell parts which are able to photosynthetise. Carbon dioxide present in air in the very low concentration 0·03 per cent. passes into the leaf by diffusion, mainly through *stomatal apertures*, small holes in the leaf surface. These apertures change in size throughout the day and night according to the behaviour of paired cells, the guard cells, which border them. One pair of guard cells and its aperture is called a *stomate*. Leaves which are held in a horizontal position have stomates mainly on the lower surface, while leaves which are upright often have them evenly on both sides.

Photosynthetising cells occupy the middle of the leaf, the *mesophyll*; they are irregular in shape and have large spaces between them, so gases readily diffuse and reach the more deeply-positioned cells.

The complete photosynthetic process takes place in the chloroplast, and depends upon a light-absorbing green pigment, *chlorophyll*. Chlorophyll changes its structure when it absorbs light, and then uses the energy of light to drive a complex chemical process in which carbon dioxide and water give rise to sugar. The process also produces oxygen, which diffuses out of the chloroplast and the cell.

Sugar produced by photosynthesis may be stored in the chloroplast in another

form, starch, or may be passed out into the cell and used for other manufacturing processes not dependent on chlorophyll and light. All these syntheses (building processes) are necessary for the life and growth of the plant. Some materials which are not required by the leaf are transported away to other parts of the body by the phloem, which lies beside the water-conducting xylem (see pages 106–107). The conducting strands lie in the veins, which form a net and provide a strengthening framework for the leaf.

While the way in which foliage leaves work is remarkably constant, their arrangement, shape and detailed structure is very varied.

For each species there is a constant arrangement of foliage leaves on a stem (*phyllotaxis*). Leaves may be attached singly or in pairs, forming two vertical rows, but more often leaves are arranged spirally. Such regular arrangement is sometimes obscured by a twisting of the leaf stalk as the shoot grows, so that one leaf is not overshadowed by another; the resulting 'leaf mosaic' allows all leaves to absorb light equally.

The shape of a leaf is fairly typical for any species, so plants can be identified in the leafy, non-flowering stage, and closely-related plants can be recognised by the similarity of their leaves. Many leaves are attached to the stem by a *petiole* (stalk) which carries the main photosynthetising part, the *lamina* (blade) above. The blade may be undivided (simple leaf), or divided into segments called *pinnae* or leaflets (making up a compound leaf) which are either *palmate* – arising from one point, like fingers on a hand – or *pinnate* – spread along the leaf in pairs. Some monocotyledons have strap-shaped leaves without a stalk, and in grasses the lower part of the strap clasps around the shoot to form a sheath.

While leaves are usually of a constant shape in each species, there are some species whose leaves vary even on one plant. For example, European ivy (*Hedera helix*) which is a creeping or climbing plant, has lobed leaves on the creeping or climbing stems, and unlobed, smooth-edged leaves on the upright flowering branches. Sometimes such variation can be related to environment. Leaves of water plants are often highly divided, and so offer little resistance to flowing water. The floating water crowfoot (*Ranunculus aquatilis*) has dissected leaves under water and entire blades above water. The rooted arrowhead (*Sagittaria sagittifolia*) and the water-plantain (*Alisma plantago-aquatica*) have strap-shaped leaves under water and broad blades above.

Those plants which live in dry conditions have a tougher and often folded structure. The heathers (*Erica*), which grow on exposed moorland, have leaf edges turned under to cover partly the lower surface; and the marram grass (*Psamma* or *Ammophila*), which grows on sand dunes, has a device for rolling and unrolling the leaf according to the dryness of the air outside. The shape of these leaves helps to control transpiration.

An even greater variation in leaf shape is seen in climbing plants, many of which grow *tendrils*, thread-like leaf parts which are sensitive to contact with solid objects, and grow around any suitable support.

Above: *The leaves of oak trees,* Quercus robur, *are lobed. They grow in bunches on the twigs, each on a very short stalk that may be hard to see. Different varieties of oak have slightly differently shaped leaves; the red oak,* Quercus rubra, *has large leaves with tapering lobes that turn red in the autumn.*

Below: *Handsworth new silver (left) is a variety of the common holly,* Ilex aquilifolium *(right). Such a variety, with pale areas, does not survive long out of cultivation.*

Flowers

To man, flowers play a large part in the beauty of nature, but they also form one of the most important parts of an angiosperm plant. They are a vital stage in the process of reproduction, and their beauty is an attraction to insects and other animals which carry out the process of pollination, or fertilisation.

A flower is the reproductive tip of a shoot, so it is similar to the cone of a gymnosperm. It differs from a cone in that it has two types of *sporangia* (spore-producing organs) in the same flower, and has in addition flower leaves (petals and sepals).

Flower leaves are carried at the bottom of the *receptacle* – the flower stem; they are broad and flat, protect the rest of the flower, and often attract animals by their bright colours and markings, and oils which make them scented. Most flower leaves are arranged in two alternating rings. In *monocotyledons* (plants with one leaf in the seed) there are six leaves, three in each ring, which are similar in any one flower; they are white or coloured but not green. In *dicotyledons* (plants with two leaves in the seed) there are four or five leaves in each ring; the lower, outer leaves (sepals) are small and green and protect the flower when it is a bud, while the upper, inner leaves (petals) are much larger, white or coloured. The ring of petals is called the *corolla*, and the ring of sepals the *calyx*. The two together form the perianth.

Above: *Wallflowers, like many other garden flowers, are members of the crucifer family.*

Below: *These catkins hang freely from the branches so that they shake, scattering pollen, in the slightest breeze. The female flowers have little or no petals, which are not needed and would obstruct the pollen grains. Many wind-pollinated trees flower early in the year; the catkins can thus spread their pollen unhindered by leaves, which open later. Wind-pollinated plants have smooth pollen grains in contrast to the grains of insect-pollinated flowers, which are textured in many ways to help them to adhere to the pollinating insect.*

The structures which bear sporangia, the stamens and carpels, are carried further up the receptacle, stamens just above the flower leaves and carpels at the top. The *stamen* has a long stalk, and at its outer end carries four long sporangia from which *spores* (pollen grains) are released. The *carpel* forms a wrapper around its sporangium, the *ovule*.

The function of a flower is to produce seeds. For an ovule to grow into a seed it must be *fertilised* – penetrated by a pollen grain; but an ovule is completely covered by its carpel, which prevents direct delivery of the grain. The problem is solved by the carpel itself; it houses one or more ovules in a swollen base, the *ovary,* and is extended into a stalk-like part, the *style,* which carries a pollen-receiving part, the *stigma,* at its tip.

The stigma is likely to receive pollen from many different species of plants, but its structure and the chemical substances it forms make sure that only pollen from the same species of plant will start to grow. A growing or germinating pollen grain extends downwards into the style and ovary as a tube and eventually penetrates the ovule, where it starts the changes necessary to convert the ovule into a seed.

Pollination – the transfer of pollen from stamen to stigma – is carried out by animals, wind and very occasionally by water. Transfer of pollen from one plant to

Above: *Hummingbirds also pollinate many flowers.*

Above: *Bees feed on nectar using their long tongue.*

Above: *Butterflies visit flowers for nectar.*

another is called 'cross-pollination', while tranfer within the same plant is called 'self-pollination'. Cross-pollination is the more desirable because it often leads to better seed and plant production. Many flowers have mechanisms or devices which encourage cross-pollination and discourage self-pollination. In some flowers the stamens and carpels ripen at different times, or the pollen may be shed in a direction away from the carpels.

Animals which act as pollinators are mainly insects, and in the tropics also bats and birds. Pollinators are attracted to flowers mainly by the colour of the flower leaves. A visiting animal foraging for food, and already carrying pollen from another flower, leaves part of its load in the flower, and some rests on the stigma.

The encouragement of cross-pollination by insects depends upon flower size and arrangement of parts in the flower. Simple flowers have parts separate from one another and laid out in a regular manner. For example, buttercup (*Ranunculus* species) has five green sepals in a ring, while above are five yellow petals in another ring, alternating with the sepals. Further up the receptacle is a spiral of stamens, followed by a spiral of many green carpels. When fully open the flower has a wide cup shape, and the different parts are fully exposed to the air. Insects visiting a buttercup land in the centre of the cup and search for nectar, which is formed in a small flap at the bottom of each petal.

Other plants have flower leaves, particularly the petals, fused together. The bottom parts of the petals fuse to form a tube, while the upper parts remain separate and spread out widely to form a broad surface, which attracts the attention of animals and provides a landing platform. Pollinators of tubular flowers are too large to crawl down the petal tube, so they obtain nectar from inside the tube by inserting only their mouthparts, while the rest of the animal sits on the platform or hovers outside.

While animal pollination is usual for flowering plants, some species are pollinated by the wind. Wind-pollinated flowers do not have elaborate coloured petals, because there is no need to attract the attention of animals, so they are small and often hardly noticeable. The pollen is light and dry and easily spread by air currents. All grasses are pollinated by wind; the flowers are tightly packed together on shoots which stand up in the air above the leaves. Many trees also are wind-pollinated; the flowers are grouped in catkins, which ripen before the foliage leaves come out of bud and shelter the pollen from the wind.

1

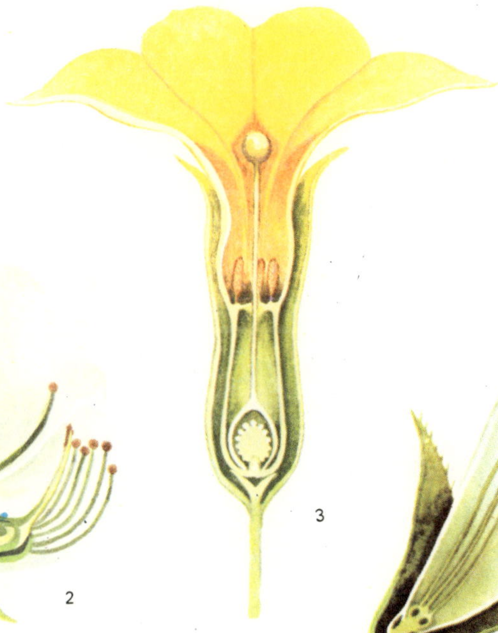

3

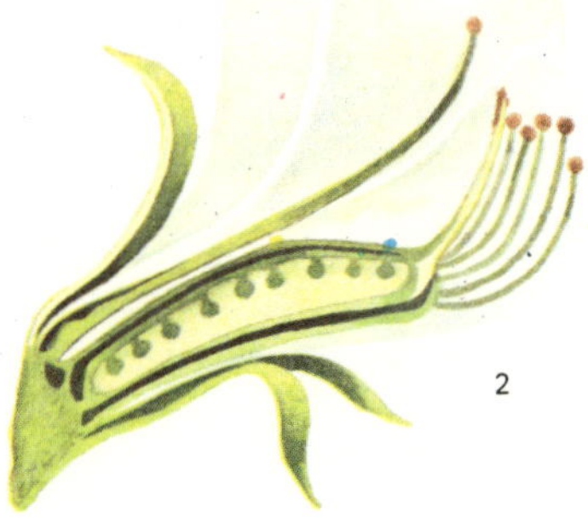

2

4

Above and right: *Adaptations for insect-pollination. Buttercups (1) are wide open flowers; insects can walk in them. Peas (2) deposit pollen on the underside of a probing bee. Some primroses (3) have flowers with stigma and stamens as here, others are reversed. Dead-nettle (4) leaves pollen on a bee's back.*

Fruits and Seeds

The function of a flower is the production of seeds from ovules and fruits from ovaries. After pollination and penetration of the ovule by the pollen grain, those flower parts which are no longer required wither and drop away. Only the ovary, with ovules inside, remains. See pages 110–111 for an explanation of the parts of a flower.

Above: *The coconut is a large seed. The part drawn here is all that we usually see, but when the nut falls off the tree it is enclosed in a very thick layer of the fibres that coconut matting is made of. These fibres trap air and thus enable the seed to float undamaged in the sea. Coconuts can be dispersed by salt water from island to island.*

Inside each ovule grows the *embryo* – a young plant. It has a *plumule* (a small shoot), a *radicle* (a small root), and *cotyledons* (one or two seed leaves). The embryo is fed from the *endosperm,* a food store in the ovule. In some ovules the endosperm is almost entirely used up during the development of the embryo, and food is passed into the cotyledons which become thick, as in peas and beans; in other ovules the endosperm largely remains and the cotyledons are thin, as in the castor-oil plant (*Ricinus*). The food stored in the endosperm and cotyledons is fat, starch and protein. It is used by the embryo when it grows out of the seed.

As the ovule changes into a seed, the outside hardens to form the *testa,* a tough and less permeable seed coat, interrupted only by one small hole, the *micropyle.* The seed becomes detached from the ovary, the position of separation being shown on the seed by a scar. At the same time the ovary changes into the wall of a fruit.

Because flowering plants are sedentary – fixed in one position for the whole of their lives – the spread of species depends upon dispersal of seed and fruits.

A few heavy seeds and fruits have no obvious dispersal devices; acorns of oak (*Quercus*), sweet chestnuts of *Castanea,* and 'conkers' of *Aesculus* in temperate woodlands, and avocado (*Persea*) in tropical rain forests, just fall down, but may be moved later by animals.

Most fruits are constructed in a way which helps dispersal. Sometimes the *pericarp,* the fruit wall, dries, and dispersal depends upon the fruit being moderately small and light in weight. In grasses the pericarp forms a tight cover over the small seed (*caryopsis*) which is dispersed by wind. Some trees, such as ash (*Fraxinus*), elm (*Ulmus*), and sycamore (*Acer*) have extensions of the pericarp which form wings, of distinctive shape in each species, and thus help the fruit to stay longer in the air so that the wind carries it further.

Dry fruits which remain on the parent plant have a variety of opening mechanisms allowing the escape of seeds. The capsule of poppy (*Papaver*) opens by a number of pores through which the enclosed seeds are ejected when the capsule is blown about by the wind. A more active ejection mechanism operates in some members of the pea family (*Leguminosae*) where the fruit is usually a flat pod which splits on two sides. In gorse (*Ulex*) when the pod is dry, and particularly on a hot day, the two halves of the pod twist away from each other with a cracking noise and fling the seeds out.

Other fruits become soft and fleshy as they ripen. At first they seem to have a chemical defence system which makes them unpalatable and even poisonous, discouraging the attention of animals, but when the seed is ready for dispersal the fruit becomes juicy, sweeter and more brightly coloured. In some plants the change from the unpalatable to the attractive state is very fast. Usually when fruits

Right: *Seeds of many trees are adapted for dispersal by wind. They are already high enough from the ground for a simple gliding sail, as in the elm (right), to carry a seed quite a long way. The goat willow, (centre), has seeds with fluffy tufts to catch the wind. Old man's beard, (far right), has long feathery plumes on its seeds, which may float for a long way on a light breeze even though the plant may be a low scrambler.*

are eaten by animals the seed passes through the gut unharmed, because it is protected by a tough coat, and so is deposited with the animal droppings some distance away. Sometimes ruminants spit out seeds when chewing the cud.

Some fleshy fruits have a two-layered wall: an outer skin and an inner thicker fleshy part; these are *berries,* such as black and red currants, gooseberry, grape and citrus fruits. Oranges and lemons are large berries in which the pericarp has an outer oily skin and an inner white flesh; each carpel forms a segment of the fruit, in which large hairs become filled with juice.

Other fleshy fruits have a three-layered wall: an outer skin, a middle fleshy part, and an inner hard layer; these are *drupes* or stone fruits. It is the innermost layer of the fruit, the stone, which protects the seed which has a delicate testa. Cherry, plum and peach are all drupes.

Juiciness or succulence is not confined to berries and drupes, but occurs in a whole range of so-called fruits which strictly include extra parts of the flower. These are *false fruits.* In apples the seeds are surrounded by a horny fruit wall, so the true fruit is the central core, but as an apple grows, the receptacle envelops it and swells out to form the flesh and skin. Other fruits such as fig and pineapple involve additional parts of the plant.

Some fruits and seeds are dispersed by water. Nearly any fruit or seed can be dispersed in this way provided it can float; a few species appear to be particularly suited to this, for they contain air or oil, which make them relatively light. Some water-dispersed seeds are quite small, such as alder (*Alnus*) but there is evidence of distribution of large fruits such as coconut (*Cocos*) by water.

Dispersal mechanisms are only effective provided the seed can remain alive during the time taken for dispersal and delivery to a suitable environment. Some seeds have a very short period of life. For example, seeds of wood sorrel (*Oxalis acetosella*), cannot stand up to drying; they germinate immediately upon release.

Most seeds have a resting stage described as *dormancy* during the winter following their liberation, and germinate only the following year. Dormancy is a result of a complicated interaction of conditions inside and outside the seed, which combine to stop the embryo from emerging at a time when the young plant would be unlikely to survive. Similarly, when the environment is unsuitable the seed remains dormant; for example, seeds buried deep in the soil remain viable, but do not germinate until the soil is turned over, when they come to the surface and are exposed to light. Seeds may persist in the soil in this way for many years.

Above: *Many plants have seeds enclosed in an edible and attractive covering to entice animals and birds to scatter them. These are the fruits. Stone fruits such as the peach (2), cherry (6) and plum (11) are called drupes. The blackberry fruit (10) consists of a cluster of tiny drupes. Gooseberry (4), grape (5), orange (1) and redcurrant (9) are all known as berries. Apples (3), strawberries (7) and figs (8) are called 'false fruits'. These divisions are based on the parts of the ovary that form the succulent part of the fruit.*

Left: *Cleavers (far left) have fruits that are adapted for dispersal by animals, being covered with tiny hooks. The poppy head (centre) shakes its seeds out as it is blown about, scattering them all around; this is called a censer mechanism, and is a form of wind dispersal. Broom pods (left) explode when the seeds are ripe, throwing them out with considerable force, as each half of the pod twists on opening.*

Buttercups, Cabbages and Carnations

About a quarter of a million different species of angiosperms are known, forming the main vegetation of the world. They are divided into two main groups, the monocotyledons (see pages 120–121) and the dicotyledons.

Dicotyledons have two seed leaves in the embryo plant, and the primary root often develops into a tap root from which most of the other roots branch out, rather than a fibrous root system in which few or none of the roots originate from the primary root. The conducting tissues of the stem are in bundles, lying in one or two circles in the ground tissue, and secondary thickening of the stems begins from tissue, the *vascular cambium*, within these bundles. Leaves may be simple or compound, often with the edges indented in various ways. Typically, each leaf or leaflet has a thick central vein from which successively smaller veins branch out, forming a network in the leaf. Flowers vary considerably in shape, with parts in twos, fours, fives and larger numbers – but rarely in threes.

The most primitive types of dicotyledons are usually taken to be those with an indefinitely large number of parts to the flower, usually spirally arranged on a long central axis and not joined together in any way. The flowers are large, solitary and pollinated by insects.

The Ranunculaceae include about 1,800 species, which form the buttercup family. Most of them are perennial herbs, with a few soft-wooded shrubs such as *Clematis* species. Most have fibrous root systems like those of monocotyledons. The flowers are very variable in shape, generally radially symmetrical and usually with a petaloid calyx, although the true buttercups (*Ranunculus* species) have clearly distinct calyx and corolla. Some, such as delphiniums (*Delphinium* species) and monkshood (*Aconitum* species), have bilaterally symmetrical flowers. The floral axis may be elongated, and stamens and carpels are usually indefinite in number, spirally arranged and free from each other, though the carpels are joined in

Above: *Annual species of delphinium are called larkspurs. The flower is markedly irregular, with a single backward-pointing spur formed from the sepal at the back of the flower. All species are poisonous.*

Below: *Each petal of the graceful columbine has a long backward-pointing spur containing nectar, to attract long-tongued pollinating insects.*

Below: *Love-in-a-mist has fern-like, much-divided leaves which partly conceal the deep-blue flowers. The carpels join to form a partly open fruit.*

Below: *The opium poppy provides poppy-seed oil, and the immature capsule gives the crude drug opium, from which morphine and codeine can be extracted and heroin prepared.*

love-in-a-mist (*Nigella damascena*). In the *Helleborus* group the fruits contain several seeds to each carpel; in the buttercup group only one.

The plants are bitter-tasting and often very poisonous, for example monkshood. They include many beautiful garden flowers such as *Clematis* species, columbines, delphiniums and anemones.

The poppy family (Papaveraceae) is probably fairly closely related to the buttercup family. The plants grow mainly in north temperate regions, producing *latex,* a white, coloured or clear juice, where injured. There are two sepals which fall off when the flower opens, four often very crumpled-looking petals, usually a large number of stamens, and an ovary which typically becomes a capsule with tiny seeds which are shaken out through small holes like pepper out of a pepperpot. Popular garden plants of this family include Shirley poppies (*Papaver rhoeas*), Californian poppies (*Eschscholzia californica*), and the beautiful blue poppies of the Himalayas (species of *Meconopsis*), while the opium poppy (*Papaver somniferum*) is the source of the pain-killing drug opium.

The cabbage family (Cruciferae) is a large and most important one with about 1,900 species, widely distributed but mainly growing in the north temperate zone. The flowers are very distinctive, with four sepals in two pairs, four petals (usually white or yellow) and six stamens, the outer two much shorter than the inner four. The ovary is divided into two parts by a thin partition, and there are usually numerous ovules. Sometimes the fruit is long and thin as in the cabbage (*Brassica oleracea*), sometimes short and wide as in the shepherd's purse (*Capsella bursa-pastoris*).

The family includes many garden favourites such as wallflowers, honesty, stock, aubrietia, alyssum and candytuft, but is mainly important because of the food plants it contains. Mustard and cress, the various species from which table mustards are derived, seakale, horse-radish, radish, watercress, cabbage, swede and turnip all belong to the Cruciferae. The swede arose as a natural hybrid between cabbage and turnip plants. The cabbage (*Brassica oleracea*) is remarkable for the variety of very different types of vegetables produced by its different strains, for common cabbages, red cabbages, savoy cabbages, broccoli, cauliflower, kohl-rabi, curly kale, marrow-stem kale and brussels sprouts are all of this one species. Rapes (used as fodder for stock) are strains of several different species of *Brassica*.

Crucifers are rich in sulphur compounds – hence the pungent smell of boiling cabbage – and vitamin C needed to prevent the deficiency disease scurvy. Indeed the scurvy-grasses, species of *Cochlearia* found commonly on northern shores, were so named because whalers and sealers discovered that they helped to ward off scurvy. A few species have also been used as dye sources, notably woad (*Isatis tinctoria*), a small yellow-flowered plant from which the ancient Britons prepared a blue dye much used in body painting.

The carnation family (Caryophyllaceae) are mainly herbs, widely distributed, with about 1,300 species. Typically they have simple opposite leaves borne on swollen nodes, with a very characteristic type of inflorescence with paired branches from below a terminal flower. The flowers are regular, typically with five sepals, five petals, ten stamens and an ovary with ovules on a central axis. The sepals may be free from each other as in the chickweeds, or united into a cup as in the carnations. The family contains many attractive garden flowers such as carnations, pinks, sweet william and gypsophila.

Below: *There are many different species of buttercup. Some have small white flowers, others have shiny golden yellow petals.*

Below: *Monkshood has helmet-shaped flowers, the helmet being formed from the sepals. The nectaries are spurred, and the flowers are pollinated by long-tongued bees. It was formerly used as a medicinal narcotic.*

Below: *The Shepherd's purse is a common weed of gardens and waste ground. It has a basal rosette of more or less toothed leaves, and many small white flowers.*

Roses, Beans and Carrots

The rose family (Rosaceae) contains about 2,000 species of trees, shrubs and herbs, widely distributed but mainly in temperate regions. The leaves may be simple or compound, and they have stipules. The flowers may be large and solitary, or small and grouped closely together. There are five sepals, often with an *epicalyx* (an overlapping series of bracts just below the flower), and stamens ranging from ten to numerous. Carpels range from one to numerous, not united but often more or less sunken in the base of the flower, which is often somewhat cup-shaped. The fruits are very variable indeed, including both dry and fleshy types. Vegetative (asexual) reproduction is very common in this family, by runners (as in the strawberry), suckers (as in many roses), and by several other methods. Most plants in the family have insect-pollinated flowers, but the salad burnet group (*Poterium* species) is wind-pollinated, and has small flowers without petals, tightly grouped together.

The family includes many important fruit plants, such as pear, apple, plum, peach, cherry, apricot, almond, raspberry, strawberry and bramble, also cultivated hybrids such as the loganberry. Some of the thorny shrubs, such as hawthorn and blackthorn, provide very good hedging plants.

The most popular garden plants are undoubtedly the roses, which have been widely cultivated for the beauty and scent of their flowers, and now exist in innumerable sizes, shapes, colours and perfumes. Other garden flowers from this family include species of *Spiraea* and *Potentilla.* Brambles (*Rubus* species) can be troublesome weeds, readily invading neglected pastures and discouraging grazing animals from coming too close to their sharp thorns.

The bean family (Leguminosae), with about 13,000 species, is one of vital importance to man. Its herbs, shrubs and trees are widely distributed. The leaves are usually compound, with stipules, and there is a tap root system. Leguminous plants have a symbiotic relationship with nitrogen-fixing bacteria, which live in nodules in the roots and supply the host plant with nitrogenous compounds in return for energy-giving carbohydrates. As a result, leguminous plants can enrich with fixed nitrogen the soils in which they grow, as well as providing their own vegetation and seeds with a high protein content.

The family is divided into three subfamilies, sometimes considered families in their own right. The Mimosoideae subfamily are mainly tropical and subtropical trees and bushes, often growing in very dry habitats. Unlike the other two groups, they have radially symmetrical flowers. The Caesalpinioideae subfamily are also mainly tropical. They include the poinciana tree, with its spectacularly brilliant flowers, and the Judas-tree, an ornamental temperate shrub in which flowers develop directly from the older woody branches.

The bean (Papilionoideae) subfamily is the largest of the three and the most important to man. The flowers are bilat-

Above: *White clover is a legume. It enriches the soil because of the nitrogen-fixing bacteria which live in nodules on its roots.*

Above: *Most members of the currant family have inconspicuous flowers. However the flowering currant is grown for its beautiful red or pink blossom.*

Far left: *Sweet pea is a legume, grown for its delicately coloured sweet-scented flowers. Like most* Lathyrus *species, it climbs by means of tendrils that are modified leaflets.*
Left: *Hawthorn is a shrub or small tree of the rose family. Its masses of pink or white blossom in spring are followed by dark red fruits: haws.*

erally symmetrical, with five sepals fused into a cup. Of the five petals, one large one is at the back, two small ones are at the sides, and two are loosely joined together at the front to form a keel on which the pollinating insects land. The 10 stamens are grouped round the single carpel, and often have their stalks fused into a tube. The carpel develops into a fruit which typically is like the familiar pea-pod, with a single row of relatively large and heavy seeds which are thrown out violently when the mature pod splits open.

The high protein content of leguminous seeds makes them a nutritious food, both for man and for domestic animals. The many different kinds of peas and beans, soya beans, ground-nuts and lentils are only a few of the crop plants grown for their seeds. In addition, many are grown as fodder crops for domestic animals, alone or with grasses. These include the clovers, lucerne, and sainfoin.

The saxifrage family (Saxifragaceae) is like the rose family, and is probably closely related to it. The 750 species are mainly perennial herbs with fused carpels. They are mostly found in north temperate regions, and there are also many Arctic and alpine species. The genus *Saxifraga* includes many species which are favourites of the rock garden. Several garden shrubs and small trees which are sometimes included in this family are by other botanists placed in small families of their own. Among these are the hydrangea, mock orange, escallonia, flowering currant, and the fruit-producing shrubs of the red currant, black currant and gooseberry.

The carrot family (Umbelliferae) contains about 2,700 species, widely distributed but mainly in the north temperate zone. They are herbs with stems which are often hollow, and leaves which are usually much divided, and with wide sheathing bases. The flowers are typically grouped in *compound umbels* (the inflorescence divides into a number of stalked units each of which ends in a number of small stalked florets). Each floret has a tiny cup-shaped calyx, five petals which are often deeply divided, five stamens and an ovary with two compartments, each containing one seed, which lies below the other flower parts.

Vegetable crop plants from this family include carrot, parsnip and celery. Many species are very aromatic, and are used as flavouring herbs, such as caraway, aniseed, coriander, dill, fennel (as seeds), fennel and parsley (as leaves) and angelica (the candied leaf-stem). However, many members of this family produce deadly poisons, notably hemlock (*Conium maculatum*), cowbane (*Cicuta virosa*), water dropwort (*Oenanthe* species) and fool's parsley (*Aethusa cynapium*), and confusion between these and the edible species has often had fatal results.

Above: *This simple floribunda rose is similar to the wild briar or dog rose after which the family is named. More exotic garden roses developed from them.*

Below: *Lupin is a perennial legume rather like gorse. It bears tall spikes of pea-type flowers above the stalked palmate leaflets. The seed pods open explosively when dry and ripe, throwing out the seeds like those of gorse.*

Right: *Raspberry and blackthorn are both members of the rose family. Raspberries have fruits with segments, like blackberries.* Far right: *The fruits of the blackthorn, sloes, are round black drupes. Both have white five-petalled flowers typical of roses.*

Potatoes, Daisies and Others

The potato family (Solanaceae) contains mainly tropical or subtropical herbs, with about 2,000 species. The flowers are regular, with five sepals (free or united), five united petals, five stamens which are attached to the corolla, and an ovary with usually two compartments and many ovules. The plants contain alkaloids, and many are consequently very poisonous, including species with edible parts such as the potatoes. A number of economically important species belong to this family, notably the potato, tomato, tobacco, red pepper and green pepper species. The Cape gooseberry and species of *Petunia*, *Schizanthus*, *Cestrum*, and *Nicotiana* are among the cultivated ornamental plants of this family. Important medicinal drugs are extracted from some of the highly poisonous species (see pages 126–127).

The figwort family (Scrophulariaceae) is closely related and rather similar to the Solanaceae, but the flowers are usually bilaterally symmetrical and strongly two-lipped, with typically only four functional stamens (two in *Veronica*). There are about 2,500 species, mostly herbs, widely distributed. They are of little economic importance, but include many beautiful flowering plants, such as species of *Calceolaria*, *Antirrhinum*, *Penstemon*, *Nemesia*, *Veronica* and *Mimulus*.

One section of the family consists of plants which develop roots that clamp on to the roots of neighbouring plants and draw off water and nutrients from them. These root-parasites include the eyebrights (*Euphrasia* species), louseworts (*Pedicularis* species) and yellow rattles (*Rhinanthus* species).

In a closely related family, the Orobanchaceae (broomrapes), the plants have become total root-parasites, without chlorophyll and entirely dependent on their host plants for their nourishment.

The forgetmenot or borage family (Boraginaceae) contains about 1,600 species, mainly herbs. The family is widespread but principally centred on lands around the Mediterranean Sea. The

Left: *The potato, a staple part of our diet, is a member of the nightshade family which contains the most deadly plants in Europe. Every part of the plant is poisonous except the tubers, which are mildly poisonous until cooked. The flowers are similar to others in the family such as the tomato and nightshades. The poisonous fruit, the 'potato plum' is like a black tomato.*

inflorescence is typically a one-sided one, and when the plant is young is curled like a scorpion's tail. The flowers are regular, with a five-lobed calyx and five-lobed corolla, five stamens attached to the corolla, and a two-celled or four-celled ovary. The forget-me-nots (*Myosotis* species) are familiar garden plants.

The bindweed family (Convolvulaceae) has about 1,000 species of herbs and shrubs, mainly tropical. Many are climbing plants, and many contain a milky latex. The flowers are often large and showy, with five sepals, a corolla of five fused petals, five stamens, and an ovary with two compartments, typically with two ovules per compartment.

The sweet potato (*Ipomoea batatas*) belongs to this family; so do a number of other species of the genus *Ipomoea* which are grown for their beautiful flowers, such as the morning glory. The bindweed (*Convolvulus arvensis*) can be a very persistent weed in light sandy soils owing to its ability to spread by long slender underground stems which grow whole new plants from quite small portions. The larger bindweeds (species of *Calystegia*) can be equally troublesome.

The dodders, species of *Cuscuta*, are sometimes placed here and sometimes put into a separate family of their own. They are parasites without leaves, roots or chlorophyll. They twine around the host

Below: *Veronica (left) is a cultivated speedwell. The four petals of its blue flowers are fused together at the base and fall as a single unit. It is a member of the figwort family (Scrophulariaceae). This family also includes the cultivated penstemon (below), a showy garden plant which is not native to Britain, and consequently rather tender. Both veronica and penstemon are usually perennials.*

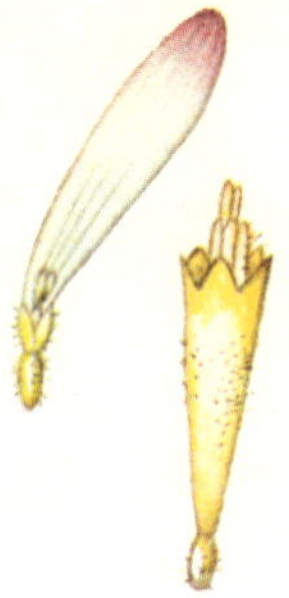

plant, and anchor themselves by sucker pads termed *haustoria* which penetrate the host, link up with its tissues and draw off food and water. The parasite branches freely and may spread to surrounding plants, causing much damage where it attacks a crop plant such as clover.

The dead-nettle or thyme family (Labiatae) probably derived from the Boraginaceae. The leaves are simple, typically opposite or in whorls on four-sided stems. The flowers often have a markedly two-lipped tubular corolla and two or four stamens. The style comes from the base of the ovary, which forms four nutlets, still protected by the persistent calyx. There are about 3,000 species, widely distributed, mostly herbs and often with aromatic glandular hairs. Many such as lavender, rosemary, mint, thyme and sage, are used as aromatic herbs for flavouring food and for other purposes. Several of the dead-nettles (*Lamium* species) are common garden weeds.

The daisy family (Compositae), with perhaps 20,000 species, is one of the largest and most advanced families of the angiosperms. It is widely distributed, and though most species are herbs it includes shrubs and even small trees. Flowers are small, grouped in heads which are often surrounded by an *involucre* (protective surround) of bracts. The florets are spirally arranged on the dish-like or conical receptacle. Each floret has a calyx reduced to hairs or scales (or absent altogether), a corolla with four or five lobes, five stamens (usually lightly joined together by their anthers), and an ovary which lies below the other flower parts, with a forked style and containing a single ovule. The florets have either a tubular corolla (tube florets) or a flattened strap-shaped corolla (ligulate florets). Some plants, such as the dandelion, have only ligulate florets; others, such as the rayless mayweed, have only tube florets. But many, such as the common daisy, have a central disc of tube florets surrounded by a fringe of ligulate (or ray) florets.

Above: *Dandelions and daisies are composite flowers. Daisies' flower heads are made up of many small florets. These are of two kinds: white 'petal' florets round the outside of a central cushion of yellow tube florets.* Below: *The florets of dandelions are all the same, with one yellow 'petal', which is really five fused true petals, and an anther tube of five fused anthers with the style inside.*

Below: *The labiate family contains many plants with aromatic leaves. A large number of our herbs belong to this family. Those illustrated are (left to right) sage; lemon-scented balm; spearmint; sweet rosemary; and thyme. These are all perennials, like the related white dead-nettle and self-heal.*

Although the Compositae are so abundant and diverse, surprisingly few species are of much use to man. Food plants include the Jerusalem artichoke, globe artichoke, salsify, endive, chicory and lettuce. An oil is extracted from sunflower fruits. The dried powdered flowers of *Chrysanthemum coccineum* form the insecticide pyrethrum powder. A rubber-yielding latex can be extracted from *Taraxacum bicorne* (a relative of the dandelion), and several species are sources of vegetable dyes and medicines. Many species with beautiful flowers belong to this family, notably the China aster, marigold, French marigold, African marigold, sunflowers and species of *Chrysanthemum, Aster, Rudbeckia, Zinnia, Cosmos* and *Senecio*.

The family also contains many serious weed species. Thistles, particularly creeping thistle, are pests of both arable and pasture land. Ragworts (*Senecio* species) can be poisonous to stock. Ragweeds, such as *Iva xanthifolia* and *Ambrosia artemisiifolia,* are among the main causes of hay fever in North America because of the vast quantities of pollen that they produce. The spiky fruits of some species, such as the bur-marigolds and the cocklebur, becomes wedged in the feet of sheep and other animals, making them lame. Daisies, dandelions, yarrow and sow-thistles may be troublesome weeds of gardens or lawns.

Left: *The most familiar monocotyledons are the grasses. In warmer climates there are monocotyledons like the banana tree. The bananas we eat are seedless, but many wild seeded varieties are known. The plant has a starchy underground rhizome from which many stems, covered with overlapping leaf bases, grow upwards.*

Monocotyledons

The monocotyledons have only one seed leaf in the embryo plant, and have a fibrous root system. The conducting tissues of the stem are in bundles scattered through the ground tissue, and there is no special provision for stems to become thicker as they grow older. Leaves are usually simple in shape, with the main veins all about equal in size and parallel to the leaf edge, while the flowers typically have their parts in threes.

It seems likely that the first monocotyledons were small herbaceous waterplants, related to buttercups and water-lilies. The most primitive families are believed to be those in which the flower has a clearly distinct calyx and corolla (the Calyciferae). These include the Butomaceae, to which the beautiful flowering rush belongs, and the Alismataceae, including the water plantain.

Some families of monocotyledons include plants specialised for living in a watery environment, such as the eelgrasses, marine plants of the family Zosteraceae which form large underwater meadows in sheltered bays and estuaries, providing food for flocks of wild geese.

Other families of monocotyledons are mainly terrestrial, though in the pineapple family (Bromeliaceae) many have left the ground to become tree-dwellers, such as Spanish moss (*Tillandsia usneoides*), which drapes trees in Florida swamps – a true flowering plant in spite of its appearance and name. The banana family (Musaceae) includes large tree-like plants with trunks mainly formed from the thick overlapping bases of the enormous leaves. The genus *Musa* includes the various species of bananas, the plantain, a very important food plant of the tropics, and manila hemp, the leaf-stalks of which produce long, tough fibres used in rope-making.

Families in which there is no clear distinction in the flower between petals and sepals (the Corolliferae) include the lily family (Liliaceae), with about 2,500 species. Liliaceae have a perianth of six petal-like parts, often forming a large and showy flower, six stamens and an ovary divided into three compartments. Many very beautiful garden plants belong to this family, including bay lilies, tiger lilies, lily of the valley, fritillaries, tulips and hyacinths. Asparagus, which has both decorative fronds and edible shoots, is also in the family Liliaceae.

The Amaryllidaceae is a closely related family, but in its plants the flowers sometimes form umbels, all growing out

Right: *Lily-of-the-valley flowers have three petals and three sepals, but these are the same colour and fused to make an apparently six-petalled bell. The plant spreads vegetatively by means of shoots from its underground rhizomes; it also produces red berries, which are poisonous. Relatives include a large range of different forms, from the spikes of asphodel to the delicate drooping bells of fritillaries, as well as edible species like onions, leeks and asparagus. Some lilies have bulbs, others rhizomes.*

from the same point like the spokes of an umbrella, and the ovary often lies below the other flower parts. There are about 1,000 species in the family, including the onion and its many useful relatives – garlic, chives, leeks, shallots – as well as the very serious pest the wild onion, which can grow abundantly in pastures and wheat fields, helping to provide onion-flavoured milk and flour. The family also contains many beautiful and well-loved plants such as the snowdrop and daffodil.

In the iris family (Iridaceae) the ovary is usually below the other flower parts, there are only three stamens, and the flower is not always radially symmetrical. This family likewise contains many beautiful garden plants such as irises, ixias, freesias, crocuses and gladioli.

The palms (Palmae, or sometimes Arecaceae) make up a very important monocotyledon family with about 4,000 species, mainly tropical and subtropical. They include trees with trunks which, like those of the banana, are mainly formed from persistent leaf bases, but also include narrow-stemmed climbing plants. Leaves can be large and featherlike, which is most unusual for monocotyledons, and in tree-like species are crowded at the crown of the plant. Flowers are small.

Palms can produce food, drink, building materials and clothing, supplying all that primitive people really need. A Tamil poem in praise of the Palmyra palm (*Borassus flabellifer*) lists 801 uses for it alone. Coconuts, dates and coconut matting are some of the more important products from members of this family.

The orchids (Orchidaceae) are the biggest family of all, with over 20,000 species, widely distributed but mainly tropical. They are all perennial herbs, growing in the ground or, in the tropics, as *epiphytes* (plants which grow on others) perched high in trees. The ground species often have thick, tuberous roots, while epiphytic species often have long, hanging roots with water-absorbing tissue, and with chlorophyll to carry out photosynthesis.

The flowers are adapted for insect pollination. The large petal on which insects land should really be at the back, but the flower is twisted round through 180° to bring it to the front. There may be one functional stamen or two, and the pollen is tied together by threads into masses called *pollinia*, which become attached to the head of an insect exploring the flower for nectar, and transferred to the stigma of the next flower visited. Often the mechanism to bring this about is very complicated indeed. In some cases insects are attracted by the uncanny resemblance of the large petal of the orchid to an insect of the same kind, as in the bee orchid.

Orchids produce tiny seeds which are so light that they may be readily carried into trees, as the epiphytic species require, but such seeds cannot contain much food for the developing seedling, which must establish a symbiotic relationship with a particular fungus at an early stage or die. The fungus enters the outer tissue of roots or rhizomes, taking over many of the functions of root hairs. The presence of such a fungus allows some orchids such as the bird's-nest orchid to do without photosynthesis, depending on the fungal partner to obtain energy for both plants by breakdown of organic materials in the soil.

The need for the precisely right fungal partner makes orchid-growing difficult, but many species are highly prized for their flowers.

Above: *The coconut palm is a very valuable plant. Almost every part of it can be used. Its fruit contains 'meat' which is rich in oil and protein. The leaves are woven into thatch and baskets, and the trunk provides a strong, tough wood. It grows on shores and its floating fruit enables it to colonise even isolated islands.*

Right: *Orchids are among the most exotic of the world's flowers. Most species grow in tropical climates, where they live as epiphytes on jungle trees. The orchids of temperate regions are smaller and so vulnerable to disturbance that many species are now protected to prevent their complete disappearance from the countryside. The lady's slipper orchid illustrated here is the largest-flowered European species, and rare in Britain where it grows mainly on limestone hills.*

Sedges and Grasses

Sedges and grasses are two similar families of monocotyledons with wind-pollinated flowers. Both have many species and are widely distributed around the world, but while the sedges are not particularly useful to man, the grasses are indispensable.

Above: *Rice is a cereal crop of great importance; it grows in wet places. This is a newly planted rice paddy.*

The sedge family (Cyperaceae) includes about 3,200 species, most of which live in temperate and cold climates. They are typically perennial, grass-like plants with fibrous roots, solid, three-sided stems and three rows of leaves. Each leaf has a basal part sheathing the stem and a narrow, grass-like blade. Flowers are very small, each protected by a sheathing bract, and are grouped together in spikelets. Petals and sepals are absent or reduced to bristles or scales. There are typically three stamens, a two-branched or three-branched style, and a single ovary containing one ovule. Stamens and ovary may be in the same florets, in different florets on the same spikelet, in different spikelets, or even on different plants.

Below: *Cotton-grasses are common on wet moorland. The floral envelope is formed of bristles which later lengthen.*

Below: *The reed-mace has commonly been called the bulrush ever since Landseer's painting 'Moses in the Bulrushes'.*

Below: *Thin strips of the pith of the paper-reed were pressed together to form the Egyptian papyri.*

The sedges are often abundant in boggy and marshy places, but they are coarse, tough plants which provide very poor grazing. The cotton-grasses (*Eriphorum* species) with cotton-like tufts of long bristles are common plants of boggy ground, and the bulrush (*Schoenoplectus lacustris*) is often abundant in slow-flowing, shallow fresh water. The common sedge (*Cladium mariscus*), the principal sedge of the fens of eastern England, was formerly much used for thatching. One sedge of particular interest is the papyrus (*Cyperus papyrus*) which grows in the swamps of the River Nile. The pith of this plant was used by the early Egyptians to make a writing material, and from its name came our modern word 'paper'.

The grass family (Gramineae) is one of the largest families, with over 10,000 species. Grasses are mostly perennial herbs, like the sedges, but include tree-like plants 40 metres (130 feet) high among the bamboos. Unlike the sedges, grasses typically have leaves in two rows, mostly on hollow rounded stems. The leaves have a portion sheathing the stem and a narrow blade which may be flat or rolled. The flowers are small, usually enclosed in two bracts, an outer one (the *lemma*) and an inner (the *palea*). The lemma may bear a long, rough bristle (the *awn*).

The florets consist of typically three stamens and a single ovary, with one ovule and two feathery styles; sepals and petals are sometimes represented by a pair of tiny scales (*lodicules*). The florets may be grouped together in spikelets, each spikelet partly or wholly enclosed in two further bracts (the *glumes*). The spikelets may be on simple or branched stalks, as in oats, or stalkless, as in wheat.

The ripe grains contain endosperm packed with starch grains, and members of this family, the cereals, provide more than half of man's food supply. The two most important cereals (each with several species and innumerable strains) are wheat, growing best in fertile soils of temperate climates with an annual rainfall of less than 750 millimetres (30 inches); and rice, growing mainly in humid tropical regions and providing 80–90 per cent of the food of its cultivators. Other important cereals are barley, rye and oats in temperate climates, maize (corn) under warmer conditions, sorghums on semi-desert land, and millets in very hot climates. Both the grain and the straw of cereals are fed to domestic animals; straw is used for thatching; and grain is fermented to produce alcoholic drinks.

One important grass crop is sugar cane (*Saccharum officinarum*). Growing in hot climates, it is the world's most efficient and cheap source of sugar. Bamboos, of which there are more than 20 genera, are grasses with many different uses. The light but strong stems are used to build houses and furniture, and provide canes, fences and containers; bamboo strips are used in basketry or weaving, bamboo fibres are used to make ropes or paper, and the young shoots are eaten.

Grasses form the main vegetation in many places where summers are hot and dry and summer fires are frequent. Great areas of natural grassland occur, such as the prairies (North America), the pampas (South America), the veld (southern Africa) and the steppes (Soviet Union). Such grasslands used to support huge herds of grazing animals, but in many parts of the world domestic animals have replaced wild animals, and crop plants have replaced wild grasses.

Grasses can be troublesome weeds, especially in cereal crops, because they are as resistant as the crop plants to selective weedkillers. Couch grass, winter wild oats and spring wild oats are among the most troublesome of such weeds.

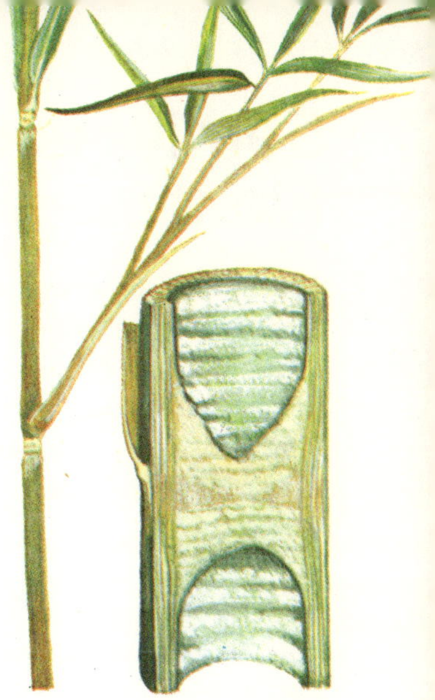

Above: *Bamboos include the largest of the grasses, and are fast-growing. They are mainly found in tropical climates. The hollow-jointed stems are strong but flexible, and used for many purposes.*

1 2 3 4 5

Left: *Grasses of the field: 1 bent grasses have feathery flowering heads with only one floret per spikelet; 2 meadow fescue has many-flowered spikelets on branched stalks; 3 rye grass has stalkless spikelets; 4 timothy grass has one-flowered strongly flattened florets on a dense head; 5 marram grass helps to build and maintain sand-dunes.*
Below: *The cereals: 6 wheat is our staple cereal; 7 rye provides grain, as well as long strong straw suitable for thatching; 8 oats can grow in a cool damp climate; 9 barley provides both food and drink.*

6 7 8 9

Carnivorous Plants

Most plants get their energy from sunlight and their nutrients from soil, water and air, but a small group supplements this diet by capturing and digesting animals. These are not the man-eating monster plants of science fiction, but small herbs which mostly capture nothing bigger than insects. This habit has evolved in five different families of flowering plants, probably to overcome a shortage of available nitrogen in the kind of place in which the species grow. In all cases it is the leaves which form the trap; the flowers, which need insects for pollination, are usually very different in appearance.

One type of trap is a pitcher into which insects may fall. Their drowned bodies are broken down, and the plant absorbs nitrogenous materials from them.

The American pitcher plants, which grow in boggy places, have their whole leaves converted into hollow containers, with the tip of the leaf expanded to form a partial lid. The rim of the pitcher is thickened, and around it there are glands producing nectar, which attracts insects. Should these insects be rash enough to wander inside the rim, they find themselves on a slippery downward path, over overlapping, wax-covered cells which give no grip to the insects' feet. Below this path lies a zone with downward-pointing bristles, ensuring that this is a one-way journey. At the bottom the insects usually drown and decompose in accumulated rainwater.

The Old World pitcher plants which live in tropical forests, especially in Malaya, have even more specialised pitchers. The leaf has a broad blade which is prolonged into a stout tendril. This tendril coils round a suitable support, then grows downward and curves back up again, forming a beautifully balanced pitcher. The pitcher also has a thickened rim with nectar-producing glands, and the upper part of the inner surface is lined with downward-pointing cells coated with loose wax platelets. Here the water in the pitcher is secreted by the plant itself, which also secretes enzymes to break down the proteins of the victim's body into soluble compounds which it can then absorb. A third type of pitcher plant, rather like the American ones but with bright red pitchers, grows in a few marshes of south-western Australia.

A somewhat similar type of trap is formed by some of the tropical members of the bladderwort genus (*Utricularia*), which produce hollow tubes lined with inward-pointing bristles. Some small animal wandering in finds itself in a

Above: *Most of the Old World pitcher plants grow in open forests or peat bogs, especially in Southeast Asia. The climbing forms frequently have differently shaped pitchers at different heights above the ground.*

Left: *Bladderwort is a rootless plant that grows submerged in acid moorland ponds. Its leaves are mostly much-divided, but some form the bladders from which the plant takes its name. Its food consists mainly of small water-fleas such as* Daphnia *and* Cyclops. *The pools in which bladderwort lives are very poor in available nitrogen and the decay products of its prey are thus essential for its growth.*

chamber which it cannot leave, and the plant claims another victim.

Aquatic plants of this genus have small bladders with an inward-opening trapdoor which has branched trigger bristles on the outside. Stalked glands inside the bladder withdraw some of the water, causing the walls to be sucked inward, and the trap is then set. Any little animal touching the trigger hairs causes the trapdoor to open, the walls to bulge out, and water to be drawn in so quickly that the unfortunate animal is sucked in also. It is not killed immediately, but eventually it dies and decays naturally, and the bladderwort absorbs the breakdown products. If the trap is sprung by an animal too big or too quick to be trapped, the trap can be reset in as little as 20 minutes.

Another kind of trap is formed by the Venus's fly-trap (*Dionaeà*), a plant growing in boggy parts of the south-eastern United States. The leaf blade of the plant is fringed with long stiff hairs which point upwards, and on the upper surface of each half-blade there are three jointed bristles. Contact with any of these six bristles causes the two halves of the leaf to snap quickly together, so that the marginal hairs interlock, forming a prison for any small insect which may have triggered off the action.

The surface of the leafblade is covered with stalkless glands which produce digestive enzymes. The closure of the trap is brought about by very rapid removal of water from rows of large cells along the midrib, and as the cells shrink they act as a hinge. A rare submerged water plant of some European lakes, *Aldrovanda vesiculosa,* traps small water animals in a similar way.

Still another kind of trap operates like fly-paper, by producing sticky substances which hold the victims firmly until they can be digested. The sundews (*Drosera*) are good examples of this. These plants have rosettes of leaves bearing 'tentacles', the fringing ones with long stalks, the inner ones with short stalks. Each 'tentacle' has a bright red glandular head from which a glistening drop of sticky fluid is secreted, very attractive to insects. If an animal sticks on to any of these, the

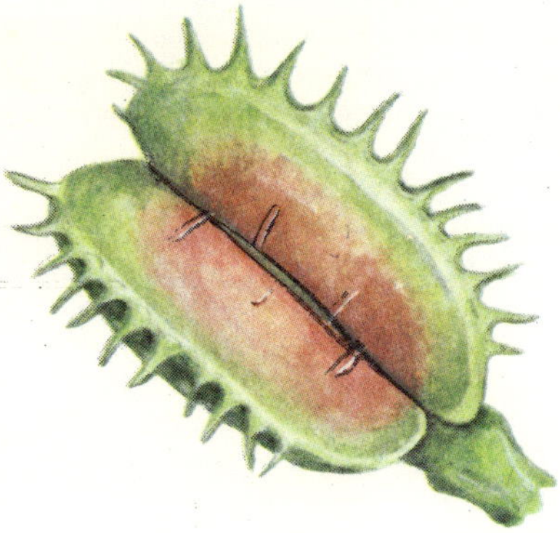

Above and right: *The three species shown on this page all live in boggy areas. Because the ground is waterlogged, decomposition is slow and nutrients are only gradually released to the plant. Here the Venus's fly trap is catching its prey. The fly touches the hair, the two halves close – and the fly is caught.*

'tentacles' begin to bend inwards, bringing the prey into contact with the central glands. Outer tentacles which have not so far been directly in contact with the prey then begin to bend inwards likewise, and unless the victim is large and strong it is hopelessly trapped. Its proteins are broken down to simple soluble substances which are then absorbed. The whole process may take several days, and the trap is then reset.

The butterworts, (*Pinguicula*), little plants forming star-shaped rosettes in open boggy ground, have a similar but simpler mechanism; here the leaf margins curl inwards to trap the prey yet more firmly.

Some very different kinds of carnivorous plants are found among the fungi, where some of the soil-inhabiting species have developed most efficient mechanisms for trapping small eel-worms. Sometimes the trap is just a sticky secretion from a single hypha or gland-cell, or a sticky network of looped hyphae, but the most efficient type of trap is formed of a stalked ring of cells like a lasso.

If a wandering eel-worm chances to push its way into this loop and make contact with the inner surface of the loop cells, these cells immediately swell up, firmly holding the unfortunate eel-worm.

Below: *The long-leaved sundew grows in the north-west of Britain in hilly regions with high rainfall, and also in boggy areas in the south-east.*

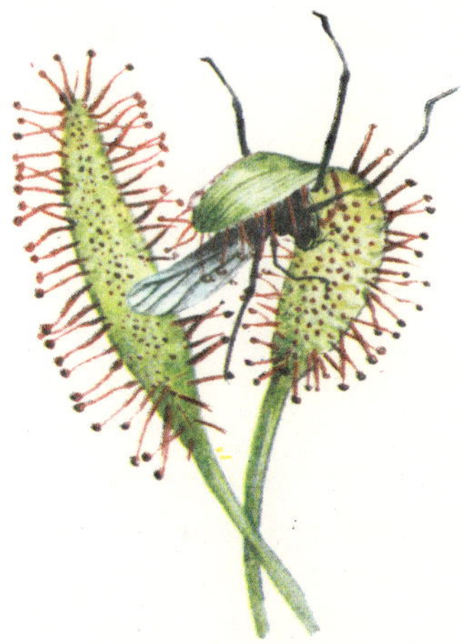

Below: *Butterworts live in similar places to sundews, but they tend to catch crawling insects whereas the sundews' prey probably fly.*

Poisonous Plants

Right: *Many familiar garden plants can be dangerous or even deadly to man and animals. Laburnum (2), monkshood (5) and thorn-apple (3) contain deadly alkaloids; foxglove (1) carries a well-known glycoside poison, digitalis. Lily-of-the-valley berries (4) are attractive to children but the whole plant is poisonous, even though it smells so sweet.*

Many plants produce poisonous substances, either kept within their own tissues or secreted. Antibiotics are used by plants to prevent the development of possible competitors in their neighbourhood, and some of those produced by certain fungi and bacteria are now extracted and used by man in his own war against harmful micro-organisms. Some plants produce poisons that discourage insects and other organisms which might damage them. Man uses some of these poisons, for example in derris dust and pyrethrum powder, in his own war against marauding insects. Many micro-organisms such as bacteria can produce very powerful poisons (see pages 86–87). Here we shall deal only with poisonous higher plants.

Poisons can be of many kinds. Some, known as *allergens*, are poisonous only to susceptible or sensitised individuals but cause little or no discomfort to other more fortunate people; for instance the pollen of ragweeds (*Ambrosia* species) can cause acute hay fever in susceptible victims, while others barely notice its presence.

Some plants may be harmless in themselves, but may pick up poisonous substances from the air or the soil and pass them on to animals which feed on them, sometimes with very serious results.

Some plants may be relatively harmless in certain conditions but very poisonous in others. Hemlock (*Conium*) and thorn-apple (*Datura stramonium*) produce their alkaloid poisons more abundantly in warm climates than in cool ones. The fruit of the may-apple (*Podophyllum peltatum*) contains a poisonous resin, podophyllin, when unripe, but when ripe is quite safe to eat. Rhubarb leaves are at best bitter and unpleasant when raw, but when cooked with salt in a mistaken effort to use them as a cabbage substitute the almost insoluble oxalates which they contain become converted to the soluble and very poisonous sodium salt.

Conversely some poisonous plants may be made safe to eat by treatment. The glycosides in buttercups (*Ranunculus*) become harmless to cattle in properly-made hay, and the deadly prussic acid in the roots of bitter cassava (*Manihot esculenta*) can be removed by grinding and careful washing to produce tapioca. Poisonous shoots of pokeweed (*Phytolacca*) can be used as a vegetable if it is well boiled in plenty of water, which is then discarded.

Often the poisons are confined to particular parts of the plant, and the other parts may be perfectly safe. Thus the very poisonous glycoside of the corn-cockle (*Agrostemma*) is found only in the seeds; tubers of potato (*Solanum*) if not green are edible, while the sprouts, fruits and greened tubers contain deadly alkaloids such as solanine.

Substances poisonous to one animal may be safely eaten by another, or may produce a quite different effect on it. Thus rabbits may nibble with impunity enough of the deadly death cap fungus to kill a whole human family.

Many of the most dangerous plant poisons are alkaloids, such as the very deadly aconitine found in all parts of monkshood (*Aconitum anglicum*); atropine from the deadly nightshade (*Atropa belladonna*); strychnine from the Indian tree (*Strychnos nux-vomica*); coniine from hemlock; taxine from the yew (*Taxus baccata*); and cytisine from laburnum (*Cytisus labur-*

Above: *Contact with black bryony causes a skin condition some time after exposure. Touching the plant, or even clothing which has itself touched it, causes inflammation which can be dangerous.*

Left: *Here are some poisonous wild plants. Two of them, deadly nightshade (1) and bittersweet (2) – also called woody nightshade – are members of the same poisonous family that also gives us potatoes and tomatoes. The other three are members of the carrot family. These three, hemlock (3), fool's parsley (4), and cowbane (5) are all very dangerous.*

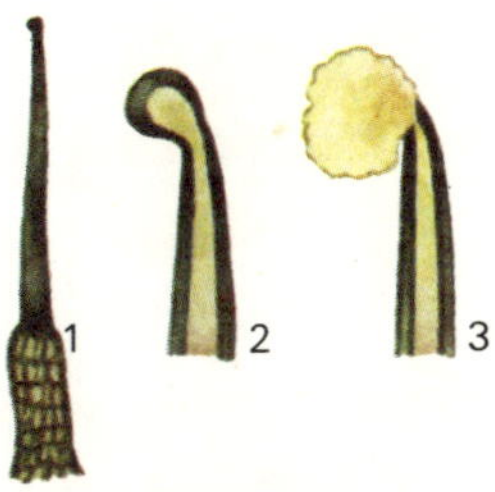

Above: *The effects of the stinging nettle are well-known. The itching rash is caused by an acid fluid in tiny hairs with delicate tips, which break off when touched. 1 hair; 2 tip; 3 tip broken.*

num). However, plants produce many other kinds of poisons, such as glycosides, for example digitoxin, found in the foxglove (*Digitalis*); and phytotoxins such as the deadly ricinin of the seeds of the true castor-oil plant (*Ricinus communis*). These seeds are often used by school classes for germination experiments, with neither students nor teachers aware of their very dangerous properties.

Plants with dangerously poisonous fruits which may appear attractive to children include deadly nightshade, bittersweet (*Solanum dulcamara*), ivy (*Hedera helix*), and privet (*Ligustrum vulgare*).

Yew is among the poisonous plants most dangerous to livestock, for all parts are very poisonous, and both horses and cattle eat it readily. Laburnum is dangerous to children, for again all parts are very poisonous and even use of the seeds in peashooters may lead to poisoning.

Some plants produce irritant poisons which can affect people who merely brush against them. Many members of the stinging nettle family, the Urticaceae, produce irritant organic acid poisons in special stinging hairs, which pump the poison into tiny wounds inflicted by their jagged broken tips, but the effects of these do not usually last very long. Some species of *Rhus*, such as poison ivy and poison sumac, can be more serious, even fatal, producing severe inflammation of the skin of susceptible people, usually some days after application. The poison is a very persistent resinous juice containing urushiol, which may be carried in smoke from burning vegetation or persist in clothing which has been in contact with poison ivy. It can produce its symptoms in new victims sometimes a year or more after the original contact. Perhaps a quarter of a million Americans are seriously affected by poison ivy every year, yet cattle, horses, sheep and pigs can eat it with apparent impunity.

Many plant poisons have been put to good use by man as medicines, pest-killers, or in hunting and fishing. Thus atropin from deadly nightshade is used to enlarge the pupil for eye operations; digitalin from foxglove as a heart stimulant; cocaine from the coca shrub and morphine from the opium poppy to relieve pain; strychnine from *Strychnos nux-vomica* as a rat-killer; nicotine from the tobacco plant (*Nicotiana tobarum*) as an insecticide; and curare (from *Strychnos toxifera* and other plants) as a potent South American arrow poison, which swiftly paralyses and kills its victims. Curine, one of the alkaloid poisons involved, is used medicinally to relax muscles.

However, many plant poisons have been badly misused. Some used in folk medicine proved too erratic in their concentration and were as likely to kill as to cure. Plant poisons such as aconite, used as a painkiller, and purgatives from members of the spurge family are now rarely used medicinally. Addictive poisons such as cocaine and opium have brought misery and death to many. Arrow poisons have been used against people as well as animals, and plant poisons have been widely used as a means for committing murder. Socrates died from hemlock poisoning, the dacoits of India used the deadly nerve-poison of the thorn-apple in their murderous activities, and the poisoners of classical and medieval times knew well how to use belladonna and hemlock to eliminate their victims.

Specialised Plants

Land plants which grow under average conditions are called *mesophytes,* but competition for light and space can be very keen and many species have become adapted to flourish under conditions in which most other plants could not even survive. Where conditions are good enough to allow tall plants to grow these become dominant, forming forests and woodlands.

Those plants which cannot grow tall and self-supporting like the trees must then grow elsewhere, make do with the limited light reaching the forest floor, or use their taller rivals for support. Climbing plants have long, relatively slender stems with wide conducting elements (for rapid and efficient conduction of water and other substances). Their stems may twine closely round supporting plants, usually in a right-handed (clockwise) spiral, sometimes in a left-handed (anticlockwise) spiral as in the bindweed (*Convulvulus major*).

These plants are attached by various means. Some are scramblers, holding on by recurved prickles and spines, like goosegrass (*Galium aparine*) and brambles (species of *Rubus*). Others such as ivy produce on the side away from light numerous little roots which grow into cracks and crevices in the supporting plant or wall, anchoring the ivy tightly to this support.

Tendrils form another very effective climbing device – long slender structures which grow rapidly on the side away from contact, thus coiling round stems and branches of suitable width. The unattached part of the tendril may then also coil, drawing the climber closer to its support. Tendrils can be produced from all kinds of organs – stems, branches, leafstalks, leaves, leaflets, midribs. Still other climbers such as the Virginia creeper (*Parthenocissus tricuspidata*) hold on by little sucker discs which are firmly cemented to the support. These have the advantage that, unlike tendrils, they can be used for climbing up a flat surface such as a cliff face or the side of a house. Big woody climbers (*lianes*) are more common in tropical jungles, but some, such as ivy (*Hedera helix*), honeysuckle (*Lonicera periclymenum*) and clematis (*Clematis vitalba*) grow in temperate woodlands.

Epiphytism (growing perched on another plant) is rare among temperate flowering plants, apart from the semi-parasitic mistletoes, but common in tropical forests. Special adaptive features of epiphytes include water storage pitchers (members of the Bromeliaceae), and in the Orchidaceae a special water-holding tissue, the *velamen*, in the roots, and aerial roots which may be green and photosynthetic.

Many plants grow under conditions in which it is difficult to get water and easy to lose it. Plants of dry places are called *xerophytes,* but taking up water may also be a problem for plants growing where soil water is frozen, or for saltmarsh plants, which cannot easily draw water in from salt water, and these often show adaptations similar to those of the true xerophytes. Xerophytes of the desert may produce deep tap roots to reach water well below the surface, or shallow but widespreading root systems to absorb water rapidly and efficiently after rainfall before it evaporates or drains away. Many xerophytes, such as cacti, become succulent, with special water storage tissue in stems or roots. These succulents have very reduced leaves. The leaf-like structures of many cacti are in fact stems.

Plants have evolved many ways to reduce water loss. Thick mats of hairs reflect sunlight and also create a zone of still air around the plant surface, slowing down transpiration. Plants may grow flat against the soil, like saltwort (*Salsola kali*), in tight rosettes or in cushions, like the sea

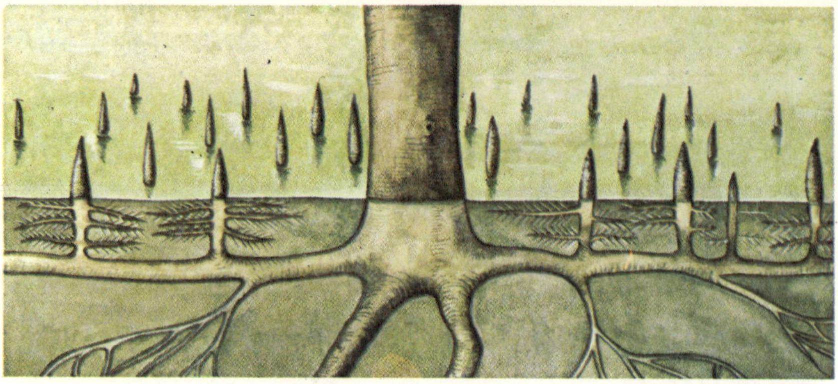

Above: *Mangroves like* Sonneratia *live on muddy river shores; their roots obtain air by sending up shoots called pneumatophores.* Below: Rhizophora *mangroves live on tidal estuaries and have prop roots to support them when the tide is out.*

Below: *Honeysuckle twines through branches of taller plants to lift its flowers where their scent can attract moths and other insects for pollination.*

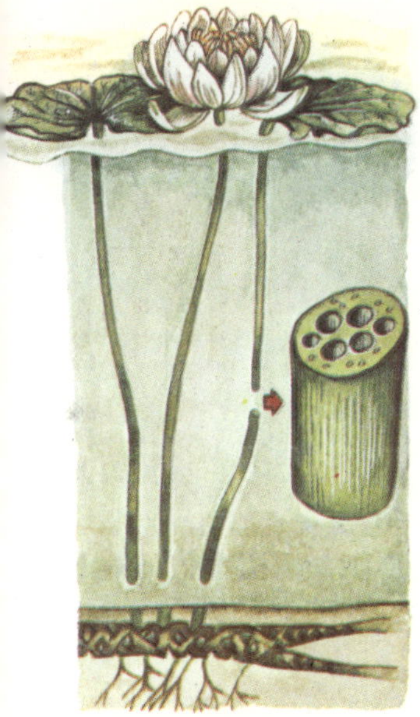

Above: *The large floating leaves of water-lilies send down air to their roots in the mud through large air spaces in the long flexible stems.*

pink (*Armeria maritima*), cutting down on exposure to drying winds. Leaves are the most serious potential source of water loss, so in many cases they are *deciduous,* shed during the season when water availability is reduced. In other cases they are provided with thick layers of protective wax, the surface area exposed to sunlight is reduced by rolling or folding of the leaf (as in marram grass, *Ammophila arenaria*), the 'breathing pores' are sunken in chambers away from direct light, and there are lots of strong, thick-walled cells which prevent the leaf from collapsing if it should lose much water. In the so-called compass plants (for example *Silphium laciniatum*) leaves are angled to lie north and south, with only their edges exposed to the direct blaze of the noonday sun.

Many xerophytes dispense with leaf-blades altogether, and instead have flattened photosynthetic *phyllodes* (leaf-stalks) or *cladodes* (branchlets), likewise growing edge-on to the noonday sun. Alternatively they may be 'switch plants' such as broom (*Sarothamnus scoparius*) with long slender ridged branches having photosynthetic tissue deep in the protected grooves. Plants growing in dry places are obvious targets for animals seeking food or water, and are often protected from would-be grazers by forbidding spines on stems and leaves.

At the other extreme we have *hydrophytes,* plants which live at least partly in water. The completely submerged plants are supported by the surrounding water, so have little or no special supporting or water-conducting tissue. Roots are only needed for anchorage, and some floating plants do without them altogether. However, light is not so strong under water as above, so underwater leaves are often very thin and much divided to expose as much surface as possible to such light as is available. Some leaves, such as those of water-lilies, float on the surface, held up by internal air cavities. Plants have to breathe, and many water plants take their air down with them through big air spaces in stems, and sometimes in special upward-growing roots called *pneumatophores,* such as mangroves and the swamp cypress (*Taxodium distichum*) have. Floating leaves have functional 'breathing pores' only on the upper surface, usually raised to avoid water-logging, and the leaf surface may be coated with wax or protected by a raised rim so that it is not readily wetted.

Above: *The beautiful leopard orchid,* Ansellia gigantea, *is an epiphyte, which means that it actually grows in the humus that has collected in the fork of this tree, and so lives nearer to the light in its jungle habitat.*

Above: *The weak stems of hops twine tightly round those of other plants in a clockwise fashion. They are covered in rough hairs, and the stems die down each year.*

Plant Communities

Plant communities begin, grow, develop, age and die just as individuals do, although sometimes the whole process, termed a *sere,* takes thousands of years. When a community begins from bare rock the first colonists are likely to be simple algae and lichens, clinging closely to the rock surface or even partly embedded in it, for only these hardy organisms can cope with temperature extremes and the lack of water and nutrients.

As the rock surface crumbles and organic and inorganic particles accumulate in crevices, conditions get easier for plants. Larger, more complex lichens, mosses and specially adapted higher plants begin to move in, crowding out the pioneer plants. These newcomers produce more waste material and trap more broken-down rock, forming a soil which gradually covers the rock surface. More herbaceous plants move in until the open community becomes a closed one, with no empty space in it. New arrivals can only enter at the expense of plants already there, and the plants are then actively competing with each other.

As the depth of soil increases it can hold more nutrients and water and support larger plants, which shade out the smaller plants. Thus tall herbs replace short ones, shrubs replace tall herbs, and eventually, if conditions permit, large trees dominate the habitat, forming a wood. But the trees produce in their shade new conditions which favour other, smaller plants specialised for these conditions, so that the community becomes increasingly complex. Eventually a stage may be reached when the community does not change significantly. As individual plants die, they tend to be replaced by similar individuals in a more-or-less stable balance, provided the general conditions (such as climate) do not become very different; this is the *climax community.*

If this community is seriously damaged, for instance by a forest fire, then new plants and animals may move in, such as fireweed (*Chamaenerion angustifolium*), but gradually the community changes until it returns to its natural climax. If man removes the forest, then plants crops or introduces grazing animals, nature bides its time; when man removes his controls the forest slowly but surely returns, and the grassy downlands, closely grazed for hundreds of years by sheep and rabbits, may in their absence quickly become overgrown by coarse herbs and bushes, and finally by trees.

Other communities develop along different lines. The loose blown sand of the seashore seems most unpromising as a support for vegetation, but plants such as sea rocket (*Cakile maritima*) can flourish among the dead seaweeds washed up to the highest tide level. Higher still, grasses such as sea couch grass (*Agropyron pungens*) can bind the sand into low dunes, through their network of creeping stems and roots and their ability to grow up through smothering sand. Behind these low dunes are higher ones, held in place by marram grass (*Ammophila arenaria*), sea lyme grass (*Elymus arenarius*) and other hardy plants. As the dry blown sand piles up around and over them, they grow up through it, producing the white dunes, with pure sand still visible around them These dunes provide shelter from the salt-laden sea breezes. The old dunes behind them become colonised by other plants, and organic matter begins to accumulate, colouring the dunes grey. Shrubs such as gorse move in, and then trees.

In a comparable way a lake may gradu-

Below: *In any plant community, like this marshland scene, every species has its own place, although at first sight there seems to be a haphazard collection of different flowers and grasses. The vetch on the right of the picture, for example, is using the tall stems of other plants, like the reedmace, to give it support. Such a community is, however, in a state of constant change; if the water level falls, some species, such as the marsh marigold, will find survival too difficult, and others, such as the fritillary, may be better off. If conditions remain the same, there may be a gradual trend over the years for some species to crowd out others, perhaps thereby providing a foothold for new species. Sometimes a stable balance can develop, and it is in this kind of marshy habitat that long-standing constant communities are often found.*

ally silt up; waterlilies and pondweeds give way to reeds and rushes, and these to bushes and small trees such as willows and alders which can live in waterlogged soils. As the soil level rises if drainage is adequate, the climax community once more becomes woodland.

Where drainage is poor the community may remain marshland – or bogland, often dominated by sphagnum moss and cottongrass (*Eriophorum* species) in acid conditions. Thin acid soils and strong winds may produce heaths or moors as their climax communities, with at best only a scattering of stunted, wind-deformed trees. The bright green grasslands of the lowlands are the result of man's activities, aided by his flocks and herds, and for most of them the true climax communities would be woodland dominated by broad-leaved trees such as oaks (*Quercus*) and beech (*Fagus sylvatica*).

Above: *The floor of this willow wood is carpeted with marsh marigolds,* Caltha palustris, *in the summer. Both marigolds and willows thrive in damp conditions.*

The typical oak-beech woodland is even more complex than at first appears. Among the dominant giants there are smaller trees such as holly (*Ilex aquifolium*), hazel (*Corylus avellana*), crab apple (*Malus* species) and hornbeam (*Carpinus betulus*); and shrubs such as brambles (*Rubus fruticosus*), hawthorn (*Crataegus* species), blackthorn (*Prunus spinosa*) and dog rose (*Rosa canina*). These also often form a fringe round the edge of the wood, where they are less shaded. Ivy (*Hedera helix*) and honeysuckle (*Lonicera* species) may form a loose covering on the ground and then climb among the trees.

The ground itself is carpeted with dead leaves and twigs in various stages of decay, with their own vegetation of decomposers – fungi and slime fungi. These also flourish on the fallen trunks of trees lying around the forest floor. Both living and dead trunks may carry communities of lichens, mosses and liverworts, and these also carpet exposed earth or stones.

These are the permanently visible inhabitants, but others only become prominent seasonally, beginning with spring flowers, going on to the full, lush vegetation of high summer and then reverting to the bare winter state.

The World of Animals

Some of the differences between plants and animals have already been described on page 84: animals can move about and feed on particles of food which they take into their bodies and digest. There are several other important differences. One relates to growth: many plants continue to grow provided conditions are right, and several plants of the same species may be very different in size, although all are mature. Most animals, however, grow to a certain size and then stop.

While plants respond to only the very simplest features of their surroundings, such as light, temperature and moisture, animals have a much greater awareness. In many animals the responses to their surroundings are merely reflex or semi-automatic reactions, but in the higher animals some choice is involved.

The kingdom Animalia is divided into three subkingdoms: Protozoa (one-celled animals); Parazoa (many-celled animals – the sponges – which do not have a true digestive system); and Metazoa (many-celled animals with digestions). There are 21 divisions of the Metazoa, ranging from the very simplest wormlike Mesozoa to Arthropoda (joint-footed animals, including spiders, crustaceans and insects), and Chordata (animals with simple or true backbones, including fish, reptiles, birds and mammals).

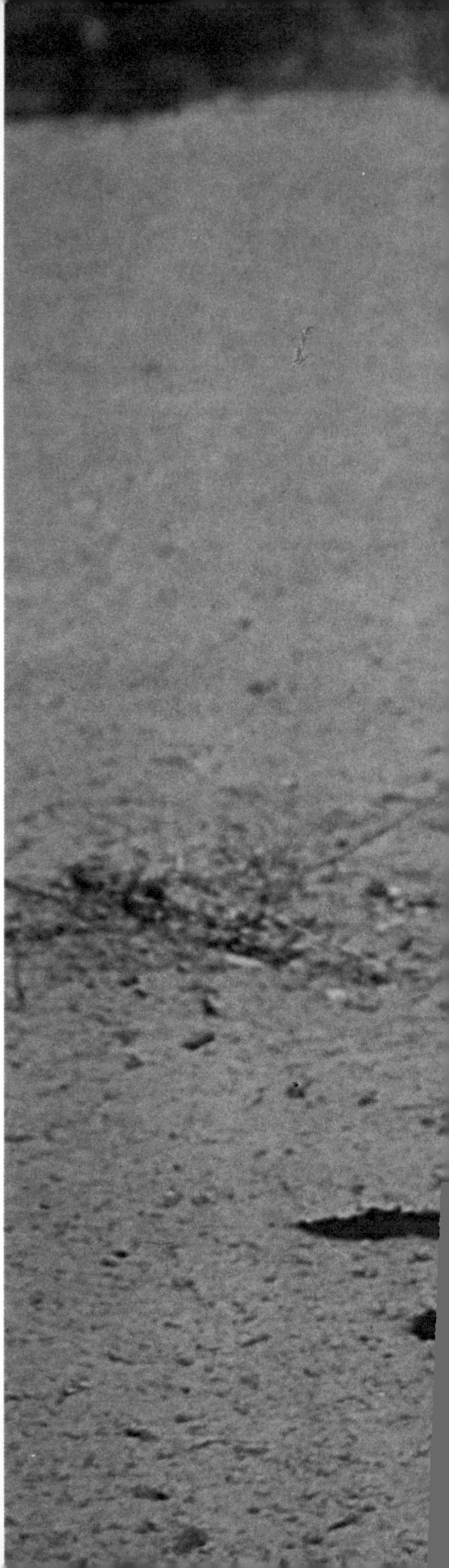

Ever-alert for danger, a nyala doe and her youngster on a game reserve in South Africa.

Protozoa

Protozoa are single-celled animals most of which are invisible to the naked eye. Because of their size, they were unknown until 1674, when a Dutch draper, Anton van Leeuwenhoek, saw them with a home-made microscope, which he had invented. While protozoa are usually microscopic, the majority being less than a tenth of a millimetre (four thousandths of an inch) in diameter, several attain the size of a millimetre (four hundredths of an inch) and the shells of nummulites (fossil protozoa) reached 100 millimetres (4 inches) in diameter.

Although the name protozoa means 'first animals' they should not be regarded as being simple – indeed modern research indicates just how complex the present-day forms really are. One proof of this is that they are able to move and to respond to stimuli in their surroundings, moving towards food and away from distasteful things. They can also trap and digest their food and reproduce.

Free-living protozoa may be found in a great variety of habitats in the sea, fresh water and the soil, while parasitic protozoa are widespread in other animals, including man, where they may be responsible for serious diseases.

Many protozoa can survive dry conditions, usually by forming a *cyst wall* or membrane around themselves to prevent evaporation of water, but no protozoon is able to feed in the absence of water. The production of cysts is a common feature of protozoa and is partly responsible for the fact that any particular species may be found in many parts of the globe. Protozoa in their protective cysts may be spread by the feet of birds and other animals, and carried by the wind.

Above: Globigerina, *a type of foraminiferan, whose shells cover vast areas of the ocean floor.*

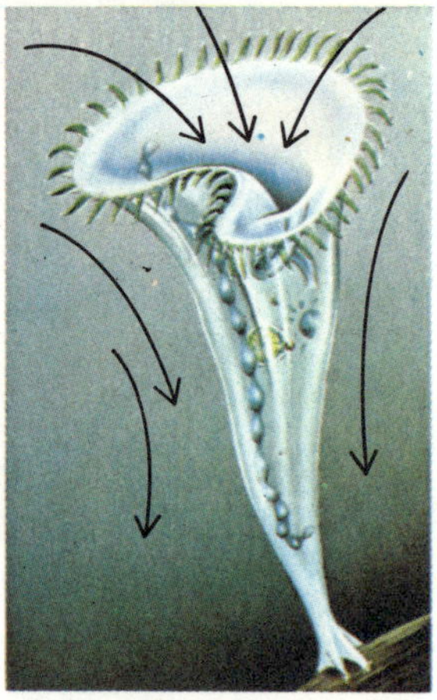

Above and below: *Stentor's steadily-beating cilia carry food into its mouth.*

All protozoa move in some way, and the structures that are used for movement enable biologists to divide protozoa into groups. *Flagellated* protozoa possess long, whip-like extensions (*flagella*) of the body surface, which they use to propel or pull themselves through the water. *Ciliated* protozoa possess hair-like processes (*cilia*) but these are shorter than flagella and occur in larger numbers so that they often cover the entire cell surface. However, modern research, using electron microscopes, has shown that flagella and cilia have the same internal structure. The well-known amœbae are like specks of jelly, often without a permanent shape, which move by producing temporary extensions of the cell (*pseudopodia* or 'false feet') into which the cell flows.

Protozoa reproduce by *binary fission* (splitting into two). In this process a cell feeds, grows to a certain size and then simply divides into two pieces, each of which is known as a daughter cell. After fission each daughter cell is capable of repeating the growth and division, and the cycle continues indefinitely. This type of reproduction is said to be *asexual* since separate sexes are not involved. Sexual reproduction is also known in some protozoa: in certain groups the sexes look exactly alike, while in others the 'male' cell is smaller than the 'female' cell.

Protozoa acquire their food in various ways. The green flagellated protozoa contain chlorophyll and are able to produce sugars from the gas carbon dioxide and water in the presence of sunlight. This process, photosynthesis, is a feature of plant life. Since these plant-like flagellates are independent of any other life for their food supply, it is likely that they evolved early in the Earth's history. Most other protozoa, however, depend upon other animals, plants or micro-organisms for their food; for example, many protozoa eat micro-organisms such as bacteria, algae or other protozoa.

The parasitic protozoa depend upon other animals for both food and shelter. Several of these parasites are of great medical and veterinary importance because they cause a number of dangerous diseases. In man, for example, the protozoon *Plasmodium* is responsible for malaria. This disease is still common, particularly in the tropics where it is spread from person to person by 40 species of *Anopheles* mosquitoes. When a mosquito bites a person to obtain a meal of blood, the malarial parasites are injected into the blood stream of the unsuspecting victim, where they invade the liver and later the red blood cells. Uninfected mosquitoes obtain the parasites from the blood of an infected person. The parasites apparently cause no harm to the mosquito, but reproduce sexually, resulting in the presence of large numbers of infective parasites in the saliva of the insect.

In Africa the protozoan parasite *Trypanosoma* causes sleeping sickness. It too is spread by a blood-sucking insect – the tsetse fly. The parasite spends much of its life in the blood stream of the victim, but eventually invades the nervous system and produces the characteristic symptom of the disease, drowsiness. A closely-related disease, Chagas' disease, in South America is also caused by a species of *Trypanosoma*. However, in Chagas' disease the parasites commonly enter the victim through the eyes from the droppings of a bed bug, the insect responsible for carrying it from person to person. Other diseases caused by protozoa include amœbic dysentry.

However, there are more than 80,000 known species of protozoa, and probably three time as many to be discovered, and only a few cause disease.

Many protozoa are useful to man. For example, some fossil protozoa enable geologists to identify rocks likely to bear oil – and it is the remains of countless millions of fossil protozoa from which oil deposits developed. Ciliated protozoa are known to play an important role in sewage-treatment processes, where they remove harmful bacteria by feeding upon them.

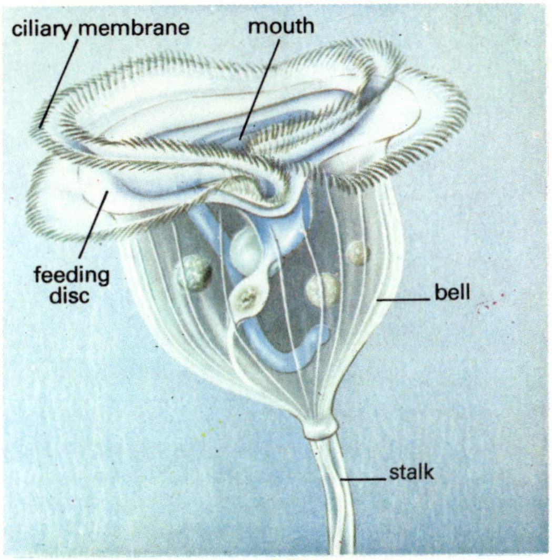

Left: Vorticella, *a ciliate like* Stentor, *shows how complex a single-celled organism can be. Its bell is supported by a contractile stalk and surrounded by a double circle of cilia on the feeding disc. Movements of the ciliary membrane cause a whirlpool or vortex of water that sweeps food into the mouth. At the slightest disturbance, the stalk coils up like a spring, pulling down the quickly closed bell.*

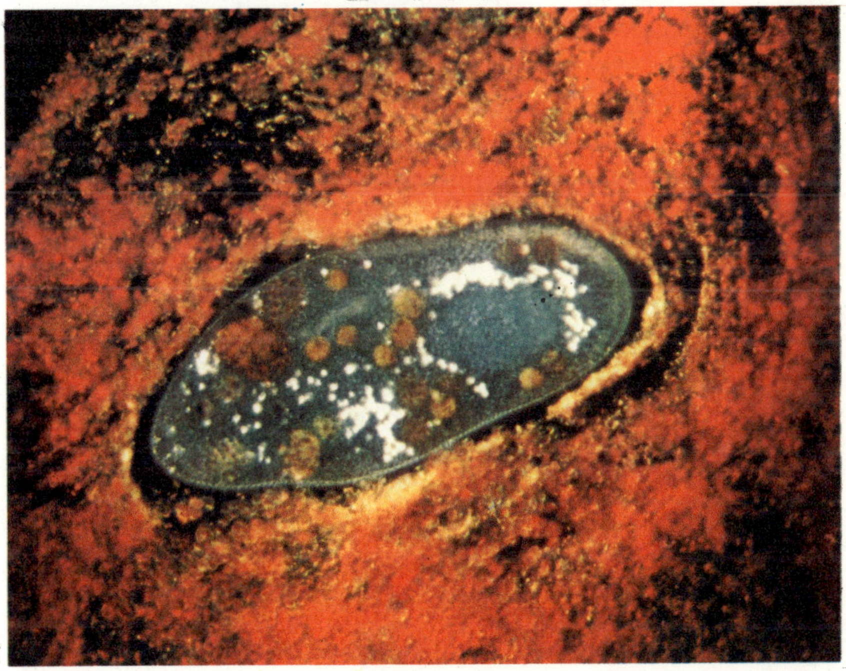

Above: *A single* Paramecium *is seen here in a mass of yeast that has been coloured red. Ciliates like this are fast swimmers; they are covered with rows of cilia that beat in a perfectly synchronised rhythm.*

Simple Water Animals

Sponges are simple animals which live attached to some solid object, such as a rock, in either salt or fresh water. They feed by extracting minute forms of life from the water, which is drawn through a large number of small holes on the surface of the sponge into a central cavity, from which it is expelled through one or more larger apertures. As the water passes through the wall of the sponge, the food particles are extracted and absorbed.

There are about 2,500 species of sponges, ranging in height from 3 millimetres (1/8 inch) to 1 metre (3 feet 4 inches). Most of them live in the sea, some at considerable depths. One common type is the yellow to yellowish-green 'bread-crumb' sponge, which has numerous large openings on its surface. This type of sponge usually forms a crust growing over rocks and the bases of sea-weeds on the lower shore. Many other sponges form encrusting outgrowths, and occur in a wide range of colours.

The familiar bath sponges belong to a group known as horny sponges because their skeletons are made of horny fibres. They live in warm waters, mainly in the Mediterranean and Caribbean seas. Divers, operating mostly from boats, collect the sponges, dry them in the hot sun, and wash them before selling them.

Cœlenterates are also simple animals living in water, mostly in the sea. They include hydroids, jellyfish and corals. All

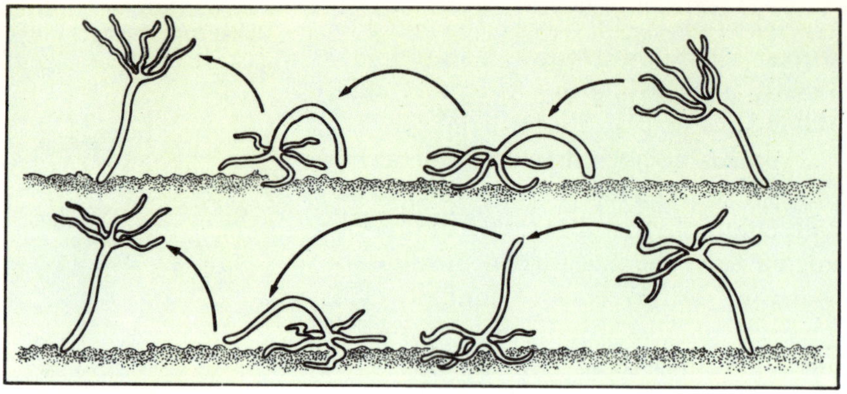

Above: Hydra *can move by somersaulting from base to tentacles. They do this for rapid locomotion.*

Above: *The plumose sea anemone,* Metridium senile, *has many colour varieties. This is a coral-pink form.*

Below: *An ovum produced by a medusa of* Obelia *grows into a swimming larva, which later settles down in polyp form to bud off new medusae.*

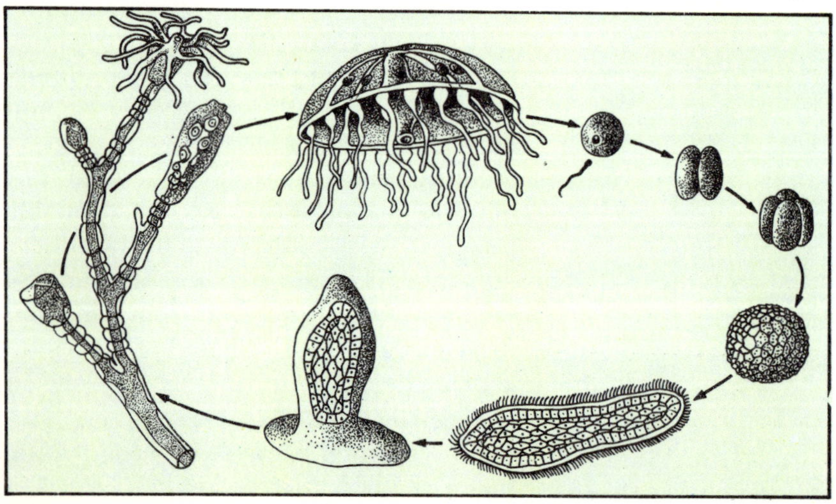

cœlenterates are built on a circular plan, with a central mouth which forms the only entrance to the very short gut. Generally, the mouth is surrounded by numerous tentacles which are armed with *nematocysts* (thread-cells), some kinds of which inject powerful poison into the prey, which is thus paralysed.

This basic cœlenterate plan is modified in some groups, but the simplest cœlenterate – the freshwater hydra – serves to illustrate the basic cœlenterate features. Small water-fleas and other animals are trapped by the tentacles and passed through the mouth. The remains of the meal after digestion are passed out through the same opening. The hydra reproduces by budding off a new hydra, and also by a normal sexual process involving eggs and sperms. It moves by bending over, attaching its tentacles near the base, which then releases its hold and loops over to a new point of attachment.

Many marine relatives of hydra form colonies consisting of several or many individuals joined together by a common living tube, which is itself attached to rock or weed. These are called *hydroids.* Many of them resemble plants in general appearance, and were once thought to be so. Some release a small, circular, swimming stage called a *medusa.* Medusae resemble jellyfish, to which they are quite closely related. They travel long distances in the sea.

Some colonial animals called *siphonophores* related to hydroids and their medusae form floating colonies in which there are up to five kinds of individuals. One kind forms a float, supporting the others in the water, while other members of the floating colony serve to sting the prey, to digest it, or to reproduce the next generation. A well-known example is the Portuguese-man-of-war, which has a very painful sting.

Another kind of cœlenterate found in the open sea is the jellyfish. Like other cœlenterates, jellyfish are built on a circular plan, the mouth being attached at the end of a tube which hangs down from the centre of the underside of the animal. Some in Arctic waters grow up to 2 metres (6½ feet) across, with tentacles up to 20 metres (65 feet) long, but most are much smaller. Some jellyfish give nasty stings, the shock of which might cause drowning, while the related 'sea-wasps' of the waters of eastern Australia have a sting which itself can be fatal.

Above: *These sea anemones,* Sagartia elegans, *are found low down on the shore, under boulders and in caves.*

The remainder of the cœlenterates

Left: *The Portuguese man o' war,* Physalia, *can be up to 40 centimetres (15¾ inches) long. Its trailing tentacles extend deep into the water carrying sting cells which can immobilise fishes. Swimmers should avoid* Physalia.

are collectively called *anthozoans* (literally, 'flower-animals'). The best known are the sea-anemones. A sea-anemone resembles a large, chunky hydra with many tentacles, but differs for example in having the gut partitioned into chambers by vertical sheets of tissue. Reproduction is usually by means of sperms and eggs, although some species produce buds from the base.

The related corals resemble anemones closely, differing most obviously in having a rigid base made of calcium carbonate which serves as a skeleton. The coral individual withdraws within the folds of the base when disturbed. Most corals grow in colonies. These are sometimes very large in tropical seas and form coral reefs.

Some anthozoans form large branching fan-shaped colonies called sea-fans (the

Above: *A gorgonian coral polyp retreats into its home. Corals feed at night; they avoid bright light and will 'close up' in this way when disturbed. Each polyp is an individual member of a colony.*

gorgonians and antipatharians). Each branch of the sea-fan supports innumerable tiny anemone-like polyps or individuals. The whole fan – which tends to grow across the prevailing ocean currents – traps any passing prey animals with great efficiency.

An unusual form is known as dead-man's-fingers. The colony consists of a broad, jelly-like skeleton that supports numerous polyp individuals, which spread their tentacles to trap passing prey. The lobed appearance of the colony, and its pink to whitish-pink colour, account for its macabre common name.

Ctenophores (comb-jellies) are mostly delicate transparent animals found swimming actively in the sea. They too are built on a circular plan. A form common around many coasts and often to be seen stranded in rock-pools is the sea-gooseberry, the size and shape of a gooseberry. It has eight rows of minute flapping 'comb-plates' on its outer surface which propel it through the water. Two long tentacles armed with sticky (but not stinging) cells catch the prey, young fish and similar-sized creatures. When prey is caught the whole animal twirls round so that the mouth is able to engulf the prey. Unlike cœlenterates, comb-jellies have an anus through which the digested remains are passed out. The sea-gooseberry forms an important item in the diet of herrings.

Various Kinds of Worms

The name 'worm' is often used for several different kinds of animals. All these worms have a head and a tail end, and a left and a right side, a kind of arrangement known as *bilateral symmetry*; but the three groups of worms we are dealing with here – platyhelminths, nematodes and nemertines – differ internally from one another.

Platyhelminths are more commonly called *flatworms,* and as that name suggests they are flat creatures. A flatworm has a muscular body wall enclosing a spongy tissue surrounding the internal organs. In most species there is a single opening to the gut which serves both as mouth and anus. The vast majority of species are *hermaphrodite,* which means that both male and female reproductive organs are present in each individual. There are four classes: *turbellarians*, which are mainly free-living, and three classes which are solely parasitic – two types of *trematodes* (flukes) and *cestodes* (tapeworms).

Turbellarians range in size from microscopic up to 500 millimetres (20 inches) long. Most are aquatic species, living on the beds of ponds or streams or on the sea shore. Many of the larger forms are land-living, and are found mainly on the floor of tropical and subtropical forests, and occasionally in moist conditions in temperate regions.

Land turbellarians are carnivores, but aquatic forms are scavengers which feed on dead and decaying animals. They may also attack and eat living creatures even larger than themselves.

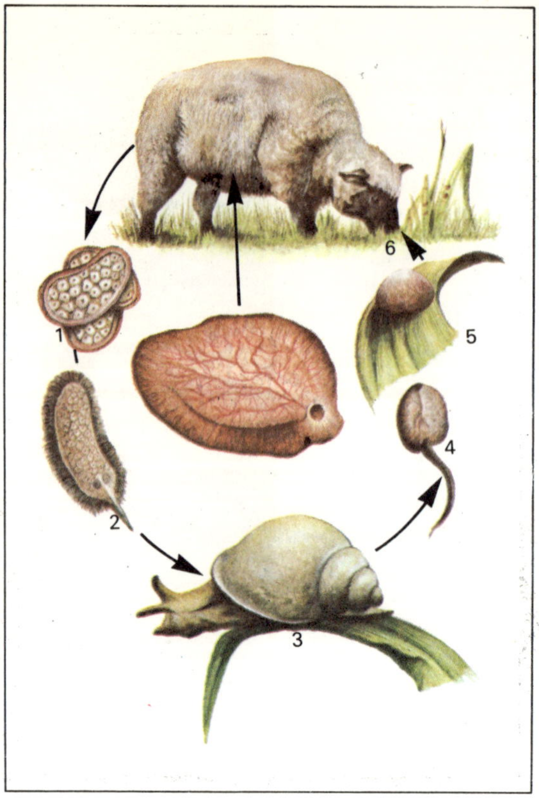

Above: *An adult liver fluke in a sheep's liver lays eggs (1) that develop into a swimming embryo (2). This travels until it finds a snail,* Limnaea pereger *(3), where it lives for a while, undergoing two transformations. A swimming larva (4) then leaves the snail, becomes a cyst (5) on the grass and, when eaten by a sheep (6), develops into another liver fluke.*

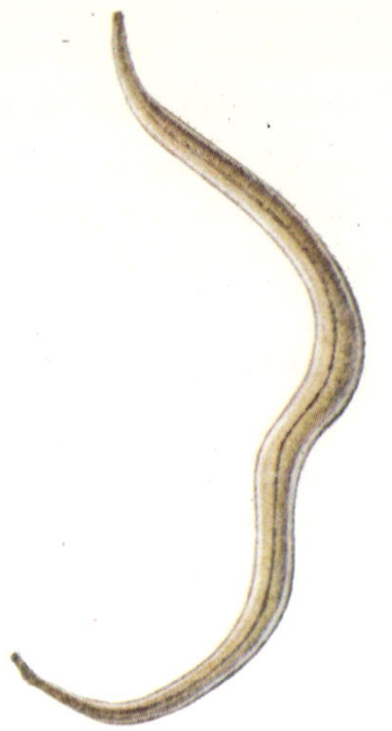

Above: *Nematodes are numerous in soil and water. Some are parasitic, like this* Ascaris *which lives in the gut of vertebrates. It causes damage by attaching the hooks on its head to the gut wall and sucking blood. A female can lay 200,000 eggs a day.*

Below: *The polyclad flatworm has a quite different way of life. It glides along the sea floor feeding on whatever tiny creatures it can find.*

Flatworms are among the most primitive animals to develop a central nervous system; in one group, called planarians, there is a concentration of nervous tissue at the front end, where simple eyes and sensory cells are located.

Trematodes (Monogenea) are flukes which live on only one host. They may be *ectoparasites* (external parasites) for many live on the skin and fins of fishes. But some are found on the gills of fishes and tadpoles, and one on the eye of the hippopotamus. Others are *endoparasites* (internal parasites) which are found in amphibians and reptiles.

Trematodes (Digenea) are the other class of flukes. They have complex life-cycles which involve one or more intermediate hosts, and have larval stages specially adapted to these hosts. The adults are found mainly in vertebrates, including man. These worms are endoparasites, occurring in many regions of the body, especially the gut.

The Chinese liver fluke is a good example of a complex life cycle, with man as the final host and freshwater snails and fish as first and second intermediate hosts respectively. Many flukes cause debilitation in their hosts and some are dangerous. One such parasitic fluke causes bilharziasis, a severe disease common to man in tropical areas. The larval flukes are carried in the bloodstream and normally end up in the small blood vessels of the intestine or the bladder.

Nematodes are usually called roundworms. They are the most numerous of multicellular animals, and they live in a wide variety of habitats. It has been estimated that a typical farm field contains many millions of terrestrial nematodes. Many nematodes are free-living. Some live in close association with other animals, while others are parasitic and live in or on a variety of hosts, including plants, wild and domestic animals, and man. These parasitic forms are of considerable agricultural and medical importance.

Most of the members of this group look very similar, and identification and classification are difficult. The general shape of a nematode is that of a cylinder tapering at both ends. This shape is maintained by a flexible cuticle or outer sheath composed of several layers. The main body muscles are arranged along the length of the body. The main body cavity is filled with fluid, this acts as a hydrostatic skeleton. In combination, the flexible cuticle, the longitudinal muscles and the hydrostatic skeleton enable roundworms to move by controlled thrashing and flexing movements. The sexes are usually separate, with males smaller than females. Free-living nematodes are usually less than one millimetre (four hundredths of an inch) in length but parasitic forms can reach up to several metres. Nematodes normally moult four times during their life history.

Above: *The deep-water ribbon-worm,* Nemertea pelagonemertea, *belongs to a family containing both very small and very large species. It has a long extensible tubular proboscis that it can shoot out rapidly to catch prey or disconcert enemies.*

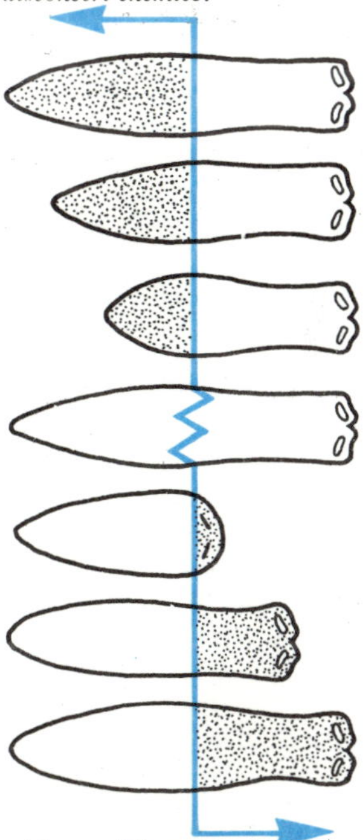

Above: *Planarians have remarkable powers of regeneration. While most animals with some regenerative ability can produce a new tail or even a stunted limb, a planarian can even grow a new head. If a planarian is cut in half, each half will grow the missing part, and there will be two planarians. In times of food shortage, planarians slowly shrink until conditions improve.* Left: *Bootlace worm,* Lineus longissimus, *is a very long ribbon-worm.*

Some free-living roundworms are carnivores; others are herbivores. Many of them feed by piercing the food with a *stylet* (spear) which can be protruded through the mouth. Some roundworms also have teeth. The roundworm sucks the contents of cells, which have been pierced, into the gut, where enzymes begin the process of digestion. This sucking mode of feeding may damage plant roots. Nematodes have a whole range of life styles, from free-living with direct development, through ectoparasitism to endoparasitism, some with intermediate hosts. Parasites include the hookworms, which feed on the host's blood by biting into the gut wall.

Nemertines are usually known as ribbon worms. Most of them live in shallow sea water, but some dwell in fresh water and a few live on land. They are unsegmented, soft-bodied creatures, and many of them reach surprising lengths. Bootlace worms from the North Sea commonly reach 5 metres (16 feet), while one specimen was more than 44 metres (144 feet) in length.

Ribbon worms are also known as *proboscis worms* because they have a large muscular tube which they can eject to pierce, poison and entangle prey. This retractable proboscis is normally sheathed in a space just above the gut. When handled, nemertines may break in pieces, and some of the fragments may then regenerate into new worms.

The Segmented Worms

The segmented worms belong to the phylum Annelida. An annelid has a soft body, divided into segments or compartments which give it a 'ringed' appearance. The body cavity is filled with fluid. At the front end many annelids have several segments modified to form a distinct head; this contains the mouth, brain, and sensory structures – which include eyes.

There are three main classes of annelids: *polychaetes,* which are mainly sea or beach dwellers, and include ragworms and lugworms; *oligochaetes,* which live on land or in fresh water, and include the familiar earthworms; and *hirudineans,* commonly known as leeches.

The name 'polychaetes' means 'many bristles', and these seashore worms carry bundles of stiff, hair-like structures on each segment. Although these worms are not often seen, they are common, and some of them can be more than 1 metre (3¼ feet) long; however, the usual size of a ragworm, one of the more familiar types, is 50–100 millimetres (2–4 inches).

There are two main groups, which have distinct life styles. The first is the errant or free-moving group, and includes the ragworms; the second is the sedentary group, in which the worms live in temporary or permanent burrows or tubes; the lugworms form the typical example.

The free-moving forms are active, but usually remain well hidden, crawling under rocks and seaweed or burrowing into the sand. The sense organs, such as the eyes, sensory tentacles and palps, are well-developed, and are suited to the active and often predatory habits of the worms. Movement is beautifully coordinated. Propulsion for swimming or crawling is provided by a pair of paddle-like *parapodia* (appendages) borne on the side of each body segment.

Above: *This large terebellid worm,* Amphitrite johnstoni, *normally lives in a burrow in the sand with only its tangle of tentacles protruding. It has bristles (*chaetae*) on its body that help it to grip the sides of its burrow.* Below: *The luminous* Chaetopterus, *builds a U-shaped burrow lined with a tough parchment-like secretion. It stays in this tube, waving the paddles at the rear end of its body to cause a current of water to enter at the head end. A bag of mucus secreted by the worm catches particles in the water, and about four times an hour the worm swallows the mucus and starts paddling again while it puts out a new mucous net.*

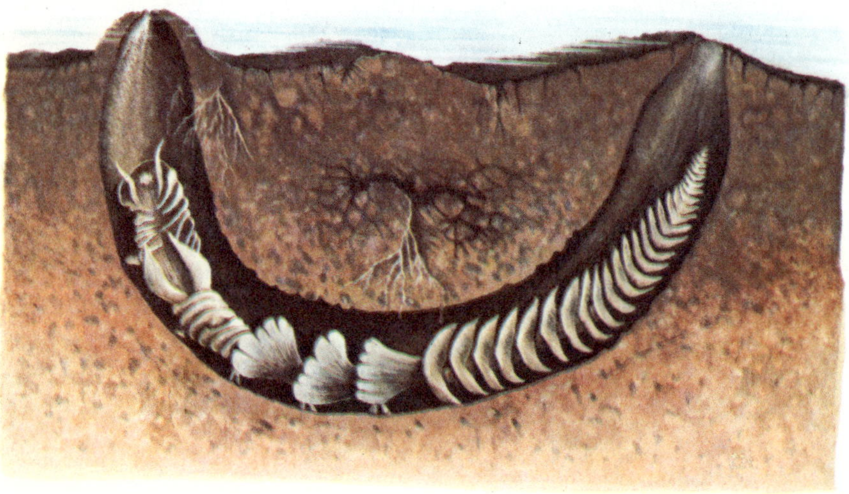

Most active errant polychaetes have a muscular tube or proboscis which can be pushed out through the mouth. Many species have, on the end of the proboscis, powerful jaws and rows of teeth which they use to seize and cut up prey. The food is swallowed by simply retracting the proboscis into the body.

Some species can regenerate parts of the body which are damaged or eaten by predators. Others are able to reproduce asexually by budding, but males and females are usually separate in errant polychaetes.

Sedentary polychaetes, such as the serpulids, construct permanent dwelling tubes of lime, while others, such as the sand masons, cement together grains of sand and small stones to form tubes.

The name 'oligochaetes' means 'few bristles', which is what the earthworms have – each segment of those apparently smooth and shining bodies has some small, hard bristles on it. Some species can develop to a considerable length, the record being an African giant earthworm found in South Africa, which measured 6·5 metres (21 feet) when fully extended.

Earthworms have an invaluable habit of making burrows by swallowing soil. Some species then deposit this soil as a cast on the surface, much to the annoyance of gardeners with fine lawns. Other species, including the common earthworm, drag leaves and other material deep into their burrows for food. These species swallow only a small quantity of soil, which is used in the gizzard for grinding up the food. Only small casts are produced by these worms, and they are often deposited below the surface. These burrowing habits of earthworms improve the texture of the soil by increasing ventilation and drainage, and adding to the organic content of the soil. It has been estimated that from 1·2 tonnes per hectare (3 tons per acre) to 15 tonnes per hectare (37 tons per acre) of 'cast' soil may be deposited at the surface in a year.

Ways in which earthworms have adapted to their underground existence are shown in the reduction of the anterior sense organs, and the reduced lateral bristles. These small bundles can still be protruded, but are used only to gain purchase in the burrow.

Earthworms are all *hermaphrodite,* which means that both male and female sex organs are present in each individual. Worms protrude from their burrows at night and, wrapped together in a tube of mucus, exchange sperms. Eggs are laid in a cocoon, which is produced by the wide,

Right: *The peacock or fan worm,* Sabella pavonina, *lives in a parchment tube. One worm here has its crown of tentacles extended in the feeding position, and the other is retracted into its tube with just the tip of a tentacle visible.* Below: *Leeches are freshwater annelids which feed by sucking blood from various other animals. They attach themselves by means of a suction disc while the sharp stylets, shown below, pierce the host's skin until blood or body fluid flows into the leech's mouth. When it has finished feeding, it lets go and swims away with an undulating movement of its muscular body. Leeches also walk along the bottom in a looping fashion, attaching by suckers at front and rear and moving them forward in turn.*

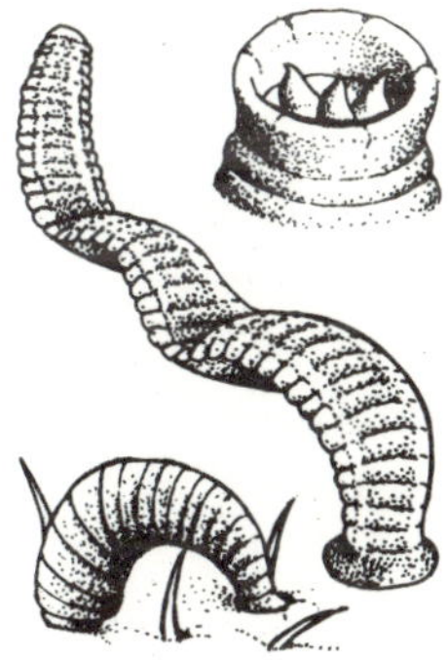

Below: *Longitudinal muscle contractions press the worm against its burrow. Circular muscle contractions in turn extend it forward.*

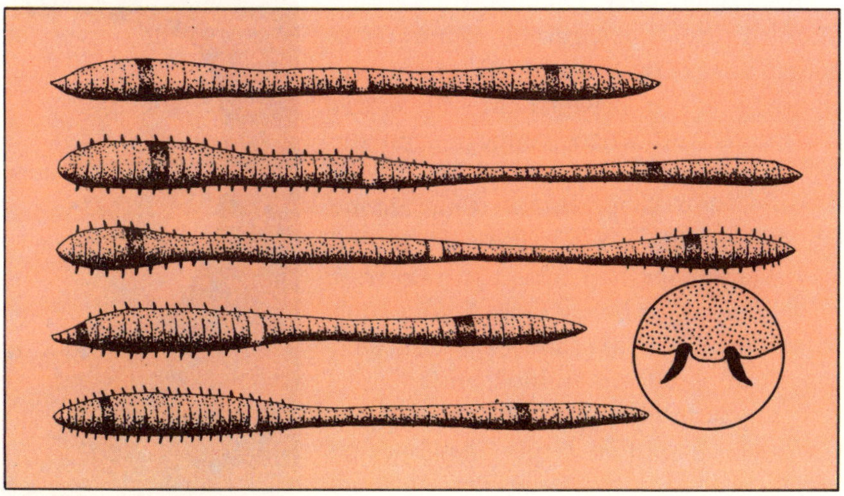

smooth part of an earthworm known as the saddle.

Leeches – the Hirudinea – are notorious for being bloodsuckers, and in tropical areas tend to lurk on damp vegetation waiting for a suitable host such as man or domestic animals to brush past. In Western Europe and North America leeches are aquatic. A common example is the horse leech. Most leeches have front and rear suckers, the front sucker normally surrounding the mouth, and move by looping along, using the suckers for attachment.

The medicinal leech (blood-letting was once thought to have wide-ranging powers of healing) has three muscular jaws which protrude through the mouth and, like miniature circular saws, make a 'Y' shaped cut in the skin. So that the host does not brush off the feeding leech, an anæsthetic is pumped into the wound. To prevent clotting an anticoagulant is also forced into the wound, and blood can then be sucked freely into the gut of the leech.

During the 1800s people used to keep leeches in lidded jars half filled with water, for use as barometers. If the leeches rose to the surface, this was a sign of bad weather. The leeches were probably responding to a drop in barometric pressure, and a consequent drop in the concentration of oxygen in the water.

Moss Animals

If you look closely at objects on the shore such as seaweed, driftwood or shells, or at plants and pieces of wood pulled out of a pond, you will often see a patchy, brownish coating. These patches may be well-organised colonies of bryozoans, which means 'moss animals'. Together with the Entoprocta they used to be known as polyzoans.

There are about 4,000 known species. Some of the colonies they form may reach 1 metre (3¼ feet) in length, but most individual bryozoans are less than 0·5 millimetres (1/50 inch) across; some are as wide as 2 millimetres (1/12 inch).

The main distinguishing character of bryozoans, and of other related groups such as phoronids and lampshells (brachiopods), is the food-catching organ around the mouth, consisting of a circle of tentacles known as a *lophophore*.

The anus of the bryozoans opens in the vicinity of the mouth, but outside the lophophore. The entoprocts look superficially like bryozoans but the anus opens within the range of tentacles. The entoprocts do not have the true body cavity of bryozoans, tissue filling the space between the gut and the outer wall. The gut in bryozoans is a compact 'U' shape, hanging in the body cavity.

To see how moss animals got their common name, use a pocket magnifying glass to examine a colony kept under water, when you will see the feathered tentacles of units in the bryozoan colony, which give a moss-like appearance. The open circles of tentacles form a pattern across the surface of the colony. Cilia (small hairs) borne on the tentacles create a water current which draws all manner of tiny food organisms such as rotifers, diatoms, ciliate and flagellate Protozoa and unicellular algae into the mouth. Through the thin walls of the tentacles oxygen is taken into the body and carbon dioxide is lost.

In times of danger the tentacles are withdrawn into a pocket enclosed by the box-like structures which form the skeleton of the bryozoan colony. These boxes are variable in shape, but consist of an external layer of leathery cuticle, perhaps with a strengthening of calcium carbonate. The compartments are somewhat like the cells of a honeycomb, and most of them have a circle of feeding tentacles.

Right: Pentapora foliacea *forms large seaweed-like colonies of double-layered plates. It is found from the Bristol Channel to the Mediterranean. There are always many other creatures ready to settle on the rough surface the colony provides. In many bryozoans, some individuals are modified into pincer-like forms, ready to remove any potential settlers, thus keeping the colony clean.*

Even after the tentacles have been withdrawn the animal is still vulnerable to attack or desiccation (drying out) unless the opening can be closed. Bryozoans have a number of closing structures, which include a pleated collar around the neck of the tentacles which unfolds and closes over after the tentacles have been withdrawn. Another structure is an *operculum* or hinged lid.

Bryozoans make colonies by asexual budding; only one species is solitary. The colonies are clustered and may encrust on stones, shells or seaweed. In calm water conditions and where support from the base is not so important, rigid fan-shaped colonies may be produced. One colony which looks like a piece of dead seaweed and is often washed up on the shore is called *Flustra,* or hornwrack. A small colony 100 millimetres (4 inches) high would consist of about one million units.

Tentacle crowns of freshwater bryozoans are often larger than marine species. In marine colonies certain units

Right: *Two sea mats. The tufted one is* Scrupocellaria scruposa, *a free-standing colony. The crusty growth on the seaweed is another type,* Electra pilosa, *which forms a colony one-polyp-cell deep, and spreads over surfaces such as the bladderwrack here.*
Below: *This shallow-water brachiopod waves its pair of tentacled arms within its shell to trap food particles; these arms show its relationship to bryozoans.*

Right: *The encrusting cheilostome* Escharella immersa *forms small circular crusts on hard surfaces, like shells and stones, down to a depth of 50 metres (165 feet) in cold seas. It is known to live off the Norwegian coast and near Scotland; this specimen was photographed at Tresco, Scilly Isles, quite far south in its range. The name cheilostome means that the opening of the cell has a cover.*

take on special functions. Some have no ring of tentacles and cannot produce sex cells, but are used to hold the colony firmly on the *substrate* (anchoring point). Some units serve as brooding compartments. Developing larvae in brood chambers are often brightly coloured, and can be seen in large patches over the colony. In one group of bryozoans the cells from the fertilised egg separate, and up to 100 larvae are derived from one egg.

Most bryozoans are *hermaphrodite,* with both male and female sex organs present in the same unit. The eggs are released from the ovary and remain in the fluid of the body cavity until fertilised by sperm, probably from another unit. In a few species the eggs are released directly into the sea, but most bryozoans brood their young for a few weeks. Young larvae may be held in the neck of the lophophore, or in the special brood chambers. When the young larva has completed its development, it is released from the brood chamber, swims towards the light and may be free-living for several days before settling on a suitable substrate selected by a tuft of sensory hairs. Cells of the larva are then rearranged to form the first unit of the colony. In freshwater species resting stages are produced, consisting of a hollow ball of cells with a dark brown leathery shell. These can overwinter and withstand desiccation.

Moss animals are most abundant in regions of the sea between 0·5 and 200 metres (1½–655 feet) in depth, but they have been found at a depth of 8,300 metres (27,200 feet). Communities of other kinds of animals develop around and within colonies of bryozoans. Moss animals are often found in association with hydroids, polychaetes and molluscs. Frequently moving through colonies of bryozoans can be found flatworms, nematodes, crustaceans, gastropods, starfish, small sea slugs and sea spiders. These either feed on the bryozoan colony, or use it for protection. Some colonies protect themselves to a certain extent with specialised units, with adapted operculum lids and muscular developments. These specialised units may be snapping beaks, or whip-like structures which sweep across the colony surface and remove sand and mud particles.

Bryozoans are world-wide in their distribution, due largely to the many millions of years they have existed and to the free-swimming larval stage.

The Molluscs

The phylum of molluscs is one of the largest in the animal kingdom, with 80,000 species, and also one of the most diverse. There is no such thing as a standard mollusc form, and the external appearance of these animals can be confusing when you are trying to classify them.

There is no one feature which is characteristic of all species of molluscs. There are, however, various combinations of characters, and to understand the molluscs it is easiest to consider these, and then the different types, before considering ways of life.

The essential mollusc features include a body divided into a head/foot with a mouth containing a *radula* or ribbon of teeth; and a *visceral* (internal organs) mass which in most species is enclosed by a shell. The shell is secreted by the margin of the *mantle,* a membrane attached to the visceral mass. A space, known as the *mantle cavity,* lies between the mantle and the body wall.

The relative significance of these features varies from group to group within the phylum; and while each animal must have its viscera, the head, foot, radula and mantle may each be lost or modified. This enormous diversity of form and function is closely linked to the ability of molluscs to penetrate and exploit almost all habitats – reefs, mudflats, rivers, lakes, deserts, forests and even underground.

The phylum may be divided into seven sub-groups or classes – the Monoplacophora, Aplacophora, Polyplacophora, Gastropoda, Bivalvia, Scaphopoda and Cephalopoda – which closely reflect differences in the mode of life.

Until the 1950s the Monoplacophora were known only from fossils, and people thought they had been extinct for 500 million years. The specimens which have recently been found have been taken from very deep water. The shell is conical like a limpet, and some of the internal organs and gills are paired. There are no eyes, but there is a radula.

The class Aplacophora consists of small worm-like species, often not recognised as molluscs although they do possess definite molluscan characters, including radular teeth and *ctenida* or elementary gills. These slow-moving animals are carnivores.

The molluscs of the group Polyplacophora are the chitons, or coat-of-mail shells. They are elongated and flattened in shape, with a strong, broad foot. The shell is divided into eight transverse plates, held together by a leathery girdle which overhangs the foot. They are very well adapted for a life spent clinging to the surface of rocks, and when dislodged can protect themselves by rolling up like wood-lice. The head and mouth are at the front and the anus at the rear. The gills are arranged in two long series. The internal organs, such as the digestive, nervous and reproductive systems, are, on the whole, very simple.

Gastropods form the largest group of molluscs, with about 30,000 species. They include the slugs and limpets and freshwater and marine snails, and they vary greatly in size, shape and form. Gastropods have adapted themselves to a wide variety of diets, which makes them able to exploit varying habitats in water and on dry land. The adaptation of certain groups of gastropods to the specific conditions of a given environment has led to various changes in their structure. One

Above: *A variety of shells from cool seas, including grey-top shells, common and flat-sided periwinkles, and a small turret shell. These have been found washed up on the beach after death.*

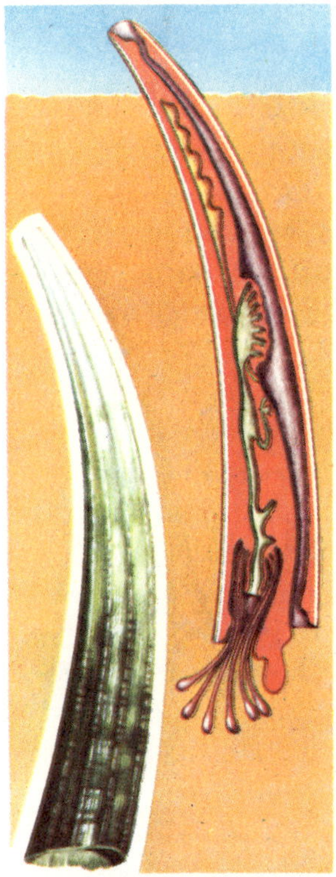

Above: *Tusk shells, made by a scaphopod mollusc. The living scaphopod burrows in the sand with its digging foot, and the small hole at the pointed end of the shell is exposed for respiration.*
Right: *Locomotion (1). The whelk glides on its foot; (2) scallops swim by using shell valves; (3) cockles have a digging foot; cuttlefish (4) and squid (5) use undulating membranes or jet propulsion.*

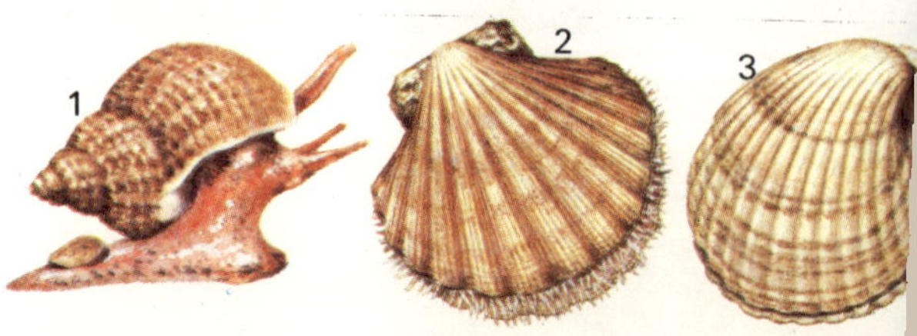

of the most striking of these changes is to be seen in those forms in which the foot has been modified into a swimming organ. Most gastropods have a one-piece univalve shell, secreted by the mantle edge and usually coiled in a right-handed spiral.

Above: Nautilus *is a cephalopod that may have remained virtually unchanged since Paleozoic times.*

In some gastropods, however, such as the slugs, the shell may be much reduced or lost altogether. The class may be divided into three subclasses: the Prosobranchia, marine snails which breathe with gills; the Opisthobranchia, the sea slugs, which have little or no shell or mantle cavity, and the Pulmonata, consisting of land snails and slugs, and freshwater snails, all of which breathe with lungs.

Slugs and land snails have a film of mucus under their single foot. The sole of the foot is covered with *cilia* (fine hair-like structures), and some snails crawl by moving the cilia through the mucus. Most gastropods, however, creep along by means of muscular contractions of the foot, which glides over the mucus. Some marine gastropods either float, or swim by means of side flaps on the mantle.

Above: *The muscular arm of a squid is equipped with rows of suckers. Squids bear two types of arm. There are eight short arms and two long ones with suckers (and sometimes hooks) confined to the tip.*

Bivalves have shells formed in two parts, called valves. These molluscs have no heads or radula; the mantle margins have taken over sensory functions; and the gills, which are enormously developed, assist in feeding. The two-part shell is joined at the mid-line by a hinge which is operated by muscles between the valves.

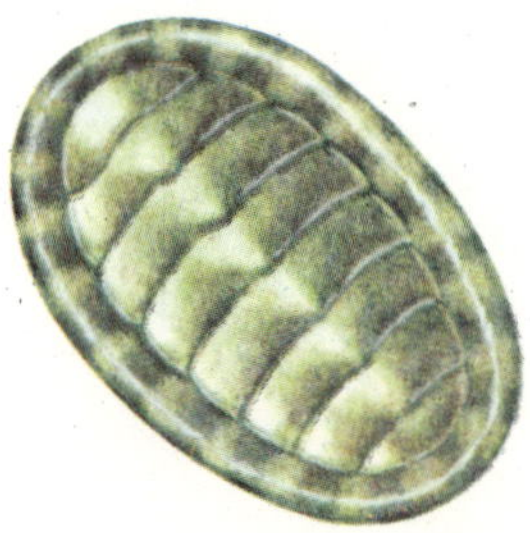

Above: *Chitons have a shell with eight hinged valves. They creep over rocks, scraping algae off as they go. Well-protected when attached to a rock, they can curl up into a ball when detached.*

Many bivalves are sedentary. Some such as mussels attach themselves to rocks by threads; oysters cement themselves to rocks; piddocks or shipworms burrow in rock or wood; while cockles and razor shells burrow in sandy or muddy ground. A few species, such as scallops, are able to move through the water at speed by clapping the valves together to produce a current of water, which propels them backwards.

As their popular name of tusk shell implies, many species of the group Scaphopoda have shells resembling elephant's tusks in shape. They are all marine, and burrow in sand. The shell is hollow from end to end, the broad end which contains the head and foot lying in the sand, while the narrow end projects into the water obliquely. They have no gills, respiration taking place through transverse folds in the lining of the mantle. The head bears several slender retractable tentacles which reach into the sand to pick up food.

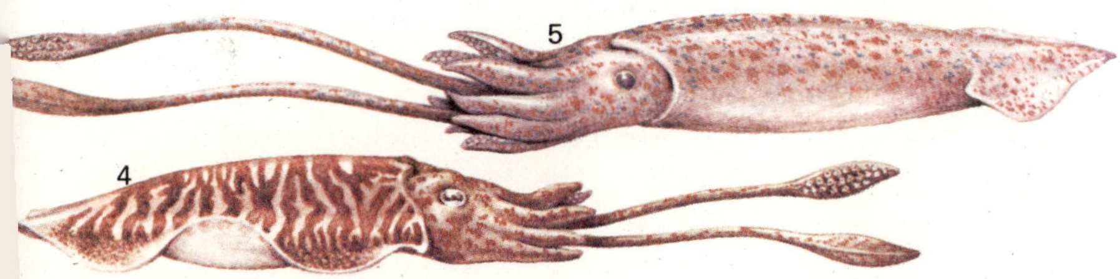

The cephalopods include squids, cuttlefish and octopus. They are the most highly developed and efficient of the invertebrates. They are almost all free-swimming carnivores, often capable of moving very quickly.

The name cephalopod, meaning 'head-foot', is derived from the close union of the head and foot, which has become much subdivided to produce two new types of highly specialised organ. Firstly there is a ring of prehensile tentacles armed with suckers around the head, with the mouth at the centre; and secondly a funnel or siphon has developed from part of the foot which controls the outflow of water from the mantle cavity, producing a kind of jet-propulsion used in swimming.

The eyes and brain of cephalopods are as elaborately developed as those of some vertebrates, and the digestive, respiratory and circulatory systems are much more highly specialised than those of other molluscs. Only the nautilus has an external shell; the other cephalopods either have internal shells – for example cuttlefish and squid – or no shell at all.

Nearly all the cephalopods can eject a globule of ink when in danger. The ink acts as a decoy or smoke screen which enables the animal to swim to safety.

How Molluscs Live

Some molluscs have separate sexes and no accessory sexual organs. They release their eggs and sperm directly into the sea, where fertilisation takes place. It is a method fraught with many dangers; eggs and sperms may be eaten by other animals, or destroyed or separated by adverse temperatures or currents. All these molluscs produce large amounts of eggs and sperm.

Hermaphroditism, the presence of both male and female sexual organs in one individual, is not uncommon among the molluscs. Many sea slugs, land slugs and land and freshwater snails are hermaphrodite. Some molluscs change sex during their lifetime, the most familiar example being the slipper limpet *Crepidula*, which lives in clusters, one on top of another. The larger individuals at the bottom of the pile are all females, the smaller and younger ones at the top are males; often the individuals in the middle of the pile are in the process of changing sex. The cephalopods have separate sexes, and some have complex courtship and mating rituals.

Molluscs deposit many kinds of egg capsules which protect their eggs. Some, including whelks, lay piles of interlocking capsules, while the necklace shells deposit a stiff gelatinous 'collar' with the eggs protected on the inside. Species of the purple sea snail carry their eggs on their raft of air bubbles. A few bivalves lay their eggs in gelatinous capsules, while some others attach them to the substrate with sticky mucus. Cephalopods lay eggs which are relatively large and yolky. Cuttlefish eggs are black, and attached in clusters to the substrate. The octopuses fix their single eggs together in masses, and squids deposit sausage-shaped egg masses attached at one end.

Right: *The courtship of the garden snail begins by both snails moving in a decreasing spiral until they meet. These snails are hermaphrodite, and each shoots a 'love dart' into the other which stimulates mating.*

Below: *The anatomy of a limpet. The body is covered by a limy shell (2) and bears a muscular foot (1) below. It feeds by scraping algae off the rock with its rasp-like tongue or radula (8). This is supported by a stiff cartilaginous rod (7), and as it wears away it is replaced by new growth from behind (5). From the mouth, food passes into the stomach (4) where digestion takes place. The gills lie in the mantle cavity (6) and the other organs are contained in the visceral hump (3).*

The eggs of many land snails are few in number by comparison with other gastropods and often very large. The typical egg-shell is tough and resilient, such as that laid by the common garden snail. Snails and slugs frequently lay their eggs in damp, shaded places or in the soil. Development is quite rapid. Limpets and top shells for example produce free-swimming larvae. Within a few hours the larvae change into shelled larvae, which may remain among the plankton for varying lengths of time before maturing. Some young molluscs remain inside the egg capsule until a shell is formed, having no free-living larval stage. Some species of molluscs bear live young.

Molluscs have many different feeding methods. Chitons and many gastropods use the radula to scrape the ground for algae and other small food particles. Many gastropods are carnivorous, preying upon animals which are alive, dying or decaying. Some groups, such as the cones, are equipped with dart-like teeth, often combined with a poison which paralyses the prey. The sting of some cones has proved fatal to man.

Most bivalves are filter feeders, pumping water through their bodies and filtering out food particles. Some boring species feed upon the material through which they burrow. The cephalopods are all carnivorous, capturing and eating fish, crustaceans, and even on occasions each other.

It is perhaps the most notable feature of this diverse group of animals that its members are found in almost every environment on Earth. They are to be found living on the world's highest mountains, and also on the deepest parts of the ocean floor.

Land snails have many ways of coping with the most demanding environments. One of these is the *epiphragm,* a covering of hardened mucus which forms a seal in the aperture of the shell. When conditions become unfavourable, the snail forms an epiphragm and becomes dormant; in winter this is called *hibernation.* In hot or dry conditions, for example in summer, some snails are able to enter a state known as *aestivation,* which may last for some months. Instances have been recorded of periods of aestivation lasting for many years.

A few land snails live well within the Arctic Circle, and some freshwater species survive severe winter conditions encased in ice. At the edges of the sea live molluscs which like brackish water, and those inhabiting the sea marshes and mangrove swamps. Their territory joins the first shore zone, the *littoral,* between the highest and lowest tide levels. At the top of the littoral zone live the gilled molluscs, surviving in areas where only the sea spray reaches. Next down the shore are those species which spend part of their lives under water, and part uncovered at low tide. One of the most widespread groups of this littoral zone is that of the periwinkles.

Most species of marine molluscs are to be found in the shallow seas of the continental shelves. Here there is light and food for many species. In tropical areas, coral reefs support the highest number of different species of molluscs to be found anywhere. Some molluscs live in the deep oceans, and some, such as many of the squids, live all their lives on or near the surface of the sea.

Below: *Fresh-water burrowing clams are adapted in two ways for reproduction in fast-running water. The small globular species, Sphaeridae, keep their eggs safe in a brood pouch until they have developed into tiny clams. Freshwater 'mussels', like this* Unio, *use freshwater fishes to keep their larvae from being washed down to the sea and at the same time to assist in distribution. In the cycle shown here, sperm cells are released into the water by the male clam (1); they pass into the gills of a female (2); the eggs are fertilised in the gill pouches and develop into larvae, called glochidia (inset right). The glochidia are released into the water (3) and, according to species, attach themselves either to fins (4) or gills (5) of a fish with the sharp hooks of their shells. Here they live as parasites for several weeks until they grow into tiny clams (6) and drop off to burrow in the mud.*

The Starfish Group

Starfishes and their relatives belong in the phylum Echinodermata, a name which means 'spiny-skinned'. Echinoderms are radially symmetrical – like a wheel – and are arranged on a *pentamerous* (five-part) plan. This arrangement is shown very clearly in such forms as starfish, but is less obvious in sea cucumbers.

There are five classes of echinoderms: starfishes; brittlestars; sea-urchins; sea-cucumbers; and sea-lilies and feather-stars. There are about 5,000 species of echinoderms.

Between the spines on the surface of an echinoderm it is often possible to see a large number of pale, soft objects waving about. These objects are called tube feet, and they serve as organs of locomotion. The tube feet are scattered over the entire surface of sea-urchins, but starfish have them mainly on the undersides of the arms. Tube feet are hydraulic in operation, and have their own plumbing system filled with water. This water system is quite complex, and opens to the outside through a perforated plate on the upper surface, called the *madreporite*.

Most tube feet have sucker discs on the end, which can be used to hold on to the surface of rock or sand as the echinoderm moves, or to hold food while it is eating. Some tube feet, especially those near the tips of the 'arms', are long and suckerless, and may be used as sensory organs.

Echinoderms reproduce by the female shedding eggs into the sea, where sperm from the male fertilises them. Most species of echinoderms produce larvae, which are free-swimming. This highly mobile period of development serves to distribute the animals to new habitats.

Starfishes form the class Asteroidea. Most starfishes have an ill-defined central disc, and five radiating arms. However, some species such as the sunstar (*Solaster papposus*) have up to 12 arms, and *Labidiaster* species may have as many as 50. The arms are not always in multiples of five. A starfish has no head, but there is a mouth on the underside of the central disc.

Like other echinoderms, starfishes can extract calcium carbonate (lime) from seawater to build a hard skeleton. This skeleton consists of many calcareous rods embedded just below the skin surface.

Starfishes mainly eat shellfish, such as oysters. A browsing starfish wraps its arms around the two valves (half-shells)

Below: *Brittle-stars (2) feed by sweeping food particles along the underside of the arms to the central mouth by means of their tube feet. They differ from most higher animals in that they have no anus; waste passes out through the mouth.*

Left and below left: *Starfish (1, 3) show the typical echinoderm pattern of five radiating arms. Jointed calcareous plates give the body rigidity, while muscles attached to these plates allow flexibility. Underneath the arms are rows of tube feet.*

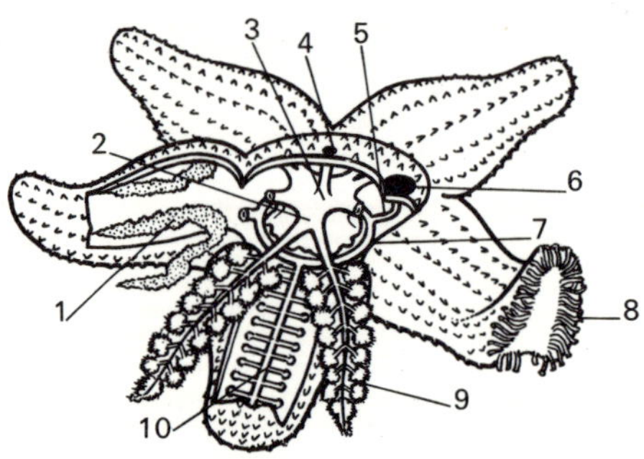

Left: *Anatomy of a starfish.*
1 Gonad or reproductive organ
2 Lower part of stomach
3 Upper part of stomach
4 Anus
5 Stone canal
6 Sieve plate
7 Ring canal
8 Tube feet
9 Digestive gland
10 Radial canal

Left: *Feather stars (5) are usually found clinging onto rocks on the sea bed, but they can swim. The central mouth faces upwards and detritus falling through the water is collected in food grooves on the arms.*

Far left: *Sunstars (4) may have 15 to 50 arms in which the basic structure of the five-armed starfish is repeated. Early crinoids had stems like present-day sea lilies, but in modern feather stars the stem is lost.*

Below: *When disturbed, the cotton spinner produces long, sticky threads from its anus in defence.*

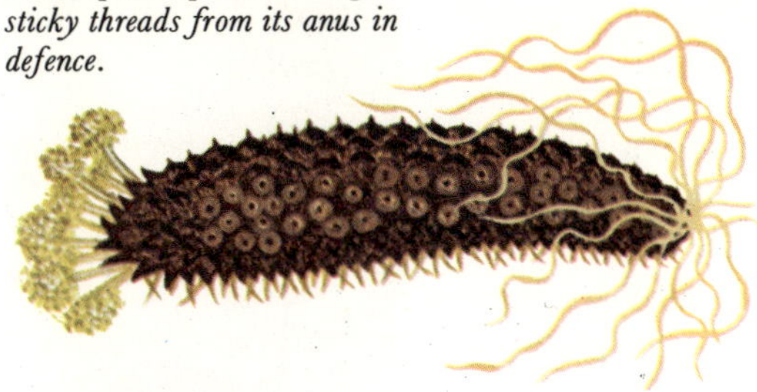

Below: *Sea cucumbers have a leathery skin, in which small calcareous plates (shown) are embedded. These give added protection to the body.*

Left: *Although sea cucumbers have a cylindrical body with mouth and anus at opposite ends, they still show the five-rayed symmetry.*

Above: *The European edible sea urchin forages below high tide mark for shellfish, crustaceans and hydroids in seas from Norway south to Portugal. Sea urchins have a rigid skeleton.*

of an oyster, and grips the valves with the suckers on its hundreds of tube feet. It forces the valves open against the pull of the oyster's own muscles which normally hold the shell closed. Once the soft parts of the oyster are exposed, the starfish pushes out its stomach through its mouth and engulfs the oyster with it. When the oyster is digested, the starfish retracts the stomach with its contents.

Brittlestars form the class Ophiuroidea. Underwater photographs show that these creatures live often in dense concentrations on the sea bed. They have small, well-defined central discs. They do not use their tube feet for locomotion like starfishes but employ them mainly for helping the movement of food particles towards the mouth. The long arms are flexible, and are made of a series of sections loosely jointed together, so that a portion can readily be detached if an enemy seizes it – hence the name 'brittlestars'. Portions broken off can be regenerated. To move about, a brittlestar moves its arms in a wave-like way, the leading arm pulling the animal forward.

Sea-urchins are in the class Echinoidea. A sea-urchin has an internal 'shell' called a *test*, made up of interlocking plates. It is located just below the surface of the animal, which is covered with many spines. The spines articulate by means of ball-and-socket joints, and are moved by tiny muscles around the base. Any predator is faced with a battery of sharp spines.

Between the spines are *pedicellariae*, numerous pincer-like structures, which are opened and closed by muscles which are under automatic nervous control. If any small object alights on the test the pedicellariae snap shut to remove it. In this way the sea-urchin can keep clear of debris which settle between the spines, or of other organisms which might try to establish colonies. Starfishes have similar protective organs. Sea-urchins use their tube feet for locomotion, but many species also use their spines rather like stilts.

Sea-cucumbers form the class Holothuroidea. They are elongated like the cucumbers from which they take their name, and cylindrical rather than star-shaped. The mouth is at one end. The tough, leathery body-wall contains small skeletal plates or *ossicles* embedded in it, and also a substance, holothurin, which is poisonous to fishes but not to man.

Sea-lilies and featherstars form the class Crinoidea. They represent the oldest class of echinoderms, fossil crinoids of almost 500 million years ago having been found. A typical sea-lily has a stalk, the bottom of which is anchored to a rock or firmly embedded in mud on the sea-floor. The mouth is in an inverted cup at the top of the stalk and is surrounded by five branch-like arms, each of which may divide to form up to 10 sub-branches. The arms are used to gather food particles and guide them into the mouth. There are tube feet on the arms, but they are used only for respiration. Featherstars are similar, but have little or no stalk, and can move about. Some featherstars live in shallow, offshore waters, but the sea-lilies are mostly deep water forms.

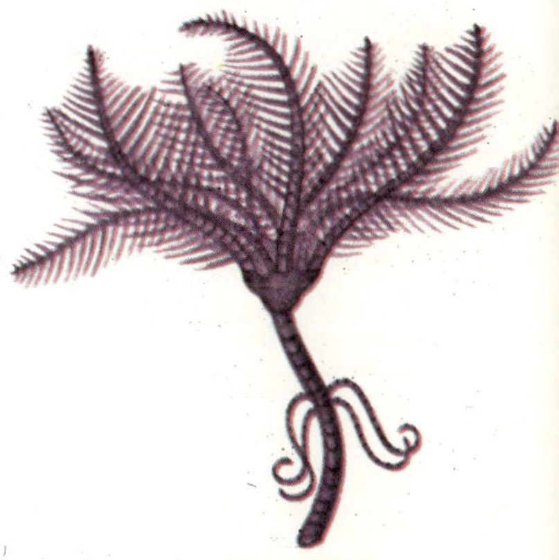

Above: *Sea lilies provide some of the earliest echinoderm fossils, but forms living today are widely distributed in deep waters. The anus is on a flexible spire and can be directed away from the mouth.*

Sea-squirts and Relatives

The most highly-developed forms of life are the vertebrates, the animals with backbones, described on pages 170–229. The Vertebrata form a subphylum of a larger group of animals, the phylum Chordata. Chordates are animals which have some form of *notochord* or stiffening rod in their bodies. There are some links between the Chordata and the Hemichordata, a small group of animals which at one time used to be considered as related to the Chordata but are now regarded as a phylum on their own.

On these pages we describe the hemichordates and all the chordates except the vertebrates.

The features linking the hemichordates with the chordates are details of internal structure and the development of larvae, and for this reason they are not obvious. The group is divided into two main classes, the Enteropneusta and the Pterobranchia, and may include the now-extinct graptolites.

The Enteropneusta or acorn worms burrow in seashore mud. They have an acorn-like proboscis, a fleshy collar and a long trunk with gill pores near the front end. They range in length from about 10 to 500 millimetres (3/8 to 20 inches), although the giant Brazilian species *Balanoglossus gigas* grows to 1·8 metres (6 feet) in length. Typical of the class is *Saccoglossus kowalevskii,* a species occurring on both sides of the North Atlantic. The soft cylindrical body has no appendages and is covered with mucus. The mouth is placed underneath.

Some species of acorn worms live among the holdfasts of seaweeds or under stones, but those belonging to the genera *Balanoglossus* and *Saccoglossus* inhabit solitary burrows in mud or sand. The burrow of one well-studied species, *Balanoglossus clavigerus,* often has more than one opening, and a coil of fæces identifies the exit. The sand or mud of the burrow wall is held together by mucus.

The eggs of some species (for example *Balanoglossus clavigerus*) hatch as small,

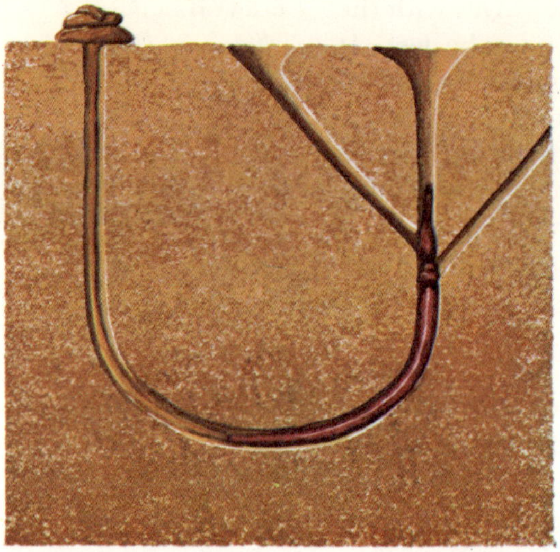

Left and below: *Acorn worms live in muddy sand (left). They have a series of paired openings (a) behind the collar (b) which are comparable with gill slits.*

transparent planktonic larvae. Each larva bears numerous bands of cilia (hair-like organs) on the body surface, and the beating of these cilia propels the larva through the water. After approximately four to five weeks of growth the larva assumes a worm-like appearance and lives on the sea bottom. Other species of acorn worms hatch as more mature larvae, which swim for only a day or so before developing into the worm-shaped stage.

The Pterobranchia have no common name. They are a small group of rarely-seen creatures. Most live in deep water in the southern hemisphere. They live inside tubes which they secrete, and are normally clustered together in colonies. They feed by filtering particles from the surrounding water by means of *lophophores,* arms bearing large fringed tentacles.

Besides the vertebrates, there are two relatively simple groups in the phylum Chordata – the Urochordata and the Cephalochordata. These two groups are described as *protochordates,* because they represent a possible stage in the evolution of vertebrates from earlier invertebrate forms of life. At some stage in its life, each chordate has a notochord, which performs the same supporting function as the more highly developed backbone in vertebrates. Above the notochord lies a tubular nerve cord, and below it is the gut.

The subphylum Urochordata contains three classes, of which the most important is Ascidiacea, the sea-squirts or tunicates. Some of these animals live solitary lives, others form colonies. Each has a sac-like

Below: Rhabopleura, *a colonial type of hemichordate often found on dead corals. They are less than 2 millimetres (1/12 inch) long, and have two tentacled arms but no gill slits.*

Above and right: *The colonial sea star squirt,* Botryllus schlosseri *(above) and the solitary form (right) share the characteristic habit of contracting when disturbed to eject a stream of water. Their larvae show some chordate characteristics, including notochord and gills.*

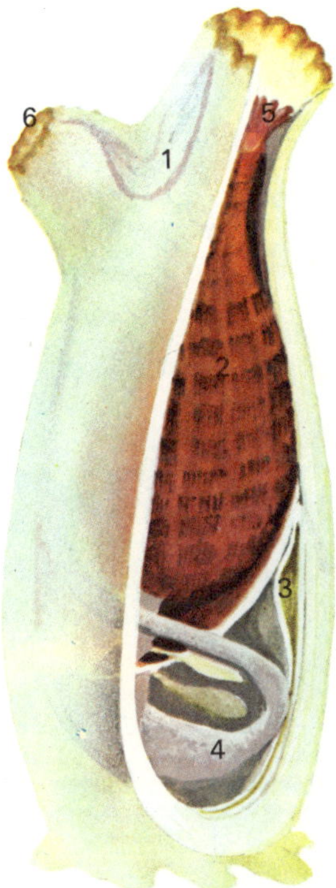

Above: *Sea squirt anatomy. Water enters through the mouth (5), is strained through gills (2) and is expelled through the other hole (6). It also has a heart (3), stomach (4) and nerve ganglion (1).*

body encased in a gelatinous teat. Much of each individual consists of the enormous pharynx which is penetrated by gill slits. Small food particles and plankton are drawn through the body with water, filtered off by cilia, and caught up in a mucous thread that carries them to the gut.

Sea-squirts are sedentary animals, living on rock surfaces, breakwaters, and other seashore objects. They acquired their popular name because some species when exposed at low tide squirt jets of water from their body-openings if disturbed.

Ascidians are hermaphrodites – that is, of both sexes at once. Many species shed their sperms and eggs into the sea, and the sperms from one individual fertilise the eggs of another. In some species the eggs are retained within the body and are then fertilised by sperms carried in by water during feeding. Each egg hatches as a tadpole-shaped, free-swimming larva. The larva has a prominent tail, a sucker in front of the mouth, and body organs that include a well-developed notochord (confined to the tail), and a nerve cord. The larva soon settles on to a suitable surface and changes into the adult form; at this time the notochord and nerve cord disappear, along with some of the other organs.

The class Thaliacea contains salps and fire-bodies. Salps are transparent, free-swimming barrel-shaped animals with conspicuous hoops of muscles. Repeated contractions of these muscles drive water through the hollow body, and propel the salp forward in short jerks. In the species *Salpa zonaria* two forms occur. The first is an asexual form that buds off chains of small individuals. These chains soon break away and develop reproductive organs; they are now in the second form. Each salp is a hermaphrodite, but the eggs and sperms of individuals ripen at different times, and the eggs of one salp are fertilised by the sperms from another. Each fertilised egg develops into the first form, repeating the alternating life cycle.

Fire-bodies (*Pyrosoma* species) form colonies in which the individual animals are embedded in the wall of a stiff, jelly-like cylinder, one end of which is open. Water, containing food and oxygen, is drawn in by each member of the colony, expelled into the common cavity of the cylinder, and leaves through the open end, propelling the colony along. Each fire-body has two luminescent organs, and colonies produce a spectacular whitish glow when disturbed.

The class Larvacea is of special interest because the mature adults retain the form of the tadpole-like larvae of other urochordates. The miniature 'tadpoles' live in transparent and extremely delicate 'houses', made from a substance they secrete. Movement of the animal's body sets up water currents through the 'house', which contains extremely fine filters for removing food particles.

The subphylum Cephalochordata consists of the lancelets. There is one genus, *Branchiostoma,* with about 24 species. Lancelets are elongated, semi-transparent animals pointed at both ends. The nerve cord and notochord extend the whole length of the body. For most of its life a lancelet lives half-buried in gravel or sand, with the head end pointing upwards. There are males and females, and sperms and eggs are shed into the sea.

The Arthropods

The most numerous phylum of animals in terms of species is the Arthropoda, which includes such varied creatures as insects, spiders and crustaceans, and myriapods – creatures with many legs. The myriapods comprise centipedes, millipedes, pauropods, and symphylans. Formerly included among the Arthropoda were the velvet worms, now placed in a phylum (Onychophora) on their own.

There are three main characteristics common to all arthropods: their bodies are segmented; their legs are jointed – the name 'arthropod' comes from two Greek words meaning 'joint' and 'foot'; and the body is cased in a hard external covering, or *exoskeleton* to give it its scientific name. In addition, arthropods have an ill-defined blood circulation system, the vital organs being bathed in blood. There is a well-developed central nervous system.

The young grow in stages: the exoskeleton is like a suit of armour, and to expand the arthropod has to moult, or shed its old exoskeleton, revealing a new, larger one which is flexible at first and hardens by a chemical process called *tanning*.

So much for the likenesses. Otherwise the arthropods vary so greatly that in recent years scientists have begun to question whether they in fact shared a common ancestor. Study of fossil remains suggests that they did not, and that they have evolved from different origins. The features that are alike are more probably the result of the animals adapting to the similar conditions in which they lived.

Altogether, arthropods form about 80 per cent. of all living animals, and they live in every possible habitat. The three biggest groups are dealt with in the following chapters: crustaceans on pages 154–155; spiders and their allies on pages 156–157; and insects on pages 158–169. Five other groups of arthropods are described on this page.

Centipedes

Centipedes belong to the class Chilopoda. Their popular name comes from two Latin words meaning 'hundred legs', but most of them have only about 30–40 legs. However, each centipede has a pair of legs on each segment of its body, and the longer the centipede the more segments, and therefore the more legs. Some centipedes have as few as 14 legs, but in southern Europe there is one species,

Below: *On land the most numerous arthropods are the insects, which make up three-quarters of all known species of animals. They are also the only invertebrates to have developed flight; flying insects were already on land when vertebrates were only beginning to emerge from the swamps. The ladybird (1) is a beetle, with large hind wings covered by hard protective fore-wings. Arachnids include mites (2) and ticks (3) as well as spiders. They are a successful and numerous group of arthropods, having eight legs as opposed to the insects' six legs, and mouth parts quite different from other arthropods. Millipedes (4) have two pairs of legs on each body segment; they are scavenging vegetarians and there are about 6,500 different species throughout the world. Centipedes (5) are carnivorous; they have venom in their 'jaws' (which are modified legs), which is used to paralyse prey such as earthworms and insects. There are about 1,500 species of centipedes.*

Below: *The majority of marine arthropods are crustaceans. Copepods (2) are very small; they live in fresh and salt water and, in the sea, form part of the plankton on which other marine creatures feed. Some copepods, like the fish louse, are parasitic. Shrimps (1) are closely related to lobsters and hermit crabs. They have narrowly compressed bodies, long antennae and pincers to grasp their food. Other narrow-bodied crustaceans are sand-hoppers (3). The primitive king-crab or horseshoe crab (5) is not a crab or a crustacean. It is most closely related to arachnids and has existed virtually unchanged for at least 175 million years. It can swim as well as walk, and the young resemble the now-extinct trilobites. Sea spiders (4) are not really spiders; they hatch with only three pairs of legs, but develop two or three more pairs. The gut extends into the legs. They prey on soft-bodied animals and are found from the seashore down to 13,500 metres (44,300 feet).*

Himantarum gabrielis, which can have up to 354 legs when fully grown.

Centipedes are carnivores, preying on insects, earthworms, and other small animals which they kill with their poison claws. There are 1,500 species altogether.

Millipedes

The name 'millipede' means 'a thousand legs' – but none of these active little animals has nearly so many! They look somewhat like centipedes, but they are really very different, and they are placed in a separate class, Diplopoda. The 6,500 species are all vegetarians, living mostly on decaying matter. They have two pairs of legs on each segment, so they have more legs than centipedes of the same length. The longest known millipedes are about 300 millimetres (12 inches) long, with up to 750 legs.

Symphyla

These little animals live under stones and logs, feeding on decaying leaf mould. Their bodies are white, they have no eyes, and only about 100 species have so far been identified. They made themselves known to man because they attack the roots of live plants, damaging crops.

Pauropods

The animals in the class Pauropoda also live in damp, rotting vegetation, on which they feed. There are about 60 species known, each 1 millimetre (3/64 inch) or less in length. They are colourless animals with secretive habits.

Velvet worms

Velvet worms are unlike arthropods because they do not have a hard exoskeleton, and they look a bit like caterpillars. They live in damp surroundings, because their unprotected bodies dry out very quickly. They belong to the phylum Onychophora, and they are often known by the name of the best-known genus, *Peripatus*.

At one time scientists used to regard *Peripatus* as a 'missing link' in the evolution of arthropods from the more primitive annelids (see pages 140–141). They are now regarded as an enigmatic group of uncertain affinities. Possessing characters which can be interpreted as typical of both annelids and arthropods, the group has been the subject of much argument. Whatever its status, it is not now regarded as a direct link between the two groups, but as an evolutionary offshoot.

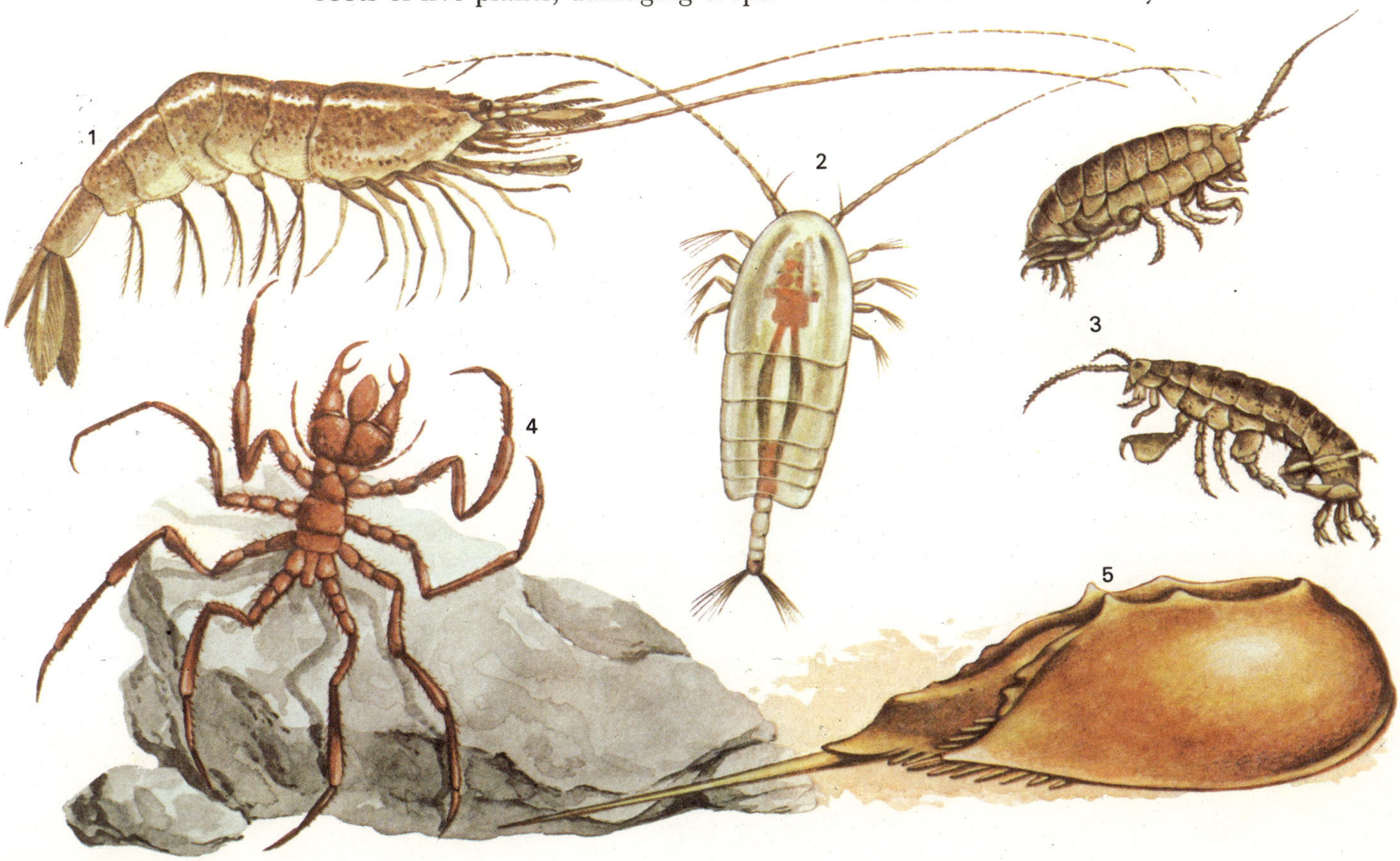

Crustaceans

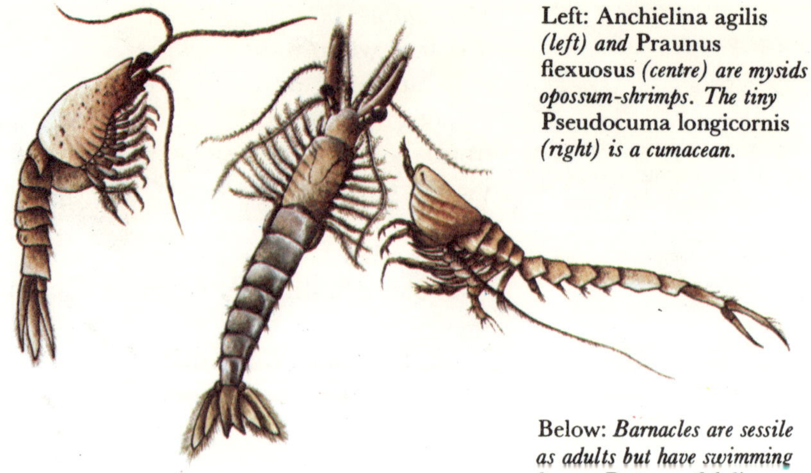

Left: Anchielina agilis *(left) and* Praunus flexuosus *(centre) are mysids or opossum-shrimps. The tiny* Pseudocuma longicornis *(right) is a cumacean.*

Crustaceans include such familiar and diverse animals as crabs, shrimps, barnacles, water-fleas and woodlice. The class Crustacea is a division of the phylum Arthropoda (see pages 152–153), and contains about 30,000 species.

Most crustaceans live either in the sea or in fresh water, though a few are land-dwellers, and some are parasites on other animals. The size of different adult crustaceans varies greatly, ranging from about 0·25 millimetres (1/100 inch) for the smallest water-fleas (genus *Alonella*) to the giant spider crab (*Macrocheira kaempferi*) of the seas off Japan, which has been known to have a claw-to-claw span of 3·6 metres (12 feet).

At some stage during their life-cycle all crustaceans have segmented bodies and limbs and an external skeleton. They also have two pairs of *antennae* (feelers). Most crustaceans breathe by means of gills, but some have no gills and absorb oxygen through their skins. The number of limbs varies greatly, and so do their form and purpose. Most species of crustaceans have males and females and reproduce sexually, but barnacles are hermaphrodite (containing both sexes in the same individual). Some crustaceans hatch from eggs as miniature adults, but most go through a series of larval stages. Crustaceans are divided into eight subclasses.

Horseshoe shrimps form the subclass Cephalocarida. They are small, blind colourless animals, with many-segmented bodies, and live in the Caribbean Sea and the waters off Japan and North America.

Water-fleas and their relatives form the subclass Branchiopoda. There are four orders, varying greatly in form; the main thing they have in common is that they breathe through gills on their feet, which are leaf-like in shape. Most branchiopods live in fresh water.

Mussel or *seed shrimps* form the subclass Ostracoda. The body and limbs of these tiny creatures (many are only 0·25 millimetres long) are completely encased in a bivalve shell. Many live in the sea, and others in fresh water habitats of all kinds.

Moustache shrimps form the little-known subclass Mystacocarida, which was discovered only in 1943. Only three species

Below: *Barnacles are sessile as adults but have swimming larvae.* Bottom: *fish lice are parasitic on freshwater fish.*

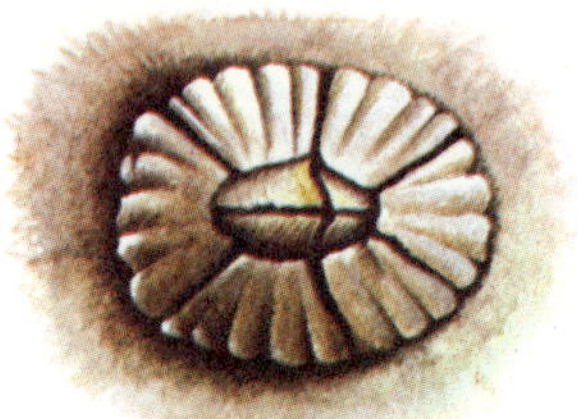

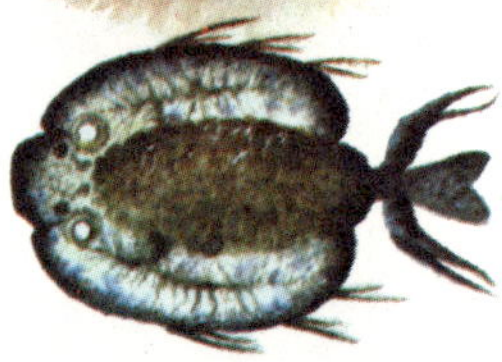

Below: *The larger crustacea are mainly marine. Examples are the hermit crab (3), the edible crab (1) and lobster (4). The robber crab adult (2) lives on land. The mitten crab (5) lives in estuaries and rivers, but the crayfish (7) is found only in freshwater. The fairy shrimp (6) is found in temporary pools.*

are known. The animals have cylindrical segmented bodies, with a pair of claws at the rear end. They live in the water-filled spaces between grains of sand on the seashore.

Copepods form the subclass Copepoda. The name means 'oar-footed', and describes the shape of their swimming limbs. There are more than 4,500 species, varying greatly in form. Many are parasitic and highly modified in form, not looking like arthropods at all. The majority of copepods are free-swimming, tiny animals living in the sea, where they form a major component of the plankton – those species of minute plants and animals which float in the open sea.

Fish lice, in the small subclass Branchiura, are all parasites, and as their popular name implies they live mainly on fishes. A typical fish louse has a broad, flat carapace.

Barnacles and their close relatives form the sub-class Cirripedia. The name Cirripedia comes from two Latin words meaning 'curly-footed', because barnacles have fine, feathery, curly limbs. There are five orders of Cirripedia. Four of them consist mostly of small parasitic animals, some of which bore into the shells of other invertebrates. The best-known cirripedes are the barnacles, in the order Thoracica. Adult barnacles attach themselves to some support, which they never leave. Sometimes the support is an animal, such as a whale, but mostly barnacles grow on rocks, the hulls of ships, or other underwater objects. The stalked goose barnacle

Above: *Crabs are crustaceans in which the abdomen is curled under the rigid protective carapace. They have claws for both defence and hunting.*

Above: *This water flea,* Leptodora, *is found in large lakes. It swims with its enlarged antennae.*

Above: *The copepod called* Cyclops *uses its antennae for swimming. This female has two egg-masses attached to her body, like saddle-bags.*

Above: *A terrestrial crustacean, the woodlouse,* Oniscus, *scavenges under stones and loose bark. It still uses gills for breathing but lives entirely on land.*

(*Lepas anatifera*) is frequently found attached to driftwood.

Lobsters, crabs and *shrimps,* with their variant forms, comprise the subclass Malacostraca, which contains all the largest and most familiar crustaceans, and also the most species – more than 18,000. There are five superorders and many orders in this subclass. Phyllocarida are small marine creatures, and mostly scavengers. Mantis shrimps form the superorder Hoplocarida, fierce little hunters which live in burrows on the sea-bottom. *Squilla mantis* has one limb developed as a 'jack-knife' which it uses for catching prey. Syncarida are shrimp-like animals which live in fresh water and are primitive compared with other malacostracans.

The superorder Peracarida contains several thousand species, including opossum shrimps, hooded shrimps, and woodlice. Females have a brood-pouch in which they incubate their young. Opossum shrimps (order Mysidacea) live in pools low down on the seashore. Woodlice or pillbugs (Isopoda) live in damp places on land, from the hottest climates to the coldest. Also among the isopods are the wood-boring crustaceans, such as the gribble (*Limnoria lignorum*) which do severe damage to submerged timber.

The order Decapoda includes all the largest crustaceans. As the name implies, these animals have ten legs, though they are not always obvious. Zoologists divide them into two groups: Natantia, or swimmers – shrimps and prawns; and Reptantia, or crawlers – more than 6,000 species, including crayfishes, lobsters, crabs, scampi and their relatives. Most species live in the sea, but there are many which live in fresh water, including river crabs and river prawns. Some crabs spend at least part of their lives on land, and the coconut or robber crab (*Birgus latro*) climbs cliffs and trees. It derives its popular name from the belief that it climbs coconut palms to cut down the nuts, which it then eats. Robber crabs have been known to grow more than 450 millimetres (18 inches) in length. Crabs and lobsters are noted for having stout pincers on one or more pairs of limbs.

The Arachnids

About 70,000 species of animals belong to the class Arachnida, an important division of the phylum Arthropoda. The most familiar are the spiders, scorpions, mites and ticks. The arachnids are related to two other classes, Merostomata (horseshoe crabs), and Pycnogonida (sea spiders). They all have pincer-like feeding appendages, called *chelicerata*.

Typically arachnids have a two-part body, consisting of a combined head and thorax, called a *prosoma*, and an abdomen, called an *opisthosoma*. There are four pairs of walking legs, and there is a pair of small limbs located just behind the mouth which are called *pedipalps*, and are developed either to seize prey, as in scorpions, or to act as sensory organs, as in spiders.

Fossils show that arachnids and horseshoe crabs have been around for a very long time – the horseshoe crabs for about 500 million years. Only five species of horseshoe crabs now survive, living on the Atlantic coast of North America and in the seas of south-eastern Asia. Sea spiders are thought to have existed for perhaps 400 million years. They live in all parts of the oceans.

There are 11 orders of arachnids, comprising scorpions; false scorpions; sun spiders; palpigrades; whip scorpions; tartarides; amblypygids; spiders; ricinuleids; harvestmen; and mites and ticks.

Scorpions form the order Scorpiones. A scorpion's hindmost abdominal segments are constricted to form a 'tail', which ends in a sting. The animal uses its sting for defence and for immobilising its prey. In some species the venom produced is harmless to man; in others it can be painful and even fatal. However, scorpions generally sting only if provoked.

Above: *Many spiders, like this jumping species, have good vision and actively pursue their prey.*

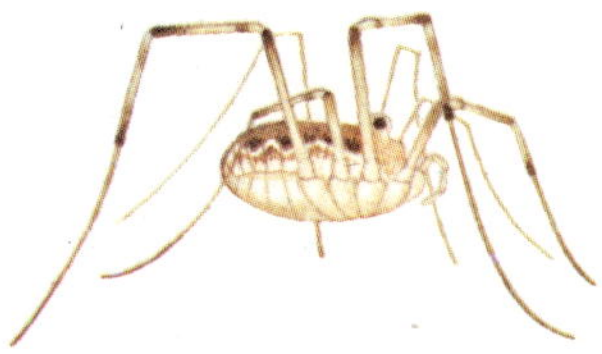

Above: *Harvestmen have no venom and spin no webs. They feed on small invertebrates.*

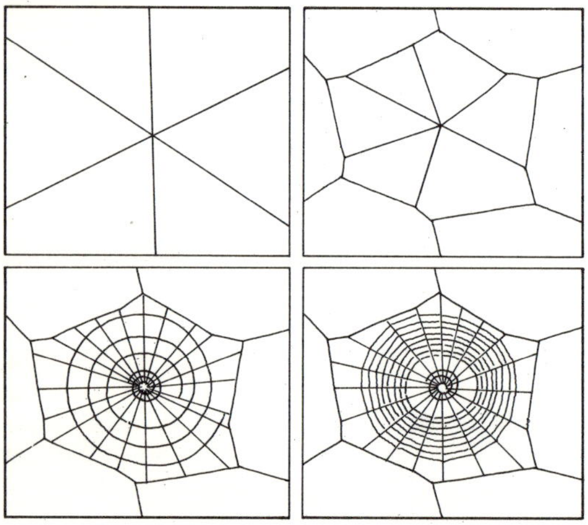

Above: *The water spider,* Argyroneta, *spins a dome-shaped nest among submerged vegetation. Her hairy body can trap a film of air, and she carries cargo after cargo of air down into her nest until it contains a large bubble in which she can live.* Left: *The most familiar type of spider's web is the orb web. The spider first sets up a radial framework of firm dry cords on which she can walk without sticking. The sticky elastic spiral is then neatly laid onto its firm base.*

Scorpions feed mainly on other arthropods, catching and crunching their prey in their pedipalps.

False scorpions form the order Pseudoscorpiones. They are small arachnids, mostly less than 5 millimetres (3/8 inch) long. They have large, pincer-like pedipalps; their general body form resembles that of true scorpions, but they have no sting. False scorpions are carnivores, and their prey includes small insects and larvae, and other small arthropods.

Sun spiders, also called camel spiders and wind scorpions, form the order Solifugae. They are characterised by their massive chelicerae. They live in desert regions in most parts of the world, but not in Australia. They are active hunters.

Palpigrades, in the order Palpigradi, are sometimes called micro-whip scorpions. They are very small, eyeless arachnids which live in damp soil and decaying vegetation in warm climates.

Whip scorpions, forming the order Uropygi, may be as long as 80 millimetres (3 inches). They have a long, whip-like 'tail' at the rear of the body. They live in warm climates and hunt by night.

Tartarides form the order Schizomida;

Right: *Horseshoe crabs are primitive armoured creatures whose ancestors lived 175 million years ago.* Below: *Mites are arachnids with sucking mouth-parts.*

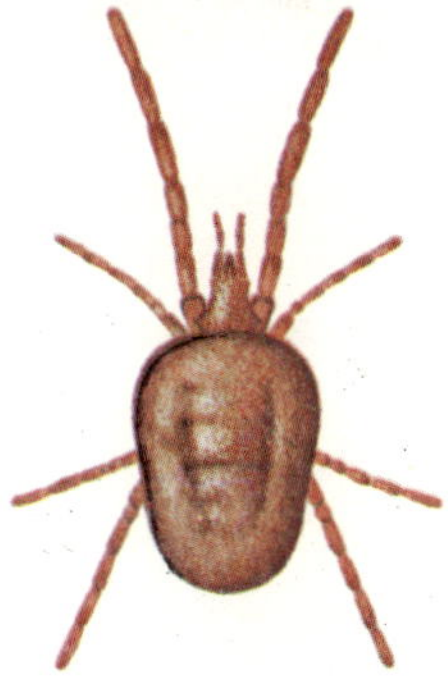

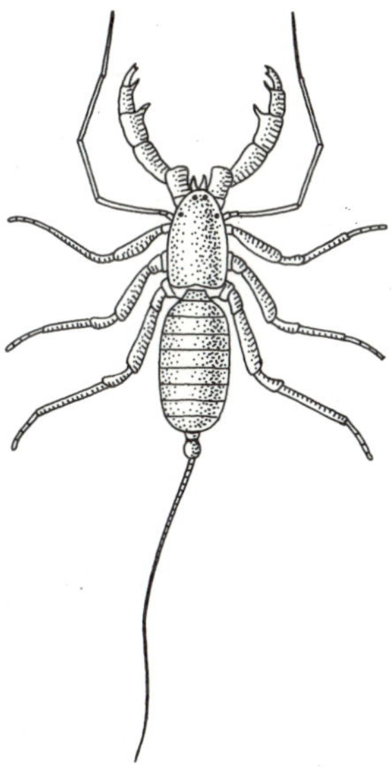

Above: *Whip-scorpions do not have a sting in their tail; they use their large strong pincers to crush spiders and insects.* Below: *Scorpions are amongst the most frightening of arachnids, armed with a venomous sting at the end of a flexible tail.*

they were formerly in the same order as the whip scorpions, Uropygi. They are small animals, and there are about 50 species, living in tropical regions.

Amblypygids are also called whip spiders or tail-less whip scorpions, and form the order Amblypygi. Like whip scorpions they are nocturnal animals living in warm climates, and range in size from 4 to 45 millimetres ($\frac{1}{8}$–$1\frac{3}{4}$ inches). They live under logs and stones or in caves.

Spiders form the largest of the orders, Araneae, with more than 40,000 known species. The body size can range from 0·5 millimetre ($\frac{1}{50}$ of an inch) up to 100 millimetres (4 inches), and the span including the legs may be twice as great. The front region of a spider's body is covered by a horny shield bearing eyes, usually eight in number. The chelicerae have movable, hook-like fangs connected to poison glands, which they use to paralyse their prey. Only one family of spiders has no poison glands. The poison of most species acts only on small arthropods and other prey. Only a few species possess poison dangerous to man. Even the notorious black widow (*Lactrodectus* species), is rarely fatal.

Spiders moult several times before reaching maturity. Young spiders travel to new habitats by 'ballooning'. A spider climbs to the tip of a twig or a blade of grass, and spins gossamer threads which catch the breeze.

Although a great many spiders catch their prey by spinning webs, there are lots of species that do not use silk in this way. The water spider (*Argyroneta aquatica*) uses its silk to make a diving bell, which it fills with bubbles of air. It feeds on tiny pond animals and even small fish. Wolf spiders chase their prey, jumping spiders leap on their victims after a slow, careful stalk, while trapdoor spiders live in underground burrows with the entrances sealed by hinged flaps. When prey comes within range the trap shoots open and the spider darts out and back in a flash.

Ricinuleids, order Ricinulei, are small arachnids with hard, thick outer casings. They are found among fallen leaves in equatorial forests and in caves.

Harvestmen, also known as daddy-long-legs (a name sometimes given to craneflies), form the order Opiliones. Most harvestmen have very long, slender legs, and their order name comes from the Latin *opilio,* a shepherd – it is thought because in some countries shepherds used stilts. Harvestmen are mainly carnivorous and hunt by night.

Mites and ticks form the order Acari. They are small animals, mostly with a body length of less than 1 millimetre ($\frac{1}{50}$ of an inch), although some ticks are more than 10 times this size. There are more than 15,000 species, some of which live in water. Many of them are parasites on plants or animals, and they are of considerable economic importance to man because of the damage they do to crops and animals.

Below: *Young scorpions, though fully formed at birth, cling to their mother's back under the protection of her sting until they are ready to face the world alone.*

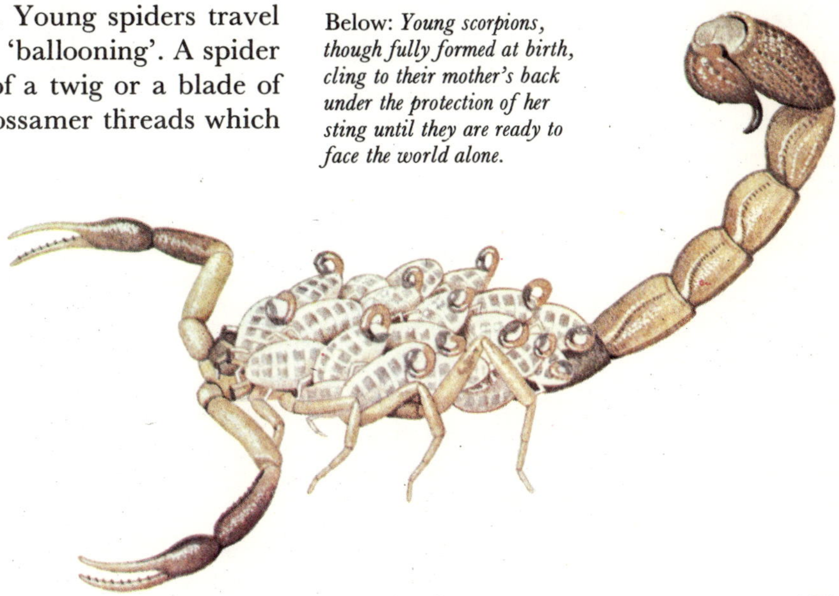

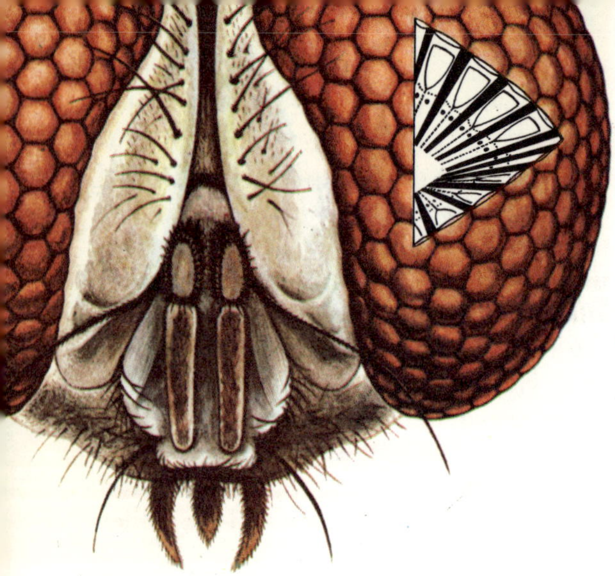

Left: *Each unit of the compound eye of an insect points in a slightly different direction, giving a wide field of vision.*

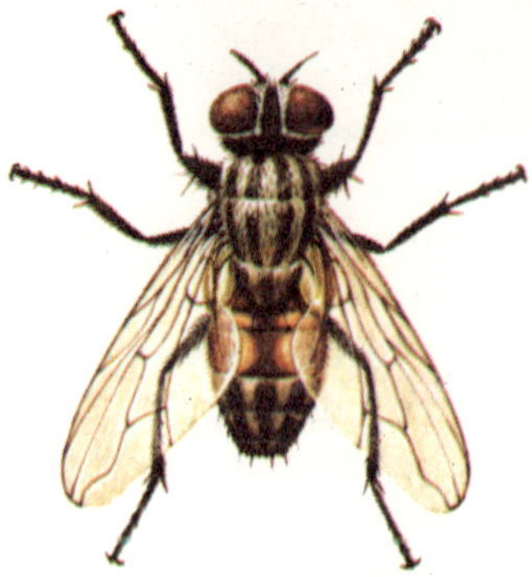

Above: *House flies feed on anything which can be digested and sucked up in liquid form. Particles stick to their legs, carrying contamination.*

The World of Insects

Insects are among the most abundant forms of animal life in every part of the world except the open sea. More than a million different species have been described, and many people believe that this is only a fraction of the number that remains to be discovered. With so many kinds it is difficult to make a simple definition of insects, but it is true to say that, like crabs and other crustaceans, they wear their skeletons outside their segmented bodies.

The body of an insect is divided into three parts; a head, a thorax and an abdomen. The thorax has three pairs of jointed legs attached to it as well as – in most species – two pairs of wings. Insects can grow only by periodically moulting (shedding their outer skeletons) and growing new and larger skeletons.

Many things have helped in the success of insects, but the most important is this outer skeleton. Although restricting their growth periods, it protects them from their greatest peril, the danger of drying up. It has enabled them to leave the moist surroundings inhabited by their ancestors and colonise almost every habitat.

Because most insects can fly at some time in their lives, they can spread rapidly into new areas, and escape from regions which have become uninhabitable through climatic or other changes. Survival is also helped by their small size. Individually they need little food, and little space to live in. They keep going when food is scarce, and often multiply enormously as soon as it is plentiful once more.

Looking at insects as a whole, their varied habits must form a major factor in their success story. A single species may be restricted in its range, but as a group, insects are found in almost every ecological niche – from mountains over 6,000 metres (19,000 feet) above sea-level to the shore line between the tides; from ponds and rivers to deep inside caves in permanent darkness.

There is hardly any plant or animal substance that is not the food of some insect. As a result they play an extremely important part in the energy turnover in nature. Without them, the decay and breakdown of dead plants and animals would occur much more slowly, and the Earth would be a much less fertile planet than it is today.

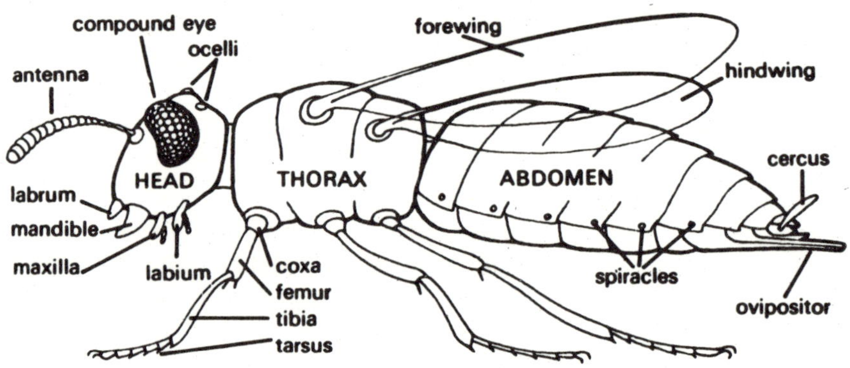

Above: *A generalised wasp-type insect showing the body parts. From a basically segmented body, the head bears appendages (modified legs) which form its mouth-parts. The three fused segments of the thorax each have a pair of legs. The abdomen is segmented, allowing flexibility, but has no appendages. Each segment of the abdomen has a pair of spiracles through which air enters the network of breathing tubes, the tracheae, inside the body. Sense organs include the antennae, compound eyes, and the ocelli which are simple light-detecting eyes, as well as some of the mouth-parts. In this type of insect there are two pairs of wings; true flies have one pair, while some insects have no wings at all.*

Although many insects damage plants by eating them, other insects are essential to the plants' existence. But flowers are not produced for our pleasure. They are a plant's means of inviting bees and other insects to perform the act of pollination.

The million or so species of insects are classified in 29 orders, arranged in two major groups according to their structure and mode of developmemt. The first group includes all the most primitive insects, and is called the Apterygota, from Greek words meaning 'without wings'. The other major group is the Pterygota ('winged'), and this group is divided into two major sub-groups, the Exopterygota and the Endopterygota.

The wingless insects are described on this page. Most of the Exopterygota are described on pages 160–161, and most of the Endopterygota on pages 162–163.

Three groups of insects, however, are important enough to have articles to themselves. They are the butterflies and moths (pages 164–165), the beetles (pages 166–167), and bees, wasps, ants and termites, many of which live in huge societies or communities (pages 168–169).

The primitive insects of the sub-class Apterygota are wingless insects. They emerge from eggs as small editions of their parents, simply growing larger each time they moult. They also have special appendages on the abdomen of a kind unknown in any other kinds of insects, and they can usually reproduce before they are full-grown. The wingless insects include four orders, the bristletails (Thysanura), two-pronged bristletails (Diplura), Protura and springtails (Collembola).

There are about 350 kinds of bristletails, the two best known being silverfish, found in dark, sometimes damp places in houses, and the firebrat which prefers warmer situations, such as bakeries. The bristletails have tapering bodies up to about 20 millimetres (¾ inch) long, and are recognised by their three long segmented 'tails' and long, thread-like *antennae* (feelers). The body is covered with slippery scales which are easily rubbed off and may help the animal to escape from the grasp of a predator. The common silverfish eats flour and other spilled food in cupboards and around sinks.

The 400 species of two-pronged bristletails are mostly smaller than Thysanura, rarely exceeding 5 millimetres (1/5 inch) in length. Unlike true bristletails they have only two rear appendages. They are blind, pale-coloured, narrow-bodied creatures living under the bark of trees, in soil or decaying vegetation, on which they feed.

The proturans have no common name, and are so small that they remained undiscovered until 1907. All the 50 species are less than 2 millimetres (3/32 inch) long. They live in damp, humus-rich soil or leaf litter. They are blind and have neither antennae nor 'tails'. As they moult to become adult, they increase the number of segments in the abdomen from eight to 11. This last feature is so unusual that it has been said that proturans are not insects, but some other kind of arthropod.

The last group of wingless insects, the springtails, is by far the largest, about 1,500 species being known. Although they differ a lot in size and general appearance, they all have one feature in common. This is a stiff, forked, tail-like structure, normally held pointing forwards under the body. When the insect is alarmed it can jump distances many times its own length by jerking the 'tail' violently downward. Springtails are widely distributed throughout the world, living mostly in damp situations.

Right: *Springtails are among the most primitive living insects. They are small and rarely noticed, but are abundant all over the world in the places where they scavenge, like leaf litter. Nearly all of them prefer damp places, some even live on coastal waters, but a few species survive in drier places; one occurs in large numbers on snow and ice. They can be recognised when they spring up almost vertically, propelled by their long forked 'tail'.*

Below: *Primitive insects. Two of these insects belong to the order Thysanura, known as bristletails. The firebrat,* Thermobia domestica *(1), likes to live in warm places and is found round chimney flues in houses. Silverfish,* Lepisma saccharina *(4), are also familiar house dwellers, often found in the bath. Both are active at night. The Dipleuran* Campodea staphyliniformis *(2) lives under bark and stones. Two springtails (3) can also be seen, one jumping.* Neanura *is slim but the short deep* Sminthurinus *is abundant in the soil.*

Insects with Nymphs

Most of the world's insects belong in the sub-class Pterygota, insects whose adult forms generally have wings. This sub-class is divided into two groups according to the way in which they undergo *metamorphosis* (changes in their pre-adult stage).

Incomplete metamorphosis is undergone by the 16 orders of the Exopterygota, dealt with here, and complete metamorphosis by the nine orders comprising the Endopterygota described on pages 162–163.

Immature forms of the Exopterygota are known as nymphs, and a nymph is really an incomplete version of the adult insect, with wings only partly developed. Every so often the nymph moults (sheds its skin) and emerges slightly more mature. Each stage between moults is called an *instar*, and there may be as many as 15 instars before the insect is fully adult. Some nymphs pass all their lives on land; others live under water, only the adults emerging from water to fly and mate.

The most important orders of this group are described here, the exception being the termites which are social insects and are described with bees and ants on pages 168–169.

Cockroaches and praying mantises belong to the order Dictyoptera. They have biting or chewing mouthparts, thread-like antennae composed of many segments, and leathery forewings which overlap along their backs when closed. Cockroaches are scavengers and are most numerous in warm climates, but have spread over most of the world. The mantises also live mostly in the tropics, but feed exclusively on other insects. They catch their prey between the spines on their front legs. Stick insects, in the order Phasmida, look superficially like mantises, but they have a differently shaped thorax, and are vegetarians.

Grasshoppers, crickets and their relatives belong to the Orthoptera and are (apart from cicadas which are bugs) the great noise-makers of the insect world. Some species produce their 'songs' by rubbing spines on their legs against small pegs on their wings; others do it by rubbing one wing against the other.

About 1,000 species of earwigs form the order Dermaptera. They can be separated from beetles by the curved 'forceps' at the end of the abdomen. Most species live in the warmer parts of the world. They are comparatively unusual among insects in that the female, having laid eggs in a batch in the soil, stays with them, feeding the young after they hatch.

Three orders of insects all have nymphs which live in water. They are

Below: *Earwigs are unusual among insects in that the female tends her eggs and takes care of the nymphs. The forceps-shaped cerci at the end of the abdomen are rarely used as a weapon, and even then only the largest tropical species are strong enough to pierce the human finger.*

Left: *There are two types of lice; sucking lice, the smaller group, live mainly on mammals – including man – while the biting lice tend to parasitise birds. None of them have wings. The biting lice,* Sturnidoecus sturni, *are from the head of a starling.*

Below: *On the bean plant, unfertilised female aphids produce live young; eventually winged males and females fly to the spindle tree, where the fertilised females lay eggs that hatch out in spring into more females, which return to the bean.*

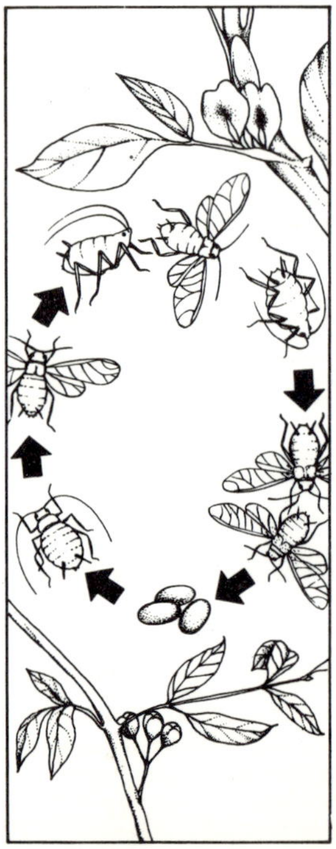

Left: *Aquatic insects. The pond skater (4) is a true bug that runs on the surface of the water, feeding on small creatures that fall onto the water. The other three are species that spend their larval lives under the surface. (1) Nymph of a dragonfly; (2) adult stonefly; (3) adult mayfly.*

Below: *An adult grasshopper. The larval stages have increasingly long wings until they are mature.*

Above: *There are many species of grasshoppers and crickets. Taking into account the differing appearances of the various instars of each species, they present a bewildering array of forms. The rufous grasshopper,* Gomphocerippus rufus *(top), has conspicuously clubbed antennae with pale tips. The mottled grasshopper,* Myrmeleotettix maculatus *(centre), also has slightly clubbed antennae, but they are uniformly dark in colour. The speckled bush-cricket,* Leptophyes punctatissima *(bottom), never has hind wings, even in the adult; it has extremely long antennae which are characteristic of bush-crickets. Grasshoppers are usually active during the daytime, while the crickets chirp at dusk and at night.*

dragonflies and damselflies (Odonata), mayflies (Ephemerata), and stoneflies (Plecoptera). Nymphs of dragonflies and damselflies are carnivorous, but those of the other two orders feed on decaying plants and algae. In each case the full-grown nymph, having moulted several times, emerges from the water before moulting again to become a flying adult. Adult dragonflies are quite long-lived, but stoneflies live only two or three weeks, and the mayfly a single day.

Thrips (Thysanoptera) and all the true bugs of the order Hemiptera (called 'true' because 'bug' is a word loosely used, often simply meaning any insect) have mouth-parts modified to pierce and suck and not to bite. Those of the thrips – minute, narrow, fringed-winged insects sometimes called 'thunder flies' – are strange in that they are asymmetrical (lop-sided). Many bugs and almost all thrips obtain their food from plant juices, often damaging fruit or flowers as they do so. Others suck animal juices, usually those of other insects, but sometimes those of mammals, including man. Nearly all the true bugs are land animals, but some, almost always predatory in their habits, are adapted to an aquatic life. The tropical watertiger, *Belostoma*, grows up to 80 millimetres (3 inches) long and is strong enough to attack quite large fish. The water-boatmen, or backswimmers, are much smaller, up to 20 millimetres (3/4 inch) long.

These bugs live under the water, but another group, called pond-skaters, have water-repellent hairs on their feet which enable them to stand and walk about on the surface, feeding on small insects. This group includes *Halobates*, almost the only truly marine insect. It is tropical and has been found at sea hundreds of kilometres from the nearest land.

Among the plant-sucking bugs, the aphids (greenfly and blackfly) are of special importance. They transmit virus diseases and cause great damage to crops.

Aphids are often called 'plant-lice', but true lice, ectoparasites on birds and mammals, belong to two quite different orders, Mallophaga (biting lice) and Anoplura (sucking lice).

Insects that Pupate

The insects of the group Endopterygota go through a complete metamorphosis (change) which consists of four stages, each unlike the others in appearance and structure. The egg hatches to produce a grub or larva (called a maggot in flies and a caterpillar in butterflies). The larva moults several times, growing larger with each moult. The insect then pupates – that is, turns into a form called a pupa or chrysalis, which is almost always one in which it does not feed but rests before producing the adult stage. Many insects spend cold winter periods in this stage. Finally, when conditions are right, the casing of the chrysalis cracks open and the adult insect emerges.

Three orders of the Endopterygota are described in the next three chapters – butterflies and moths, beetles, and social insects. The others are dealt with here.

Scorpion flies (Mecoptera) are distinctive in appearance, with long wings and their heads prolonged into a sort of 'beak'. The males of some species have their hind end curved upward like a tiny scorpion; hence the name. They are of great interest scientifically because they are known to have existed from early fossil times (the Permian period, which began 260 million years ago). The larvae of scorpion flies are carnivorous and live in the soil, one generation a year being usual in temperate climates.

Alder flies, snake flies, lacewings and antlions (Neuroptera) are another group with interesting early stages. Lacewings attach their eggs to the leaves of plants by long, thin threads, presumably to help protect them from enemies. The larvae which hatch from them are voracious feeders on aphids and other insects. Alder flies live near water. They lay their eggs on land in masses, on stones or leaves, and when hatched the larvae have to make their own way into the water. The larvae are carnivorous and, when ready to pupate, come out of the water and burrow into the soil.

In contrast, snake flies lay eggs on trees, usually conifers, and the larvae live under the bark, feeding on other insects and spiders. The carnivorous antlion larva makes a shallow pit in sandy ground, burrowing into the bottom, but leaving its jaws just showing. When an unwary insect stumbles on the edge of the pit the antlion throws sand grains at it. The insect falls into the pit and is sucked dry by the antlion's sickle-shaped jaws.

Adult caddis flies (Trichoptera) are difficult to identify, mostly looking like small, brownish moths. They are usually found near water, in which they spend their entire larval and pupal lives. The larvae usually make some sort of shelter, although a few are free-living and more active. Some shelters are tubes of silk covered with sand or mud, which the larvae drag around. Others are silken nets attached to stones or underwater plants; one net may be the fixed home of several larvae. These nets also collect food.

The pupal stage of the caddis flies is unusually active. When ready to turn into an adult fly it swims or crawls to the surface of the water. Caddis fly larvae are eaten by many species of fish and birds and are thus an important part of the freshwater food web.

The true flies (Diptera) are by far the

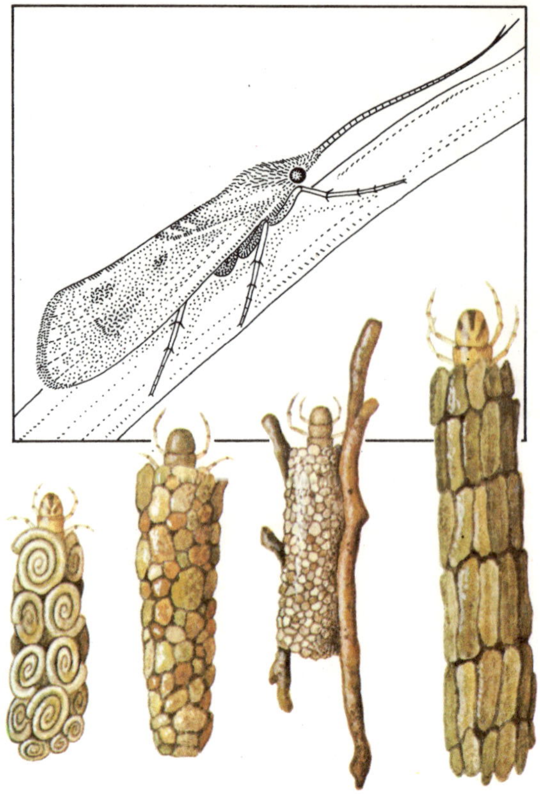

Left: *Caddisflies are the only entire order of pupating insects with aquatic larvae. Adult flies look rather like moths, but with hairy wings, and are all very similar. They can always be distinguished from the smaller moths in that caddisflies always rest with their antennae directed forward.* Below left: *It is simpler to identify caddisflies by their larvae, which make tubes to live in either from silk or other materials like stones, sticks and leaves that they pick up. The larvae and cases shown here are (left to right)* Limnephilus – *the larva of the fly above* – Stenophylax, Anabolia, *and* Phryganea.

Above: *Bluebottle flies,* Calliphora *spp., are scavengers. The adults feed on almost anything easily digested; they lay their eggs on decaying animal matter and the larvae feed and pupate there.*

largest group in this section, almost 80,000 species being known. The adults are extremely varied in appearance from large 30 millimetres ($1\frac{3}{16}$ inches) long crane flies to minute gnats, and from bulky horse flies to tiny *Drosophila* (fruit-flies). Many flies are a dull brown or grey colour, but some, like the greenbottles, are metallic green while others, such as hover flies, bear warning colours of black and yellow.

All adult flies have two features in common. The first is that, provided they can feed at all, they can only take in liquid nourishment. Some species have mandibles, but they are quite unlike the pincer-type jaws of cockroaches and grasshoppers; they form the piercing needles of the female mosquitoes, the horse flies, and related species. Mostly the mouthparts are even more specialised, designed for piercing and sucking (stable flies, for example) or for lapping (house flies).

The second common feature is that the hind pair of wings has become reduced to two tiny, club-shaped stalks called *halteres*. These halteres can be vibrated very rapidly and act as gyroscopic balancing organs, giving the flies great mobility in flight.

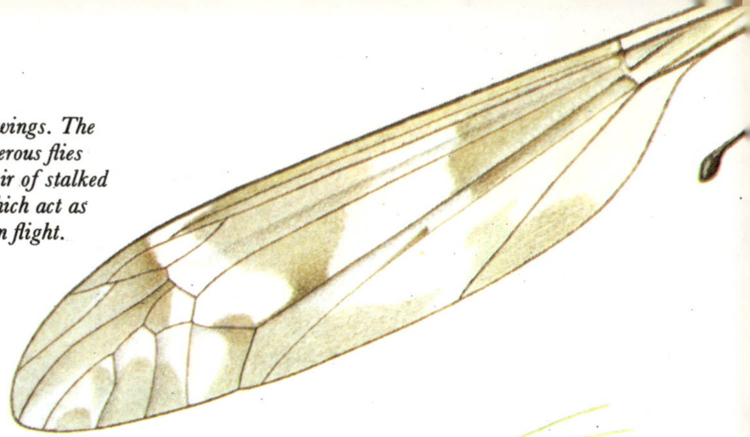

Right: *Crane-fly wings. The hind wings of dipterous flies are reduced to a pair of stalked knobs, halteres, which act as balancing organs in flight.*

Right: *Delicate-looking lacewing flies have voracious larvae which eat great numbers of aphids; they are thus of enormous benefit to man. Their equally pretty habit of laying eggs separately on slender stalks is thought to be a method of ensuring that the larvae do not eat each other on hatching.*

Most flies lay many small, spindle-shaped eggs which hatch very quickly, but a few species, external parasites on birds and mammals, produce living larvae, one at a time, the egg having hatched inside the parent's body. Fly larvae are more varied in their appearance and habits than any other insect order, but they never have any legs and have to move by wriggling.

The heads and feeding organs of larvae are suited to their various ways of life. The mosquito larva, hanging upside down under the surface film of still water, has a large head and chewing mandibles. The grubs of the blood-sucking horse flies (*Tabanidae*) have only moderate-sized heads and mouthparts. They live in damp soil, eating insects and other small animals.

Among the important, flower-pollinating hover flies is the drone fly, whose aquatic larva is called the rat-tailed maggot because it has a long, telescopic breathing tube extending upward from the back end of its body.

A large number of other fly larvae have tiny heads and mouthparts reduced to two small hooks. Many of them live in rotting fruit, decaying carcasses, in the stomachs, nasal cavities and under the skin of some living mammals, or inside the bodies of other insects.

Below left: *Hover-flies frequently have black and yellow wasp-like markings, like* Syrphus ribesii, *and they are in general useful to man, the adults pollinating flowers and the larvae feeding on aphids.*

Above: *Many of the flesh-fly family, like* Sarcophaga carnaria, *deposit live larvae directly onto meat. Some flesh-flies lay eggs, and yet others have larvae which are parasitic inside living animals.*

Left: *Adult fleas are blood-sucking parasites; their larvae are scavengers, usually in the nest of the host. This hedgehog flea has an unusually soft cuticle, since its host makes little attempt to harass it. Most fleas are extremely tough and slippery, and they can swim.*

Butterflies and Moths

About 150,000 species of moths and butterflies have been described. Together they form the order Lepidoptera. They range in size from minute creatures with a wingspan of a few millimetres to others with wings more than 300 millimetres (12 inches) across. They are found in most parts of the world from the Arctic to the tropics and from deserts to swamps. Some are very feeble fliers, but others are regular migrants, covering more than 1,600 kilometres (1,000 miles) during their short adult lives.

Moths and butterflies are the best-known large group of insects and are the least likely to be mistaken for anything else. With few exceptions they have two pairs of large wings, big compound eyes, and mouthparts formed into a *proboscis* (sucking tube).

Clearwings and a few other species have transparent wings in which the veins – important aids in classifying the different species – can be seen. In the vast majority of species, however, the wings are covered with flattened hairs called scales, which overlap like the tiles on a roof. Some scales contain pigments, but others have minutely grooved surfaces which reflect light in a way that produces iridescent colours.

The Lepidoptera are divided into about a hundred families, of which fewer than ten are butterflies. There is no simple division between moths and butterflies, but most moths are night-fliers with thread-like or feathery antennae, while most butterflies fly in the daytime and have knobs on the ends of their antennae.

Like beetles and flies, Lepidoptera have true larvae and pupae. The larvae are called caterpillars and are, in many ways, the most important stage of the insect's life. All the growth and most, sometimes all, of the feeding occurs during this period. Caterpillars are the Billy Bunters among the insects, often feeding almost continuously, except for brief periods just before they moult.

Some adult insects do not feed at all and those which do take only liquids, mainly nectar. Some butterflies and moths are

Below: *The monarch butterfly,* Danaus plexippus *(1), is distasteful to birds; its bright colouring helps to warn them. The large copper,* Lycaena dispar *(2), belongs to a family in which the caterpillars may be partly carnivorous; they secrete a sweet substance which ants like, and can thus live in ants' nests where they feed on larvae. The Camberwell beauty,* Nymphalis antiopa *(3), is a member of the tortoiseshell family and has the typically bristly caterpillar of this group. The swallowtail caterpillar,* Papilio machaon *(4), repels enemies by extruding an unpleasant-smelling organ from its tail.*

Below: *The peacock butterfly,* Nymphalis io, *has a brilliantly iridescent eyespot on each wing. This marking is thought to deter predators, allowing the butterfly to escape unharmed.*

Right: *Many hawk moth caterpillars have the 'tail' that can be seen on this spurge hawk moth caterpillar,* Celerio euphorbiae.

Below: *The viceroy,* Limenitis archippus, *is a member of the peacock family of butterflies. Many species in this family, which are palatable to birds, resemble other butterflies which are extremely distasteful. This viceroy, for example, resembles the monarch (far left). Birds who have learned that the common monarch is distasteful will also avoid the less common viceroy.*

important in the pollination of flowers. Many species simply play their part in nature's system of checks and balances, but the larvae of a large number have become pests to man, devastating crops, forests, stored food and manufactured articles such as clothing.

Butterflies, moths and fat caterpillars would appear to be attractive food for insectivorous vertebrates. They are, and many millions are eaten each year, but they have developed remarkable ways of escaping attention or deterring predators.

Many kinds of caterpillars feed only at night, hiding in the soil or dead leaves by day. Night-flying adults may hide in crevices while their predators are on the prowl, but many species protect themselves by more sophisticated means. Certain moths lie immobile on their sides, pretending to be dead, when danger threatens. Other species have improved their chances of survival by pretending to be something uninteresting. Dull-coloured looper caterpillars stretch out rigid on a host-plant and look like dead twigs. Some adult moths resemble bird-droppings when sitting still upon a leaf.

Many moth larvae live in cases or webs. Some, such as the bagworms (family Psychidae) build a portable home and enlarge it as they grow. Others make shelters in which they hide when at rest.

Colour and shape are also used as deterrents to predators. Some butterflies and moths give startling displays of bright colours or of eyespots by suddenly spreading their wings if disturbed. Certain caterpillars, such as that of the puss moth, also have large, eye-like markings, while others are equipped with spikes and horns designed to discourage predators. Larvae of cinnabar moths and milkweed butterflies (monarchs) are brightly coloured, often in black and yellow stripes. This is a warning system which is no idle threat, for many species accumulate poisons in their bodies from the plants on which they feed.

Mimicry is a special form of camouflage based on these poisonous or unpleasant-tasting species. If an edible butterfly looks like a common unpalatable one it will be left alone by predators.

Below: *Most hawk moths are nectar-feeders, some have such long probosces that they alone can penetrate certain flowers. The death's head hawk moth,* Acherontia atropos, *however, has a very short strong proboscis, which it uses to pierce honeycombs and suck honey.*

Beetles

Beetles, forming the orders Coleoptera, are the most successful and varied of all insects. So far, about 300,000 species have been described. Many kinds of beetle are seldom seen because they shun the daylight. their larvae (grubs) are even less well-known, for a lot of them spend their lives hidden in plants, in the soil, in water or in various kinds of decaying material, both plant and animal.

Although the larvae are very varied in appearance, they can generally be identified by their yellow or brownish heads, with biting mouthparts, and by the fact that they never have more than three pairs of legs, sometimes none at all. Many larvae grow to change into pupae after just a few weeks, but some, especially those living in dead wood in cold climates, may take several years to mature. Adult beetles often have relatively long lives.

The two most important features in the success story of beetles are also those which, taken together, separate adult beetles from other insects. Firstly, they have biting and chewing mouthparts not unlike those of grasshoppers and cockroaches. Variations of these simple jaws have enabled them to become carnivores, plant feeders, scavengers and, in a few cases, external parasites.

But it is the modified forewings that have really made the beetles what they are today. These forewings are short and thick, meeting down the middle of the back, and serve as wing-covers for the folded hind wings which are used in flight. These wing-covers, *elytra* as they are called, not only protect the delicate flight wings, but usually form a shield for the whole of the hind body. This armours the insect against attack from predators and, in addition, enables some beetles to live under water and others to survive the rigours of hot deserts.

Most beetles have highly developed sense organs of one kind or another. These senses, together with chemical repellents, threatening attitudes, strange body shapes, remarkable colours and other special attributes, have enabled beetles to seek their prey, find their mates and hide

Left: *Common British beetles. (1) Cockchafer,* Melolontha melolontha; *(2, 11) comb-headed cardinal* Pyrochroa serraticornis; *(3)* Rhagium bifasciatum; *(4) seven-spot ladybird* Coccinellia septempunctata; *(5) lined click beetle* Agriotes lineatus; *(6) nettle phyllobius* Phyllobius urticae; *(7, 13)* Christolina polita; *(8)* Stenus bimaculatus; *(9)* Hoplia philanthus; *(10) green tortoise beetle,* Cassida viridis; *(12) leaf beetle,* Donacia aquatica; *(14, 16) great diving beetle,* Dytiscus marginalis; *(15) whirligig beetle,* Gyrinus marinus.

from their enemies or frighten them away. The familiar black beetles of gardens and fields have striking relatives in the predatory caterpillar-hunters (*Calosoma*) with their shining green wing-cases and their ability to climb trees in search of food, and the bombardier beetle (*Brachinus*) which terrifies potential enemies by discharging a repellent spray, with a small explosive noise, from glands at the back end.

Right: *The bombardier beetle,* Brachinus crepitans *(left), ejects a pungent gas when surprised. The devil's coach horse,* Ocypus olens *(right), rears up and fights, with its formidable jaws ready.*

Left: *The caterpillar hunter,* Calosoma inquisitor, *often climbs high trees in search of the caterpillars it preys on. Related species have been tried in America in an attempt to control some of the destructive moths in orchards there.*

Carnivorous water beetles such as the great diving beetle (*Dytiscus*) have evolved a smooth, streamlined shape and powerful, flattened legs for swimming. They carry a bubble of air beneath their elytra and so can breathe under water. In contrast, the rove beetles, such as the Devil's coach-horse (*Ocypus*), have long, flexible bodies and very short wing-cases, enabling them to move freely in confined spaces.

The great group called the lamellicorns, more than 20,000 of them, include such giants as the Hercules beetle, with males over 80 millimetres (3 inches) long. Their C-shaped grubs feed on rotten wood in the forests of Central America and the West Indies. The males use their fierce-looking horns to fight each other when competing for a mate. They are otherwise harmless, feeding on overripe fruit.

Many beetles are coloured to match their backgrounds, but some contrast strongly with their surroundings and others, like the ladybirds, have developed patterns of red, yellow and black which tell the world that they are either dangerous or unpleasant to eat.

Among the beetles with specially developed sense organs are such strange creatures as the male of *Callirhipis philiberti*. It looks like a click-beetle or skip-jack, but has enormous, fan-like antennae with which it detects the presence of a suitable mate. When the antennae are not in use they are carried for protection beneath the body between the legs, making the animal less conspicuous. This beetle and others like it live on islands in the Indian Ocean and in Malaysia. They are generally active at dusk and have very large eyes.

The largest beetle eyes are those of the fireflies and glow-worms. They cover almost all of the head, enabling the males to detect the cold, greenish, chemically-produced light emitted by their mates. The European glow-worm is unusual in that the female has no wings or wing-cases. She spends her adult life among grass tussocks on chalky soils, climbing up a blade of grass at night and signalling to a prospective mate with light produced by chemical action inside her abdomen.

The plant-feeding longhorns and weevils include the strangest-looking beetles. The first group contains one of the largest beetles of all, *Titanus giganteus*, up to 150 millimetres (6 inches) long and weighing at least 100 grammes (3½ ounces). Its legless larva, which lives in decaying wood in the Amazon forests, is about 150 millimetres (6 inches) long.

The weevils, of which there are more than 35,000 species, all have one feature in common. The front of the head extends into a snout with tiny jaws at the far end. In extreme forms, this snout is longer than all the rest of the body. It is used by the females as a drill, boring holes in trees or nuts to provide a safe start in life for their eggs. Because of their plant-feeding habits, many weevils are regarded as pests, but the group also includes some of the most beautiful of all beetles. They have on their bodies flattened hairs or scales which, by altering the light which falls on them, produce shimmering, metallic tints of green, gold or pink.

Above: *The hercules beetle,* Dynastes hercules. *The fearsome horns of the male are used only in combat with other males at mating time.*

Above: *While the forewings of beetles are hardened into elytra, their hind wings can carry even large species like this stag beetle into the air. Biologists do not yet understand what benefit the beetle derives from having such large unwieldy jaws.*

Left: *A honey bee worker,* Apis mellifera, *collecting nectar to take back to the hive. Its long proboscis is inserted into a floret.*

Above: *The common bumble bee,* Bombus terrestris, *is moderately social. The colonies are about 10 centimetres (3½ inches) in diameter and may number 100 or more individuals, but only last one summer season.*

Social Insects

Some of the most highly-organised communities in the world are those of the so-called social insects – bees and wasps, ants and termites. Bees, wasps and ants belong to the order Hymenoptera, which also includes a great many insects that do not live in large social groups. The termites belong in the order Isoptera.

The order Hymenoptera includes well over 100,000 species, spread over much of the world. Many look like flies and have legless grubs with small heads. Most adults can fly and have two pairs of wings, the hind pair smaller than the front ones.

The order is divided into two sub-orders: Symphyta – sawflies and wood-wasps – and Apocrita – all the others. The social insects – bees, wasps and ants – belong in a sub-division of the Apocrita called the Aculeata.

Most species of bees and wasps are solitary, doing no more than making a nest for their grubs and providing a store of food, but some of them and all ants are social. The social insects live in large family groups, or colonies, usually the offspring of a single mother, or queen.

Primitive bees found colonies which last a single year. The queen begins the nest and rears the first few grubs. These grow into workers – non-breeding females – who take over the tasks of nest-building and feeding the grubs while the queen simply goes on laying eggs. Later in the year a few grubs develop into fertile males and females. They fly off to mate, and the females found new colonies.

The most highly-developed colonies are those of the honey bees. A honey bee colony may continue for many years, surviving the winter, or times when there are few flowers, with stores of honey and pollen. A prosperous colony may contain some 60,000 workers, a few hundred drones (males), a single queen, and thousands of grubs. Workers live only a few weeks or months. The queen normally survives for several years and may lay up to 200,000 eggs a year.

The workers do all the jobs in and out of the hive. They build cells for stores and as

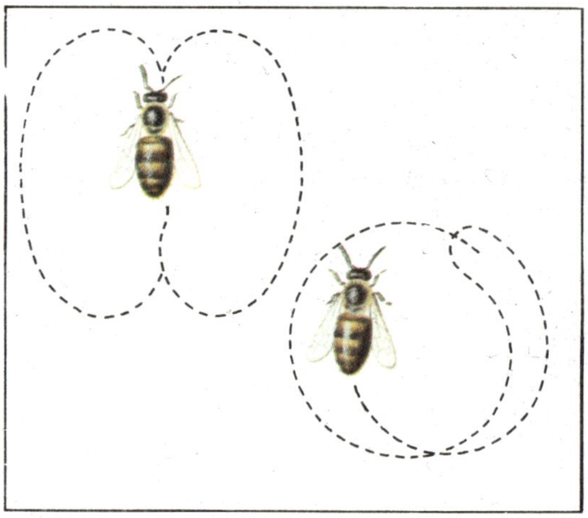

Above: *Honey bees, returning from newly discovered food, communicate their whereabouts by the round-dance (right) for nearby food, or the waggle-dance (left) for distant food. The angle between the waggle-run and the vertical is that between the food and the sun.*

Below: *Honey bees make hexagonal wax cells in layers; each layer is sealed off, cell by cell, before another layer is built up and filled with honey.*

nurseries for grubs, and collect honey and pollen and, if necessary, water. They feed the grubs and the queen, and keep the place clean, warm, ventilated and defended. The queen lays eggs. Drones are there to mate with new queens.

In temperate climates social wasps make colonies which last only until the next reproductive generation is produced. In some tropical species the 'family' continues for many years and may include several queens at once, although only one lays eggs. Wasps' nests are built of paper, made from wood scrapings and saliva.

There are about 3,500 species of ants. The non-breeding females in their colonies are wingless and basically of two kinds, workers and soldiers. Unlike their equivalents among the bees, workers and soldiers may live for several years, foraging, tending the young and enlarging or defending the nest. The fertile male and female ants have a brief winged life, mating in the air during a nuptial flight, but shedding their wings on landing. The male dies, but the female becomes queen of a new generation, either beginning a new nest, or entering an existing colony.

Ants build many types of nests. Those of the tropical driver ants are temporary, hardly more than a space under a log or stone. Other kinds of ants build mounds of earth, or make a complicated series of underground galleries and chambers. Desert-living species often tunnel deep into the soil in search of water. Many tropical species make nests in parts of plants, and at least one sews leaves together, using as thread silk produced by their larvae. Soil-nesting ants, with colonies sometimes numbering more than 100,000 individuals, often have definite territories surrounding their nest, over which they forage for food.

Ants' food varies with the species. Many are carnivorous, some voraciously so. Others eat grass or seeds. Leaf-cutter ants make underground compost-heaps of chewed leaves, on which they grow a fungus. The ants feed on the fungus. Pastoral ants milk aphids of a substance called honeydew, and protect the aphids from predators. Some build shelters for their 'cattle', and carry their eggs down into the ant-nest during winter.

Termites have a social life even more highly developed than that of the ants. The termite colonies, which in some species contain several million individuals, have a 'king' as well as a 'queen'. The long-lived workers and soldiers may be either male or female, but are always immature and wingless. The foundation of new colonies follows the emergence and mating of flying adults. There are 1,700 species, mostly tropical.

Termite nests vary widely. The most primitive species make galleries in moist, decaying conifer logs, but others attack dry wood, including buildings and furniture. Some species build huge mounds of soil mixed with saliva and fæces, while yet others burrow in the soil, or make nests in trees with mud-covered tunnels leading to the ground. The large mounds can last a very long time. One in Australia is known to have existed for more than 60 years, but there is evidence that another in Rhodesia (Zimbabwe) was begun over 600 years ago.

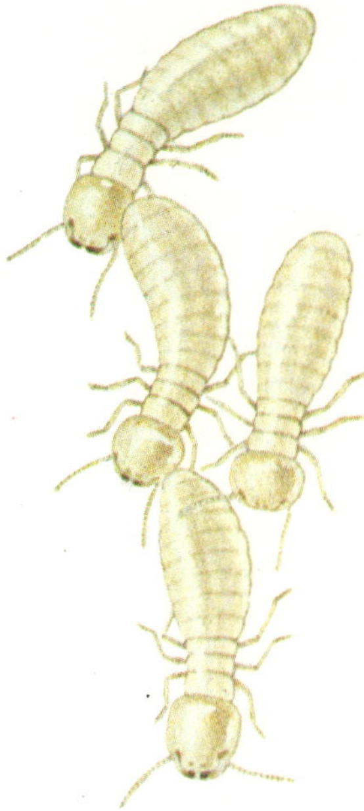

Above: *Termites belong to a different order – the Isoptera – from the other social insects on this page. Some types form primitive colonies in rotting wood while others build enormous permanent earthen structures.*

Below: *There are many species of ants. The large wood ant,* Formica rufa *(left), is the one that is supposed to bite, but actually discharges irritating formic acid. The other three ants are the black ant,* Lasius niger, *the red ant,* Myrmica ruginodis, *and the yellow meadow ant,* Lasius flavus.

Animals with Backbones

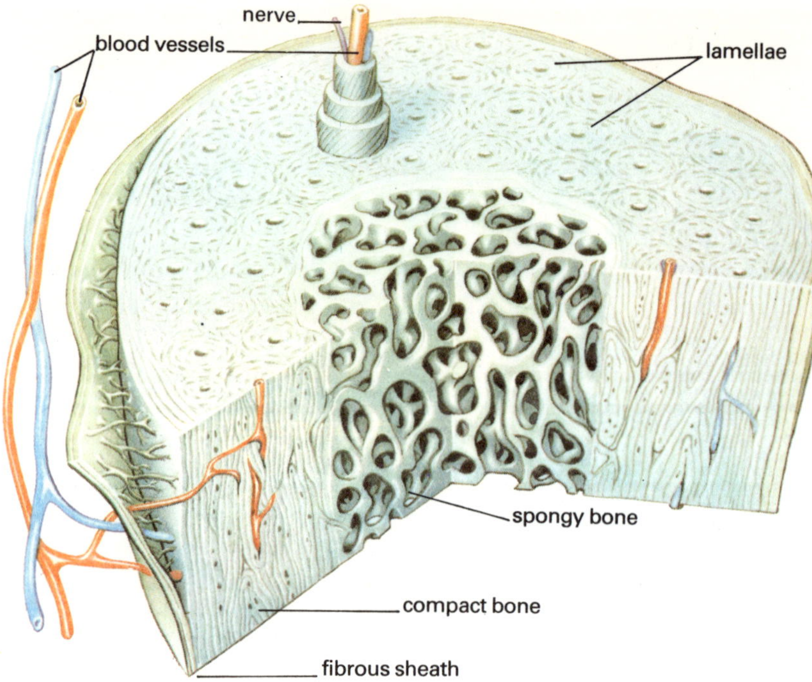

Vertebrates are animals with backbones made up of separate bones, the *vertebrae*, and hard bony *crania*, cases for the brain. Two groups of vertebrates have vertebrae and crania made of cartilage, a softer material than bone.

The vertebrates are a sub-phylum of the phylum Chordata, which includes several kinds of marine animals described on pages 150–151. The Chordata evolved from earlier invertebrate forms, that is, animals without backbones. Many invertebrates have bodies which are soft, with no supporting tissues of any kind. Animals like this are bound to be small, or to live in water, which holds them up. Some of the more active and large invertebrates have hard tissues, but these are almost always external to the body and have a dual function, acting as a support and also as an armour.

The echinoderms (see pages 148–149) include some animals with a skeleton which is more like that of the vertebrates, in that it is internal – and in the starfishes, jointed – to allow the body of the animal to be flexible. It is not surprising, therefore, that the vertebrates, which have developed an internal jointed support system called the skeleton, should have evolved from animals related to the echinoderms.

The vertebrata comprise seven main groups: the jawless fish-like cyclostomes; cartilage-fish; the true fishes; amphibians; reptiles; birds; and mammals. In all these animals there is, at some stage in their development, a stiff jelly-like rod, called the *notochord*, above which lies the spinal cord. The main muscles of the trunk are supported by the notochord, but are further supported by cartilage in some animals and replaced by bone in others. Besides this, all vertebrates possess gill structures at some time in their lives, although in mammals, including man, these gills disappear long before birth.

Above: *A section of a long bone of a mammal. Bone is a living tissue, and it is provided with a blood supply to nourish it. The reinforced lamellae are arranged around blood vessels and nerves, and there is a protective fibrous sheath over the whole bone. The spongy core helps to reduce the weight without loss of strength.*

Below: *Antler growth in the red deer. Antlers are completely different from horns – they are made of bone and are shed at the end of each year. The next year, a new, larger and more complex set of antlers is grown. Here are six successive fully grown sets of antlers showing the increasing maturity of a stag.*

The *cyclostomes*, which include the lampreys and the hagfishes, are the most primitive of the vertebrates. In them, the notochord survives throughout the life of the animal, but is somewhat strengthened by a series of isolated pieces of cartilage on either side of the spinal cord. Lampreys and hagfishes also have cartilaginous skulls, but these do not support lower jaws, as is the case in all other vertebrates. Instead, at the front of the head is a funnel-like mouth, strengthened by cartilage. In the lampreys this funnel acts as a sucker, the inside of which is lined with a large number of horny, tooth-like projections. There are more of these 'teeth' on the piston-like tongue. Together they are used to rasp the flesh of living fishes, for the lamprey is a parasite.

The adult hagfish has no sucker. Its

mouth is surrounded by a number of small tentacles, for the hagfish feeds on small invertebrates and is also a scavenger of decaying animal remains on the seabed.

Lampreys and hagfishes breathe with gills which lie in seven pairs of pouches behind the head. Water taken in through the mouth can pass over the gills, but when the lamprey is feeding its mouth is buried in the flesh of its prey. It is then able to draw water directly into the gill pouches from outside.

The skeleton, which supports the body of all other sorts of vertebrate, may be made of cartilage. The first support to the body in the developing embryo is always made of cartilage, but it is later replaced by bone in most vertebrates. Cartilage is softer than bone, but is sometimes found in those parts of the body which need some support, but which have to take little strain. In humans, it is found towards the end of the nose – you can feel how soft this is compared to the hard bone at the top of the nose – and also the last few ribs, although these are a little more difficult to feel.

Cartilage is made of proteins arranged in twisted strands, three of them together. Each strand lies very close to the others and binds to it at frequent intervals along the length. Because of this, the strands do not slip past each other and are very strong under tension, but they can be bent easily, because the fibres are not stiff. Cartilage can be hardened with *apatite*, a form of calcium phosphate, but even then, it is not nearly as strong as bone.

Above: *The river lamprey,* Lampetra fluviatilis, *is generally considered to be among the most primitive of living vertebrates. It has a braincase and a notochord but no limbs or jaws. The sucking disc with rasping tongue that it has instead can be seen here, as well as the gill openings and simple eyes.*

Below: *A snake's skeleton is like one long backbone on which the head is the only really specialised part. Each joint of the spine has its pair of ribs.*

True bone is a living substance, which, like cartilage, is made of fine fibres. These fibres are usually arranged in layers called *lamellae* and are always stiffened with minute, needle-shaped crystals of calcium phosphate or other inorganic salts. The bulk of the bone is made up of this non-living material, but the live fibres occupy spaces in it. These spaces are called *lacunae* and interconnect through narrow passages called *canaliculi*. Sometimes the live substance in a bone may die, but even then the bone continues to support the body, although it becomes very brittle and does not heal easily if it breaks. The bone of many sorts of fishes does not contain any of these living cells, or *osteocytes*, and as a result, broken fish bones do not heal.

The general construction of bone, with hard minerals and soft fibres, gives it two sorts of strength. It can stand great compression, when the crystals prevent the fibres from deforming under the stress, but it can also stand great tension, for although the crystals would develop cracks, like those of a metal showing fatigue, the elastic fibres would hold them in place. In a way, bone is like glass fibre, which has a similar combination of hard and flexible substances. Bone cannot stand shear stress very well, but this is minimised by the jointed structure of the skeleton. Weight for weight, bone is stronger than steel.

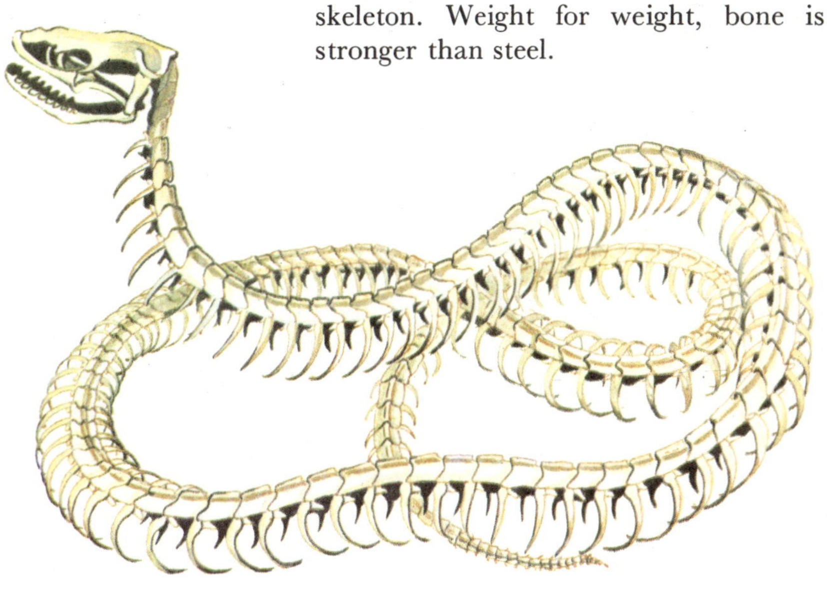

Sharks and Rays

Sharks and rays are an important group of vertebrate animals. Like the other vertebrates they have a backbone which helps to keep the body rigid but, more importantly, provides attachment for the body muscles. In both sharks and rays, and in a smaller third group, the chimaeras or ratfishes, the vertebrae and the remainder of the skeleton are composed of *cartilage* (gristle), not bone. For this reason they are often known as cartilaginous fishes.

Above left: *Many shark-like fishes lay large yolky eggs with long tendrils for anchorage.*
Left: *The blue shark can grow up to 3½ metres (11½ feet).*

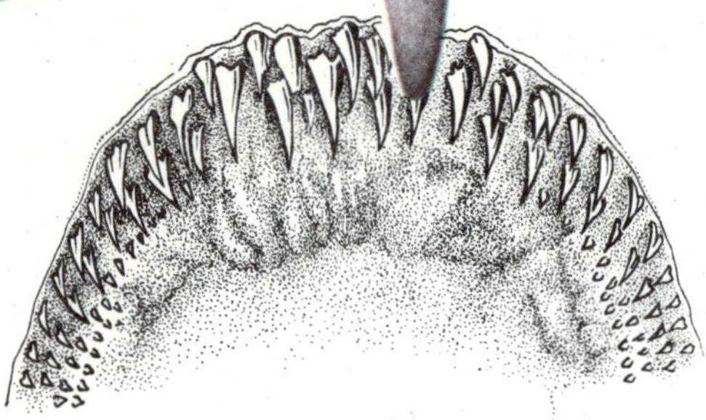

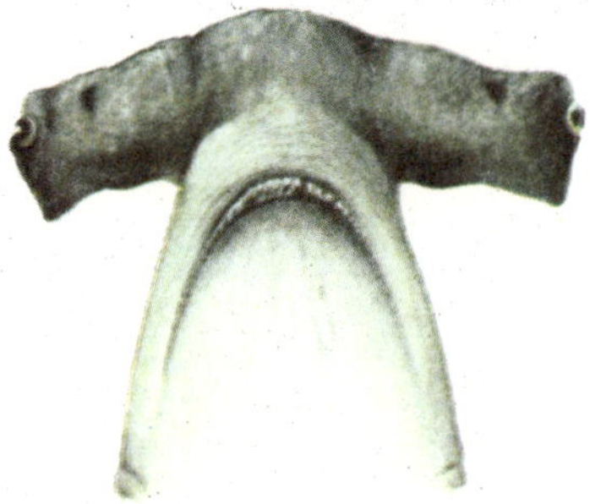

Above: *The frightening teeth of sharks are continually replaced as old ones break or wear out; the typical pattern can be seen in the lower jaw of a blue shark (top left). The mako, (above), which has very long central teeth and is extremely fast, and the hammerhead shark (top right) are extremely dangerous – the shaped nose is no ornament.*

Sharks and rays differ from the bony fishes in other ways. They have five, six, or seven pairs of gills in the throat, with the same number of openings on the outside which are known as gill slits. In sharks these gill slits are in the sides just behind the head; rays have them underneath the body because their pectoral fins are very large and join on to the head.

The teeth in both sharks and rays are very numerous, lie in rows and are continually being replaced; as new teeth form in the gums the older, worn or broken teeth fall out. The fishes' bodies are covered not by normal fish scales, but by small scales which have the structure of teeth, and which give the body surface a rough feel.

Sharks and rays form the class Elasmobranchiomorphi. There are about 300 different kinds of sharks (orders Hexanchiformes, Heterodontiformes and Lamniformes) and about 350 rays (order Rajiformes); it is not possible to be certain of the exact numbers because some of the rarer, mostly deep-sea, species are not well known, and previously unknown kinds are found from time to time. Most are large fishes, and few are as small as even medium-sized bony fishes.

The largest shark is the whale shark which can grow to 18 metres (60 feet) and is found in tropical seas, but the basking shark which lives off the British coast and elsewhere, is the second largest and may be as long as 12 metres (40 feet). The largest of the rays is the manta, a surface-living fish of tropical seas which may be 6·7 metres (22 feet) across, although its body is shorter than this. In contrast to these giants the smallest shark is a mid-water species, the dwarf shark, which grows to 230 millimetres (9 inches) in length; one of the smallest rays is the hedgehog skate of North America which measures at most 530 millimetres (21 inches) from the tip of the snout to the tail tip. These are, however, large fishes when compared with the hundreds of much smaller bony fishes.

Both sharks and rays are essentially marine fishes. The only representatives of either group to live entirely in fresh water are the river rays found in the lakes and rivers of eastern South America. These are small – up to 300 millimetres (12 inches) across the body – and have a sharp, daggerlike spine in the tail fin. Some sharks and other kinds of sting-rays are found in fresh water in tropical regions, but they migrate to the sea at times.

At sea, both sharks and rays live in most of the habitats available. Thus in tropical seas the manta rays, whale sharks, and white-tipped sharks live at the surface in the open sea. Many requiem sharks, such as the black-tipped shark and tiger shark, live in shallow, inshore waters or around reefs, where sting-rays and cow-nosed rays either lie concealed in the sand or feed on buried shellfish such as clams.

In temperate seas fewer sharks are found, but rays are often very numerous, living close to or on the bottom in shallow water. Very few sharks are found in the polar seas, although some, such as the Greenland shark, seem to thrive in cold water, and bottom-living rays are fairly common.

The waters over the continental shelf in tropical and temperate seas are inhabited by numerous kinds of sharks, and on the sea bed are large skates. In general these fishes are not very numerous in the deep sea, but this is the least-explored part of the oceans and it is possible that there are more and larger sharks living there than have so far been discovered.

All the cartilaginous fishes are carnivorous, but the diet varies from one kind to another, and these differences are reflected in the shape and arrangement of the teeth in the jaws. Sharks are best known as fierce predators on fishes and other sea creatures such as whales, porpoises, and turtles, and on man. Some kinds, such as the sand shark and the mako, have pointed teeth, especially in the front of the jaws. These sharks eat smaller fishes and squids which are stabbed by the long teeth and swallowed whole.

Other large sharks, such as the great white shark and tiger shark, and many smaller species, have triangular cutting teeth which interlock with those in the other jaw. This type is particularly well arranged for cutting flesh off larger animals, and the two species named are well known for their ability to bite huge chunks out of larger fishes and animals such as whales, porpoises, and seals. Sometimes such sharks attack human bathers or divers and may cause dreadful injuries which can be fatal. Such attacks are comparatively rare, however.

In some sharks, such as the smooth-hounds and the Port Jackson sharks of the Indian and Pacific oceans, the teeth in the jaws are rounded and form a crushing mill; these sharks feed on hard-shelled animals such as crabs and molluscs.

It is perhaps surprising that among all those fierce predators the very largest sharks eat the smallest food organisms, for the whale shark and the basking shark eat plankton which they filter from the water by special sieves in their throats. Most of the basking shark's food is small crustaceans about the size of a pin-head, but it also swallows large numbers of fish eggs and larvae. The whale shark may also catch larger fishes.

The feeding habits of the rays show similar variations. Again, the largest species, the mantas, are plankton eaters. Several species, such as the cow-nosed rays and sting-rays, have flattened crushing teeth and feed on hard-shelled shellfish. Most rays eat a variety of small crustaceans, fishes and worms, and do not possess very specialised teeth. However, those such as the skate and the shagreen ray, which eat fishes, mostly have longer stabbing teeth than other rays.

Compared with bony fishes, sharks and rays produce very few eggs, mostly fewer than 20 at a time, and rarely more than 50 in the big sharks. The largest sharks and rays produce only one or two young at a time. This means that they very quickly become rare if many are captured.

Below: *One of the Australian carpet sharks called wobbegongs. These are nurse sharks that feed at night. During the day, they rest on the sea bed, so well camouflaged by their mottled colouring that they are something of a hazard to swimmers who may innocently tread on them. Their attractive skins are sometimes used in the shark-leather industry.*

Above: *Skates and rays live on the sea bed, where they feed on small fishes and shellfish. Their teeth are rounded – more so in rays – and well adapted for crushing rather than biting. The sting ray,* Dasyatis pectinatis *(left), defends itself against attack from above with a venomous spine on its long whiplike tail. Some skates (above) have small electric organs in their tails – possibly used for orientation.*

The Bony Fishes

Almost all the fishes that you see in everyday life, from the herring, cod, and plaice in the fish shop, to the goldfish and the guppy in aquaria, are bony fishes, which form the class Pisces. Unlike sharks and rays, they have a proper bony skeleton, the brain and other vital head organs are protected by hard bone, the jaws are strong and well-developed, the body muscles are attached to vertebrae, ribs and spines, and the fins are composed of hard spines and branched rays.

The possession of a bony skeleton is not the only difference from the sharks and rays. Bony fishes have proper scales on their bodies (or none at all), not scales which resemble teeth like those of the sharks. Their upper jaws are formed by different bones and are more or less fixed to the head skeleton, whereas in sharks and rays the jaws are only loosely attached. Bony fishes also have a swim-bladder, a slim balloon-like organ in the body cavity.

How successful are they? The number of different kinds of bony fishes is hard to state for certain, partly because there are so many of them and partly because scientists are still describing previously unrecognised forms. A conservative estimate of their total number is over 20,000 species – more, that is, than all the species of birds, mammals, reptiles, and amphibians together. Most of these belong to the one major group, called the *teleosts*, but to some people the most interesting are the few 'living fossils', also bony fishes, but possessing features which can be seen in those 'early' fishes now mostly extinct and preserved as fossils.

One of the most exciting living fossils is the coelacanth, a fish living in the Indian Ocean near the Comoro Islands, close to East Africa. It lives on the steeply-sloping rocky bottom and can only be caught on lines and baited hooks; it grows to about 1·8 metres (6 feet) in length. It has many features which are primitive, and is the only living member of a group of fossil fishes which otherwise became extinct about 90 million years ago. From fishes of this type the earliest amphibians evolved, and from them evolved the other vertebrates.

Other primitive fishes related to the coelacanth are the lungfishes. Like the coelacanth, lungfishes are members of the tassel-fin group, so-called because they do not have rays of the usual kind in their fins. There are only seven kinds of lungfishes living today, one in Australia, another in South America, and the rest in Africa. All live in fresh water and have a lung-like swim-bladder which allows them to breathe air. The South American and some of the African lungfishes live in

Below: *The great diversity of fishes is illustrated here. They include freshwater fish (1, 7, 11) from rivers and lakes, marine fishes (2, 3, 4, 5, 6, 9), and some which spend part of their lives in the sea and part in fresh water (8, 10). Fish are found in cool waters (e.g. 2, 6, 8) and warm waters (e.g. 9, 11), near the surface (e.g. 6) or deep in the ocean (e.g. 3).*

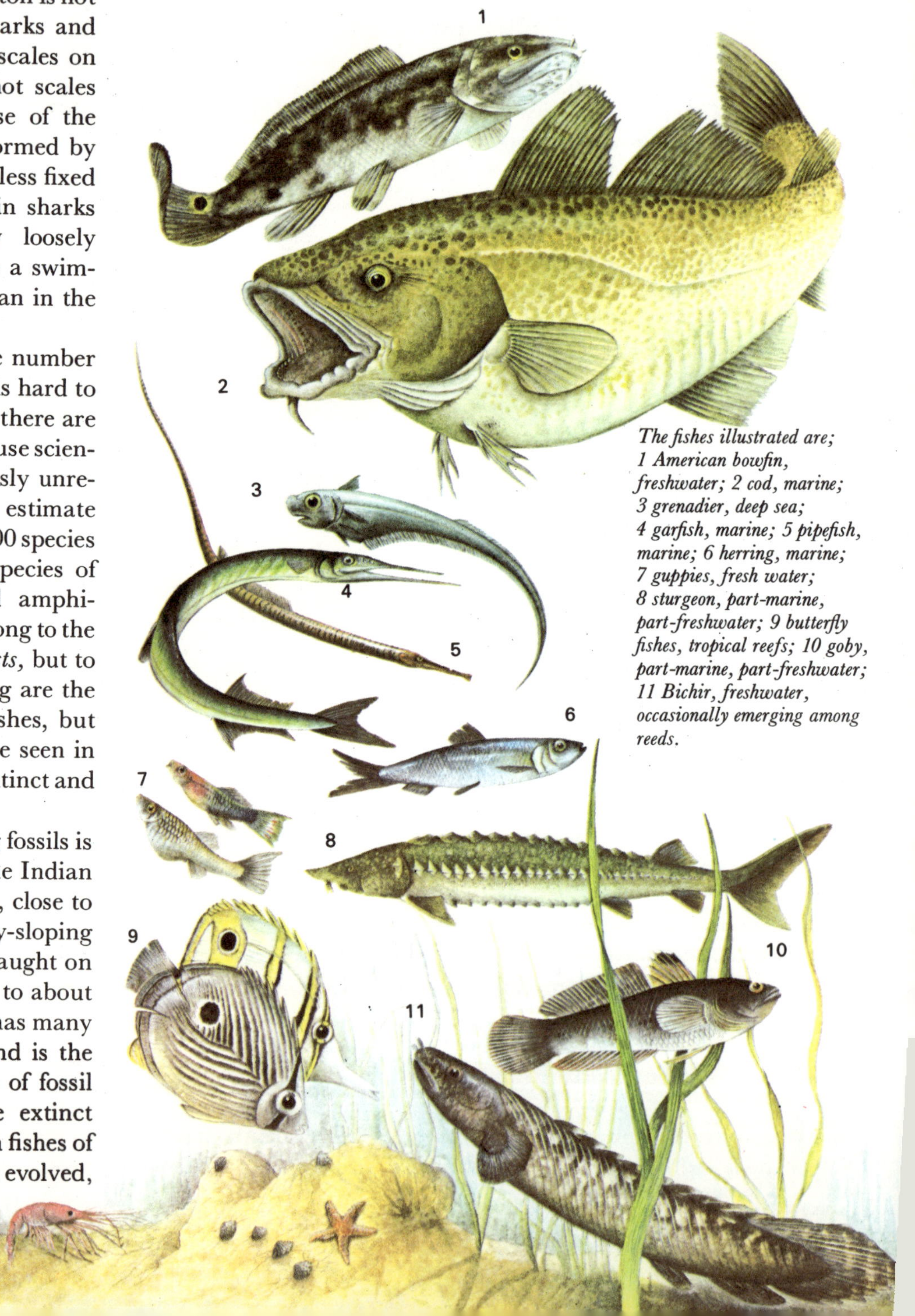

The fishes illustrated are; 1 American bowfin, freshwater; 2 cod, marine; 3 grenadier, deep sea; 4 garfish, marine; 5 pipefish, marine; 6 herring, marine; 7 guppies, fresh water; 8 sturgeon, part-marine, part-freshwater; 9 butterfly fishes, tropical reefs; 10 goby, part-marine, part-freshwater; 11 Bichir, freshwater, occasionally emerging among reeds.

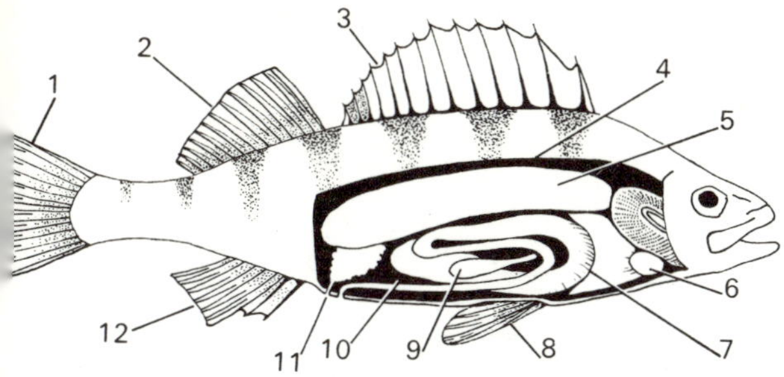

Left: *Perch, showing parts of a bony fish. 1 caudal fin; 2, 3 dorsal fin; 4 body cavity; 5 swim bladder; 6 heart; 7, 10 intestine; 8 pelvic fin; 9 spleen; 11 genital pore; 12 anal fin.*

Above: *This coelacanth,* Latimeria, *is a deep-water carnivore. When it first came to the attention of scientists in 1938 it was recognised as the living counterpart of Carboniferous-age fishes.*

swamps which dry out in summer, and they survive by air-breathing.

There are three groups of ray-fin fishes, of which by far the most numerous (possibly 20,000 kinds) are the true bony fishes (teleosts). Two smaller groups are recognised, mostly showing primitive features and all mainly freshwater fishes. The reed fish and the bichirs of African swamps (11 species), the sturgeons which live only in the northern hemisphere (20 species), and two paddlefishes, one in North America and the other in China, make up one group (orders Polypteriformes and Acipenseriformes) which could all be called living fossils. Another group of 10 species, the garpikes (order Semionotiformes) and the bowfin (order Amiiformes) all live in North American lakes and rivers.

Clearly it is the teleost fishes which have proved to be the most successful of all the living fishes. Why is this ? One reason is their small size. Small fishes can use all kinds of little living spaces, such as the dense weed-beds of a pond or the intricate winding hollows of coral reefs.

Another advantage of the bony fishes which is denied the cartilaginous fishes is the possession of a swim-bladder. In most bony fishes this is a gas-filled, slender tube in the body cavity which can be pumped up or let down so that the density of the fish is close to that of the water in which it is swimming. When a lantern fish, for example, which lives in the deep sea during the day and comes near to the surface at night, swims upwards it constantly regulates the amount of gas in the swim-bladder as the water pressure changes. This means that it can virtually float at any level it requires, and for this reason it saves energy.

The extra mobility of the fins of the true bony fishes is also a constant factor in their success. In having such movable aids to swimming they have attained a mastery of their environment. This is denied the cartilaginous fishes, which can swim fast and powerfully, but lack precision in turning and slow stalking.

Even such fishes as the seahorses or pipefishes, slow and stately swimmers as they may appear, are capable of turning exactly so that they are in the correct position to snap up a single pin-head sized crustacean. Such subtle adaptations to special life-styles and habitats are the major factors in the success of the bony fishes.

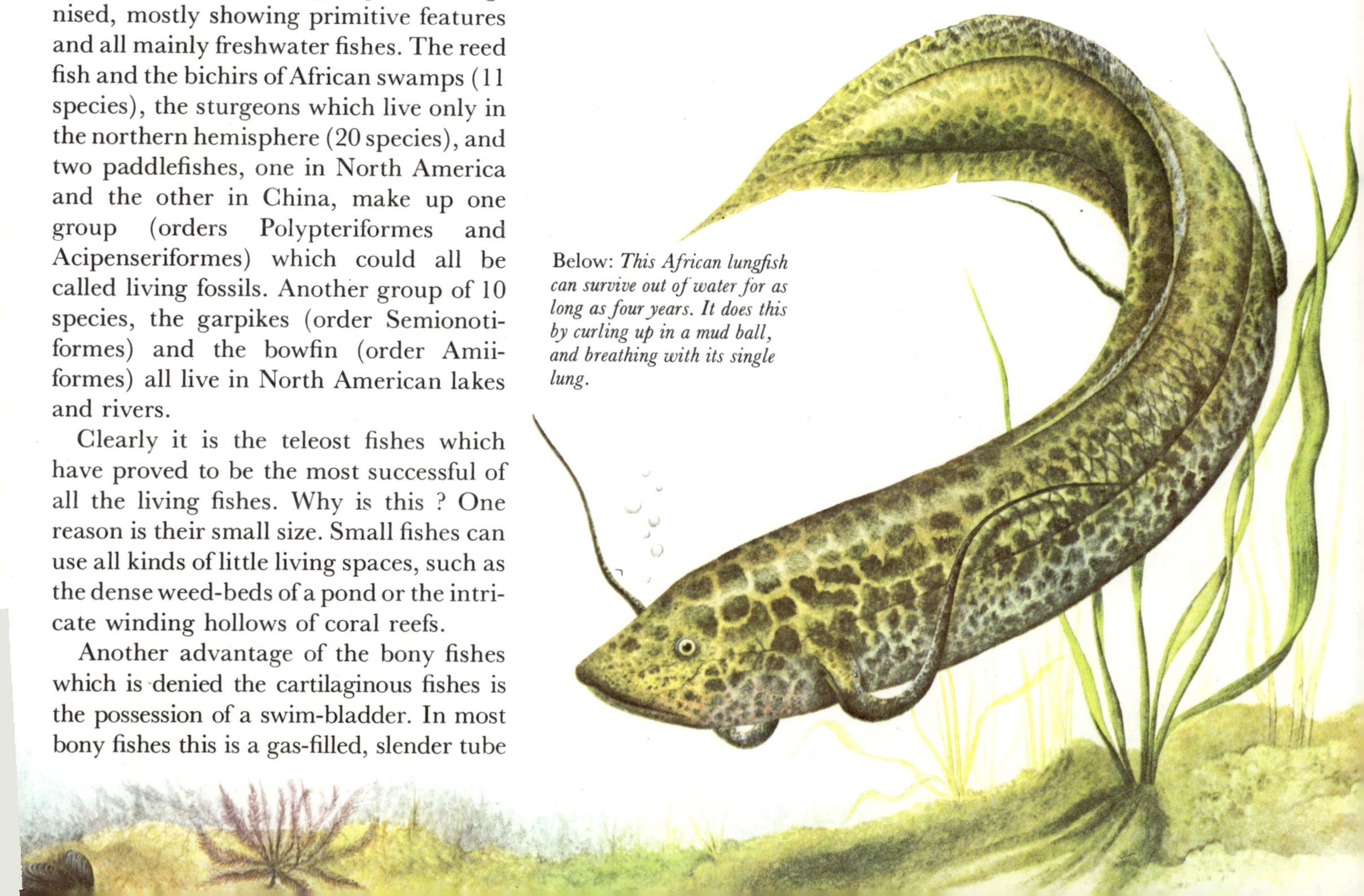

Below: *This African lungfish can survive out of water for as long as four years. It does this by curling up in a mud ball, and breathing with its single lung.*

How Fishes Live

One of the major problems for any animal is how to stay alive long enough to reproduce. Fishes have solved this problem in a variety of ways, many of which have parallels in other animal groups.

Many kinds of smaller fishes which live in the open waters, such as herrings, anchovies, dace and minnows, form schools. Usually such a school consists of a number of fishes, sometimes even thousands, all of approximately the same size. This size matching gives the fish an advantage, because if large and small fish were mixed together then clearly the smaller fish could not swim at the same speed or for as long, and they would weaken and drop out of the school, to be captured by predators.

Living together also means that there are many eyes to watch for danger, many nostrils to sense food, many brains to assess the signals they receive, so a school of fish becomes in effect a 'superfish' in its own right. Often when threatened by a larger predator, a school bunches together and the individual fishes continually change their place in it. So the predator becomes confused with what seems to be a never-ending relay of prey becoming visible and then disappearing.

Puffer-fishes can swell themselves up to enormous proportions by swallowing water, and they also have prickles in the skin on the sides and belly. It is probably the impossibility of swallowing a prickly balloon that deters many predators, but the fish are also poisonous.

Puffer-fishes are not the only fish to be poisonous. The cabezon, a large scorpion-fish, living on the Pacific coast of North America from Alaska to California, lays its eggs in clumps at communal nesting sites on the shore. The eggs are guarded by the male fish, but there is little necessity for this as the eggs are very poisonous and never seem to be even approached by likely predators.

Below: *This burr-fish is a kind of puffer fish with spines. When alarmed, it takes in water until it is a round prickly ball. If taken out of water, it can inflate itself just as easily with air. There are about 15 different kinds of burr-fishes – or porcupine-fishes – known from tropical seas.*

In the Red Sea a small flatfish called the Moses sole has similar and equally effective defensive weapons. A series of glands along its sides produce a milky fluid which is poisonous to predators, and probably to man as well.

The anemone fishes, which live in the tropical Indian and Pacific oceans, have evolved another way of staying alive in seas abounding in larger, hungry fishes. These brightly-coloured banded fishes live beside large sea anemones, whose stinging cells are normally fatal to any small fish. Most of the time the fishes

Left: *A male seahorse delivers a brood of young. The female lays her eggs directly into the male's brood pouch, where they are fertilised and remain until the young seahorses mature. They are then released from the pouch by the male.*

hover very near the anemone, but if danger threatens they actually take refuge within the mass of waving tentacles.

Anemone fishes lay their eggs in a compact mass close to the base of the anemone, and the eggs are guarded by a parent. Many other fishes, especially those which establish territories, guard their eggs in some kind of nest. Possibly best known is the stickleback which builds a small, cotton-reel-sized nest of plant fibres and leaves in which the eggs are laid. The male guards the nest and, for a while, the young fish.

Other nest-builders, or more precisely egg-guarders, are the gobies of the seashore, many of which lay their eggs on the hollow side of an empty sea-shell. Blennies have been known to make a nest inside a hollow marrow bone on the sea bed, but they usually adopt a crevice in the rock or among stones.

In general, fishes which guard their eggs produce very few of them. This is nowhere better seen than in the seahorses, where the eggs are carried by the male in a brood pouch, but only 200 eggs or fewer are laid. The male worm pipefish, which is common on rocky shores in Britain, carries as few as 50 eggs. Other fishes, such as several African freshwater cichlids, a number of catfishes, and some tropical coral reef cardinal fishes, take the eggs in the mouth (usually the male's) and protect them in this way. Naturally, the number that can be so looked after is low.

As we have seen, many sharks and rays give birth to fully-formed young fishes, and a few bony fishes have also adopted this strategy as a means of protecting their young. The best-known are the livebearing toothcarps of South and Central America, popular in the aquarium as guppies, mollies, and platies. In European seas the viviparous blenny, which can be found on the shore and in shallow water, also gives birth to fully-formed tiny young.

Right: *The boxfish or cowfish is related to puffer fishes. When they are alarmed, they release a poison in the water that can kill other fishes close by. The conspicuous colouring may serve as a warning to other fishes.*

In contrast to the coelacanth, which probably produces fewer than 20 young at a time, most bony fishes lay thousands, even millions of eggs. This again is a response to the need for survival of the species. These egg-layers shed their eggs and swim away. The eggs are not protected, but they are shed in places and at seasons favourable for their survival. In most species it is doubtful whether more than one or two adult fish are produced from a single fish's spawn – and a cod, for example, may produce 9 million eggs! Mortality during the egg stage, and more particularly immediately after hatching, is usually so high that the number of survivors may be halved each day.

Although this seems an incredible waste when compared with live-bearing fishes, and more particularly birds and mammals, it has proved to be an efficient way to solve the problem of survival, as witness the enormous quantity of bony fishes that inhabit the waters today.

Below: *Sticklebacks are well known for their nest-building. The male fish builds the tube-shaped nest (below) with weeds bound by a gluey thread he secretes. When it is completed he persuades a gravid female to enter it and lay her eggs. The male then follows the female through the tube and fertilises the eggs. He remains on guard by the nest, tending the eggs until they hatch, and then protecting the young until they can fend for themselves. Nine-spined stickleback,* Pungitis pungitis *(left), three-spined stickleback,* Gasterosteus aculeatus *(right).*

Amphibians

Amphibians are animals which live partly in water and partly on dry land. They include frogs, toads, newts and salamanders. There are about 2,000 species, most of which live in the tropics. Amphibians were the earliest group of vertebrates to live on the land. They possess smooth slimy skins, normally without scales, although one group (the Apoda) has little scales embedded in the skin. The skin is not waterproof, and an amphibian must avoid situations where water loss is rapid, and must also be able to remove excess water from the body when submerged.

As adults, most amphibians live on the land and have lungs to breath air. These lungs are not very efficient, and often extra breathing methods are used, the animal absorbing oxygen through its damp skin or through the membranes of its mouth and throat. In some species these methods of gaining oxygen are more important than lungs. Some amphibians live in water as adults and retain gills for breathing. Amphibians are cold-blooded, unable to generate warmth within the body, which has about the same temperature as their surroundings.

A typical amphibian starts life as an egg laid in water but not cared for by the parents. After a short time a tadpole emerges. It looks like a little fish and is equipped with gills for living in water. The gills are first external, then internal. After growing for several weeks the animal *metamorphoses* (changes) and emerges from the water as a miniature adult. In the common frog the tadpole stage lasts about 12 weeks. Towards the end of this period first the back legs and then the front legs grow, and the tail is absorbed into the body. Finally the tiny frog becomes air-breathing.

In the common newt the process is a little quicker. The eggs are laid singly and from each a tadpole with external gills hatches. By eight weeks first two front legs, then a pair of back legs, develop, and by 10 weeks the gills have disappeared, giving a lung-breathing adult.

Most amphibians develop in this way but there are some extraordinary variations. Some frogs lay their eggs in pools of water held in tree branches or even in leaf-bases. The male of the midwife toad wraps strings of eggs from the female round his back legs and carries them till hatching time, when they are placed in water. The female Surinam toad carries the eggs embedded in her back. The tadpole stage and metamorphosis take place in the egg.

There are three orders of amphibians – Apoda (caecilians), Urodela (newts and

Right: *Typical amphibian development can be seen in the life-cycle of the common frog. The female lays a large number of eggs which are externally fertilised by the male clinging to her back. These fertilised eggs are coated in a covering which swells in the water to become the familiar frog spawn. When the developing embryo has used up the yolk in the egg, it breaks out, emerging as a tailed tadpole, breathing by means of external gills. The external gills are later replaced by internal gills and the tadpole develops hind legs. The tail shrinks slowly as the front legs develop, and it is finally a tiny frog ready to breathe air with the lung which has been growing inside. Many variations on this theme are found in the amphibian world, some of them quite bizarre; some salamanders, for instance, remain in the tadpole condition, with external gills.*

Below: *When Surinam toads mate the male and female cooperate in manoeuvering the fertilised eggs onto the female's back. She then sits quietly while the thick skin there swells and envelops each egg. When the eggs mature, the tadpoles develop inside their capsules and emerge one by one as fully formed tiny toads.*

salamanders), and Anura or Salientia (frogs and toads).

Caecilians are a little-known group of limbless, rather worm-like burrowing animals living only in the tropics. They have no trace of limbs, and instead of eyes they have sensory tentacles. Fertilisation is internal and eggs are laid in damp soil, or in some cases retained by the females until hatching.

Newts and salamanders have long tails in the adult form, which aquatic species use for swimming. Fertilisation of the eggs may be internal or external. The eggs hatch to tadpoles.

The common newt and the European fire salamander are fairly typical. Probably the most remarkable are some species of mole salamanders of North and Central America. The larval form of these species is called an axolotl, which looks like a giant tadpole with legs. Although not a fully-developed adult, the axolotl can breed. The axolotl has gills; if its surroundings dry up it develops lungs and turns into an adult salamander. For many years axolotls were thought to be an independent kind of amphibian.

There are three other families of entirely aquatic urodeles: the congo eels, which have minuscule limbs and live in swamps in the United States; the sirens, which have small front limbs, but no hind limbs, and are found in Mexico and the United States; and the mud-puppies, rather like overgrown tadpoles with legs, also from the United States. The olm, a close relative of the mud-puppy, lives in underground streams in the extreme south of Austria, and in northern Italy and Yugoslavia.

Above: *The North American spotted salamander lives entirely on land, going to water only for one or two days each year to lay its eggs. The larvae hatch after about 40 days, and mature in about three months.*

Below: *The European smooth newt also lives mainly on land. At mating time males and females find their way to water, and the male displays his fine tail and breeding colours in an elaborate dance. At the end of the dance the male and female mate and the female sticks fertilised eggs singly onto stones or water weed and then leaves the water. The eggs hatch in two weeks and the young newts leave the water after four months. This is usually in late June or early July in the South but rather later in the North or in mountains.*

With the exception of one primitive family all adult *anurans* (frogs and toads) have no ribs or tails, and most of them have short backbones. Many species have long back legs, ideal for jumping, though some anurans habitually walk.

The terms *frog* and *toad* strictly belong to the true frogs, which form the genus *Rana*, and the true toads of the genus *Bufo*. The names are applied to many other anurans, and are sometimes confused – tree frogs are occasionally called tree toads.

The common frog (*Rana temporaria*) belongs to a world-wide family, the Ranidae, with a large number of species. The toads of the family Bufonidae are also numerous, and are found in all continents but Australia. They generally walk rather than hop, and have a warty skin, harder and drier than that of frogs. Toads are more independent of water than many amphibians.

Members of the large tree frog family are well adapted for climbing. Most have large eyes, and there are pads on the tips of fingers and toes and extra cartilages within which help the grip. The pipid toads, which include the African clawed frog, used as a laboratory animal, are entirely aquatic.

Several families of anuran are burrowers, such as the small spade-foot toads of the northern continents, and the Mexican burrowing toad.

Reptiles: Turtles and Crocodiles

There are about 6,000 species of reptiles. The most obvious external characteristic of these animals is the body covering of scales, on a skin which is much more waterproof than that of amphibians. Many reptiles live away from water and some never need to drink. Nor do reptiles need water to reproduce: most of them lay eggs on land. Reptiles breathe air, using lungs. Like amphibians they are cold-blooded and cannot maintain a constant body temperature by internal energy production.

The skeletons of reptiles differ from those of mammals in several respects. The bones harden first in the middle, and the ends may remain soft as cartilage, allowing even old animals to continue to grow. Ribs may extend from neck to tail, not just in the chest region. There are differences in the soft parts too: for instance, the heart has only three chambers, allowing some mixture of oxygenated and deoxygenated blood.

The brain of a reptile is small. A large crocodile may have a brain little larger than your thumb. As might be expected, most reptiles show little intelligence, but many of them have complex instinctive behaviour, sometimes including displays and colour signals, like those of birds.

Many lizards have sharp colour vision, and crocodiles have good hearing. Most reptiles are silent apart from hissing, but crocodiles and their relatives make booming roars, and geckos make a variety of clicks and cheeps.

Reptiles regulate their temperature surprisingly well by the way they behave, basking in the Sun to gain warmth, and changing posture or retreating to shelter to escape excessive heat or cold. In this way, a lizard in the tropics may be able to keep within a degree or two of its best working body temperature.

The reptile class is divided into four orders. Firstly there are the Chelonia, the tortoises and turtles, with about 250 species. There are only 21 species of crocodiles and alligators in the order Crocodilia. The order Rhynchocephalia is smallest, with only one living species, the tuatara. The largest order is the Squamata, the lizards and snakes. There are about 3,000 species of lizards, and nearly as many snakes.

The tortoises and turtles have existed for more than 200 million years with very little change. They have solidly-roofed skulls and a shell which covers and protects the body. This is formed of an internal shell made up of backbone, ribs and bony plates from the skin fused together, which makes a box over and under the animal. Covering this are modified scales, forming the visible horny shell. The upper shell is called the *carapace*; the lower shell is called the *plastron*. Land tortoises may

Right: *Soft-shelled turtles,* Trionyx *sp., are freshwater reptiles. Adults only come out of the water to bask in the sun.*

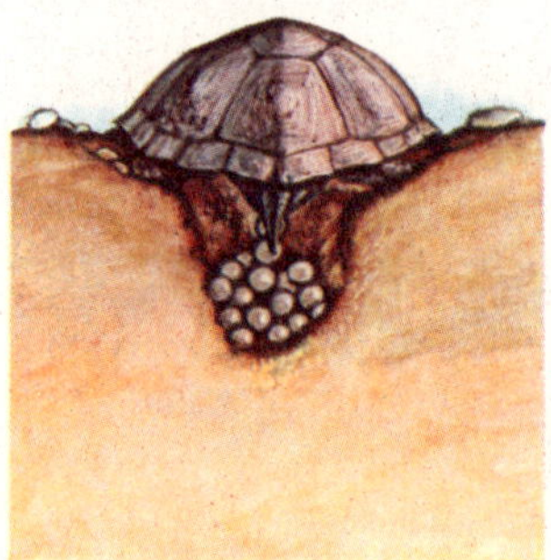

Below: *Sea turtles come ashore to lay their eggs in the warm sand. The female turtle digs a deep hole with her hind feet, depositing about 100 eggs in it. She then pushes the sand back over them, and smooths the surface before returning to the sea.*

Below: *The turtle (left) and the Galápagos giant tortoise (right) are both sadly depleted species. Their palatability, slowness of movement and habit of leaving eggs unattended have all contributed to their near-extinction. The harvesting of turtle eggs is now strictly regulated, and the Galápagos Islands are carefully guarded.*

have heavy shells, move slowly and be vegetarian. Sea-turtles and freshwater tortoises (terrapins) often have lighter shells and may be meat-eaters.

Two families of primitive sidenecked turtles live in freshwater in South America, Africa and Australia. They get their name because they withdraw the head into the shell by a sideways bending of the neck. The other seven families of tortoises fold the neck vertically when withdrawing the head.

The largest tortoise family, the Testudinidae, with over 100 species found all over the tropics except Australia, ranges from giant tortoises of the Galápagos and Indian Ocean islands, with shells over 1 metre (3 feet 3 inches) long and weighing 200 kilogrammes (440 pounds), to the Mediterranean tortoises often kept as pets, and includes many freshwater species. In the North American box turtles the plastron is hinged and the animal can close the ends. An African genus, *Kinixys*, has a hinge towards the rear of the carapace. One of the oddest shells is that of the African pancake tortoise, whose bones are so reduced that the tortoise, which wedges itself among rocks to avoid enemies, can inflate to prevent itself from being pulled out.

Sea-turtles' legs have become efficient flippers for swimming. These turtles only come to land to lay eggs, up to 200 in a clutch. The enormous leathery sea-turtle, whose curious degenerate shell is a mosaic of little bones, may weigh up to half a tonne. It feeds on jellyfish.

The soft-shelled turtles are well adapted for life in freshwater. Found in Africa, southern Asia and North America, they have long noses drawn out as breathing tubes, and there are no horny plates on their shells.

Crocodiles and alligators are the largest of the living reptiles. Formerly some species grew to 9 metres (30 feet) in length, but now a crocodile over 6 metres (20 feet) would be considered a giant. With powerful tails for propulsion, and eyes, ears and nose set right on top of the head, crocodilians are well equipped for life in the water, but sometimes bask out of water. They must come to land to lay eggs. A nest may contain 30 to 40 eggs and in some species the female remains near the nest to guard it.

Crocodiles differ from alligators in having fewer teeth and in having the fourth tooth in the bottom jaw visible outside the upper jaw. The alligator group has bony plates in the skin of the belly. Alligators, which include caymans, are found only in the Americas, except for one small rare species, the Chinese alligator. Crocodiles live in America, Africa, Asia and Australia. Those crocodilians such as the Indian gharial which feed mostly on fish, have longer, narrower snouts than those with more catholic tastes.

All crocodiles, unlike most reptiles, have the nose cavity separate from the mouth, and have flaps of skin at the back of the mouth which can close it off from the throat. Because of these flaps, crocodiles can breathe with their mouths open under water. The nostrils can be closed on submerging.

Most crocodiles live in fresh water but the estuarine or salt-water crocodile of South-East Asia and Australia is capable of sea journeys. It is one of the larger living crocodilians. The smallest are the African broad-fronted crocodiles, at about 1·3 metres (4 feet 3 inches) long.

Right: *Alligators – and crocodiles too – attack creatures too large to swallow whole. They manage to twist off small pieces by grasping a limb of the victim in their jaws, and spinning themselves on a longitudinal axis until it breaks off.*

Right: *There is not much difference between an alligator and a crocodile. They both have an enlarged fourth lower tooth; alligators (above) have their upper teeth fitting inside the lower ones so that when the mouth is closed no teeth can be seen. Crocodiles' teeth are more or less in line, and when a crocodile closes its mouth the enlarged lower tooth fits into a notch outside the snout where it is clearly visible. At a quick glance, crocodiles appear to have more retroussé snouts than alligators.*

Below: *Alligators lay eggs in a kind of compost heap enclosed in mud. The heat produced by rotting vegetation incubates the eggs. When the young are ready to emerge they squeak and the mother then tears open the nest to release her young. A 20-centimetre ($7\frac{3}{4}$-inch) baby alligator emerges from an 8-centimetre ($3\frac{1}{4}$-inch) egg, armed with two fine rows of teeth ready to eat small water creatures.*

Reptiles: Lizards and Snakes

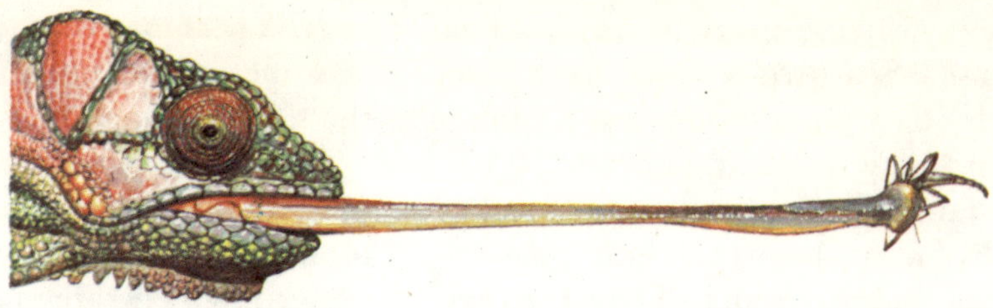

Above: *The chameleon can shoot out its remarkable sticky tongue to a distance of about its own length, often further, in a split second. Its vision is correspondingly accurate.*

The tuatara now lives only on a few islands off the coast of New Zealand. It is the sole survivor of the order Rynchocephalia, which flourished in the time of the dinosaurs but became extinct about 100 million years ago. It is active mainly at night, often at low temperatures.

Lizards and snakes form the order Squamata. Most lizards have four legs, small scales below the body and above, and well-developed eyes and ears. Snakes are thought to have developed many millions of years ago from lizards which burrowed underground. This ancestry may explain some of the differences between typical lizards and snakes. Snakes have no legs, but large scales beneath the belly extend across the underside to provide a grip on the ground as the animal moves. The eyes are covered by a transparent scale, and the external ear is absent, so snakes are deaf to airborne sounds.

Lizards are in the sub-order Lacertilia or Sauria. One of the largest families is that of the iguanas, with about 700 species found in the Americas and Madagascar. The common green iguana of the South American forests may grow to more than 1·2 metres (4 feet) long. Most lizards are meat-eaters, but this species eats much vegetable food.

The agamas (family Agamidae) fill the same ecological niche as the iguanids in the Old World. They too are active, four-legged lizards which may be spiny or crested, and brightly coloured. The frilled dragon of Australia can run fast on its hind legs and has a throat fan used in threat.

The family Lacertidae includes the typical small lizards of Europe and northern Asia. The common lizard found in Britain is a hardy species that can live as far north as the Arctic Circle. The female is ovoviviparous – that is, she retains the eggs within her body until hatching, so effectively the young are born alive.

The geckos (family Gekkonidae) are found all over the tropics, and there are about 400 species. They are nearly all nocturnal and good climbers, for their toes have flattened tips with ridges underneath. These ridges have tiny hair-like projections which grip, even on apparently smooth surfaces.

Chameleons are a mainly African family (Chamaeleonidae) with about 80 species. Most are excellent climbers with opposable toes, and some have prehensile tails. Many species have great colour-changing ability, the colour being affected by mood as well as surroundings.

Another large family, with 700 species, is that of the skinks (Scincidae). Many

Below: *Monitors (5) are a good example of lizard form – they are unspecialised and quite closely related to the snakes. Agamas (4) and the related frilled dragon (1), use shock tactics to deter enemies. The stump-tailed skink (2) bears live young. The leaf-tailed gecko (7) has toes adapted for climbing, even across ceilings. Slow-moving Gila monsters (3) have a venomous bite. Only the marine iguana (6) has taken to the sea.*

burrow in sand or the soil surface. Members of the family have legs of varying length, and some are completely limbless.

The Old World monitors (family Varanidae) are a small family of large powerful carnivorous lizards, including the Komodo dragon of Indonesia which grows to 4 metres (13 feet) long, the largest lizard. Distantly related are the Gila monster and the Mexican beaded lizard, the only venomous lizards.

Snakes form a sub-order, called Ophidia or Serpentes. Nearly 300 species belong to primitive families of burrowers, half of these being blind-snakes.

Of the more 'normal' main groups of snake, the boas and pythons (Boidae) have some primitive features, having two lungs and traces of hind limbs. They are constrictors, trapping the prey with the head and then wrapping their bodies around to suffocate the victim. Like most snakes they have very flexible jaws and skulls, and can swallow prey much larger than their heads.

The Colubridae, the largest family with well over 1,000 species, includes all the typical snakes such as the grass-snake. Most are fairly small and harmless to man. They catch prey by simply grabbing and swallowing, or by constriction. A few of this family, such as the boomslang, have developed venom glands and small fangs at the top of the rear of the mouth.

The cobras and sea-snakes have more efficient venom apparatus, with fixed fangs at the front of the mouth which inject venom. The fangs are short and the snake may need to hold on and chew at the prey, but the venom is powerful. Cobras (family Elapidae) live in Africa and Asia. Most cobras feed on rats and mice. The sea-snakes (family Hydrophiidae) have some of the most powerful venom of any snakes, but are rarely dangerous to man. They swim by means of flattened tails. Some species bear live young in the water, and never come to land.

The best developed venom apparatus is found in vipers and rattlesnakes (Viperidae). In these snakes the poison fangs are so long that they have to be folded along the roof of the mouth when it is closed, but when the mouth is opened they form a formidable hypodermic which can inject enough venom at one stab to kill a victim. The venom affects mainly the blood and circulation.

Rattlesnakes are similar to vipers, but the end of the tail bears a horny rattle which is vibrated when the snake is alarmed. Rattlesnakes have a pit on each cheek sensitive to warmth, and can use this to detect warm-blooded prey.

Above: *The green python,* Chondropython viridis, *of New Guinea is adapted to arboreal life by having a prehensile tail and very long front teeth. In these and in its way of balancing on a branch in coils as it is doing here, there is a marked similarity to the emerald boa,* Boa canina, *which lives in the same way in American forests.*

Above: *The fangs of venomous snakes are modified teeth. The poison runs in grooves from the salivary glands.*

Below: *Although the majority of snakes are harmless to man, there are four families with dangerously venomous members. These are the sea-snakes (1) and cobras (2) which are front-fanged, and the vipers (3) and rattlesnakes (4) which have folding fangs.*

Left: *The skeleton of a bird. The sternum (1) has a large keel for attachment of the powerful flight muscles, and the body and tail bones are short. The bones of the wing have humerus (2), radius (3) and ulna (4); the hand is much reduced but three fingers remain – the second (6) is long and carries primary feathers, while the first carries one or more feathers (5). The foot bears four toes.*

Birds and Their Ways

Below: Archaeopteryx *was the earliest-known bird. Its tail was long and bony, it had teeth and hollow bones, but its clawed wings were weak. Feathers were clearly an early and important bird characteristic.*

Birds are vertebrate animals with feathers – but there is much more to them than that simple definition. The first birds, known from fossils, evolved from their reptile-like ancestors about 150 million years ago. To this day, birds still retain a number of reptilian features, such as scaly skin on the feet. Feathers consist almost entirely of keratin – the same protein as in skin, nails and hair – and are apparently modified and highly specialised scales.

Like mammals, birds are *homoiothermic* (warm-blooded), which has enabled them to survive in cold areas (even better than mammals) where the bodily processes of cold-blooded creatures would cease to function.

Feathers are extremely important as insulators, as well as serving to streamline the body during flight and to propel the bird through the air. A feather is a remarkable structure. The main shaft is hollow, and is light, flexible and extremely strong. The vane of the feather is made up of a great many interlocking side branches forming the main insulating and flying surfaces. *Down* is the small, very soft feathers under the outer layer. It traps a layer of warm air next to the body and reduces heat loss.

Apart from feathers, there are many other ways in which birds differ from other vertebrates. Most of them relate to the needs of flight, which demands lightness and strength. Weight is reduced in many ways, the most obvious being in the skeleton, which is proportionately lighter than that of a mammal. Many bones in a bird's skeleton, including those of the limbs and skull, are hollow, sometimes with internal supporting struts – compare the lightness and strength of a bicycle frame. There are numerous air spaces or sacs in the body, some connecting with the inside spaces of the bones. The skull is very small, with small jaws which lack teeth. The food is ground up in the gizzard, a muscular bag which may contain grit and is positioned near the bird's centre of gravity. A small head does not need a large tail to counterbalance it; the fleshy part of a bird's tail is extremely short, and the long tails which some birds have are almost entirely feathers.

There is a great deal of *fusion* (joining up) of bones in the backbone and limbs, and many bones in the feet of the birds' reptile ancestors have been entirely lost during evolution. The skeleton of a bird's main trunk is like a firm but flexible basket, protecting and supporting the delicate internal organs, but still permitting breathing. It provides a firm base against which the wings can work, yet with enough 'spring' to prevent jarring as the bird lands. The breastbone is particularly well developed. It has a keel like the bottom of a sailing boat, providing a large, firm area for the attachment of the enormous muscles necessary for flight. These muscles may make up half the body weight.

Weight is kept down in many other ways. Undigested food is kept to an absolute minimum by a very rapid and efficient digestive system, and waste products are removed at frequent intervals from the body as droppings. The reproductive organs develop only when needed for the breeding season, withering away to very small structures at other times. The young are not carried around during their embryonic development; the fertilised egg is laid with a rich food supply in a protective shell within which the chick develops.

Flight is a highly strenuous activity, and the powerful wing muscles use enormous amounts of energy. This energy is provided when the body *metabolises* (converts) the fats, proteins and carbohydrates in the food. Birds eat a great deal, usually of energy-rich foods such as seeds, fruit, fish, insects or mammals.

A bird's active way of life is possible only because its metabolism is so rapid, and its body temperature is high – compared with a man's 36·9°C (98·4°F), that of a bird is 37·7–43·5°C (99·86–110·3°F), the majority of species being between 40–42°C (104–107·6°F). The flight muscles' great demands for energy mean that the oxygen which releases it by oxidising the food must be absorbed from the air and transported to the muscles very quickly. The waste carbon dioxide must be taken away to the lungs equally fast. Consequently, birds breathe rapidly; their lungs are more efficient than those of mammals because the air passes through them into the air spaces, and the pockets of stale air found in other creatures' lungs are largely avoided.

The heart rate is also especially rapid (man at rest, about 78 heartbeats a minute; average bird, 300–500 beats; some hummingbirds, more than 600 beats, or 10 a second). As in mammals, a bird's heart has four chambers, and there is a double circulation of the blood, first to the lungs for exchange of gases (oxygen and carbon dioxide) and then back to the heart before making the main journey around the body.

In flight, birds move at speed and need to take quick avoiding action; their bodies take up an amazing variety of positions while on the wing. To enable them to do all these things, birds have a highly-developed nervous system. The cerebellum – that part of the brain controlling movement and enabling the bird to re-adjust its position instantly in the air – is very large proportionately compared with that of any other kind of animal. A bird's eyes are enormous in relation to its overall size when compared with those of other vertebrates.

With such quick reactions and acute sight, there is no great need for a keen sense of smell in most species, but the sense of hearing is very well developed.

The ability to fly has many advantages, such as escaping from enemies, and moving to feeding and breeding areas a considerable distance away. However, the requirements of an efficient flying machine do not allow much room for variation in size and shape, and so as a class birds are much more uniform in both respects than mammals.

Above: *Flamingoes fly with their legs trailing behind them and the head held low on an extended neck. Three flamingoes here are flying down to join the flock; that on the right has its wings 'feathered' to lose height, and stall for landing as the feet are about to be brought forward. Fossil flamingoes have been found dating from 70 million years ago.*

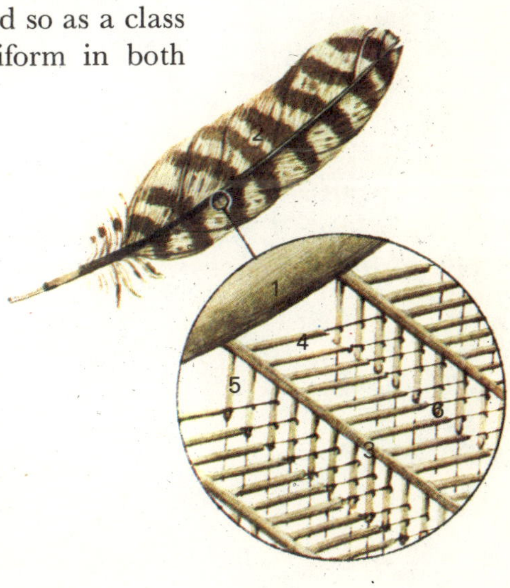

Right: *A feather with a section greatly enlarged. The centre stem or* rachis *(1) bears* barbs *(3) which in turn bear* barbules. *The barbules on one side (5) have a stiff outer edge and those on the other side (4) bear tiny hooks or* barbicels. *These barbicels hook over two or more barbules of the adjacent barb to form a strong yet easily reparable network (6), which with the barbs comprises the vane (2).*

The Social Life of Birds

Below: *The weaverbird resembles the English house sparrow, for sparrows are members of the weaverbird family. Some weavers build communal nests, others like this one build an individual family nest.*

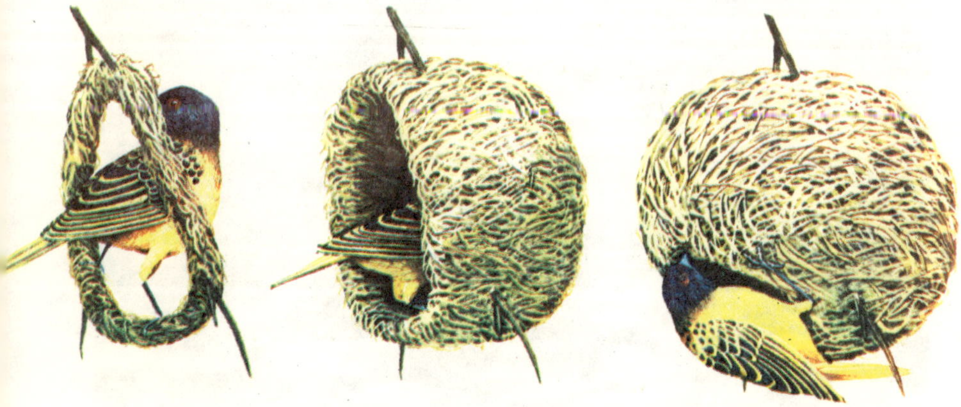

Birds, as we have seen, are highly specialised creatures. Their structure is often dictated by the requirements of an efficient flying machine.

In most cases the ability to fly gives such an advantage that sacrifices have had to be made – in evolutionary terms – in other directions. Birds' mobility enables them to disperse to new areas or to migrate away from unfavourable circumstances, but with the flying ability go such disadvantages as the production of eggs. This immediately presents such problems as protecting the very edible eggs and young from predators. Other difficulties, such as raising and protecting the young at a time of year and in a place where there is plentiful food, are shared by all vertebrates and many invertebrates.

At the start of the breeding season it is usual for the male bird to claim a *territory*, an area of ground where the young will be raised. In land-birds the nature and size of the territory will depend on the breeding habits – whether the birds live solitary lives or in colonies – and the feeding habits – that is, where food is available in relation to the nest. The territory of solitarily nesting species, such as the European robin (*Erithacus rubecula*), may be quite large and defended aggressively against all other individuals of the same species and also against certain other species of birds.

The communally nesting species such as weaverbirds (family Ploceidae) may have scores of pairs nesting in the same big nest; they defend only the immediate vicinity of their nest. This is true also for most communally-nesting sea-birds; for example, gannets (family Sulidae) sitting on the nest are just out of reach of each other. In such species the feeding area is away from the nest. In feeding areas birds may show territorial behaviour both during and outside the breeding period. Birds generally defend their territories by posturing, threatening and singing or calling rather than by actual physical combat, but vicious fighting does occur in some species.

The exact functions of territory and singing are not yet fully understood. They are probably as variable as the nature of the territorial behaviour, song and display. One key effect of territory is to cause the birds, whether singly, in pairs or colonies, to be spread out more than they would otherwise be, thus preventing overcrowding. The ownership of a territory means that the birds have a site to which they return, becoming familiar with its advantages and dangers; it also helps to keep the pair together as a unit.

Most birds breed only once every year, so that at the start of the breeding season, the male usually has to attract a female into his territory while deterring rival males. To do this he uses various and often elaborate displays, for which special plumage is developed. The variety of songs, calls and other noises is truly bewildering. The females of species in which the males do all the courting are generally drab by comparison with the cock birds. Species where both sexes dis-

Left: *Bitterns are wonderfully adapted both in colouring and in posture to blend into the reeds. A bittern hiding in this way will turn so that it always presents the thinnest view of its body.*

play at courting time generally have both sexes equally adorned with fancy plumage. In the phalaropes (family Phalaropodidae) the sexual roles are reversed and the female is brighter than the male.

Birds protect their eggs and young in a variety of ways. The nest may be placed high in a tree, over water, in a prickly bush or on a cliff face, in fact anywhere which makes it difficult to approach. Additionally it may be well camouflaged with vegetation, or well hidden among herbage or rocks. In species nesting in open habitats, the eggs are often laid on the bare ground and are in size and colour much like the stones among which they are laid.

The types of materials used for nests are extremely varied, but mostly they are vegetable matter, ranging from mosses and lichens up to large sticks. Other species, such as some of the swallows, build nests of freshly-gathered soft mud strengthened with grass, which hardens into a strong cup or pitcher-shaped structure.

Young birds can be grouped into two main types, depending on whether they leave the nest almost as soon as their down has dried after hatching (*nidifugous* chicks), or whether they remain for a lengthy period being cared for by the parents (*nidicolous* chicks, or nestlings). In nidifugous species such as waders and ducks the dangers of remaining in one spot are too great. The chicks are generally camouflaged and remain flightless for many weeks. In nidicolous species, the chicks are usually safer from predation because of the nature or position of the nest. The division between the two types is not firm and intermediate types occur.

One highly fascinating aspect of bird biology is migration. Birds undertake a variety of journeys, but true migration occurs when a species regularly leaves its breeding area and moves, sometimes vast distances, to more climatically favourable areas. Not surprisingly, the habit is best developed in species inhabiting areas where there is a distinct winter and summer.

Other movements may be more in the nature of local dispersal away from areas of potential overcrowding.

The means by which birds find their way across vast distances, often returning the following year to the same nest site, is still partly a mystery, but much progress has been made recently in research into the subject. It is known, for example, that birds can use star-patterns and the position of the Sun in relation to the time of day for navigation, and some species appear able to detect differences in the magnetism of the Earth.

Below: *Two movements in the courtship dance of grebes. The toe dance (left) shows the birds running side by side on top of the water, ending the run with a great splash. The second movement (right) follows a submerged swim in which each partner picks up a piece of weed.*

Above: *The robin is a highly territorial bird. A mature male defends a territory of about 2,000 square metres (21,525 square feet), preserving its boundary with ritual aggressive displays where it meets the robin on the adjoining patch.*

Left: *Swallows nest and rear their young in Europe. They spend the winter in Africa, making the long trip over land and sea by a route that is constant for any one group. The mature birds may leave before the younger ones but young birds follow the route their parents took.*

Flightless Birds

A bird learns to fly only gradually after hatching, because its wings are relatively undeveloped at first. Some species are unable to fly when moulting (changing their feathers) because they lose so many feathers all at once. Some species are incapable of flight at any stage in their lives. Presumably all had flying ancestors and so the ability to fly has been gradually lost over thousands or millions of years.

While some whole orders of birds, such as the penguins (Sphenisciformes) and emus (Casuariiformes) are flightless, in general one or a few species from entirely different and unrelated families are involved. These flightless birds have evolved in habitats where the ability to fly has apparently proved to be unnecessary for survival. It may indeed be a definite hazard; some birds on small islands would face a distinct danger of being blown away from land and out to sea if they were able to take to the air. Flightlessness is not an all-or-none condition however, as some species fly so reluctantly or so weakly, if at all, that they would appear to be evolving in the direction of flightlessness.

Perhaps the best-known family of flightless birds is that of the penguins (Spheniscidae), containing 17 species. Penguin wings are shaped like curved paddles and cannot be folded as in most birds. Instead they are held at the sides or spread out like arms for balance during progress on land. Because the legs are far back on the body (they act as a rudder during swimming) the penguin stands upright and walks or waddles very much like a human being when ashore. The body is long and streamlined and thickly covered in a dense, compact layer of tiny, shiny feathers which form a very efficient waterproof and insulating coat.

All species are greyish or black on the back, and white on the underparts, reminiscent of western male evening dress and further enhancing the human appearance. The sexes are similar in appearance. Differences between species are chiefly to be found in the head and neck region, where the pattern and colour of marking vary. The largest species, the emperor penguin (*Aptenodytes forsteri*) is about 1·2 metres (4 feet) long and weighs from 22 to 45 kilogrammes (50 to 100 pounds). It breeds only in Antarctica.

The female lays a single egg which is incubated by the male. He balances it on top of his feet to protect it from the chill of the ice, and covers it by a flap of skin on his belly. Meanwhile the female departs to sea to feed. Only after a 60-day incubation period does she return to feed the hatched chick and relieve the male, who leaves for the sea.

The smallest species is the little blue penguin (*Eudyptula minor*), a mere 400 millimetres (16 inches) long, and slate-blue in colour with white underparts. It occurs in southern Australia, New Zealand and the Chatham Islands. It nests, like many other penguins, in a crevice or burrow – some make a nest of stones on the open ground – laying two eggs which take about six weeks to hatch.

The second large group of flightless birds is often given the name *ratites*. The ratites do not have the keel-shaped structure on their breastbone to which flying muscles are attached, whereas penguins do. The ratites are the ostrich (*Struthio camelus*) of Africa and Arabia, placed in its own family, Struthionidae, the two species of rheas of South America (family Rheidae) and the two emus (Dromiceiidae) and three cassowaries (Casuariidae) of Australasia.

There is much discussion on how closely related the ratites are. All have much reduced wings, which may however be used like sails when the birds run before the wind. Their very powerful legs can also be used for defence, being capable of delivering a vicious kick. The ostrich is the largest surviving species of

Above: *The owl parrot or kakapo,* Strigops habroptilus, *lives in the forests of South Island, New Zealand. It feeds and nests on the ground, sometimes climbing trees for fruit; its wings are only used to help it increase its hopping stride.*

Left: *The rock-hopper,* Eudyptes crestatus, *is a small penguin found on islands of the Southern Hemisphere. Like all penguins it is incapable of flight; its wings are completely adapted for swimming, with fused bones and no quills. The rest of its feathers are barbless, scale-like and evenly distributed over the body.*

Above: *The Galápagos cormorant,* Nannopterum harrisi, *is the only flightless cormorant. It walks on land in a penguin-like style.*

Left: *The wings of New Zealand kiwis are too small to be seen. Kiwis, like the extinct moas, lay enormous eggs – up to a quarter the weight of the hen.*

Above: *The now-extinct great auk was a large flightless bird. This Audubon painting shows it to have been like a penguin in appearance.*

bird, some 2·5 metres (8 feet) high and weighing as much as 140 kilogrammes (300 pounds). All the ratites eat mainly vegetable matter, such as grass, with occasional insects or slugs. Large clutches of eggs are laid but in some cases these clutches may be the product of several females. Clutches of up to 25 ostrich eggs and 30 rhea eggs are known while more modest clutches of 3–12 are more usual for emus and cassowaries. The ostrich is unusual among birds in having only two toes on each foot.

The three species of kiwi (family Apterygidae) are the national birds of New Zealand. They are curious nocturnal birds with fur-like plumage. Their long tapering bills have nostrils near the tip, and the birds have an apparently well-developed sense of smell. The wings are extremely small and obscured by the body plumage.

Apart from these well-known flightless birds, there are many others scattered throughout the world. A few can be listed: the kagu (*Rhynochetos jubatus*) of New Caledonia, a relative of the rails, which is apparently flightless; the flightless grebe (*Centropelma micropterum*) of South America; the flightless cormorant of the Galápagos Islands (*Nannopterum harrisi*), two species of steamer ducks of the genus *Tachyeres*, of South America and the Falkland Islands, which can only flap along the water surface when alarmed; the kakapo (*Strigops habroptilus*) which is a New Zealand parrot; two Australian species of parrots; and a number of rails (family Rallidae) from New Zealand and various oceanic islands.

Left: *These steamer ducks are a flightless type of shellduck, found in the Falkland Islands.*

Below: *Ostriches (3) are very large and long-lived birds. Their inability to fly is compensated by their powerful legs which carry them across the grasslands where they live, at speeds of up to 64 kilometres (40 miles) per hour. The claws of the two-toed African ostriches, which are also effective weapons, are hoof-like in appearance.*

Above right: *The only surviving species of emu (1) is at risk from Australian cattlemen, because it competes for food with grazing cattle.*

Above right: *Cassowaries (2) of New Guinea and North Australia are fast-running powerful birds.*

Above: *The brown pelican of the New World is perhaps the most marine of the half-dozen species. They are among the largest flying birds. Their bill is unique, its floor is formed into a large pouch for engulfing fish. Although ungainly on land, they are extremely graceful in flight.*
Top right: *The red-tailed tropic-bird is one of three species of the genus* Phaethon, *the others being the red-billed and the yellow-billed. They breed on islands in the warmer tropical and subtropical seas, and range far out to sea at other times. Individual yellow-billed tropic-birds of Ascension Island in the Atlantic are unusual in breeding at intervals of less than a year.*
Above right: *The African skimmer is one of three species of the genus* Rhynchops *which inhabit mainly tropical ocean shores, large rivers and lakes. They are closely related to gulls and terns.*

Seabirds

All seabirds face much the same problems in their daily lives – moving about in the air or on the water for feeding; avoiding predators; and breeding. There are, therefore, many similarities in distantly related species. The majority of seabirds are white, black and white or various shades of grey, or a combination of these colours, which makes them hard to see against greyish seas and skies. High winds, frequent at sea, mean that seabirds must be strong fliers. Webbed feet are needed for efficient swimming.

Most seabirds spend their lives and get all their food at sea, and so they breed on islands and cliffs, where they are incidentally safer from ground predators such as foxes. Since suitable breeding sites are scarce, breeding colonies are often crowded.

The seabirds consist of three main groups or orders of bird families: the albatross order (Procellariiformes), the cormorant order (Pelecaniformes), and the gull and auk order (Charadriiformes). The last group also includes the waders, called 'shorebirds' in North America.

The Procellariiformes are strictly marine birds, often remaining at sea all the time except when breeding on sea-cliffs and islands. The order consists of more than 50 species of shearwaters, 14 species of albatrosses, and more than 25 species of storm petrels and diving petrels. The albatrosses (family Diomedeidae) are large, heavily-built birds from 600 millimetres to 1·8 metres (2–6 feet) long, with enormously long, very narrow wings. The wandering albatross (*Diomedea exulans*) has a wing-span of up to 3·5 metres (11½ feet). The wing shape is an adaptation enabling the bird to spend hours at a time in flight, gliding on the gales frequent in the southern oceans where most species live.

The Shearwaters (family Procellariidae) are so called because of their flight, skimming from side to side low over the waves. These birds occur throughout most of the world, and are 280–910 millimetres (11–36 inches) long. The diving petrels (family Pelecanoididae) are only 150–250 millimetres (6–10 inches) long and inhabit the southern oceans. They dive from the air into the water to catch their animal food, and pursue it using their wings as paddles. The storm petrels (family Hydrobatidae), of similar small size, have a fluttering flight, dipping to the surface without actually alighting.

The second order of seabirds, the Pelecaniformes, is made up of about 55 species. Not all species in the group are in fact marine; the darters, long, slim swimming birds with long tails and snake-like necks, frequent rivers and lakes; some cormorants and pelicans prefer inland water, though often with a high salt content.

Feeding methods vary considerably. Gannets and boobies (family Sulidae) and tropic birds dive from the air into the sea to catch fish or squid; frigate-birds (family Fregatidae) feed on similar food picked from the surface while in flight. They may also steal food from other birds or eat their chicks when on land. Cormorants and shags (family Phalacrocoracidae) dive from the water surface, swimming with their feet to chase fish. Pelicans (family Pelecanidae) employ two feeding methods, either plunging from the air or swimming in 'U' formation, dipping their enormous scoop-like bills to trap fish.

The order Charadriiformes includes all the other seabirds and the waders, and

Left: *The puffin of the north Atlantic is perhaps the most colourful of seabirds. It can catch a succession of fish, arrange them neatly in a row across the ornate bill, and carry them back to its chick.*

consists of 16 families. The skuas, gulls and terns, and skimmers (families Stercoratiidae, Laridae, and Rhynchopidae) are very similar, medium-sized birds 200–760 millimetres (8–30 inches) long, with mainly white, pied or grey plumage, stout bills often hooked at the tip, long, narrow wings and strong graceful flight. Food consists chiefly of animal matter but feeding methods vary; in this way competition is reduced.

The auks, guillemots and puffins (family Alcidae) are mostly medium-sized, 150–760 millimetres (6–30 inches) long. They are plump black or black-and-white birds which can be regarded as the northern hemisphere equivalent of the penguins and diving petrels of Antarctica.

The waders and relatives number about 200 species, the majority in the plover and sandpiper families (Charadriidae and Scolopacidae). Small to medium-sized birds, 125–610 millimetres (5–24 inches) long, with fairly long necks and short tails, they are typically found near water, either inland or on the coast, living and usually nesting on the ground in the open. In many species the plumage and eggs are camouflaged against predators.

Bills of many species are long and tapering and may be down-curved as in curlews or up-turned as in the avocets. Long legs are adaptations for feeding in deep water, and long bills are for deep probing in soft mud. The shortest-billed species, the plovers, feed by picking food from the surface.

The seven species of jacanas and lilytrotters (Jacanidae) have greatly elongated legs and the toes and claws are even longer in proportion. The birds can walk about on floating plants such as water-lilies without sinking through their thin supporting platform, because the long toes spread the weight.

Some waders are boldly marked, the oystercatchers (Haematopodidae) and stilts being conspicuously black and white. Oystercatchers can open cockles and mussels by stabbing through a weak part of the hinge of the shell and the muscles holding the shell closed.

Above left: *The sooty shearwater flies with its wings stiffly outstretched. It visits its island nesting burrow at night.*

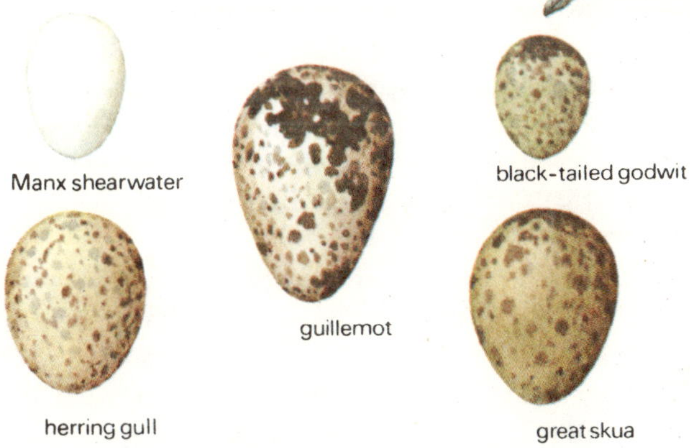

Below: *Various eggs.*

Below: *The black-browed albatross uses the same nest each year which may thus reach 1 metre (3 feet) in height. Colonies may number many thousands.*

Below: *The greater black-backed gull eats almost anything. The speckled brown and white juveniles take several years to acquire adult plumage.*

Below left: *The avocets feed by sweeping the bill from side to side through the water, sieving out minute organisms.*
Below: *The jacanas and lilytrotters swim readily and will also dive. They eat insects, snails and seeds.*

Wildfowl, Storks and Others

Above: *To take off from water, the tufted duck (above) first lifts its body by running with its wings high until it angles up from the surface. On landing, the mallard (above right) stalls over the water, using its webbed feet to brake and skid along until it has lost enough speed to settle on the surface.* Below: *Black Swan,* Cygnus atratus, *Australia (below); black-necked swan,* Cygnus melanocoriphus, *South America (centre); Coscoroba swan,* Coscoroba coscoroba, *South America (bottom).*

Ducks, geese and swans are grouped into the order Anseriformes. The order also includes the screamers (family Anhimidae), three species of South American birds with only very slightly webbed feet, and large bony spurs on the leading edge of their wings. The rest of the order form the family Anatidae; the swans, geese and whistling ducks in one sub-family; the remaining ducks in another; and one species, the magpie goose (*Anseranas semipalmata*) of Northern Australia and New Guinea, in a group by itself. The magpie goose is a pied, goose-like bird with only slightly webbed feet and many internal anatomical features quite different from the rest of the order. Ducks, geese and swans are often collectively called wildfowl.

The Anseriformes include species from 280 millimetres to 1·5 metres (11–60 inches) in length. All are aquatic and, outside the breeding season, gregarious. They feed on plants or animals. The birds nest on the ground, in hollow trees, or on rocky ledges, laying usually large clutches of pale white, buff or greenish unmarked eggs, which are camouflaged and prevented from chilling with a plentiful layer of down feathers provided by the female. The young are downy and can swim as soon as they are dry.

The geese are a fairly uniform group, divided into 'grey' forms and 'black' forms. The grey species include the Asian swan goose (*Anser cygnoides*), which is the ancestor of the domestic Chinese goose, and the greylag (*Anser anser*), the ancestor of other domestic geese. Not all species in the group are actually grey: for example the snow goose (*Anser caerulescens*) and Ross's goose of northern North America are white with pink legs and bills, though the lesser race of the snow goose (*Anser caerulescens caerulescens*) occurs also in a bluish-grey form.

The grey geese breed in the high Arctic of Europe, Asia and North America, migrating southwards to warmer climates for the winter. The black geese also inhabit northern latitudes, but the ne-ne or Hawaiian goose (*Branta sandvicensis*), rescued from extinction with the help of the Wildfowl Trust in England, is non-migratory.

The swans are another fairly uniform group for colouring. Most have white plumage, long necks and black webbed feet and live in northern latitudes. The black swan (*Cygnus atratus*) of Australia and New Zealand, black with white flight feathers, and the black-necked swan (*Cygnus melanocoryphus*) of South America are the only species with any black plumage. The black-necked swan is unusual in having pink feet, a characteristic which it shares with the coscoroba swan (*Coscoroba coscoroba*), also of South America.

The whistling ducks or tree ducks have typically duck-shaped bills and feet, but are particularly long-necked and long-legged.

The rest of the order Anseriformes – the 'duck-half' of the order – consists of a wide variety of ducks throughout the world, some in freshwater habitats, and some at sea. The shelducks are intermediate in size between typical ducks and geese, and are mostly colourful with patches of conspicuous white, black, grey or orange. Closely related are the sheld geese, mainly

of South America, and notable for their finely-barred black and white or brown and white plumage; and the crested duck (*Lophonetta specularioides*) and steamer ducks of South America, two species of which are flightless.

The vast majority of the ducks are termed *dabbling ducks*. They feed by swimming along, sieving the water for tiny aquatic forms of life with their broad bills, the insides of which are equipped with special filtering 'combs'. Many of these species have clearly defined male and female plumages. The drakes (males), particularly in the northern hemisphere, are especially colourful with distinctive, often musical calls, and the females have sombre camouflaged colouring and mainly 'quacking' calls.

A large number of other species feed by diving below the water surface in search of food (diving ducks). They include the eiders, large, marine species; the scoters, jet-black sea ducks; and the sawbills, such as the smew and mergansers.

The order Ciconiiformes contains all the stork-like birds, and also includes the flamingoes, which some zoologists think are related to the geese. Like other members of the order, flamingoes have very long legs and necks, but they have webbed feet and they do not have the typical long dagger-like bill. Instead, the flamingo's bill is adapted to filter feeding; it is rather like a duck's bill bent downwards in the middle, so that it is at the right angle for feeding when the flamingo hangs its head down.

The most familiar species in the order are the herons, storks and ibises. They are referred to in North America as 'wading birds', because they feed by wading in the water, stealthily approaching their prey, and finally shooting out the bill to catch the frog or fish which is usually swallowed whole.

Above: *Herons feed their young by regurgitating half-digested food. They are gregarious nesters; even different species nest together.* Below: *The whooping cranes belong to a different family. The females join in the spectacular bowing-and-leaping courtship dance.*

The herons (family Ardeidae) often have beautiful plumes of feathers on their necks and backs, but are generally of sombre colours. They nest in colonies which are located in trees, bushes or sometimes in reeds or on the ground. Three to seven pale, unspotted eggs are laid, and the young remain in the nest for some weeks before they can fly.

The storks (family Ciconiidae) are large birds 750 millimetres to 1·5 metres (30–60 inches) long with long necks, legs and bills. There are 17 species ranging from Central America, Africa, Europe and Asia to Australia. Most species have bold black and white plumage, the black feathers often having a beautiful gloss. Many have brightly coloured legs and bills.

The ibises and spoonbills (family Threskiornithidae) differ mostly in the bill shape, the ibises having strongly down-curved bills and the spoonbills, as their name suggests, having bills with a large flat spatulate tip, adapted for filtering food from the water.

The crane order (Gruiformes) are with the exception of the rails (family Rallidae), mainly stork-like birds. The 132 species of rails, some 140–500 millimetres (5½–20 inches) long, are a fairly uniform group typified by the moorhens, coots and gallinules. They have medium or short straight bills.

Another fairly large family is that of the bustards (Otididae). There are just over 20 species. They are ground-living and can run very fast and fly strongly.

Hunters of the Sky

There are two groups of birds which may be described as hunters: the birds of prey (order Falconiformes), such as hawks and eagles, which are mainly diurnal (day-time) hunters; and the owls (order Strigiformes) which are mainly nocturnal (night-time) hunters. These two unrelated groups of birds have evolved separately; but the needs of their common way of life have produced birds which are superficially similar in many respects.

Although the smaller species of hunting birds eat insects and worms, the majority prey on vertebrate animals – that is, mammals, other birds, amphibians, reptiles and sometimes fish. Consequently, the bill is typically short, strong and markedly hooked for tearing flesh, and the feet are strong with talons for grasping.

Most hunters are very strong fliers, but their habits vary according to the particular types of animals which they normally eat. For example, many of the falcons (family Falconidae) fly rapidly to overtake smaller birds in flight and catch them with their feet, or dive on their prey from above at high speed; others hover before pouncing on creatures on the ground. Some of the hawks (family Accipitridae) fly rapidly through trees to take their prey.

The osprey (*Pandion haliaëtus*), a species occurring throughout the world, which is often placed in a family of its own (Pandionidae), plunges into the water of lakes and rivers to catch fish, which it grasps with its specially-adapted spiny feet. Some owls also specialise in fish prey, but the majority eat land animals such as insects, earthworms, mammals and birds.

Vultures also are members of the Falconiformes, but their habits are different from the ordinary hunters; they feed on

Above: *The osprey feeds on fish and differs from other hunting hawks in having a reversible outer toe as owls do. All its talons are curved and have sharp scales underneath to help grip slippery fishes. Ospreys nest in trees in America, but usually on cliffs in Europe; a pair may use the same nest site for many years.*

Left: *The old-world griffon vulture, (below left), and to a lesser extent the yellow-headed vulture, (left), of America have featherless heads and long necks. This is an adaptation for reaching into carcasses.*

Right: *The crowned hawk eagle,* Stephanaetus coronatus, *lives in African forests. It is a booted eagle, with powerful feet and legs, capable of killing mammals such as duiker. Its short wings and long tail are adaptations to forest life. It breeds about once in two years, having a very long cycle of display, incubation and rearing its young; the fledglings may be fed by their parents for nearly a year after their first flight.*

Below: *The secretary bird is a snake-hunter, although some of the birds eat tortoises, and others feed on rodents, lizards and insects. They will also take young birds of other species. The nest is a large construction about 7 metres (22 feet) up in a thorny tree, used by the same pair for a number of years. The young – usually two – are fed by regurgitation for about three months, when they leave the nest almost fully grown.*

Right: *The peregrine,* Falco peregrinus, *one of the long-winged hunting falcons, was reserved for the use of noblemen in medieval Britain. It is the most widely distributed bird of prey, ranging from the Arctic Circle to the southernmost tips of the continents of the Southern Hemisphere. It keeps mostly to coastal regions, nesting on cliff ledges and feeding on sea birds taken on the wing.*

carrion. There are two main types of vultures. Those found exclusively in North and South America (the New World vultures) are grouped in the family Cathartidae, while the rest (the Old World vultures) are grouped with the hawks and eagles in the Accipitridae.

Vultures rise from the ground in thermals (currents of rising hot air) and therefore live in hot climates where such thermals are common. The vultures circle and gain height until their keen sight detects a dead or dying animal. They then descend to feed, or, if the animal is still alive, to await its death. A flock of vultures can pick a dead donkey clean of everything edible in 20 to 30 minutes.

Since owls hunt mostly at night or in poor light they need special attributes to enable them to find and catch prey. They have specially soft plumage and a fine, comb-like leading edge to the flight feathers, permitting them to fly silently. The senses of sight and hearing are adapted for nocturnal use. Inside the back of any eyeball is the retina, a sensitive layer of nerve endings which are of two types: rods, sensitive to light and movement; and cones, concerned more with clear images and colour-vision. Owls and other night-feeding creatures have extra rods so that they can see clearly in what appears to us to be total darkness.

Owls' ears are similarly highly-developed, with large openings – though not external flaps like those of mammals – and it is thought that the shape of the face may help to collect sounds. The 'ears' on the tops of some owls' heads are only tufts of feathers and not concerned with hearing. Experiments have shown that some owls probably hear about ten times better than we can, and that some species have one ear larger than the other. The ears are so developed that the sounds made by prey, such as high-pitched squeaks, seem loudest when coming from straight ahead.

Two members of the hawk group deserve special mention. One is the lammergeier or bearded vulture (*Gypaëtus barbatus*), of southern Europe, Asia and Africa, which has a wingspan of 2·4–2·7 metres (8–9 feet). The lammergeier drops large animal bones from a great height to break them open, exposing the bone-marrow, which the bird then eats. The other is the secretary bird (*Sagittarius serpentarius*) of Africa, which is placed in a family of its own, the Sagittaridae. It stands about 1 metre (3¼ feet) high. It has long, powerful legs, on which it walks about rapidly to hunt. Its prey ranges from termites and wasps to frogs, rats and birds. Snakes are a favourite food. The bird kills large prey by stamping on it.

Above: *Golden eagles,* Aquila chrysaetos, *once lived in most of the northern mountain ranges; they are now greatly reduced in numbers and carefully protected. This eagle nests in trees and on high mountain ledges, usually laying only two eggs which are incubated by the female for eight or nine weeks. Carrion forms a large part of its diet.*

Below: *The largest European owl is the eagle owl,* Bubo bubo, *with a wing span up to 1½ metres (5 feet). It lives in open country and on the edge of forests, preying on small mammals and birds, and nesting on the ground under rocks or bushes, sometimes in hollow trees. Eagle owls are becoming rarer throughout their range, possibly due to the effect of agriculture on their habitat.*

Right: *The best-known owl of Eurasia, the little owl,* Athena noctua, *hunts mice and insects both by day and at night. It nests in hollow trees and old buildings, and can be seen perching in exposed places. It is one species which is apparently increasing.*

Left: *The European sparrow-hawk,* Accipiter nisus, *is quite a small bird of prey; the male is about 30 centimetres (12 inches) long and the female a little larger. It hunts in woods and open country, preying mainly on small birds but sometimes taking mice and frogs. It hovers low over hedgerows and suddenly drops onto its victim. The nest, in which about five eggs are laid, is made of sticks, usually in a tree but occasionally on a cliff ledge.*

Below: *Snowy owls live on the northern tundra, and feed mainly on lemmings. They nest on hillocks, even in snow.*

Nightjars

The nightjars (family Caprimulgidae) and their relatives belong to the order Caprimulgiformes, a group of birds superficially similar in appearance. The order also contains the frogmouths (Podargidae), owlet frogmouths (Aegothelidae), potoos (Nyctibriidae) and the oilbird (*Steatornis caripensis*) which is the sole member of the family Steatornithidae.

The nightjars are represented everywhere in the world except the more northerly parts of America, Europe and Asia, southern South America, New Zealand and many other oceanic islands, and Antarctica. Species breeding in the northern parts of the temperate regions migrate southwards before the onset of winter.

The plumage in all 70 or so species is soft-textured and of camouflaged pattern, being basically buff, rufous (reddish brown), greyish or almost black, sometimes with white patches.

Most nightjars have long tails and long pointed wings, and their flight is effortless-looking and silent. They are flat-headed birds with tiny beaks which can, however, gape enormously. Most species have on each side of the mouth stiff *rictal bristles* (modified feathers) similar in appearance to a cat's whiskers and serving a similar purpose – that is, providing a sense of touch, necessary for birds flying mainly at night and catching insects such as moths while in flight.

The nighthawks of the New World form a separate subfamily, the Chordeilinae. They differ from most of the Old World nightjars in lacking the rictal bristles, but have very large eyes, like those of owls.

Many species, like the European nightjar (*Caprimulgus europaeus*), utter sustained churring or 'jarring' songs – hence the name. Others in the Americas have whistling calls which have been translated into human phrases to give them their common names, for example – the whip-poor-will (*Caprimulgus vociferus*) and the chuck-will's widow (*Caprimulgus carolinensis*).

The poor-will (*Phalaenoptilus nuttallii*) of North America hibernates in rock crevices during the winter. At one time it was thought that no birds hibernated. During this dormant period, the poor-will's body temperature drops by almost half and it becomes and remains torpid (dormant).

The 12 species of frogmouths, occurring in Australasia and South East Asia, differ from the true nightjars in building stick nests and laying white eggs (nightjars lay camouflaged eggs on the bare ground). Frogmouths feed by picking up food, up to the size of mice and small birds. Three species in the genus *Podargus* – often called moreporks from their cry – react to danger by sitting stiffly upright to look just like broken-off dead branches.

Probably the most remarkable species in the order is the oilbird or guacharo of Central America. Its true relationship to the nightjars is still uncertain, because it has some owl-like characteristics. A large bird, some 450 millimetres (18 inches) long and with a wingspan of 900 millimetres (3 feet), it eats fruit exclusively, and is the only nocturnal fruit-eating bird. It has a large, owl-like beak and navigates in pitch-dark caves, using echo-location, like a bat.

Below: *Nightjars spend much of the night flying in search of insects, mainly moths, on which they feed. Their wings are extremely long and the shoulder joint is unusually mobile and allows the wings to be raised high above the head as illustrated here. This combination is found in many others of the nightjar group. The long wings are an adaptation to rapid flight in open country, and the mobility is an adaptation to flying in woodland, where they frequently nest. The white patches on the wings of the flying nightjar are very conspicuous; compare this with the camouflage of the sitting bird (below).*

Above: *The oilbird,* Steatornis caripensis, *which nests in dark caves in South America, has characteristics of both owls and nightjars.*

Below left: *Camouflage is well developed in nightjars. When on the ground – resting or nesting – they sit with closed eyes and blend perfectly with their surroundings.*

Swifts

The order Apodiformes is divided into two suborders, the Apodi containing the swifts (family Apodidae) and crested swifts (Hemiprocriidae), and the Trochili containing in one large family (Trochilidae) the hummingbirds.

The swifts are a fairly uniform group, bearing a superficial resemblance to the swallows (family Hirundinidae) due to *convergent evolution* (unrelated species evolving to look alike because of similar life-styles). Both swifts and hummingbirds have a very short but stout humerus (the bone of the base of the wing, equivalent to the human upper arm). The shape of the wing is adapted in both forms for high-speed flight, but the longer swift wing is adapted more for sailing through the air to catch flying insects, while that of the hummingbirds, relatively shorter, is used for hovering at flowers to lap up nectar.

The swifts are the most strictly aerial of all birds, performing most of life's functions on the wing. Feeding is entirely airborne. Some species collect nest material while in flight by dipping to the ground, and some regularly spend the night on the wing. The plumage is mainly sooty black or brown in colour.

A swift's nest may be in a hollow tree or a chimney, attached to the inside vertical wall, or in a cave as in the *Collocalia* species of southeast Asia, famous for supplying the nests from which bird's nest soup is made. All swifts use some saliva to cement their nests together, but *Collocalia* use virtually nothing but saliva. They also use echo-location to find their way in the murky darkness of the caves.

The 10 Old World species of swifts usually nest in holes in cliffs or buildings. The Old World palm swift (*Cypsiurus parvus*), which has a long, forked tail, builds a small, shallow-cupped nest attached to the inner side of a palm leaf, the eggs being glued to it with saliva. Others build bag- or sleeve-like nests suspended from a branch or rock.

Hummingbirds are well known for their hovering flight, their ability to fly backwards for short distances, their tiny size and their often brilliant plumage. There is an enormous range in detail of colour and form, and quite a range in size, but their life-style means that they are basically very uniform in structure. Their name comes from the buzzing sound made by the wings, which beat extraordinarily rapidly – up to 50 or more times a second in small species – so as to blur completely.

The hummingbird family includes the smallest warm-blooded vertebrates. The body of the bee hummingbird (*Mellisuga helenae*) of Cuba is a mere 50 millimetres (2 inches) long, including a proportionately long bill and tail which together make up about 25 millimetres (1 inch).

Hummingbirds are entirely confined to the New World, with a stronghold – in terms of the number of species – in Ecuador. Some species migrate.

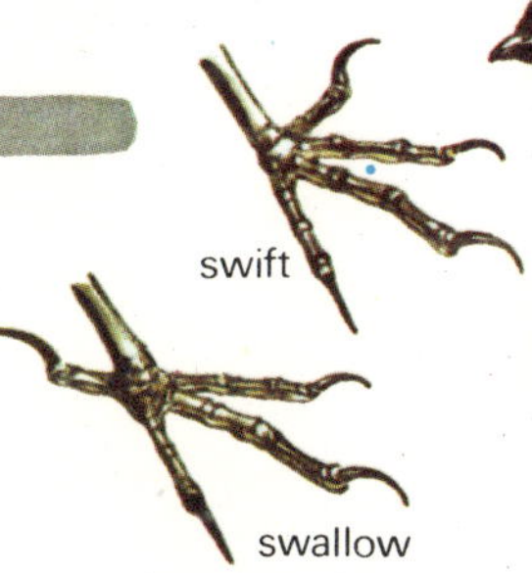

Left and below: *Tails and feet. Swifts have feet too weak to stand on; their tails are less forked than swallows. The falcon has an unforked tail.*

Below: *Swifts are related to hummingbirds and nightjars, but not to swallows. They fly fast, apparently erratically, seizing insects as they go. The common swift,* Apus apus, *winters in Africa and Madagascar and breeds throughout Europe.*

Below: *The three species of crested swifts differ from true swifts in having strong legs, soft plumage and solitary nesting habits.*

Kingfishers and their Relatives

Kingfishers, woodpeckers and their relatives include many of the world's most colourful and interesting birds.

Kingfishers (family Alcedinidae) are in the order Coraciiformes. They live mainly in warm parts of the world; the European kingfisher (*Alcedo atthis*) is an isolated adventurer into cooler climates. Kingfishers find food by watching patiently from some vantage point. Usually fish is the prey, because most kingfishers live by water, but some inhabit wooded places far from rivers or sea, and eat insects or lizards. The kookaburra (*Dacelo novaeguineae*) of Australia is one of these; its raucous cackling has earned it the name of laughing jackass.

The five species of todies (family Todidae) are tiny birds found in parts of Central America and the West Indies. Though they look a bit like small kingfishers in shape, they feed quite differently by catching insects among leaves. Central America and South America are the homes of the motmots (family Momotidae), eight species of medium or large birds, beautifully marked in blues, greens and russet. Most motmots have long, often racket-shaped tails, which they swing in a pendulum motion while perching.

Bee-eaters (family Meropidae), as their name indicates, eat many bees and other stinging insects. They capture the insects in the air, but may take them back to a perch for 'de-venoming' – causing the insect to expel its poison by rubbing it on a branch. Bee-eaters live in the Old World.

Rollers (family Coraciidae), like bee-eaters, belong to the Old World, and have a single European species, *Coracias garrulus,* with ten others in Africa and Asia.

Hoopoes (Upupidae), wood hoopoes (Phoeniculidae) and hornbills (Bucerotidae) seem to be closely related to each other. There is only one species of hoopoe, *Upupa epops,* which lives in Europe and Asia. It is a striking black, white and orange bird with a fan-shaped crest and a long curved bill, with which it probes the ground for food. The six species of wood hoopoes are confined to Africa; they probe rotten timber for food.

Most species of hornbills are large birds, the biggest being the great Indian hornbill (*Buceros bicornis*) over 1·5 metres (5 feet) long. Most hornbills have an extraordinary growth on top of the bill called the *casque*.

Hornbills nest in holes in trees, and their early life history is among the strangest of all birds. The female (sometimes aided by her mate) seals herself into the nest chamber with mud and dung, leaving just a slit for air, and for the male's deliveries of food. This wall is retained

Above: *The European kingfisher,* Alcedo atthis, *tunnels into an earth bank, nesting at the end of the tunnel. The young queue at the entrance to be fed.* Below: *The nest of the green woodpecker,* Picus viridis, *is typical of the woodpecker-type of home. It is drilled by the male bird, who also does most of the work of incubating and rearing the young.*

Below: *The woodpecker's tongue has a cartilage skeleton with two long horns, each extending round the head and sheathed in muscle. When the muscle contracts, these horns shoot out, extending the tongue.*

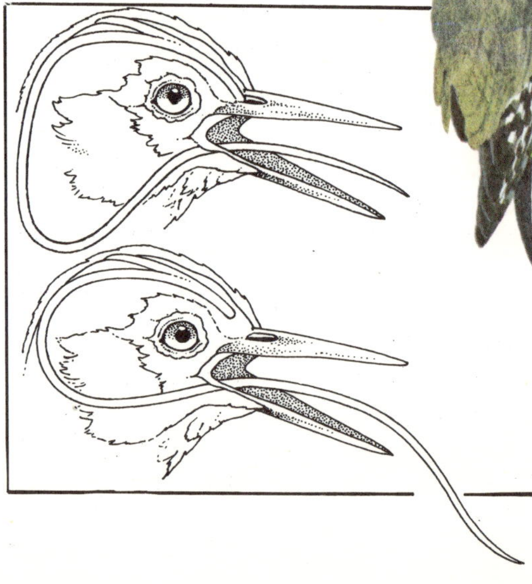

until the young are ready to leave, when it is broken away.

Woodpeckers and their relatives form the order Piciformes. They differ from all the birds on this page except the cuckoo roller in having the outer toe reversed, so that two toes point forward and two back.

Woodpeckers (family Picidae) feed mainly on insects obtained from wood, or sometimes the ground. They use their strong bills as chisels to get at their prey, and are further aided by their enormously long tongues with barbed tips.

Jacamars (Galbulidae) and puffbirds (Bucconidae) live in Central and South America. Though closely related, they differ in life-style. The brightly-coloured jacamars hunt flying prey such as butterflies, while the more sombrely-clad puffbirds wait stolidly for less nimble prey among foliage or on the ground.

Barbets (Capitonidae) live throughout the tropics. Closely related to woodpeckers, they resemble them in their gaudy or spotted plumages, but differ in their more conventional feeding methods, used to obtain insects or fruits.

Toucans (Ramphastidae), which live in Central and South America, resemble large barbets, but have enormous, brightly-coloured bills, which they use to pluck fruit. They are noisy birds.

Honey-guides belong to the family Indicatoridae. Like cuckoos, they are nest parasites, and the nestling honey-guide is provided with sinister hooks on its bill with which it attacks its nest mates – usually barbets. The 11 species live in forests in Asia and southern Africa, mostly eating insects. Some species feed on beeswax and bee larvae, and rely on other animals to break open the bees' nests so that they can reach their food.

Above and below: *The kingfisher order includes such different birds as the heavy kookaburra, (above), and the acrobatic rollers like the lilac-chested roller, (below). Both include snakes in their varied diet.*

Above: *Bee-eaters feed on insects. This African red-throated bee-eater, is a primitive type.*

Below: *Todies catch insects on the wing and have come to resemble flycatchers; the brilliant red of the chin is characteristic.*

Above: *Mot-mots feed on insects. They also use their serrated bills to shape their tail feathers. This is a blue-crowned mot-mot.* Right: *The hoopoe is unique; its crest, long curved bill and brightly barred plumage combine to make it an unforgettable sight.*

Pigeons, Parrots, Cuckoos and Game Birds

The order Columbiformes is made up of two families of birds, the pigeons and doves (Columbidae), of which there are almost 300 species, and the 16 species of sandgrouse (Pteroclidae).

The Columbidae are represented throughout the world, except the Arctic, subarctic and Antarctic regions and some oceanic islands.

Pigeons are plump birds with small heads and dense, soft plumage. The bill is small with a patch of soft, bare skin at the base, called a *cere*, found also in the parrots and birds of prey. The legs are generally short except in some of the ground-living species, which are outnumbered by the tree-living species.

Pigeons, doves and sandgrouse differ from most other birds in being able to drink while the bill is immersed in water; most birds have to tilt the head back to swallow liquids.

The racing pigeon and the city or domestic pigeon are descended by selective breeding from the rock dove (*Columba livia*) of northern Africa, southern Europe and north-west Britain, and south-western Asia.

The sandgrouse, though grouped with the doves, are of somewhat uncertain relationships. Some zoologists consider them more closely related to plovers (family Charadriidae). Superficially they are similar to small birds, such as grouse, but many have long pointed tails. The majority of species live in dry, open or even desert and semi-desert regions of Africa and Asia.

The parrot family (Psittacidae) forms an order of its own, the Psittaciformes. Almost everyone must be familiar with at least one species of the group, since in regions where they do not occur naturally they are usually kept as cage birds. Many species survive well in captivity, and some have the ability to mimic sounds including the human voice. Perhaps the best-known species is the small budgerigar.

Most parrots are plump, and their tails vary from extremely short to extremely long, as in the macaws (genera *Ara* and *Anodorhynchus*) of Central and South America. The bill is short and strongly hooked, similar to that of birds of prey, but adapted for cracking open nuts and seeds. It is also used by most species in climbing among the branches. Some species feed on fruit and other vegetable matter, including nectar.

There are over 300 species in the Psittacidae, living in the southern hemisphere and tropical and subtropical parts north of the Equator. They range in size from about 100 to 1,000 millimetres (4–40 inches), and vary greatly in colour, some being uniformly grey or green and some with bright patches of colour as well. Others, such as the macaws, are brilliantly coloured in reds, blues or yellows.

Above: *Domesticated pigeons like the racing pigeon (top) are descendants of the rock dove (left) which lives on sea and inland cliffs. Sand-grouse (above), near relatives of the doves, live in arid country.*
Below: *The emerald cuckoo lives in Africa.*

Below: *Parrots are among the most colourful birds. They range from the large tropical blue and gold macaw to the tiny budgerigar shown here.*

The cuckoo family (Cuculidae) and the touraco family (Musophagidae) make up the order Cuculiformes. The name cuckoo derives from the familiar call of the European cuckoo (*Cuculus canorus*). There are 127 species ranging in size from 150 to 680 millimetres (6–27 inches) long. They are generally sombre-plumaged in various shades and combinations of brown, grey, black or olive, often with streaking or barring. One of the notable exceptions is the emerald cuckoo (*Chrysococcyx cupreus*) which is brilliant golden green with bright yellow on the body.

The 'typical' cuckoos, numbering 47 species, are noted for their nest-parasitism. The female lays her eggs in the nests of 'foster' species which incubate them and rear the resulting young, the fosterer's own eggs or young being removed by the cuckoo chick.

The game birds (order Galliformes) sometimes called gallinaceous birds, are a fairly uniform group consisting of brush-turkeys (megapodes), curassows, grouse, pheasants, partridges and quails, guinea fowls and turkeys, and the South American hoatzin (*Opisthocomus hoazin*). They are mainly ground-living or partly tree-living birds of medium size, being represented virtually throughout the world.

The brush-turkeys of Australasia form the family Megapodiidae. They are notable for the way they incubate the clutch of 6–24 eggs. The eggs are laid in a hole in the sand and covered with decaying vegetation, which provides the heat necessary for hatching. The temperature of the nest is controlled by the male, which adds vegetation to the heap or removes it.

Above: *Pheasant (above left), red grouse (above right), wild turkey (below left) and helmeted guinea fowl (below right) represent four families of game birds. The pheasant is one of the family that includes peacocks. Red grouse are the only ptarmigans not to have white winter plumage. Wild turkeys are the ancestors of domestic turkeys.* Below: *The hoatzin resembles both game birds and cuckoos. It is unique in having young with functional claws on their wings which enable them to scramble around in trees before fledging.*

Some species – generally those living in open habitats – are cryptically coloured, such as the partridges, quail and some grouse. Others, such as the pheasants, are some of the most brightly coloured of birds.

Most male game birds have a strong, pointed bony projection above the foot, at the back of the tarsus, called a spur, which they use for fighting during the breeding season. The hen lays large numbers of eggs, but sometimes extra-large clutches are the result of several females using the same nest. The wings are short and rounded, permitting rapid acceleration and high speed over a short distance.

The typical game bird food includes seeds, grain, berries, buds, leaves and fruit, with insects, worms and snails.

The hoatzin of northern South America is generally grouped with the gallinaceous birds, but in a family of its own (Opisthocomidae); it is of somewhat uncertain relationships. In a number of features it resembles the pigeons. The wing of the young bird is armed with two claws, resembling those of the fossil bird *Archaeopteryx*. The claws help the chick to clamber about in the trees.

Perching Birds 1

There are approximately 8,600 species of birds known in the world today, so if one is to study them, there must be some way of dividing them into groups. Some species fall readily into groups, such as the penguins, owls, parrots or humming birds, and these groups are the zoologist's *orders*. Within these orders, certain features are used to group species into smaller, more manageable units called *families*.

With the perching birds, placed in the order Passeriformes, there is a problem in that more than 5,000 species are involved; in other words more than half of all living birds are perching birds. Just to add to the difficulty, not all perching birds perch readily – some spend much of their time on the ground – and many non-passeriform birds do perch, spending their entire lives in trees.

If the same type of characteristics used for grouping non-passerines into families were used with the passerines, then most, if not all of them, would be in the same enormous family. This would obviously make them very difficult to study and so they are grouped in families by using much more detailed features. If you compare all 67 or so families of the perching birds with one family of non-passerines, such as the cranes and their relatives (order Gruiformes), there is at least as much variation of form in the cranes as in all the perching birds. The passeriforms are therefore a very uniform group.

Some species live in virtually every habitat, and often near to human dwellings. They are found throughout the world, with the exception of the extreme polar regions of the oceans.

The group is characterised by such species as crows (family Corvidae), flycatchers (families Tyrannidae in the New World and Muscicapidae in the Old World), thrushes (family Turdidae), starlings (family Sturnidae), tanagers (family Thraupidae), weaverbirds and sparrows (family Ploceidae) and finches, buntings and grosbeaks (family Fringillidae).

A few groups have become so specialised in their way of life and especially their feeding as to resemble some non-passerine groups more than the rest of their closer relatives. As examples, the passerine swallows (family Hirundinidae) have become adapted to feeding entirely while in flight on their long wings, catching insects. In these respects they resemble the unrelated non-passerine swifts (family Apodidae).

Secondly there are the passerine woodcreepers (family Dendrocolaptidae) of the Central American region and the tree creepers (family Certhiidae) of the Old World and North and Central America. Both these families have evolved a lifestyle and hence a superficial appearance rather like the non-passerine woodpeckers (family Picidae), climbing tree-trunks with ease in search of small animals living on and in the bark.

Since there is so much uniformity, it is possible to give a good account of the order Passeriformes by describing only representative families. The order is divided into four suborders, based mainly on anatomical details such as muscles, tendons and bones. Three of these suborders, the Eurylaimi, the Menurae, and the Tyranni, make up the so-called *sub-oscine* families, because they are held to be less highly developed than the rest of the Pas-

Below: *Crows, like this carrion crow,* Corvus corone, *have been regarded by some biologists as the most advanced of birds. They are certainly the most intelligent of the perching birds – which are themselves currently the most successful order of birds. When not breeding, crows gather to sleep in flocks, with sentries posted to keep watch. In the spring, pairs build solitary nests in high places; the female incubates the eggs but both parents share in feeding the young. They are long-lived, and spend a comparatively long time 'growing up', as do most of the crow family. Old birds can pass on information to the less experienced ones in the flock in a more specific form than just an alarm call.*

seriformes in the fourth suborder, the Oscines.

The Eurylaimi consists of only one family (the Eurylaimidae), containing 14 species of broadbills, ranging from 125 to 280 millimetres (5–11 inches) in length. They are brightly coloured in various combinations of green, blue, black, white, yellow, orange, grey and chestnut. The bill, as the name suggests, is broad.

Broadbills eat fruit or various types of animals, from insects to frogs. They are non-migratory, inhabiting open wooded country and forest edges in Africa, the Himalayas, China, Malaysia and the Philippines. The nest is a pear-shaped structure, often suspended from a branch over water and decorated with moss and other vegetation.

The second suborder, the Menurae, contains the two species of lyrebirds (family Menuridae) and the two species of scrub-birds (family Atrichornithidae). The lyrebirds live only in eastern Australia, and are well known for the enormously developed tail feathers – especially in the superb lyrebird (*Menura superba*) – which give them their common name. They are exceptionally good songsters, with rich, fluty voices and remarkable powers of mimicry. They build large shed-like nests of sticks.

The scrub-birds also live only in Australia. As with the lyrebirds, their exact relationships with other birds are still under discussion. Both families lack a clear affinity with any other orders and indeed have most in common with each other. The Western or noisy scrub-bird (*Atrichornis clamosus*) was the first species to be discovered; it has an exceptionally loud voice, which perhaps makes up for its drab appearance. It is mainly terrestrial in habit.

The third suborder is the Tyranni, which contains a mixed group of families, some of uncertain relationships. These families include woodcreepers (family Dendrocolaptidae), ovenbirds (Furnariidae), ant-thrushes (Formicariidae), antpipits (Conopophagidae), pittas (Pittidae), New Zealand wrens (Xenicidae), New World flycatchers (Tyrannidae), manakins (Pipridae) and bellbirds (Cotingidae).

The woodcreepers, numbering almost 50 species, are a very uniform group presenting ornithologists with considerable problems of identification. The plumage is brown with various amounts of streaking or spotting with black, grey or white. The bill is usually fairly long and slender, downcurved in many species, adapted for picking out food from the trunks of trees. The birds climb trees with great agility, using their strong-clawed feet to grip and their stiff tail feathers as a prop.

Below: *Most tanagers sing very poorly, if at all, but the American scarlet tanager,* Piranga olivacea, *has a pleasant song. It is also unusual amongst tanagers in being migratory, wintering southwards to Peru.*

Below: *A male superb lyrebird, (left), stands underneath his gorgeous umbrella of tail feathers at the peak of his courtship display. The relatively drab female (below) will do all the work of building and raising the young.*

Below: *Broadbills, primitive perching birds, are great nest architects. Long-tailed broadbill, (above); lesser green broadbill, (centre, and nest, right); African broadbill, (below).*

Perching Birds 2

The ovenbird family, consisting of over 200 species of small brown birds, is extremely variable in terms of habitat, behaviour and breeding biology. The true ovenbirds in the genus *Furnarius* build large domed mud nests – which become rock-hard – on the tops of posts or on branches. Most species of spinetails (subfamily Synallaxinae) build huge nests of sticks, out of all proportion to the birds' size. For example, the so-called firewood gatherer (*Anumbius annumbi*), a mere 215 millimetres (8½ inches) long, builds a very large nest using sticks which it may have difficulty in carrying.

The pittas are among the most gaudy of bird families. The 23 species, found in the Old World tropics, are all plump, thrush-like birds with short tails and longish, sturdy legs suited to their terrestrial habits. Their bright plumage, shaded with large blocks of colour such as scarlet, blue, green, purple, black, white and chestnut, has led to their popular name of 'jewel-thrushes'. They are shy birds, their loud, distinct calls often being the only clue to their presence in dense vegetation.

The New World flycatchers are a diverse group of well over 300 species, which superficially can be distinguished from the Old World flycatchers only by the leg structure and the pattern of the *primaries* (outer flight feathers). Some species are cryptically coloured in pale shades of green, brown, yellow, white or grey, but some are almost black.

Kingbirds in the genus *Tyrannus* are dark on top – olive, grey, reddish brown or almost black – and white, grey or yellow on the underparts. Some kingbirds, such as the great kiskadee (*Pitangus sulphuratus*), eat small birds, mice, frogs and lizards, but most species are chiefly insectivorous, though some also eat fruits and berries.

The manakins (family Pipridae) – not to be confused with the weaver finches in the family Estrildidae, termed mannikins – are a fascinating group of 59 species which live in the New World tropics. They are small birds some 75 to 150 millimetres (3–6 inches) long. The males are mainly black, with patches of brilliant blue, orange or red; the females are a pale greenish colour. Manakins are stocky little birds with short wings, tail and bill.

The bellbirds, numbering about 90 species in Central America, are closely related to the manakins and the New World flycatchers. They range in length from 90 to 460 millimetres (3½–18 inches). They vary greatly in external appearance, but all have broad bills, slightly hooked at the tip, short, stout legs, and rounded wings. In some species both the sexes are dull-coloured, but in others the male has brilliant plumage, with wattles or areas of brightly-coloured bare skin. The calls, as the name suggests, often resemble metallic sounds. Others make musical whistles or cow-like lowing calls. Because most species live high in the forest canopy, little is known about them except their general appearance and calls.

Above: *Male manakins perform communal courtship dances. Yellow-thighed manakins,* Pipra mentalis, *congregate on trees, and each male provocatively exposes his yellow legs as he pirouettes.*

Above: *Pittas, or jewel-thrushes, are vividly coloured birds. However, they are difficult to see on the floor of the dark, deep jungles where they live. They are generally reluctant to fly, preferring to hop under cover when alarmed, and it is therefore surprising that many of them are migratory. The Indian blue-winged pitta,* Pitta brachyura *(above), is known to winter in Ceylon, fiercely defending its feeding territory there until it returns to India in the spring. Gurney's pitta,* Pitta gurneyi *(left), is a little-known species.*

Birds in the suborder Oscines are sometimes referred to collectively as 'songbirds' to distinguish them from the rest of the perching birds (sub-oscines). They are divided into 40 to 50 families according to the method of classification used. In the Oscines the sound-producing apparatus, called the *syrinx* (plural *syringes*) is highly developed. The syrinx is located at the base of the windpipe, and has internal and external muscles which act to produce the song. The exact position and degree of development of the syrinx and the two types of muscles are important aids in classifying the passerines, and especially the Oscines.

The larks (Alaudidae), numbering 75 species, are a distinct group, being ground-living, mainly brown birds. Many species are noted for their beautiful songs, often performed while soaring.

Some families are notable for their

bright plumage, particularly the 43 species of birds of paradise (family Paradisaeidae) of the New Guinea region. Less gaudy but also handsomely feathered are the orioles (Oriolidae), with black and yellow plumage, and the bell-magpies (Cracticidae) of Australasia with black and white plumage.

Yet other families are noted for their nests, the weaverbirds (Ploceidae), numbering over 300 species, being the most obvious example. Weaverbirds' nests range from elaborately woven, hanging, flask-shaped structures to massive colonial nests occupying the whole of a tree-crown and inhabited by scores of pairs.

Left: *Larks are famed for their airborne singing. The European skylark,* Alauda arvensis *(left), flutters and drifts high in the sky, sometimes so high that it is almost invisible, yet the gloriously cheering song of the male bird carries clearly to the ground. The woodlark,* Lullula arborea *(far left), is a smaller bird with a different pattern of flight; it climbs in a looping spiral, not very high above the ground, singing its wistful notes. Both birds nest on the ground, an adaptation to the treeless open country which followed the Ice Age in Europe. The skylark's brown speckled eggs are more heavily marked than those of the woodlark.*

Similar in general appearance to the weavers are the finches and buntings, often placed in the one family (Fringillidae), with their short, conical bills. The most famous finches are those studied by the British naturalist Charles Darwin on the Galápagos Islands off Ecuador. The typical finch-type bill is adapted for crushing seeds and fruits of varying size and hardness, but some have become adapted to eating softer foods like buds or insects. One of Darwin's finches, *Camarhynchus pallidus*, uses a twig or thorn held in the beak as a tool for winkling grubs out of crevices – a rare example of a tool-using bird.

The tanagers constitute another large family (Thraupidae) of some 200 species, included by some zoologists in a family (Emberizadae) with the buntings. The bill is short and conical, and the plumage of many species is brightly coloured.

The crows (Corvidae) comprise some 100 species, including the largest passerine birds, mostly black or pied.

The tits or titmice (Paridae), termed chickadees in North America, are small, sometimes brightly-coloured birds, which are extremely agile and active. The 65 species are widespread, one species or another occurring in most parts of the world except South America and Australia.

The bulbuls (Pycnonotidae) are over 100 species of colourful birds in Africa and Asia. The thrushes (Turdidae) number over 300 species throughout the world, excepting New Zealand.

The Old World warblers (Sylviidae) number almost 400 species, being generally sombre-plumaged birds, often difficult to identify. The 119 species of New World wood-warblers (Parulidae) are by comparison relatively brightly coloured, yellow, orange, red or blue often figuring in their plumage.

The Old World flycatchers (Muscicapidae) number over 300 species. The typical flycatchers, varying from 90 to 230 millimetres (3½–9 inches) in length – though some species have extremely long central tail feathers – are often brightly coloured. They get their name from the habit of darting out from a perch to catch an insect, either in the air or on the ground.

The mockingbirds (Mimidae) of North and South America are thrush-like birds, though with longer tails and bills but with similar fluty musical songs. Several species of mockingbirds have great powers of mimicry.

Below: *Ovenbirds, which live in South America, build a variety of nests in many locations. The rufous ovenbird,* Furnaria rufus, *builds a two-roomed mud oven with a side door. It is often found near human dwellings. The other species within this subfamily generally nest in tunnels or crevices.*

The Mammals

The name 'mammal' comes from the Latin word *mamma*, a breast, and the important feature of all mammals is that the females have mammary glands, or breasts, which secrete milk. With two exceptions, mammals give birth to live young, instead of laying eggs like the reptiles from which mammals evolved. The babies develop inside the mother's body, and she feeds them on milk for the early parts of their lives.

Some baby mammals, such as horses and antelopes, can walk almost at birth; others, such as kittens and puppies, are naked and blind at birth and have to be kept warm by their mothers.

In the majority of mammal species, the developing animal or embryo is nourished by the mother before it is born by means of a *placenta*, a mass of tissue attached to the wall of the *uterus* (womb). Inside the placenta blood vessels from mother and embryo intertwine, so food and oxygen pass into the embryo's system, and waste products are removed. The embryo is attached to the placenta by the *umbilical cord* which enters its body at the *umbilicus*, or navel.

There are about 4,000 species of mammals alive today, many fewer than either birds or reptiles. About half of them are rodents – rats and their relatives.

There are three main kinds of mammals, grouped according to the way in which they reproduce. Most mammals are *placentals* or true mammals; the kangaroos and their relatives are *marsupials*, which nurture their partly-developed babies in pouches; and there are two *monotremes* which lay eggs as reptiles do, although when they hatch the babies are fed on milk by their mothers.

Above: *Sheep frequently give birth to twins. Ewes usually have only enough milk to feed two lambs; if three are born the shepherd can either rear the extra lamb on a bottle, or he can foster it onto a ewe with only one lamb.*

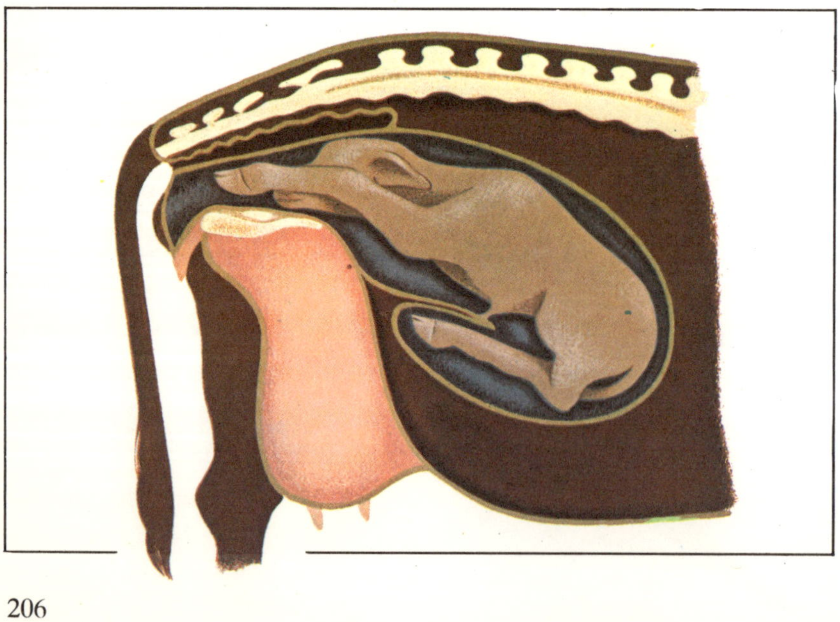

Below: *A calf in its mother's uterus. In the early stages of pregnancy the calf lies with its head forward, but as it nears term it moves around to a head-backwards position, ready to be born head first.*

In their evolution from reptiles, the bodies of mammals have changed little compared with those of birds. Most mammals run on four legs, with a tail to act as a balancer, and have jaws lined with rows of teeth. Nevertheless, there are very distinct differences between the bodies of mammals and reptiles. These are mainly adaptations by the mammals for efficiency in a very active way of life.

The most striking difference is that the scales of a reptile have been replaced by a thick covering of hair. All mammals have at least some hair; even baby whales and elephants have a few sparse hairs. The coat of hair or fur helps to keep the body warm, but it sometimes has secondary functions. The mane of a lion and beard of a man are male sexual characteristics.

Keeping warm is the secret of the mammals' success. Some reptiles can keep warm by basking in the sun and hiding in holes at night but mammals, like birds, are warm-blooded. This means that they keep their body temperature constant despite changes in the surrounding air temperature – for example, human body temperature stays within a few fractions of 36·9°C (98·4°F).

In animals with thick coats, the fur acts

as an insulation by trapping a layer of air next to the body. In cold weather, it is fluffed out to increase the thickness of the insulation. If the mammal gets too hot, it sweats or pants and loses heat by evaporation.

A high temperature enables the muscles, nerves and other parts of the body to work well even if the air temperature is low. Heat for maintaining this temperature comes from burning food in the body. This process needs oxygen, and the breathing and blood systems of mammals are arranged to carry large amounts of oxygen to the muscles and other organs. The rib cage is strengthened and a muscular diaphragm helps to pump air in and out of the lungs. The heart has four chambers which separate the blood circulation to lungs and body.

Because food has to be burnt to provide heat, mammals must eat more than reptiles. Some mammals, particularly small species, are not very good at keeping warm, especially in winter when the weather is cold and food is scarce. So they go into hibernation, a state in which their heartbeat and breathing slow down and they become almost cold-blooded, thereby saving their reserves of food and so surviving the winter.

Above: *A chipmunk curled up in its winter sleep. Chipmunks live in the northern forests of North America and Siberia. They hibernate because the winter food supply is not sufficiently reliable.*

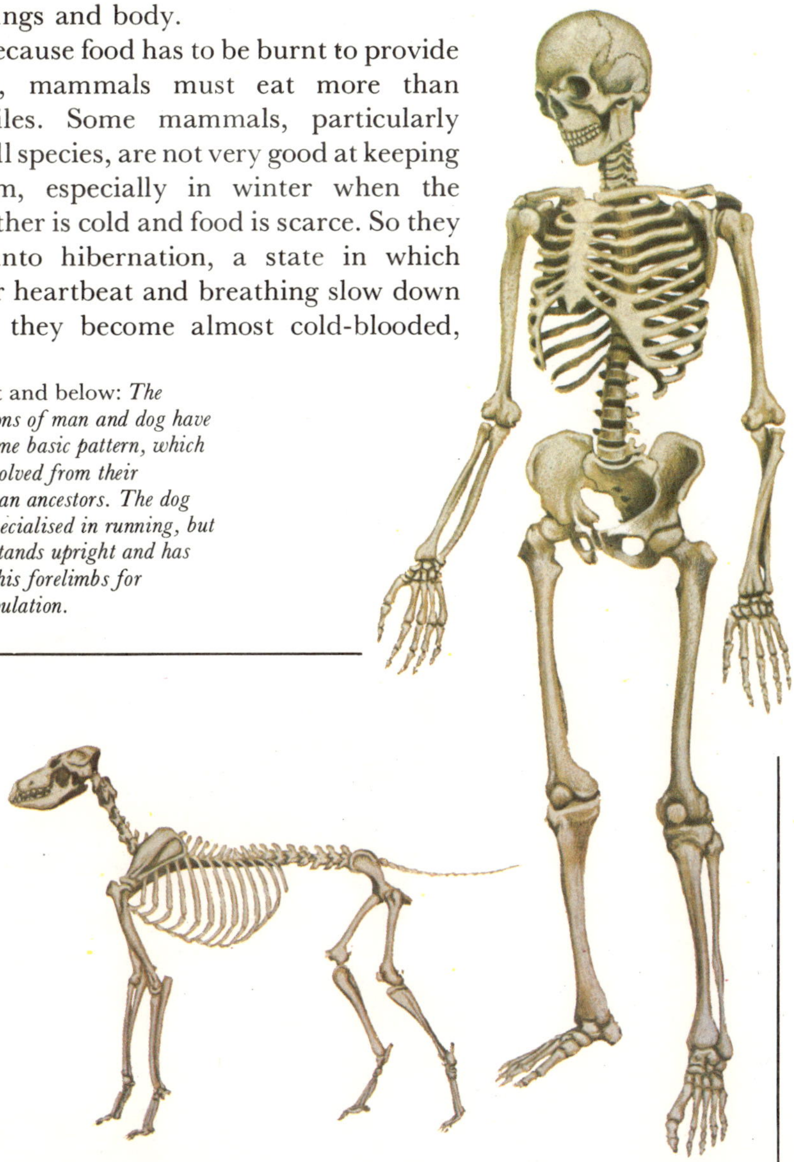

Right and below: *The skeletons of man and dog have the same basic pattern, which has evolved from their reptilian ancestors. The dog has specialised in running, but man stands upright and has freed his forelimbs for manipulation.*

The mandible (lower jaw) of a mammal is formed from a single bone on either side, strongly joined together in the middle. Two of the several bones which make up the reptilian jaw-joint have in mammals become *ossicles* – tiny bones in the middle ear – and now transmit sounds from the eardrum to the inner ear.

The teeth are set in sockets in the jaws and are of several different kinds. The mammal may have *incisors* in the front of the mouth, which are chisel-shaped and are used for biting. Next to them are the *canines*, one in each corner of the mouth, used for stabbing. They are well developed as fangs in carnivorous mammals. Along each side of the mouth lie the cheek teeth, the *premolars* and *molars*. They have points, called *cusps*, for chewing. The mammal has two sets of teeth in its lifetime. The first set, the milk-teeth, usually erupt just after birth and they are replaced as the animals grow up.

Scientists use the arrangement of the teeth to help them classify mammals. Anteaters, for instance, have no teeth, and the rodents (rats, mice and squirrels) have well-developed incisors for cutting tough plant food.

The limbs of mammals are brought under the body and give better support and agility than the sprawling legs of reptiles. The *pelvic* and *pectoral girdles* (hips and shoulders) are stronger and lighter. The structure of the joints combines strength with mobility.

The mobility and activity of the mammals demands good senses and quick thinking. The most primitive mammals have brains little more advanced than those of reptiles, but the majority are quick-witted and intelligent, particularly the primates (monkeys and apes) and cetaceans (whales and dolphins) which have large brains, whose capacity is increased by the surface of the cerebral hemispheres being folded. Brain capacity culminates in man himself.

The development of the senses differs from one mammal to another. Many depend on a good sense of smell, while the tree-living monkeys have good eyesight.

Monotremes and Marsupials

Australia is the main home for two primitive kinds of mammals, the monotremes and the marsupials. A few species of both kinds also live in neighbouring New Guinea, and there are some marsupials in South America which have spread northwards to the United States and Canada.

Monotremes are the most primitive mammals. They lay large, yolky eggs, and they get their name because their digestive and reproductive organs have a *monotreme*, or single opening. The only living monotremes are the echidna, or spiny anteater, and the duck-billed platypus.

Monotremes have several reptilian characters, such as the bone structure of the shoulders. However, other features confirm that they are mammals. They have a coat of fur and are warm-blooded although the temperature is likely to vary more than that of other mammals. The heart and lungs are separated from the other internal organs by a diaphragm, and the female suckles her young with milk.

There are two species of echidnas, one in Queensland and New Guinea, the other in more temperate Australia. They look like hedgehogs or porcupines, with a covering of long, sharp spines and a long snout. The animal uses its strong forelegs for tearing up hard earth in search of termites and ants, which it then captures with its long sticky tongue that whips out of a tiny mouth on the end of the snout. Echidnas have no teeth, but chew the insects by rubbing them between the tongue and the roof of the mouth, both of which are set with spines.

The single egg is laid in late summer and is incubated in a pouch on the mother's belly until it hatches 10 days later. At first the baby echidna clings to its mother, but when it gets too large she leaves it in a burrow while she goes out to feed.

The platypus is such a strange-looking animal that when the first specimen arrived in London it was thought to be a fake with a duck's bill sewn to a mammal's skin. It is found in the rivers and lakes of eastern Australia and Tasmania, where it swims with its webbed feet. It catches insects, snails and other small animals, which are crushed in the horny bill. The male bears a poison spur on each ankle. When not swimming, platypuses live in burrows. Here the female lays her two or three eggs.

Marsupials get their name from the *marsupium* (pouch) on the female's abdomen; the marsupium covers the mammary glands. Marsupials give birth to live babies which are minute and incompletely developed. As soon as it is born, a baby marsupial crawls through its

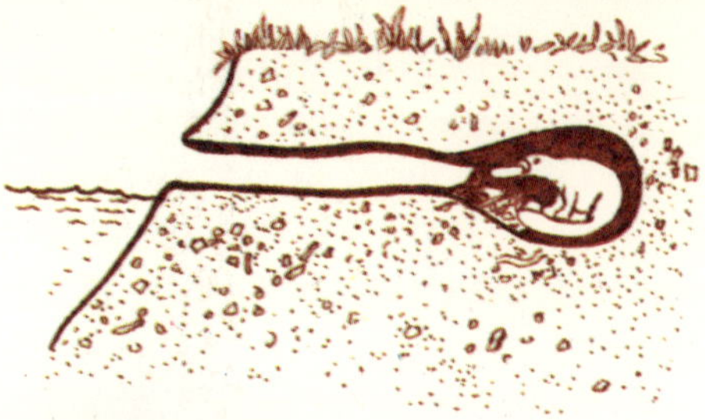

Right: *The platypus digs a burrow in the river bank in which to sleep, but when the female is ready to lay her eggs, she blocks the entrance with earth. She remains there until the young have hatched and are partly grown.*

After the birth of her young, the female mates and conceives again. However, so long as the young in the pouch is suckling, the fertilised ovum remains free in the uterus as a ball of cells. When the young leaves the pouch and is weaned, this ball begins to develop.

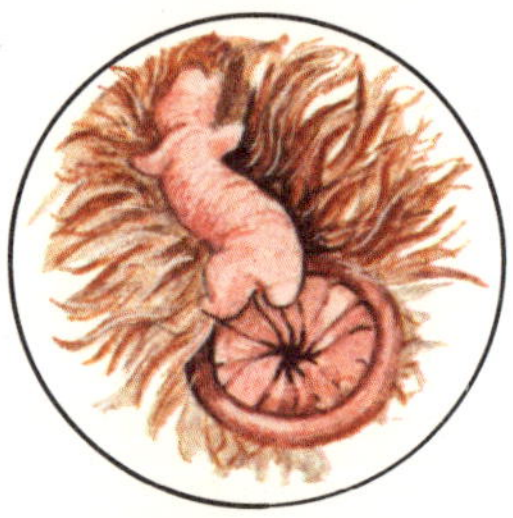

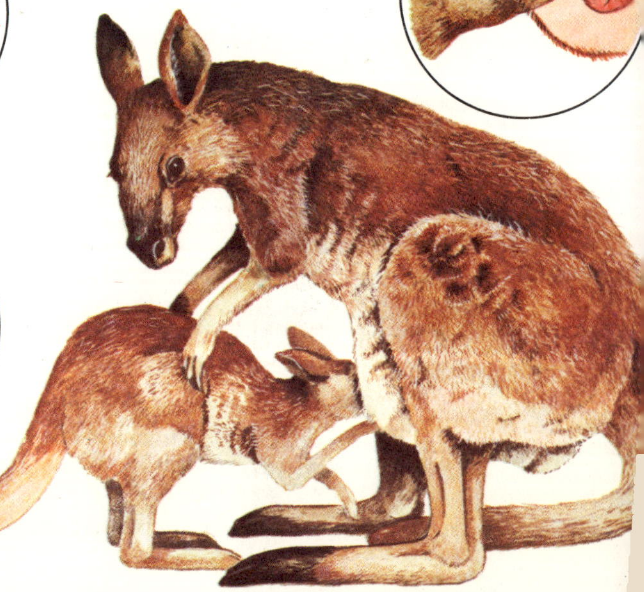

Below: *The tiny newborn kangaroo has powerful arms which it uses to crawl through the mother's fur and into her pouch. There it becomes securely attached to one of her teats. When much older the young kangaroo still returns to the pouch for food and safety.*

mother's fur to the pouch and takes a teat in its mouth. There it completes its development while being fed with milk. A few marsupials do not have a pouch, and the babies are exposed as they cling to the teats.

Marsupials were once much more widespread than they are today. They probably reached Australia about 50 million years ago across the sea from Asia, long before the placentals arrived. In their isolation they evolved into many different forms.

The process by which members of one animal group adopt varied ways of life is called *adaptive radiation*. Some of these marsupials are remarkably similar in appearance or habits to the placentals of other continents. The adaptation of two or more unrelated groups of animals for the same way of life is called *convergent evolution*.

The so-called marsupial mice really resemble the placental shrews; the marsupial mole lives in underground burrows; and the dasyures (the Tasmanian wolf and Tasmanian devil), are hunters equivalent to members of the cat and dog families. The numbat or banded anteater catches termites on its sticky tongue, like a true anteater, and the wombat looks rather like a marmot. Although their appearance and hopping locomotion are so different, the kangaroos and wallabies are the Australian counterpart of grass-eating cattle and sheep.

There is no real distinction between kangaroos and wallabies; large species are generally called kangaroos and the smaller are termed wallabies.

The largest kangaroos are the red and great grey kangaroos. The males are called boomers, the females flyers and the babies are joeys. Kangaroos live in herds called mobs. When moving slowly a kangaroo balances on its front legs and tail while swinging the hind-legs forward. For fast movement it hops on its back legs, using the thick tail as a balancer. The maximum speed is about 40 kph (25 mph) and large kangaroos can clear fences 2·7 metres (9 feet) high.

The koala is a small, bear-like marsupial belonging to the Australian possum or phalanger family. It lives in eastern Australia, where it feeds on the leaves of eucalyptus or gum trees.

Above: *Wombats are now very rare in the grasslands and mountains of Australia where they used to be common. They are great diggers; many of their burrows are up to 30 metres (100 feet) in length. Wombats bear a remarkable similarity to rodents such as the marmots and prairie dogs of the American mountains and prairies. This similarity also extends to their burrowing habits and diet – grasses, roots and fungi.*

Below: *The koala is familiar throughout the world, yet in its native Australia it is much reduced in numbers. One reason for this is that it will only eat the leaves of certain species of gum tree* (Eucalyptus). *Koalas bear one young at a time, which after six months in the pouch rides on its mother's back. Mother koalas punish their young by spanking them across their knee!*

The most common possum is the brush possum, which has also been introduced to New Zealand, and the family includes the monkey-like cuscuses and the flying phalangers or gliders. Flying phalangers are like the placental flying squirrels, having flaps of fur-covered skin between the legs which enable them to glide long distances.

The American opossums live mainly in South America, but one species, the Virginia opossum, is North American, extending into Canada. It is famous for its habit of 'playing possum' – when frightened it feigns death. Its body goes limp, its eyes close and its tongue lolls out.

The yapok or water-opossum of South America is the only marsupial to live in water. The mouth of the pouch closes tightly, so the babies do not drown.

Above left: *Sloths have no incisor or canine teeth and their cheek teeth are simple and without enamel. There are two-toed and three-toed (shown here) sloths. All sloths are slow-moving, with a characteristic way of hanging upside-down. As a result of this, their fur grows the opposite way from other mammals.*

Below: *Hedgehogs are related to moles and shrews. They root around in the undergrowth in the dark, often following the same path night after night, in search of slugs, snails, worms and beetles. When a hedgehog is suddenly alarmed, it rolls into a ball, and nothing except the most foolish dog will try to harm it.*

The Insect Eaters

The insectivores are the most primitive of the placental mammals. All are small and most, as the name suggests, feed on insects and other small invertebrates.

The most abundant and widespread insectivores are the shrews, which are also the least specialised. Most of the 200 species lead a retiring life, looking for insects and snails among the grass and leaf litter, but some live in water. A shrew's long muzzle projects beyond the teeth in a mobile snout. Its ears and eyes are small but the sense of smell is good.

Shrews lead a very active life, hunting almost incessantly, with only short breaks for sleep. While on the move they communicate with high-pitched squeaks. Many live for no more than one year, surviving only one winter and dying not long after their first breeding season. The Etruscan shrew, weighing no more than about two grammes (1/14 ounce), is the smallest mammal in the world.

The hedgehog is the most familiar Old World insectivore. The true hedgehogs have a coat of spines, which are modified hairs, but the related gymnures of Asia are merely hairy. Hedgehogs can roll into a prickly ball by means of a ring of muscles which pull the loose skin together like the drawstring of a kitbag. Baby hedgehogs are born naked and the spines appear shortly afterwards.

The tenrecs are spiny, hedgehog-like insectivores which are confined to Madagascar and the nearby Comoro Islands. They can roll into a ball like hedgehogs. The young of one species of tenrecs communicate by rattling their spines together.

The moles of Europe, Asia and North America, and the golden moles of southern Africa live in underground tunnel systems where they feed on earthworms and insects. The American moles also eat bulbs and roots. The tunnels run either just under the soil surface, where they can be seen as a low ridge, or deep underground so that the excavated soil has to be thrown out and dumped, forming the familiar molehills. Some moles are blind; the rest have poor eyesight.

The American star-nosed mole has a ring of 22 pink tentacles on its snout. It lives on marshy ground.

There are several groups of mammals only a little less primitive than the insectivores and unusual in many respects. The tree shrews of south-east Asian rain forests were at first classed as insectivores, then they were linked with the monkeys, and now it is thought that they should be placed on their own. In appearance and habits they are very like squirrels, with bushy tails and large eyes. Some are flesh-eaters, others are vegetarian.

Another inhabitant of these forests is the colugo or flying lemur – which is not a lemur and does not fly. It is a glider, with a membrane of thin skin that stretches from the ears to the front legs, back to the rear legs and thence to the tip of the tail. The colugo spends the day asleep, hanging upside down, and is active by night.

The Edentata are distantly related to the insectivores; the name means 'toothless ones', but only the anteaters are toothless. The other members of the group, the

Left: *Hedgehogs find their food mainly by scent, but they have good ears and can hear the movement of small edible creatures. They themselves make a great deal of noise whilst hunting, snuffling around and crunching snail shells.*

Left: *Shrews (left), like this common European shrew, are extremely ferocious for their size; they are only about 7 centimetres (2¾ inches) long, and have to eat a great deal to make up for the heat lost by their bodies. The European mole (centre) also needs a great deal to eat; it lives in a system of tunnels, regularly patrolling them for earthworms. Its whole body is adapted to living underground. The star-nosed mole (right) lives in eastern North America; it has similar habits.*

sloths and armadillos, have some teeth.

The anteaters of South America have peculiarly long snouts and all feed on ants and termites. They tear open the nests with sharp claws and mop up the insects with their long tongues. The giant anteater lives on the ground in forests and savannahs, whereas the tamandua and the pygmy anteaters live in trees.

The sloths also live in American forests, but are confined to the tropics. They are as sluggish as their name suggests and they spend their lives hanging upside down from branches by their hooked claws.

Twenty-one species of armadillo are protected by an armour of small bony plates embedded in the skin. Some species can roll up like a hedgehog to protect the soft underparts, and others when disturbed cling to the ground with their sharp claws or wedge themselves into holes and crevices. Their diet is mainly insects, but some armadillos eat larger animals, carrion or fruit. Armadillos are found all over South and Central America.

The pangolins used to be classed as edentates, as they are toothless, but they are now placed on their own branch of the zoological family tree. The skin is covered with an armour of overlapping, horny scales and the pangolin can curl up to look like an outsized pine cone. Pangolins live in Africa and Asia, and they eat ants and termites.

The last member of this oddly-assorted gathering is the aardvark. It is another ant- and termite-eater and it used to be classed as an edentate. Although common in many parts of Africa, its habits are not well-known. It looks like a pig but has a 600-millimetre (2 foot) tail and long rabbit-like ears.

Below: *Armadillos are great diggers, using their powerful front paws to excavate burrows to live in as well as for digging out food. The nine-banded armadillo (below right) almost always has a litter of four, born in a nest at the end of a burrow; they are identical, well-developed at birth, and weaned at two months. The nine-banded armadillo (right) cannot roll up as well as other armadillos, but when alarmed it plunges into one of its burrows and humps its back to wedge itself in firmly. The fairy armadillo (below left) is very small indeed – only about 12 centimetres (4¾ inches) long; it lives a mole-like existence, rarely being seen above ground.*

The Flying Mammals

With their ugly faces and leathery wings, bats are not the most popular animals, but few groups of mammals can have more unusual and interesting habits.

The bats are the only mammals to have mastered powered flight (the flying squirrels, flying lemurs and flying phalangers are merely gliders) and this has made them supremely successful. By taking to the air they have invaded a world previously denied to mammals and, by flying only at night, they avoid competition with birds.

There are about 800 species of bats living in all parts of the world, except Antarctica, and bats are the only mammals to have reached New Zealand without man's assistance. Unfortunately many species live in tropical forests, which are rapidly being cut down, and some bats may become extinct before they have been studied. In other parts of the world bats also suffer greatly from destruction of their roosts.

The biggest bats have wingspans of over 1·5 metres (5 feet), but most bats are small, mouse-sized animals. They have solved the problem of flight in a quite different way from birds. The wing surface is a thin membrane of skin which runs from the arm to the leg, and most bats have a secondary membrane between the legs and tail. When the arms are extended, the membrane is stretched and supported between the four fingers. The small thumb is free and is used when the bat is crawling. Each finger can move independently to make subtle alterations to the configuration of the wing surface, so bats can manoeuvre more nimbly in flight than any bird.

The wing also acts as a radiator, to lose heat produced by the muscular exertion of flight. On landing, elastic filaments in the membrane collapse the wing and it folds up, reducing heat loss. The back legs of the bat are adapted for clinging upside down by the toes.

In temperate regions bats spend the winter months in hibernation. Even during everyday sleep, many bats let their body temperature fall almost to that of the surrounding air, thus conserving energy. When they wake up, they shiver to warm up before taking to the air. During hibernation heart-beat and breathing drop, but bats do not sleep non-stop through the winter. They sometimes come out because they must not get too hot or cold. If the air is too cold, the bats die; if too warm, they use up their food reserves too quickly. A few species such as the European mouse-eared bat make long migrations to their hibernating quarters.

A female bat bears a single baby at a time. At first the mother carries it on her nightly flight but, when it is too heavy, she leaves it hanging up in the roosting place.

There are two sub-orders of bats, the

Below: *Bats find their prey in the dark by echo-location. In most insect-eating bats, such as the long-eared bat shown here, the bat emits a short pulse of very high frequency sound. Each pulse is only a few thousandths of a second long, and is about two or three octaves above that which the most sensitive human ear can detect. Because of their intensity, they are sometimes said to shout. Some of the pulses are reflected back by insects and, because the echoes received by the two ears are slightly different, the bat can deduce the direction of the insect. The bat probably deduces distance from the time taken for the echo to return. The long-eared bat feeds mainly on insects picked off leaves, and needs particularly sensitive hearing – hence the extra large ears.*

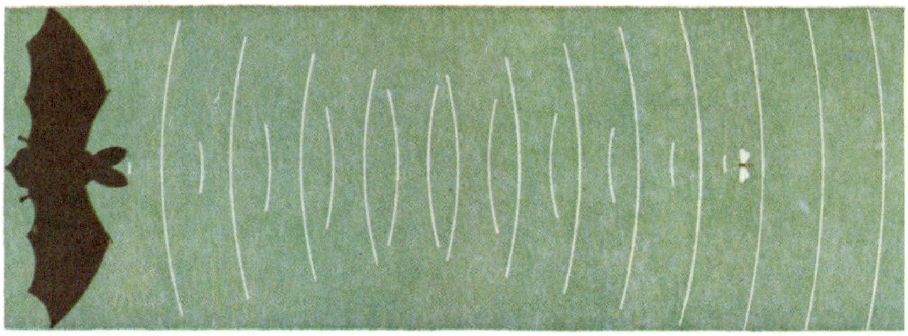

Below: *This horseshoe bat shows the typical structure of a bat wing. The second and third digits are very close and strengthen the leading edge of the wing tip. On the face there is a horseshoe shaped flap of skin surrounding the nostrils. This acts as a kind of 'megaphone', concentrating the bat's sounds, which it emits through its nose, into a narrow beam immediately in front of the bat. The pulses of horseshoe bats are longer than those of other bats.*

Megachiroptera and the Microchiroptera, literally the big-hand-wings and little-hand-wings. The Microchiroptera are the more abundant and widespread, and are the bats familiar to people living in temperate countries. The majority of the microchiropteran bats eat insects, which are caught in flight or are plucked from leaves as the bat hovers close by.

Bats are not blind as is sometimes supposed but their eyes are useless for catching flying insects at night. The insects are tracked down by an incredibly sensitive system of echo-location or sonar. The bat emits a stream of sounds through its mouth or nose and listens for the faint echoes returning from insects or obstacles in its path. The sounds are ultra-sonic – too high-pitched for human hearing – so they can be studied only with special instruments.

It is now known that bats can avoid flying into wires only 0·1 millimetre (1/250 inch) thick and that their sonar systems have the same sophisticated techniques as modern radar for determining the movement and speed of targets. However, some moths can hear an approaching bat and take evasive action.

The diet of insects results in the floors of bat roosts – caves, the roofs of houses, hollow trees – becoming covered with a layer of *guano* (droppings) containing the hard skeletons of countless insects. In some parts of the world the guano has been excavated for the manufacture of fertilisers and explosives, and it forms the food supply for many small cave-dwelling animals.

Some of the American microchiropteran bats feed on fruit or nectar. Others hunt animals larger than insects, for instance mice, birds and even other bats. A few species hunt fish by flying low over the water and grabbing their prey with their long-clawed feet as it breaks the surface of the water.

The strangest diet is that of the blood-feeding vampires. Native to tropical and subtropical America, vampires are a considerable pest. A vampire settles on its sleeping victim, often a domestic animal, and slashes its skin with razor-sharp incisor teeth. So deft are the bat's actions

Below right: *The vampire bat lives on a diet of blood. Without awakening the victim, it slits into flesh and laps up the blood with its tongue, which has two grooves in it.*

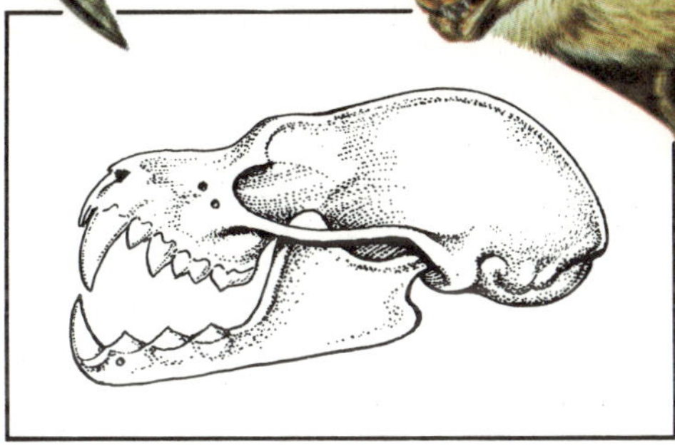

Left: *The vampire slices out a chunk of flesh with its razor-sharp upper incisors. The tongue then slides through the gap between the upper and lower incisors.*

that the victim is not awakened, and the vampire proceeds to lap up blood with its tongue, which is rolled into a tube. The flow is maintained by pumping in an anticoagulant. When the vampire is bloated it drops off its host.

More serious than the loss of blood is the fact that vampires carry rabies. Several other species of bats also carry rabies and other diseases, and there are fears that they could cause epidemics among other animals, including man.

The Old World is the home of the megachiropteran bats. They are almost entirely vegetarian, and feed on fruit and flowers. Some are nectar drinkers and hover in front of flowers to sip the nectar with their long tongues. A general name for most of these species is fruit bat, and the largest are called flying foxes because of their narrow, pointed muzzles, which look very much like that of a fox.

Some fruit bats roost in huge numbers in caves or trees and swarm out at dusk in search of food. Instead of sonar, fruit bats rely on good eyesight for navigation, although some species are known to use a simple form of echo-location, clicking the tongue instead of squeaking.

Above: *A fruit bat hangs upside down from a branch. To take off, it merely opens its wings and lets go. Landing is more difficult, and the bat has to turn upside down and seize the perch with its feet.*

The Primates

Man is a primate and, although we may not like to think so, the primates are primitive animals. The possession of five fingers and toes and a collarbone are primitive characteristics inherited from our distant ancestors.

The first primates are believed to have been shrew-like animals that were arboreal (tree-dwelling), and the majority of primates still live in trees. Some primates have, however, left the trees to live on the ground, the baboons and man for instance.

As an early adaptation for tree life, the primates gradually lost the long snout and good sense of smell, and developed good eyesight with stereoscopic or three-dimensional vision, which is useful when judging a leap from branch to branch. They have also developed large brains and are the most intelligent animals.

The primates are divided into the prosimians or 'lower primates' and the anthropoids (literally man-like creatures) or 'higher primates'. The prosimians include the lemurs, lorises and tarsiers, and the anthropoids the monkeys, apes and man.

The lemurs are confined to Madagascar and neighbouring islands. Most are tree-dwellers and nocturnal, but the ringtail lemur, a familiar inhabitant of zoos, comes down from the trees at dawn to feed on fruit, flowers and leaves. Ringtail lemurs live in groups, the females carrying their babies on their backs.

The lemur group includes the indri and the sifaka, and the mysterious aye-aye. The aye-aye is now very rare. It eats fruit and insects, which it removes from crevices by means of an extra-long finger on each hand.

The lorises of Asia and the potto, angwantibo and the bushbabies of Africa are also nocturnal tree-dwellers. The two lorises, the slow loris and the slender loris, are slow-moving animals with long legs and no visible tail. The index finger is reduced to a stub, probably to give the thumb and remaining fingers a better grasp on branches. The bushbabies are more active and leap from branch to branch. They also leave their offspring in nests instead of carrying them.

The tarsiers are the prosimians most nearly related to the higher primates. They live in the forests of south-east Asia and feed on insects and fruit. Compared with the lemurs and lorises, tarsiers have flat, monkey-like faces and they have huge, round eyes.

The monkeys are divided into New World monkeys and Old World monkeys. New World monkeys have flat noses, small faces and rounded heads. All have long tails which, in some species, are prehensile and can be used as an extra 'hand' for gripping branches or even holding food. In the isolation of the forests of South America, the monkeys have undergone adaptive radiation, developing ways of life equivalent to the prosimians, monkeys and apes of the Old World.

Some of the New World monkeys walk along branches on all fours like the prosimians. They include the marmosets, sakis, titis and capuchins. The titis live in pairs, running through the trees like squirrels or sitting side by side with their tails hanging down and intertwined.

Capuchins live in groups and are extremely intelligent, almost as bright as chimpanzees. Other monkeys are leapers

Right: *A prehensile tail is only found in South American monkeys such as this red spider monkey.*

Below: *Ring-tailed lemurs are among the most terrestrial of the otherwise tree-living lemurs.* Below centre: *Hamadryas baboons are large monkeys which live in the horn of Africa. They have a well-developed social life, each troop consisting of a group of harems led by dominant males.* Bottom left: *Gorillas are the largest primates. They live in extended family groups.*

or swing from branch to branch with their arms. The douroucouli, or night monkey, is the only nocturnal higher primate.

The spider monkeys have very long arms, which give them their spidery appearance. They spend their lives in the tops of trees, where they feed on fruit. Howler monkeys live in troops which have shouting matches with neighbouring troops. To help younger monkeys to cross from one tree to the next, adult howlers make a living bridge.

The Old World monkeys are of two

Above: *(left to right) The rhesus macaque lives in large troops with a curious matrilineal structure – each female belongs to her mother's sub-group. Chimpanzees are the most exuberant apes, and are probably the most intelligent of the primates. They have a most catholic diet and will occasionally kill small antelopes. The tarsier and the slow loris are both nocturnal. They feed on animals but unlike the tarsier, the loris catches food by stealth.*

kinds: the Asian langurs and the African colobus which are leaf-eaters, and the rest which have a varied diet. The langurs include the proboscis monkey, which has an extraordinarily long nose, and the golden langur, which has a lion-like mane. These monkeys live in troops led by an old male; young males live in separate groups. Of the Old World monkeys, the macaques of Asia are used for medical research. The rhesus monkey which lives around Hindu temples is probably the best known of the macaques.

The Barbary ape is an African representative which also has a toe-hold in Europe, where it lives on the Rock of Gibraltar. The African baboons are interesting because they have 'come down from the trees' and live in open grasslands, as did man's ancestors. Baboons live in large troops under the charge of old males.

The apes are not so numerous as the monkeys. There are six species of gibbons, the orang-utan, the gorilla and the chimpanzee. The apes are distinguished from monkeys by the lack of a tail, a broad chest and a big toe widely separated from the other toes. The arms are longer than the legs and all the limbs are supple.

The gibbons are the smallest and most abundant apes. They live in Asia in families of a mated pair with their children. Gibbons have exceptionally long arms with which they swing rapidly through the branches.

The orang-utan, whose name means 'man of the jungle', lives in the rain forests of Sumatra and Borneo and is another tree-dweller. Only the big males, who develop grotesque flanges on the face, spend much time on the ground. Adult orangs lead solitary lives, but the young spend four years with their mothers.

Contrary to their reputation, the gorillas are peaceful animals. They spend most of their time on the ground, but retire to nests of woven branches at night. Their food consists of bark, roots, fruit and leaves and, unlike chimpanzees, they never eat meat. Both these kinds of apes live in the forests of western Africa. They can swing from branch to branch when young, but they are normally quadrupedal – walking on their feet and the knuckles of their hands.

The chimpanzee is man's nearest relative. It uses tools such as small sticks for fishing termites from nests.

Right: *The black rat, or ship rat, reached Europe from Asia before the brown rat, and is now found mainly in seaports.*

Rodents, Rabbits and Hares

Below: *The house mouse is found almost wherever man lives. They eat almost anything, and have been transported around the world by ship and plane. 'White mice' are albinos bred specially for laboratory use.*

Rodents are gnawing animals. They have a single pair of incisor (cutting) teeth in both upper and lower jaws. Each incisor has a thick layer of hard enamel on the front surface only, covering the softer dentine of which the tooth is made. Constant wear removes the dentine more rapidly than the enamel, so the tip of the incisor is kept as sharp as a chisel edge.

The incisors grow continuously at the roots, so they never wear down to the gums, no matter how much they are used. The incisors are separated from the cheek-teeth by a gap, the *diastema*. By pulling the lips into the diastema a rodent can gnaw inedible material without filling its mouth. A squirrel does this when it is opening a nut.

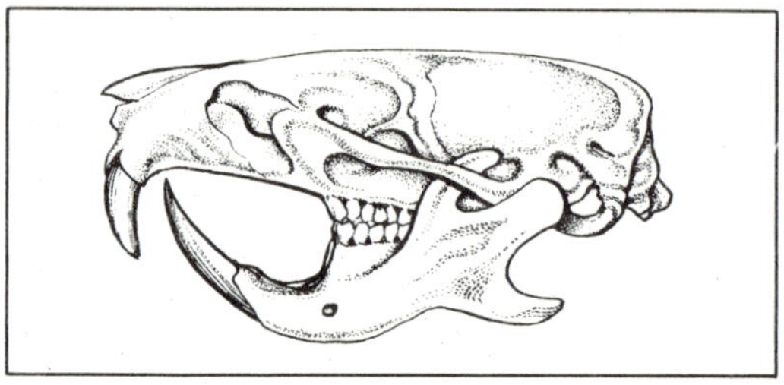

Right: *A hamster skull shows the typical teeth of a rodent. There is a pair of long, continuously growing incisor teeth in both upper and lower jaws. These are always sharp and are used for gnawing tough food. The cheek teeth are for chewing.*

The rodents are an amazingly successful group of mammals. There are about 1,500 species, and they have invaded almost every part of the world. Apart from the bats, they are the only placental mammals to reach Australia without man's assistance. The success of the rodents is partly due to their *adaptive radiation* (evolution to fit into many ways of life). There are the running springhares and agoutis, the aquatic water voles, beavers and coypus, the tree-dwelling dormice and squirrels, the aerial flying squirrels and the burrowing mole rats.

Other rodents are successful because they are not specialised; they are opportunists which can take advantage of any new resource. The brown rat and the house mouse have been carried around the world, even to subantarctic islands, and are serious pests because they go anywhere and eat anything. Some house mice have grown thick coats and live in cold-stores.

The abundance of rodents is aided by their rapid breeding. A house mouse starts to breed at six weeks old and can have five litters, each with five or six young, every year, although it is short-lived and never normally survives for more than two years in the wild.

There are three main groups of rodents, which are classified according to the structure of their skulls and other details of anatomy.

The Sciuromorpha includes the squirrels, pocket gophers, kangaroo rats and beavers. Not all squirrels live in trees, nor do they all have bushy tails to help them balance. There are many ground squirrels which live in burrows, including prairie dogs, marmots and chipmunks.

The Myomorpha encompasses the huge assembly of rats, mice, gerbils, ham-

Below: *Hares (left) and rabbits (right) are very similar. The hare is a faster runner and has longer ears. Hares and rabbits are not rodents; they have two pairs of incisors in the upper jaw, and they eat mainly tough grasses and herbs.*

sters, voles, dormice and jerboas – the whole range of 'mouse-like' rodents. There is no real difference between rats and mice except for size, but they can be distinguished from voles and lemmings by their larger ears and sharper muzzles. Many are of economic importance because they invade crops, either when they are growing or when they are stored. A very large proportion of the world's grain crop is eaten by rats and mice every year. These animals may also carry such diseases as bubonic plague, typhus and food poisoning.

The Hystricomorpha is the third major group of rodents and includes South American rodents such as the capybara – the largest rodent – the viscacha, guinea pig, tuco-tuco and agouti. The chinchilla and coypu are farmed for their thick, soft fur. The group also includes the porcupines. Porcupines are well protected by their barbed spines which easily come loose and work into the flesh of any animal struck by them. The American porcupine has short spines compared with those of the African and south European porcupines.

At one time rabbits and hares were thought to be rodents because they have gnawing incisors and a diastema, but there are many differences, including a second pair of incisors in the upper jaw. The teeth have enamel on the back, unlike those of rodents, so they do not have such a sharp cutting edge. Nowadays rabbits and hares are placed in a second group, the Lagomorpha, along with the pikas.

Rabbits and hares are running animals, with long hindlegs and long ears. There is no real difference between the two; the American snowshoe rabbit is also called the varying hare, and the volcano rabbit, living on two Mexican volcanoes, is also called the Nelson hare. In Europe brown and mountain hares are distinguished from the rabbit by their longer, black-tipped ears and their life above ground.

Left: *The brown rat is also called the common rat and Hanover rat. It reached Europe in the 18th century and is now found everywhere, both in towns and in the countryside. Rats are intelligent, and albino 'white' rats are used in laboratory studies of animal behaviour.*

European rabbits make extensive burrow systems called warrens or buries, but hares rest in a hollow in the grass or undergrowth called a form. The young of rabbits are born naked and helpless but baby hares – leverets – are born with a coat of fur and their eyes open, and are able to move around shortly after birth.

Rabbits, hares and pikas live in open, dry country, with the exception of the forest rabbit of Brazil and the marsh and swamp rabbits of North America.

The food of lagomorphs is grass, leaves and bark, and they increase their digestive efficiency by eating their own droppings. This practice, called *refection*, increases the amount of protein, carbohydrate and vitamin B extracted from the food.

Left and below: *The beaver is a marvellous engineer. It can cut down trees, using its incisor teeth and use the logs to dam a river and make a lake. Within this lake it builds its home or lodge, a huge pile of sticks and mud. Inside the lodge there is a nest chamber reached by underwater passages.*

Sea Mammals

Four kinds of mammal have forsaken the land for life in the sea. They are the sea otter, which lives along the shore, the whales and sea cows which are completely at home in water, and the seals which return to land to give birth.

The whales, dolphins and porpoises, often known collectively as cetaceans from the scientific name of the order, Cetacea, are the most completely adapted to a marine environment. They spend their whole life at sea and cannot go ashore without dying, but there are dolphins living in the fresh waters of the Amazon, Ganges, Plate and Yangtse rivers. Most species live near the surface, but a few dive to great depths.

The cetaceans have evolved the same basic shape as the fishes. Their bodies are streamlined, often with a dorsal fin for stability; the forelimbs are reduced to flippers for steering and the rear limbs have disappeared completely. Swimming is achieved by the broad tailflukes which beat up and down, rather than side to side as in fishes. Excellent streamlining allows some dolphins to reach speeds of 55 kph (30 knots). The nostrils are placed on top of the head and form blowholes; cetaceans must come to the surface to breathe or 'blow' at intervals.

A single baby, the calf, is born tail first, instead of head first as is more usual. As soon as it is clear of its mother's body the calf must swim to the surface to fill its lungs with air.

There are two kinds of whales: the whalebone whales and the toothed whales.

Whalebone whales have no teeth, but their upper jaws bear a fringe of bristly plates called whalebone or baleen. The plates are used to strain small animals from the water. The whale takes a mouthful of water, or charges through the seas with its mouth open, then shuts its mouth and raises its tongue to squeeze out the water, leaving the small animals on the baleen plate. Most whalebone whales live on shrimp-like crustaceans, such as 'krill' and sea snails, but a few catch fish.

Below: *The bowheads, or right whales were so-called because they were the right whales to catch. They were slower than a rowing boat, floated when dead, and bore long baleen.*

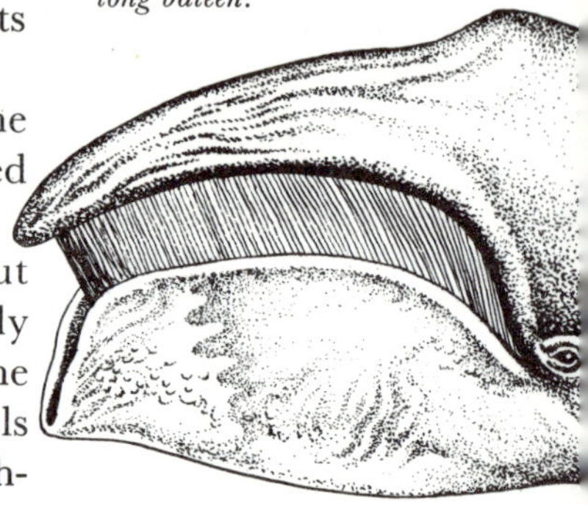

Below: *Dolphins are small toothed whales which feed on fish. They are famous for their superb acrobatics and for their intelligence, which makes them popular entertainers.*

Left: *The rorquals such as the blue whale, are faster moving than the bowheads (below left). The throat grooves in rorquals extend over much of the under-surfaces.*

Whalebone whales spend the summer in the rich waters of the Antarctic and Arctic, where they feed and develop a thick layer of blubber. Then they migrate to the tropics to give birth to their calves.

The whalebone whales include the world's largest animals. The blue whale grows to over 30 metres (100 feet) long and 100 tonnes weight and is the largest animal that has ever lived. The humpback whale has a strange knobbly skin and huge flippers. It sometimes jumps clear of the sea.

The toothed whales include the sperm whale, the beaked whales, the narwhal with its long spiral tusk, the related beluga or white whale, and the many kinds of dolphins and porpoises. The killer and pilot whales are large dolphins.

Whales are very intelligent and, because they are curious and usually friendly animals, they are easy to train. From experiments with captive dolphins it has been learnt that some, at least, possess a system of echo-location or sonar as good as that of bats.

The sea cows are so named because they are vegetarians. They are slow-moving, placid grazers, like their land counterparts, and they live in warm, shallow seas and rivers. Their food consists of marine grasses and herbs.

The dugong has a notch in its tailflukes, as in whales. It is found in the Indian Ocean, from Madagascar and the Red Sea to the Philippines and northern Australia. The manatee, which has a single spade-like fluke, lives in rivers and coasts of the tropical Atlantic.

The seals are descended from land carnivores and are basically fish-eaters. The true seals or hair seals are found mainly in colder waters, except for the monk seals of the Mediterranean, the West Indies and Hawaii. The Caspian and Baikal seals and some common seals live in lakes.

True seals use their hindflippers for swimming. They cannot turn them forward and, as the foreflippers are rather short, true seals can move over land only with difficulty.

At the beginning of the breeding season the seals gather on beaches or icefloes to bear their single pups. Harp seals gather in large numbers on top of the Arctic ice, whereas each ringed seal cow bears a pup in a den under the snow. Grey seals and elephant seals gather in thousands on beaches.

The pups of several species are born with a coat of white fur, but the common seal pup sheds the white coat before it is born. Seal pups spend very little time with their mothers – about one month on average – before they are abandoned.

Left: *When Christopher Columbus first saw manatees in the West Indies, he mistook them for the mermaids of legend, but he found them uglier than he expected.*

Left: *The dugong is entirely marine but usually stays close inshore. They frequently bear a pair of walrus-like tusks.*

The eared seals and the walruses swim with their foreflippers, and they can turn their hindflippers forward so the body can be raised when they gallop overland. The eared seals include the sealions and fur seals, which also differ from the true seals in having a dense, waterproof coat of underfur as well as a layer of blubber to keep them warm.

Huge 'rookeries' of bulls and cows gather on beaches during the breeding season. Each bull keeps a harem of cows. The cows give birth soon after hauling themselves on to the beach, then mate again. After this they spend several months suckling their pups. The walrus of Arctic seas suckles its pup for over a year. It uses its tusks for grubbing cockles and clams out of the mud on the seabed, and to help climb onto icefloes.

Below: *True seals cannot walk on their flippers like sealions, but the foreflippers can be used to haul the seal's heavy body up the beach.*

Carnivores: Cats and their Allies

The word 'carnivore' means flesheater, and sums up the essential character of these animals, although a few, for example the giant panda, do eat plant food.

Carnivores' canine teeth are enlarged to form fangs for seizing and tearing flesh. The incisors are used not so much for cutting food as for picking up small items, including carrying babies from place to place. Cutting lumps of flesh and cracking bones is undertaken by the cheekteeth.

One tooth in both upper and lower jaw, on each side of the mouth, is larger than the others. These four teeth, called carnassials, have a sharp ridge so that they act as scissors for slicing through meat.

Most carnivores are hunters. Intelligence and keen senses are needed for stalking or seeking out elusive prey. Speed is often a requisite, and the body of many carnivores is adapted for running. The slow, heavy-bodied bears walk on the soles of their feet, but the swift dogs and cats walk on tiptoe.

Meat is a rich, easily-digested food and carnivores typically have rather short digestive systems and swallow lumps of food with little chewing. The larger hunters feed only infrequently; they gorge themselves at a kill, then digest at leisure.

There are two main groups of carnivores. The cat-like superfamily Feloidea includes the cats, hyaenas, civets and mongooses; the dog-like superfamily Canoidea includes the dogs, foxes, bears, raccoons and weasels.

The cat family Felidae numbers nearly 40 species. Cats have good eyesight, the pupils dilating at night to allow as much light into the eyes as possible. The face is flat so that the eyes look forwards to give good binocular vision. The claws are sharp and, except in the cheetah, can be retracted into sheaths.

Five cats are known as the 'big cats'. These are the lion, tiger, leopard, snow leopard and jaguar. There is no real distinction between big and smaller cats.

The lion is the only sociable cat. It lives in extended family groups called prides. Each pride consists of several lionesses and their cubs and one or more adult males. At intervals the dominant male lion is replaced after a fight.

Lions are lazy animals, particularly in the open savannahs of Africa where they suffer from the heat. The lionesses do the hunting. They stalk up to their prey and leap on it but, if they miss on the first charge, they give up the chase. After the kill the male lions feed first.

Tigers are found in the Manchurian mountains of China, where they have thick, shaggy coats of fur, as well as in forests of south-east Asia and India. They

Below: *Young carnivores have a comparatively long childhood. While it is important for young herbivores, like antelopes, to run with the herd as soon after birth as possible, these lion cubs have no such problem. They begin to play hunting games when very young. This is an important part of growing up to be a successful carnivore. A few big cats, like the cheetah, rely on speed to run down their prey; lions, like most cats, hunt by carefully stalking their chosen victim until only a short run is necessary to secure it.*

Below: *The clouded leopard is one of the least known of the big cats. It lives in south-east Asia and feeds on birds and rodents.*

dislike excessive heat and lie up in dense cover, or bathe in pools. The main prey of the tiger is blackbuck and, as these antelopes have been reduced, so the tiger has been forced into retreat.

The leopard, sometimes called the panther, lives in both Africa and Asia. It sometimes hides its prey in trees so that it cannot be stolen by lions or hyaenas. The jaguar of South America is another good tree climber. It is very similar to the leopard in having rosettes of spots on its coat, but the jaguar's rosettes have a spot in the middle, whereas those of the leopard do not. The snow leopard or ounce of the Himalayas and central Asia is not a true leopard. Its thick, whitish fur is a protection against the cold.

Above: *The mongoose is an enemy of snakes, but attempts to get rid of snakes by importing mongooses have not worked.*

Above: *Cheetahs once ranged over most of Africa and the Near and Middle East, but are now rare except in Africa south of the Sahara. Cheetahs feed mainly on small and medium-sized antelopes of the savannahs and semi-deserts.*

Of the smaller cats, the puma, cougar or mountain lion, which ranges from Canada to Argentina, is nearly as large as a lioness. The cheetah, another of the smaller cats, is extremely fast, although if the prey is not caught quickly the chase is abandoned. The accepted speed record is 105 kph (65 mph) although faster speeds have been suggested. Unlike other cats, the cheetah cannot retract its claws properly.

Other cats are more the size of a large domestic cat. These include the European wild cat; the bobcat of North America; the leopard and marbled cats of Asia; and the margay, jaguarundi and pampas cat of South America. Intermediate in size are the long-legged serval and the caracal of Africa, and the lynx of Europe and North America.

The hyaena family, Hyaenidae, consists of the striped, brown and spotted hyaenas and the aardwolf. The hyaenas of Africa and Asia are heavily built and have powerful jaws and teeth which can crunch up the large leg bones of zebra and wildebeest. They are mainly scavengers and steal the prey of other predators, but spotted hyaenas hunt in packs to kill large animals, and may have their own prey stolen by lions. The aardwolf of southern Africa has very weak teeth and feeds on termites.

The mongoose and civet family Viverridae contains a large number of short-legged, long-tailed, often spotted or striped carnivores. Most live in Africa or Asia, but one species each of mongoose and genet lives in southern Europe. Apart from mongooses and civets there are palm civets, linsangs, the toddy cat – which is particularly fond of fruit – the kusimanse, the meerkats whose underground colonies often overlap with those of ground squirrels, the fossa of Madagascar and the fish-catching otter civet. Many climb trees and are nocturnal. They feed on small mammals and birds, or any other small animals that come their way, as well as a variety of vegetable foods.

Below: *The wild cat of Europe has a reputation for ferocity but it usually avoids people, and lives in remote forests and mountains.*

Dogs, Bears and Weasels

The dog-like carnivores are distinguished generally from the cat-like carnivores by their longer snouts, and in features of the internal anatomy. The dog family, Canidae, includes the dogs, foxes and wolves, which are among the noisiest of mammals with their barks and howls.

Domestic dogs are descended from the wolf, an animal which was once widespread through North America, Europe and Asia. Wolves live in packs of up to 30 individuals. Each pack has a territory of several square kilometres and is led by a dominant male and female. This pair may be the only wolves in the pack to breed. The cubs are cared for by all members of the pack, who bring food and keep guard when the mother is hunting. Prey ranges from mice to moose.

The coyotes are smaller cousins of the wolf living in North America. Despite persecution their numbers are increasing and they are becoming a pest in suburbs.

Jackals live singly or in pairs in territories. Although they are often described as scavengers and the name 'jackal' is used to mean a scrounger, jackals are also hunters.

The Cape hunting dog is one of the most ferocious animals. It lives in packs in savannah country in Africa south of the Sahara. The pack hunts animals up to the size of wildebeest. In Asia the wild dog or dhole has similar hunting and social behaviour to the hunting dog.

The red fox of Europe and North America is, like the coyote, a carnivore which flourishes despite persecution. Quick thinking and adaptability are the reasons for its success. To the north of the red fox lives the Arctic fox, whose thick fur turns white in winter.

The bears, Ursidae, have largely given up hunting, and now eat anything in the way of insects, fish, mice, berries and roots. Even the polar bear, which spends much of its time hunting seals in the Arctic seas, sometimes eats leaves and berries. Bears are slow and clumsy compared with other carnivores, but they can be surprisingly agile for their bulk, and the smaller bears are good tree climbers. In winter they lie up in dens but do not hibernate.

The brown bear lives in Europe, Asia, and in North America, where it is known as the grizzly bear. The American black bear is smaller, as is the Asian black bear. Other Old World bears are the sloth bear

Above: *The maned wolf is one of several little-known South American dogs. It has extremely long legs.*

Above: *Cape hunting dogs are of great interest because of their communal way of life. They live in packs, usually of around a dozen, which lead a nomadic existence. The pack settles in a temporary home, then hunting parties set out, leaving the pups under the care of some adults. Food is shared among the pack*

Left: *The giant panda is unusual among the carnivores in subsisting almost entirely on vegetable matter. Although it eats a certain amount of animal matter, its principal diet is the young shoots of bamboo. To aid it in dealing with these there is an extra thumb-like projection on the side of each front paw. This allows the giant panda to grasp bundles of shoots and to manipulate them. Very little is known about the habits of giant pandas in the wild.*

which feeds mainly on termites, and the sun bear. The rare spectacled bear lives in the South American Andes.

Despite its popularity, the giant panda is a mystery animal. Not much is known about its life in the bamboo forests of China, and even its position among the carnivores has been uncertain. Nowadays, the giant panda is generally thought to be an unusual kind of bear, but for a long time it was classed in the raccoon family, Procyonidae, along with the lesser or red panda. Red pandas are small carnivores with long tails, quite unlike the giant panda.

The raccoon family also includes the coati, kinkajou, olingo and the cacomistles of America. The raccoon's habit of washing its food only occurs in captivity.

The weasel family, Mustelidae, contains an assortment of animals.

The stoat, called a weasel in America and Ireland, is distinguished from the weasel of Europe and Asia by its larger size and the black tip of its tail. Both stoats and weasels living in the more northerly regions turn white in winter, the stoat in its winter white coat being called an ermine. The least weasel of North America is the smallest of all carnivores.

The black-footed ferret feeds exclusively on prairie dogs. The polecats, from which the domestic ferret of gamekeeper and poacher is descended, and the two minks – one American, the other Eurasian – are similar to the weasel, but the polecats have taken to the trees and the minks to water. Martens are like large, bushy-tailed weasels. They include the fisher of North America, the Russian sable and the South American tayra. The martens are good climbers and can hunt squirrels through the trees. The otters are web-footed and aquatic and one, the sea otter, is marine.

The largest relatives of the weasels are the badgers, the ratel and the wolverine. The badgers look like small bears and they, too, include vegetable food in their diet of small animals such as earthworms and insects.

The ratel or honey badger of Africa and India has a strange association with a bird called the honeyguide. The bird leads the ratel to a bees' nest, which the mammal breaks open, and both feed on the contents.

The wolverine or glutton lives in pine forests around the world. It is a scavenger, relying more on cunning than speed for a living. It has a reputation for ferocity.

Above: *Stoats are agile, strong predators which can kill animals larger than themselves. This has given them a reputation for being bloodthirsty hunters, but their main prey are mice and voles. In northern latitudes stoats turn white in winter, except for the black tip of the tail. The white fur is a camouflage.*

Below: *The dingo is the wild dog of Australia. It is thought that dingos are the descendants of domestic dogs which were brought by the early human settlers. They have probably been in their present wild state for many thousands of years, and have greatly reduced many native marsupial carnivores.*

Left: *The brown bear lives in the forests of Europe, Asia and North America. The bears are flesh-eaters which have turned to eating mainly plant food.*

Hoofed Animals and Elephants

Above: *The rock hyrax lives in rocky outcrops and cliffs, where it runs up steep slopes with great agility. Its hoof-like claws and padded feet get a good grip on the rock. Although hyraxes look like rodents, their closest relatives are the elephants and rhinoceroses.*

Below right: *The Malayan tapir lives in many parts of southeast Asia, but it is becoming rare where jungles are being cleared. It is usually found near water and it swims well, heading for water when disturbed. The snout, like a smaller version of an elephant's trunk, is very flexible and sensitive and is used for exploring ground.*

Below: *Rhinoceroses are the heaviest land animals after the elephants. Despite the fact that the African rhinos weigh up to two tons, they can gallop, with all four feet on the ground.*

The forests, plains and deserts of the world are stocked with a vast assembly of large plant-eating animals. They are collectively called the *ungulates*, or hoofed animals, because they walk on the tips of their toes, and their toenails are transformed into solid hoofs.

The ungulates are divided into two groups: the Perissodactyla, odd-toed animals which have either one or three toes; and the Artiodactyla, even-toed animals which have two or four toes. Distantly related to the hoofed animals because they share a common ancestor are three very different kinds of animals: the elephants and their relatives the hyraxes, and the sea-cows, all of which are descended from a forerunner of the hoofed animals.

Elephants, Proboscoidea, are the largest land animals. Large bulls can weigh over 5,000 kilogrammes (11,000 pounds) and stand over 3 metres (10 feet) high. The weight is supported on legs built like pillars and the soles of the feet have a fatty cushion. There are two species, the larger African elephant and the smaller Asian elephant. The Asian elephant is distinguished among other things by its smaller ears.

The tusks are enlarged upper incisor teeth and grow throughout life. The record weight for a tusk is 107 kilogrammes (236 pounds). Until recent years elephants were still abundant in the wild, but destruction of their habitat and killing for their ivory has made their survival precarious.

The elephant's trunk is an elongated nose with a variety of uses. It can investigate objects closely by touch and smell. It sucks up water and squirts it into its mouth, and plucks grasses and leaves from trees. The trunk is strong enough to lift heavy objects, but it is also used for gentle caressing in courtship.

The hyraxes or dassies are the conies of the Bible. They are small guineapig-like animals, about the size of a rabbit, which live on rock outcrops or in trees in Africa. The toes bear a stout hoof-like claw which helps in climbing, and the sole is covered with a pad of skin kept moist by a gland to give a firm grip. The upper incisor teeth are tusks and the lower teeth are useful only for grooming, so food has to be bitten off with the cheekteeth.

In the perissodactyls or odd-toed ungulates, the axis of the foot passes through the third toe. The side toes are lost. The horses stand on a single toe on each leg, the flanking toes having been reduced to splint bones.

Horses once lived throughout the world, but they died out in America where they had originated, and were brought back by the Spanish *conquistadores*. The only truly wild horses, as distinct from the

mustangs and brumbies which are domestic horses gone wild, are the tarpans, and Przewalski's horses of Mongolia. The tarpan used to be widespread in much of Europe and Asia and was the ancestor of all domestic horses. The last European wild horses were killed more than 70 years ago and only a few Przewalski's horses linger on in Mongolia.

The asses are small horse-like animals with long ears. The African wild asses used to live in desert and semi-desert areas of northern Africa, but now they are almost extinct. Donkeys are domesticated descendants of the African wild ass, and have retained the black cross on the back. A male is called a jack-ass, the female a jenny.

The Asiatic wild asses have been persecuted so that only small populations remain. The three subspecies that survive are known by their local names: the onager of Iran to western India, the kulan of Mongolia, and the kiang of the Himalayas.

Above: *Asian elephants are smaller than the African species and have smaller tusks – the females being usually tuskless. The head is domed and the back humped.*

Below: *The African elephant has large ears which it flaps to keep cool. It lives in small herds, mainly in the savannah.*

Compared with the wild horses and asses, zebra are still abundant and flourish in Africa. One species, the quagga, was wiped out in the last century and some races of the three surviving species – Grévy's, Burchell's and mountain zebras – are nearly extinct. The species are distinguished by the pattern of stripes.

The remaining odd-toed ungulates, the rhinoceroses and tapirs, are heavy animals compared with the horse family. Although ponderous, however, the rhinoceroses are surprisingly speedy and agile. The skin is thick and almost hairless and the horns are composed of a mass of hair-like fibres but, despite such armament, rhinoceroses are usually timid and rarely charge. As they are mainly nocturnal they do not often clash with man.

Of the two African species, the white rhinoceros (which is grey in colour) is the larger. The 'white' comes from an Afrikaans word for 'wide' and describes the shape of the mouth. Neither is the black rhinoceros properly black. Both species have two horns and smooth skins.

All three Asian species are now very rare and little is known about them. The Indian rhinoceros and the Javan rhinoceros have single horns but the Sumatran rhinoceros has two horns.

The tapirs were once spread over the world, but they now survive only in the tropics of America and Asia. They are heavy-bodied, like well-built pigs, and have a long nose resembling a short trunk.

The Cloven-hoofed Animals

The even-toed ungulates or artiodactyls are often called cloven-hoofed animals, because their weight is born on two central toes, each capped with a hoof, giving the appearance of a single split hoof. Two extra toes may also be present, the false hoofs or dew claws.

The artiodactyls are vegetarian and form three groups: pigs, peccaries and hippopotamuses; camels and llamas; and the rest, called the ruminants – the chevrotains, deer, giraffe, cattle and antelope.

Vegetable food needs more time for digestion than meat and the artiodactyls have a system of stomach chambers where digestion proceeds. The most complicated system is found in the ruminants. They have a *rumen*, or paunch, where food is stored as it is eaten. After feeding, when the animal is at leisure, it brings its food back into the mouth and gives it a second, very thorough, chewing before swallowing it again and proceeding with digestion. This is called chewing the cud, or ruminating.

The second stomach, the *reticulum* assists in the regurgitation of food. The third stomach, the *omasum*, acts as a kind of sieve, allowing only fine particles into the fourth stomach, the *abomasum*.

Camels chew the cud, but they and the pig group have different systems of stomach chambers compared with the ruminants.

True pigs live only in the Old World. The wild boar ranges from Central Europe and North Africa to Japan. It is greatly feared in many parts because of the ferocity of the males. The canine teeth grow into long, razor-sharp tusks in adults. Wild boar live in family parties which may gather into large groups. They are active by night and feed on almost anything. Domestic pigs are the descendants of the wild boar.

Africa boasts three more pigs, the bush pig, the giant forest hog and the warthog. The warthog is active by day, unlike the others, so it is often seen on the plains of East Africa, running away with its tufted tail held aloft. The babirusa lives in the Celebes of Asia. The male has exaggerated canines – the upper ones grow upward to the forehead.

Above: *Hippopotamuses usually live in groups of about 15, but herds may be much larger. They spend the day wallowing and feed at night.*

The American equivalents of the pigs are the two peccaries, which range from the southern United States south to Argentina, and live both in forests and on open savannahs. Peccaries have a reputation for ferocity.

The great African hippopotamus looks like a massive pig, but has a broad head. The feet bear four toes which all touch the ground as the animal walks. Hippopotamuses live in lakes, rivers and swamps throughout Africa south of the Sahara, and come on land at night to feed, sometimes causing considerable damage to crops. When in the water they float almost submerged, their eyes, ears and nostrils being on top of the head. They can remain under water for up to five minutes and can adjust their buoyancy to swim at the surface or to walk on the river bed.

Above: *The foot and footprint of a red deer. The two large central toes bear the weight on normal ground. When the deer treads on softer ground, such as a forest floor, the two remaining toes also meet the ground – preventing the deer from sinking too far.*

Camels are remarkable animals and are adapted for a desert life. The hump or humps on the back provide a store for fat but camels do not, as is popularly supposed, store water. They can go for long periods without drinking (over one month has been recorded) because they can lose water up to a quarter of the body weight, and then restore it quickly by drinking many litres at a time. Camels have broad feet well able to walk on soft sand, long eyelashes and closable nostrils which keep out flying sand, and a thick coat of hair for insulation.

The Bactrian or two-humped camel is used as a pack animal in Asia. The one-humped Arabian camel exists only as a

Left: *The warthog is an unattractive animal. It is a wild pig which lives on the plains of Africa. The warts of gristly tissue have no known use, but the four tusks are formidable weapons.*

domestic animal. The dromedary is an Arabian camel bred for riding purposes.

The only living relatives of the camels are the guanaco and vicuña of South America. The llama and alpaca are domestic breeds of the guanaco, the llama being a beast of burden, while the alpaca is bred for its fine wool.

Ruminants have no incisor teeth in the upper jaw and the lower incisors rub against the upper gum, which is a hard pad.

The deer, of which there are 40 species, are ruminants characterised by their antlers. Unlike horns, antlers are made of bone. They are shed and regrown each year. In most species only the male deer carries antlers, which are used for display and fighting. The exceptions are female reindeer and caribou, which also carry antlers.

The largest deer is the elk, called a moose in North America, and the smallest is the Chilean pudu of the Andes, which is 340 millimetres (13½ inches) tall at the shoulder.

In a further confusion of names, the wapiti, a deer very closely related to the European red deer, is sometimes called the elk.

The chevrotains or mouse deer are not true deer. They are delicately-built animals, seldom more than 300 millimetres (12 inches) high at the shoulder, with tusks instead of antlers. Their home is in West Africa, India and Malaysia.

Outstanding among the hoofed animals, the giraffe can feed on leaves 5 metres (16 feet) above the ground, and it tears them off with a tongue 450 millimetres (18 inches) long.

The okapi is a cousin of the giraffe which lives in West Africa. Its neck is not nearly as long as that of the giraffe.

Below left: *Cloven-hoofed animals occur in many sizes. From left to right: the pudu is the smallest of all deer, while the red deer has a magnificent spread of antlers. The wild boar's tusks make it very dangerous. The Bactrian camel still lives wild in the Gobi Desert. The giraffe can crop the highest leaves.*

Cattle, Goats and Antelopes

One family of even-toed ungulates, the Bovidae, has dominated the world's open spaces. The Bovidae includes the American bison, which used to roam the prairies in huge herds, the many different antelopes, one of which, Thomson's gazelle, still exists in millions, and the wild and domesticated sheep, goats and cattle. They are all ruminants. Horns are carried by both sexes, each one consisting of a sheath growing over a bony core. The horns are shed once in each animal's lifetime, during its adolescence.

The largest bovids include the American and European bison, the European species now surviving in the wild only in a Polish forest; the yak of Tibet; the African and Asian buffaloes; and the anoa, gaur and banteng of India, South East Asia and the Philippines.

Above: *A formidable animal weighing nearly a tonne, the African buffalo lives in herds, sometimes of hundreds. A charging buffalo is difficult to stop with a rifle because its head is protected by the broad bases of the horns.*

European cattle are descended from the now extinct aurochs, and the eastern humped cattle came from the banteng or gaur. The yak is the common domestic animal of the Himalayas, and only a few survive in the wild. The African buffalo is eminently unsuitable for domestication; it is one of the most dangerous animals.

The second group of bovids to have yielded domestic animals is the goat and sheep tribe, whose horns are placed farther back on the head than those of cattle, and are ringed along their length.

Both sheep and goats live in mountainous areas, where they feed on sparse, tough vegetation. Wild sheep include the bighorns and Dall's sheep of western North America, the snow sheep, argali and urial of Asia; and the mouflon which is native to Sardinia and Corsica in Europe. Domestic sheep are derived from the mouflon and have been bred to give a very long woolly underfur.

Wild sheep spend most of the year in groups of separate sexes. Each group is led by an old animal who knows the trails and feeding grounds and is blindly followed by the rest. During the rut (mating season), the rams fight by battering each other with their horns, but little damage is done because the horns and the thick skull absorb the blows.

Goats are distinguished from sheep by the scimitar or spiral shape of the horns, which never grow outwards as in sheep, and which are similar in males and females, and also by the male's beard and pungent odour. True wild goats, sometimes called beyoar goats or pasangs, live only in the mountains of the Middle East, from Turkey to Pakistan, but domestic goats have become wild in many parts of the world. They are very destructive animals, as they crop grass to the ground and churn up the soil with their hoofs. They even climb trees to eat the leaves and, when they chew off the bark as well, the tree dies.

Below right: *The duiker is a small antelope. Its name is Afrikaans for diver, and refers to its habit of diving for cover in thick vegetation when disturbed.*

Close relatives of domestic goats are markhors and ibexes, and the sheep-goat tribe includes many other animals living in harsh conditions. The takin and tahr live in Asia, the Rocky Mountain goat in North America and the chamois in the mountains of Europe.

The musk-ox, so-called for its musky smell, is mid-way between an ox and a sheep. It lives on the Arctic tundra of the New World. It is protected from blizzards by its extremely long hair, and from wolves by the herd's habit of closing into a tight defensive bunch, facing outwards, called a *karre*.

The majority of bovids are antelopes. This is a name which means little because it covers an immense variety of animals whose only common feature is a generally slender build and upward-directed horns. The main home of the antelopes is the savannahs and bush of Africa. Some live in huge herds. Springbok used to migrate across the South African veld in their millions.

Large numbers of different antelopes can live in one region because each kind has its own preferred food and so avoids competition. In this way the African savannahs support a far greater number of animals than the other grasslands of the world, and are the home of 45 species of antelopes.

Some antelopes are grazers, which feed on grass and herbs. As they lack upper incisors, they cannot crop the toughest grasses. These grasses are left to the zebras. The wildebeest can pull at the lower, softer leaves. Smaller antelope like Thomson's gazelle follow and eat the lowest parts of the grass and the low, broad-leaved-herbs. This is called a grazing succession.

Other antelopes are browsers, and eat the leaves of trees and bushes. Dik-diks are tiny antelopes, only 350 millimetres (14 inches) tall at the shoulders. Being small they do not need much food, and select the most nutritious morsels. Gerenuks have long necks to feed from higher branches.

Water supply is another factor which helps to sort out the antelopes. Gemsbok and Grant's gazelle can go for long periods without drinking, and live in the driest parts of the savannah. Wildebeest need to drink every day and during the dry season they migrate long distances to wet areas. Impala also have to drink regularly and they are never found far from water. Waterbuck and lechwe live in marshy places, and the sitatunga has splayed feet so it can live in swamps.

On cliffs above the plains, klipspringers leap agilely from rock to rock on the tips of their tiny hooves and the deserts are the home of addax and oryx, with magnificent sweeping horns. They are as well adapted for desert life as camels. Outside Africa, gazelle live from Arabia to Mongolia. Blackbuck are among the main plant-eaters of India, and on the central Asian steppes there lives the odd-looking saiga, with its bulbous nose.

An antelope that is not a true antelope is the pronghorn or American antelope of North America. It differs basically from the bovids by shedding its horns every year. The pronghorn rivals the cheetah for speed, cruising at 48 kph (30 mph) and exceeding 80 kph (50 mph) in a sprint.

Below: *Wild sheep live in mountainous parts of the world. Their coats are thick but not woolly as in domestic sheep. From left to right: mouflon, dall sheep, bighorn sheep.*

Below left: *Various cattle. Highland (top), Hereford (centre left) and Longhorn (centre right) are beef breeds; Friesian (bottom left) is a prize dairy cow; the zebu (bottom right) is used in hot countries to pull carts.*

Living Things and Man

In terms of the effect that they have on the Earth, human beings are by a long way the most successful and powerful animal species that ever lived. Man's giant brain, of which he is so proud, has enabled him to subdue the world in which he lives, exploiting land and ocean alike.

Man seems always to have regarded his environment as a limitless resource and, as his technology improved, his powers for destroying the environment increased too.

As organisms, human beings are omnivores, capable of eating a very wide range of plant and animal foodstuffs, an attribute shared by few other animals. In many respects, man is still a straightforward predator, catching and killing animals for food as he did in prehistoric times. The sea-fishing industry is the largest present-day example of this predatory behaviour, but man also takes furs and skins for clothing, and pearls, ivory and many other animal products for adornment. He also takes wood from natural forests, though few people now gather wild-grown seeds and fruits for their staple diet.

On the other hand, man has entered into association with many kinds of plants and animals. Domestication and cultivation have not only made his survival easier, but have also lessened his depredations on the natural world. The following pages discuss briefly man's relationships with the other living things with which he shares the Earth.

This view of the Sussex Downs shows the relationship of man and other living things with the natural landscape. A path has been worn across the fields and fencing installed to prevent grazing sheep from straying.

Domestication of Animals and Cultivation of Plants

Right: *British breeds of sheep today have inherited much from the Soay sheep, a creature very like the mountain species, and still living wild on the rocky islands of St. Kilda.*

Man's earliest relationships with other animals was as a hunter, but there is little doubt that he was impressed by their power, speed and beauty. These attributes became interwoven into early superstitions and magical beliefs.

The first real association of man with any other animal other than for food was almost certainly with the wolf. Wolves were probably attracted to human campsites by the waste food lying around. Occasionally, when there was no better food available, man ate the wolves, and it may be that, from the motherless cubs of a she-wolf that had been killed, we must look for the ancestors of today's domestic dogs. At a certain stage of their development wolf cubs can be trained to learn to live with humans.

Men may have tolerated domesticated wolves at first because they were a future possible source of meat when times were hard. They must also have realised that the wolf had a built-in knowledge of how to hunt, that it could run faster than a man, and would guard anything it thought of as belonging to its own tribe against outsiders. There is evidence from the Middle Stone Age that wolves were kept in captivity in Denmark and probably in many other places as well. It was from these animals that the many types of dogs known today were developed.

Below: *Dogs have been found in association with man in Europe as far back as the Stone Age. Man and dog are able to live together because dogs are social animals that naturally accept and welcome the firm guidance of a leader. They have been diversified by selective breeding for various purposes, originally connected mainly with hunting, into the large range of breeds we have today. Beagles (left) are suited for running in hunting hares on foot; retrievers (centre) can recover dead game without damaging it in their mouth; short-legged dachsunds (right) are able to hunt in burrows.* Tomarctus *(top) was an earlier relative of the modern dogs.*

Many other wild creatures have been domesticated by man. Sheep, goats and cattle were among the earliest to be exploited. These were first farmed by men of the New Stone Age, not less than 9,000 years ago.

Goats were favoured by early farmers because they browse on young trees, which constantly threatened to invade the farmsteads that had been laboriously carved out of the forests.

Among the early civilised peoples the ancient Egyptians were outstanding animal keepers. They tried to domesticate many species, including gazelles and hyaenas. Asses and horses were first domesticated in western Asia, but their use quickly spread to the rest of the Old World. The horse, used in war for pulling chariots and carrying soldiers and in peace for agriculture and transport, has probably influenced man's history more than any other animal.

Today we have many animal partners. Some such as honeybees are not tame; we merely offer them a place to live in and some food in exchange for the honey and wax that they can provide. Others, such as sheep and goats, are kept for their wool as well as for their meat and skins. Cattle, camels and yaks are kept for their meat, milk, hair and hides. Horses and donkeys, largely used for recreation in the western world, are still used for transport elsewhere, and in some places their flesh and milk are valued as well. Dogs work for man in many ways as well as being companions, like the domestic cat.

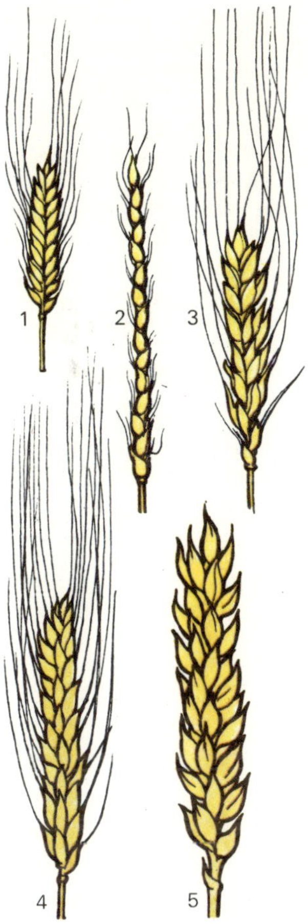

Above: *Different kinds of wheat. 1 emmer, a bearded form known to date from 6000 BC; 2 and 3 wild and cultivated spelt from central Europe; 4 durum, used for pasta; 5 bread wheat, high in gluten, used for white bread.*

Man has constantly changed his domestic animals and their ability to provide the things he needs by selective breeding. Any creature which showed a particular feature that man found useful – greater strength, heavier fleece, or the ability to produce and rear more young – was kept and bred from. In time, groups of animals with these special characteristics were developed and are still being improved by careful cross breeding.

At about the time when man began living in settled communities and domesticating animals, he also started to grow crops. Before this, he had gathered many types of plants for food, but the discovery that seeds could be sown and the desired type of plants grown from them was a great step forward. The most important crops to be cultivated were various types of grasses. Wheat, barley and oats were all natives of an area lying between the Mediterranean Sea and the valleys of the Tigris and Euphrates rivers. Rice comes from further east and maize is native to America. All modern civilisations are founded on the crops produced by these and related cereals.

Plants are also grown for the sugars which they produce, for oils, for aromatic substances and for the alkaloids used in the drug industry. Other plants are grown for fibres used in textiles and other products while a great number are cultivated as vegetables and fruit.

An interesting fact about almost all important domestic animals and cultivated plants is that their wild ancestors are now very rare, or even extinct. The forebears of modern cattle became extinct several centuries ago. The direct ancestors of the horse were killed off. Wild camels with one hump are unknown, wild sheep and goats are now very rare and even wolves are almost extinct.

It is the same with plants, the strangest case being that of maize, now very important for human and animal food, but with no close relatives among wild grasses; for cultivated maize has no way of dispersing its seed. The form that we know must be the result of long-continued selection for large cobs with big grains.

The reason why man has exterminated wild forms of domesticated animals and plants is that wild and tame species can interbreed – and once man has started to select qualities he wants and breed to get those and no others, the qualities of wild species are as a rule considered a bad thing. For instance, a tame mare mated by a wild stallion would probably produce a foal less tractable and possibly less strong than one born of a domestic sire. As for plants, man tends to regard all wild ones as 'weeds'.

Above: *The aurochs or uros,* Bos primigenius, *is known from Pleistocene remains throughout Europe. It appears to have been tamed or at least domesticated by Neolithic Man during the Bronze Age. This species has passed on many of its genes to modern cattle.*

Left: *Two of the most successful of specialised breeds of cattle. The shaggy, hardy, heavy-bodied highland cattle (below), which are bred for beef, are probably similar to ancestral cattle. The small Jersey cow (above), is famous for the large quantity of rich milk it gives.*

Plants and Animals in Folklore

In the past when man was primarily a hunter, he learned to know the plants and animals which surrounded him. Seeing that they had the quality of life, he often imagined them to be possessed of a spirit akin to his own, with powers comparable to, and sometimes outstripping, his own.

When an animal showed a particular strength, such as the ability to run fast, or to hide successfully from its enemies, or a plant was able to survive the gales on a mountain cliff, the living things possessing such powers came to stand for the powers themselves. Thus a tree would stand for the strength it possessed and by associating with the tree in some way – perhaps by carrying a twig or putting a branch up over the door – man thought he could carry or be protected by the tree's strength. This symbolism is known as *sympathetic magic,* and it is widespread in religions and superstitions.

When the powers for which the plant or animal stands are far greater than those of man himself, then the symbolic object may be elevated into something which can be influenced by prayer, worship or sacrifice. Even today, many peoples regard some animals as sacred, or as having strength-giving properties which they can pass on to those who eat them or perform the correct rituals. There is an example in English folklore: John Bull, the archetypal Englishman, typifies the strength of a real bull, and gets this strength by eating roast beef.

Left: *Thoth was the Egyptian god of wisdom; he was a moon god, patron of science and literature, and messenger of the gods. He was usually represented with the head of an ibis, occasionally as a dog-headed ape. This statue here is from the tomb of Prince Khamwast, son of Rameses III, in the Valley of the Queens.* Below left: *American Indians believed every plant, animal and bird had its own specific power which it could exert on other beings. Some tribes held certain animals to be spirits of dead heroes. The totem is a force of nature looked on as the ancestor of a group or individual; the totem pole is symbolic of the totem.*

Left: *Dragons appear in many cultures as mythical beasts representing power – usually evil. In China, however, the dragon was the symbol of the Imperial House. This badge bearing the dragon symbol would have been worn by a high-ranking official.*

Sometimes a tribe or group considered themselves to be under the protection of a particular creature. This was called their *taboo,* which they in turn had to protect and not hunt. In practical terms this often led to conservation of various species of animals.

Often the abilities of animals were exaggerated into supernatural powers – hence stories of flying horses, or of creatures which were able to divine the future.

The obvious similarities between animals and men led to the invention of many mythical creatures which were said to be part human, such as the sphinx or the manticora. The centaurs of ancient Greek mythology were perhaps the most famous of this sort of mixture: half-horse and half-man, they must have been invented by a horse-orientated people who believed that horses could weep at the death of their masters and were the only animals to feel the same emotion of sorrow as humans. In other cultures dogs were credited with this ability. Centaurs were always kindly and wise beings, unlike many of the other man-animal mixtures.

Many stories of animals in folklore are the result of unscientific observation. A widely-held belief, in northern Europe for instance, was that cuckoos turned into hawks in the winter time. People noticed that the cuckoos were no longer around,

and perhaps, with the leaves off the trees, some hawks were slightly easier to see.

Another bird myth was that nightjars sucked milk from animals pastured in the fields. These birds are still known as goatsuckers in some areas. The nightjars may fly near to cud-chewing animals, but they are merely picking insects out of the air near to the cattle. Yet another belief was that barnacles grew into geese – indeed, some are still called goose barnacles. Stories were told of how people had seen black geese hatching from barnacles. What had actually been observed is difficult to guess.

European travellers of the Middle Ages often brought back garbled stories of the wondrous things that they had seen. Some of these were clearly a confusion between two or more sorts of animals, such as the cameleopard, a mixture between a leopard and a camel. One of the most mixed-up of these mythical beasts was the leucrota, which was supposed to be the size of a donkey, to have the haunches of a stag, the breast and shins of a lion, the head of a horse, a cloven hoof, and a mouth opening as far as its ears. Instead of teeth, it had a continuous bone in its jaw; its voice was like the sound of people talking and it could run faster than all other kinds of animals!

Even fossil animals enter into folklore. The bones of dinosaurs, exposed on the surface of the ground in some parts of

Above: *Taueret was an Egyptian goddess of childbirth. She was represented as a hippopotamus. This painting on papyrus depicts a dead lady praying to Taueret, while Hathor, goddess of love, appears as a cow.*

Above: *The flecks on the petals and leaves of St. John's wort are said to be the blood of St. John the Baptist; the herb has been used to protect houses and people from danger.*

North America, were thought by the Red Indians to be the remains of evil giants, defeated in battle by the gods in ancient days. In China, fossil bones and teeth found in caves were thought to have powerful healing properties. They were known as dragons' teeth, and were ground up and put into all sorts of medicines.

Plants also are important in folklore. A forest is often a rather spooky place and in many parts of the world there are stories of wood spirits or demons of various kinds. The dryads of ancient Greek and Roman beliefs were nymphs which lived in groves of trees, but ancient men of northern Europe believed that less-friendly demons haunted their dark evergreen forests. Often a tree which grew alone on a mountainside, stunted because of the exposure which it suffered, would be thought of as being under the protection of fairies who would take revenge on anybody harming it. In recent years there was a strike on a building site in Ireland because the area contained one such tree and the workmen would not destroy it.

A plant which was thought to possess special powers was the common St John's wort (*Hypericum perforatum*). If you hold a leaf of this plant up to the light, you can see little pale-coloured dots, which make it look as though somebody has been sticking pins into it. Perhaps because of the plant's ability to thrive in spite of this apparent ill-treatment, St John's wort was until fairly recently regarded in Western Europe as a plant which would protect people against evil.

The strength of a plant often caused it to be revered. Thus the size and strength of the oak led to its being regarded as a sacred tree. Anything which could subdue the oak was thought of as being still more powerful. *Polypodium* ferns, which sometimes grow on the branches of an ancient oak, were thought of in this way. Mistletoe (*Viscum album*) was held in great awe, partly at least because of its ability to grow on other trees.

We may laugh at many of these old superstitions and beliefs, yet many of them linger on today. Lucky black cats and lucky four-leafed clovers are part of a long and ancient tradition.

Rare Plants and Animals

It is in the nature of individuals to die and for species to become extinct. Indeed, extinction is part of the great progression of life. Any species which can no longer compete successfully within its environment will become extinct, and its place will be taken by better adapted or more efficient competitors. The story of the geological past is largely one of species which are extinct.

At the present day many plant and animal species are on the verge of extinction, but the cause for this, in most cases, lies not in the natural sequence of events, but in human intervention in the natural world. Since man became civilised – that is, living in settled communities – his impact on the world around him has increased and is growing still greater.

A few species of animals are naturally rare, living in restricted areas, and their extinction seems to have little or nothing to do with man. An example is the pink-headed duck, a native of parts of northern India. It lived in remote and sparsely populated areas and seems never to have been common. It has not been seen in the wild since the middle 1930s.

These species have been reduced by three different means. The Siberian tiger (above) *has been reduced by hunting; the peregrine falcon* (right) *by pesticides; and the dodo* (below) *by careless interference with the natural ecology and breeding.*

Some animals may have become extinct as a result of hunting. As a rule, however, hunting merely reduces the level of the population to very small numbers over most of its range, driving the survivors into less favourable terrain, where they may have more difficulty in surviving. Beavers, for instance, were exterminated in Britain in the 1300s, but they survived in other parts of Europe.

Many marine creatures seem to be specially vulnerable, particularly those birds and mammals which have to return to land to breed. In the crowded breeding colonies they may be quite helpless against attack and many species both of birds and mammals have been brought to very small numbers, or even to extinction.

Perhaps the best known creature destroyed in this way is the great auk. This flightless bird existed in huge numbers in the North Atlantic until the early 1800s, when ruthless hunting at its breeding grounds by meat-hungry sailors brought it to very low numbers indeed. The last pair and their egg are said to have been destroyed in 1844 by a sailor, who gave as his reason that he had never seen anything like them before.

Destruction by the ignorant in the name of fear or superstition has brought many creatures to the edge of extinction. Rhinoceroses are among them. In some parts of the world it is believed that the rhino is a beast of powerful magic. The horn, powdered, is considered to be an aphrodisiac, and almost every other part of the rhino's body is regarded as having magic or medicinal properties. Killing rhinos and poaching them from reserves has become a profitable business for hunters who exploit such beliefs.

Hunting and direct persecution, especially when the animal concerned is felt to

Above: *The douc* Pygathrix nemaeus, *is a leaf-eating langur native to the forests of Vietnam. Recent human activities in this area have caused extensive defoliation in the forests, and the douc langur is in grave danger of becoming an accidental casualty. It does not thrive in captivity, which makes it difficult to preserve.*

Above: *A mass of spring gentian,* Gentiana verna, *a beautiful sight which nobody would wilfully wish to destroy. Alpine species such as this, however, depend on the thin topsoil of mountains. This suffers from skiers and snowploughs, which break the turf under ice and snow when the plants are not visible.*

Above: *Drooping saxifrage,* Saxifraga cernua, *is a rare British species which grows in wet mountain areas. Plants like this are in great danger from heedless activities of rock-climbers, ramblers and holidaymakers, who may pick them or simply tread on them without realising how close to extinction they might be.*

Above: *Orchids are much sought after by botanists because of their exotic appearance. They do not usually survive replanting as they are very particular as to habitat. This fly orchid,* Ophrys insectifera, *is not as rare as some other species.*

be a direct competitor for the possession of farmland, have been the cause of many extinctions, including several African antelopes and zebra. Nevertheless the most important reason for extinction is destruction of the habitat.

This can affect even very numerous species, such as the passenger pigeon. This American bird used to exist in such numbers that in 1813 the American naturalist John James Audubon watched a flock on migration that took three days to pass. The birds were slaughtered for food and for sport in unbelievable numbers – 1,000,000,000 were estimated to have been killed in Michigan alone in 1879. But what really sealed the bird's fate was the destruction of its forest habitat, which was cleared to increase the area of farmland. The last passenger pigeon died in a zoo in 1914.

The spread of farming has caused the decline of many animal species, and the situation is made the more desperate if direct animal competitors are introduced. In some parts of the world browsing and grazing animals have been dispossessed by introduced goats and sheep. Predators, their normal food supply lost, kill farm animals and dire reprisals are taken for this. Almost all predatory mammals and birds have been wiped out from areas where they were abundant with the spread of man and agriculture.

Once an animal population has reached a very low level its chances of survival are poor. If the species is a social one, in-breeding can cause a decline. If it is solitary, as with the Javan rhinoceros, it is possible that males and females may never meet.

The animals which are at greatest risk are those which live in small, closed communities, such as remote oceanic islands. Large numbers of such creatures are among the world's endangered species because their environment has often been drastically changed by the coming of man.

Even without meaning harm, man's arrival can often result in the destruction of a species. A classic example is the dodo, a clumsy, flightless bird which lived on the island of Mauritius in the Indian Ocean. The dodo was apparently not good to eat and so it was not hunted, but the sailors introduced pigs which they set free so that any other seafarers calling at the island should find a supply of meat. They also introduced the rat, by accident. These two sorts of animal destroyed the large nests and eggs of the dodo, which, deprived of any chance of breeding success, became extinct in about 1682.

The disappearance of plant species is often more difficult to document, for, as with tiny animals, the small species may pass unnoticed in the general habitat destruction. It is said, for example, that the native forest on the island of Barbados was completely destroyed within 40 years of the island's discovery. Apart from the trees, a large number of lesser plants must also have vanished.

Because plants cannot run away or hide from danger they are often destroyed by people who claim to like them. In Britain, the annual toll taken of spring flowers by those who dig them up or pick them so rigorously that the plants never have a chance to set seed has meant a great reduction in these attractive flowers anywhere near big centres of population. The destruction of the flowers reduces the overall richness of the environment, for the blossoms give food to insects which in turn nourish birds and mammals.

Conservation

Man's destruction of his habitat began to show in early historic times. For example, by the Middle Ages many large areas of the great woodlands which covered much of Britain and other parts of northern Europe had been cleared for use as farm land. It was not until comparatively recently that any serious attempt was made to control the damage or to protect any species of plant or animal from dying out.

One of the pioneers of conservation was St Cuthbert, an Englishman who died in AD 687. He lived as a hermit on Farne Island, off the Northumberland coast; there he took a keen interest in birds and other animals and is reputed to have taken the eider ducks on the island under his special protection, and to have prevented people from killing birds or taking their eggs. His orders were remembered for many years after his death.

Later, medieval kings in Europe set aside large tracts of forest land for hunting, an example being the New Forest in southern England, which was placed under royal control by William the Conqueror in 1079. The killing of animals in these forests by anyone other than royal hunting parties was savagely punished, but at least these areas were kept in a nearly natural state, and many small animals, as well as the woodlands themselves, were able to flourish unmolested.

As the numbers of people in the world increased they not only destroyed their natural surroundings for their towns and farms, but their waste and refuse polluted land and water and, with the onset of the Industrial Revolution, the air too. This pollution led to a great reduction in the numbers of wild animals and plants.

The United States led the way in conservation. In 1872 its government established Yellowstone National Park in Wyoming, 8,992 square kilometres (3,472 square miles) of great beauty and interest, 90 per cent of which is forest. This was a new approach to the preservation of wildlife. Before that time, man concentrated mainly on preserving wild animals he needed for food or sport; today, conservationists are concerned with the preservation of wildlife for its own sake.

Above: *Zoos and game parks have taken on a new role in recent years. They are now our most important resource for conserving many species of animals. The Nairobi Game Park has an animal hospital where a leopard is recovering from treatment.* Left: *San Diego Zoo is a series of canyons where creatures like the sealions can be kept in near-natural conditions.*

By 1900, a group of European countries which together ruled most of Africa was calling for the preservation of that continent's wildlife, and in 1903 the Fauna Preservation Society, with headquarters in London, was founded. Today, one of the main international organisations concerned with conservation is the World Wild Life Fund, established in 1961 to raise money to help conservation in any part of the world. Another body is the International Union for Conservation of Nature and Natural Resources (IUCN), founded with United Nations' aid in 1948.

There are a great many organisations in most countries devoted to conservation work in their own areas. Some are government sponsored, such as the United States Fish and Wildlife Service, and the Forestry Commission in Britain; others are voluntary bodies, such as America's National Audubon Society, Britain's Royal Society for the Protection of Birds, and France's *Ligue pour la Protection des Oiseaux*.

Following the American example,

Below: *In the centre of Berlin, the zoo uses water barriers instead of bars to keep the animals safe. Here is the new tiger enclosure.*

Above: *Nara, in Japan, is well-known today for its deer park which is situated among the ancient temples of this former capital city.*

countries in all parts of the world have established national parks and game reserves, some to preserve a whole area and the wildlife within it, others to safeguard the existence of a few threatened species.

Some of the most striking parks are in Africa, a continent particularly rich in wildlife. More than two million animals roam the 14,750 square kilometres (5,700 square miles) of Serengeti National Park in Tanzania, while in the same country the Ngorongoro Conservation Area includes a gigantic volcanic crater, the inaccessibility of which has preserved its natural animals and plants against man for thousands of years.

Asia has comparatively few national parks; one of the most important is at Gir, in India, where the last remaining Asian lions survive. Europe has a growing number of reserves, only small in comparison with those of Africa and North America, but important for their work in a part of the world where there is little room for wildlife.

North America has by far the largest number of nature reserves and national parks, ranging from the sub-tropical Everglades in Florida to the huge Wood Buffalo National Park in northern Alberta, 44,800 square kilometres (17,300 square miles) of bleak, sub-Arctic wilderness.

Preserving wild animals is not enough in itself. Man's efforts to foster species that are endangered sometimes result in over population, because the natural enemies which would normally keep an animal's numbers in check are absent or restrained. This situation has arisen in the Tsavo National Park in Kenya, where elephants have overgrazed the land because there are too many for the food resources. As a result, hundreds die whenever there is a severe drought. In smaller areas, such as the deer forests of Scotland, it is necessary to resort to culling (killing old or weak members of the herd) in order to make sure the numbers are kept at a reasonable level.

Another problem is tourists. The money they pay to see the wild animals is essential for the upkeep of the reserves but their presence in large numbers can upset the animals and destroy the very habitat that is being preserved.

What You Can Do

Above: *Birds, especially migrating species, are particularly badly hit by human activities. Bird reserves, like this one in the Seychelles, are vital to the conservation of birds of passage. Here, on an isolated group of islands, many birds break a very long sea journey; if they had nowhere safe to rest they would die before reaching their destinations. The establishment of a chain of bird reserves along migration routes will help to counteract the many strains put upon birds by man's activities.*

Conservation of the world's plant and animal life is an activity in which everybody can help. It begins with understanding what causes plant and animal species to become rare and die out, and which of mankind's actions are the most harmful.

Pollution of the environment and the unnecessary destruction of plants and animals are two of the chief causes of trouble. The two often go together: the insecticide DDT, once hailed as the farmer's friend because it could easily kill off large numbers of crop-eating insects, has proved to have much wider effects. In North America, DDT from over-sprayed farmland has leaked into rivers and lakes. There it is absorbed by tiny plants and animals, which in turn are eaten by fish. Animals which eat the fish, such as the United States' national bird, the bald eagle, absorb quite heavy concentrations of DDT, and the poison affects their ability to breed.

The destruction of wild plants as weeds in a cultivated garden is necessary to grow flowers and vegetables, but wild flowers in their natural habitats should be left alone. Apart from their beauty, they all have a part to play in the balance of nature. It is particularly important to protect in this way rare plants, such as the wild peony which in England is found only on one tiny island in the Bristol Channel.

You can gain a better understanding of wild things by studying them in their normal habitats. If you find a wild animal in need of care, do not try to rear it as a pet, but return it to its natural habitat as soon as it can fend for itself again.

You can get a good idea of plant life and also that of insects and other small invertebrates in your own garden or in any patch of uncultivated ground. But to study larger animals you need to visit a zoo.

In old-fashioned zoos animals were kept in clean conditions in cages, where people could gaze at them without getting much idea of how they normally behaved. Today, zoos are designed as far as possible to recreate natural surroundings, so that visitors – and scientists – can really study animal behaviour. Special exhibits in many zoos – such as those in London, Amsterdam, and New York City – even simulate nocturnal conditions so that bats and other night-living creatures can be watched in action.

Many zoos – such as Whipsnade in England – provide a park-like environment for their animals. Safari parks take this idea a stage further and allow the animals to roam around freely while the visitors are confined to safe quarters, which may be their own cars.

In addition to watching animals in zoos or in the wild, you can read more about them in specialist books. To learn even more, you can join a society, where you will meet experts who can tell you and show you far more than you can find out merely by reading. Your local library can generally put you in touch with any groups, societies or clubs in your area.

Through zoos and societies you can find out more about what other people are doing to conserve wild plants and animals. In recent years there have been many outstanding success stories. Zoos and nature reserves have become the last refuge for many endangered species, and breeding in captivity has in many instances saved a species from extinction.

An example is the ne-ne, or Hawaiian goose. In Hawaii this bird, originally numbering many thousands, dwindled to only 50 by the 1940s. Two females and a male were taken to the Wildfowl Trust at Slimbridge, in the West of England, where they bred so successfully that a

large flock of ne-nes was sent back to Hawaii a few years later.

A similar breeding programme in Poland, begun in the 1920s, saved the European bison from extinction. There were then only 56 of these animals left, all in a private herd. Today there are more than 1,000. The Arabian oryx, reduced to only 32 animals by 1960, was saved by capturing some of them and breeding them in the Phoenix Zoo in Arizona.

In two instances extinct animals have been 'recreated' by selective breeding, in much the same way as a breeder of domestic animals such as dogs or cattle can 'create' an animal with particular characters, such as long ears, or with a high milk yield. The aurochs, the wild ox of Europe, survived in Poland until the 1600s; in recent years German breeders have produced an animal closely resembling this historic beast. Other German breeders have recreated in a similar way the tarpan, the European wild horse which died out in the early 1900s.

One of the major causes of dwindling numbers of plants and animals is the destruction of their natural habitats. Fortunately, not all modern development and technology is completely destructive, and sometimes there are unexpected bonuses. For example, apparently idle land bordering railways and motorways can provide a haven for many species of plants and small animals. Britain's leading nuclear plant at Windscale, in Cumbria, contains a man-made pond which unexpectedly provided a breeding ground for the rare natterjack toad, whose numbers have been dwindling rapidly in recent years. When the pond had to be filled in a new one was dug and the spawn and tadpoles transferred to it.

This is an instance of the ways in which modern technology can be adapted to be helpful to wildlife. Others include the provision of tunnels under motorways to allow animals such as badgers and foxes to cross them in safety, and crossing places which have been provided in Alaska so that migrating herds of caribou can pass the otherwise impenetrable 'wall' of the great oil pipelines.

Above: *The saiga antelope was once common throughout the semi-desert areas east of the Caspian Sea. It is a very fast runner and relies so heavily on speed that it had no natural enemies before the advent of men with guns. It nearly became extinct, but was saved just in time by being made a protected species. This photograph was taken in the Highland Wildlife Park in Scotland, where a breeding population exists.*

Left: *The Hawaiian goose, tens of thousands of which were killed in the last hundred years, has been saved by breeding in wildlife sanctuaries. Its numbers are now increasing and some geese have been returned to Hawaii from the Wildfowl Trust at Slimbridge in England. Its relative the Labrador duck was not so lucky. The last bird was shot on Long Island, New York in 1875.*

Glossary

Words in italics are listed elsewhere in the glossary.

A

Abdomen Region of the *vertebrate* body containing the digestive organs; the posterior section of the arthropod body.
Adaptive radiation *Evolution* of varying forms, with their own ways of life, from one primitive ancestor.
Aestivation Summer sleep.
Agglomerate A cluster of large, coarse volcanic rocks cemented together.
Alkaloids Organic compounds found in plants, used as medicines or poisons.
Aminoacids Fundamental organic compounds which make up *protein molecules*. Some are made in the body; **essential aminoacids** have to be eaten in food.
Antennae The pair of feelers on the head of an arthropod.
Anther The part of the *stamen* containing *pollen* grains in sacs.
Anticoagulant Any substance that prevents blood from clotting.
Arboreal Living in trees.
Arenaceous rocks *Sedimentary rocks* composed mainly of sand grains.
Argillaceous rocks *Sedimentary rocks* composed mainly of clay, eg *shale*.
Articulation The junction between two or more bones of the skeleton.
Asphalt Black, tarry mineral formed in oil-bearing rocks.
Auxin Hormone regulating plant growth.

B

Bathyscaphe A steel sphere attached to a propeller-driven hull, used for deep-sea exploration.
Bivalve An animal with a hinged shell in two parts.
Bract A modified leaf below a flower.

C

Calyx The outer part of a flower which protects the unopened bud.
Cambium The growing layer of *tissue* just under the bark of a tree or shrub.
Camouflage Coloration or shape of animals and plants which makes them hard to see against their background.
Capsule Part of a plant which splits open to release seeds or *spores*.
Carapace The upper shell of an animal such as a turtle, tortoise or crab.
Carnivorous Meat-eating.
Carpel Female reproductive *organ* of a flowering plant.
Cartilage Gristle; flexible part of skeleton such as that forming the nose.
Cell The basic unit of *protoplasm* that makes up *organisms*; growth and reproduction are due to cell division.
Cellulose Fibrous material forming the *cell* wall of plants and giving support to plant *tissues*.
Character A feature which may be passed on by the *genes* from parent to offspring.
Chelicerae The biting mouth-parts of spiders; they have various uses in other arachnids.
Chlorophyll The green *pigment* in plants, necessary for *photosynthesis*.
Chloroplast *Photosynthetic* unit of a *cell*, containing *chlorophyll*.
Chromosomes Thread-like bodies which occur in the *nucleus* of animal and plant *cells*; they carry the *genes* and are constant in number in each species.
Chrysalis *Pupa*; inactive stage between *larva* and adult of some insects.
Cilium Fine hair-like projection from the surface of a *cell*.
Clastic rocks Rocks made up of fragments of earlier rocks.
Cocoon Envelope spun by some insects to protect the eggs or *larvae*; silk comes from the silkworm moth's cocoon.
Colony Individuals living together as a group and dependent on each other.
Commensalism A *symbiosis* without much mutual influence; literally 'feeding at the same table'.
Conglomerate A cluster of rounded pebbles cemented together.
Coniferous Bearing cones.
Convergent evolution Development of similar characteristics by creatures living in a similar environment but having different ancestors.
Corolla The inner part of a flower, made up of *petals* within the *calyx*.
Cotyledon A seed leaf forming part of the plant *embryo*.
Crustose Having a crust.
Cryptic coloration *Camouflage*.
Cuticle The outermost, non-living layer of an animal or plant.
Cyst A capsule containing a liquid; or *cells* enclosed by a *membrane*.

D

Deciduous Shedding leaves at a certain time each year.
Detritus Waste from decomposing plants and animals or crumbling rocks.
Diastema A natural gap in the jaw between teeth.
Dicotyledon A plant with two seed leaves in its *embryo*.
Dominant Of a *character*, one which will show itself in the presence of a corresponding *recessive* character.
Dyke A vertical intrusion of volcanic rock through the Earth's crust.

E

Ecology The study of animals and plants in relation to their environment.
Embryo An immature animal developing in the egg or womb; a young plant contained in its seed.
Endospore A *spore* formed inside a *cell*.
Enzyme One of many substances produced in the body that promote specific chemical changes during *metabolism*.
Evolution Gradual development through successive generations.

F

Fauna The animal population present at a particular time or place.
Fermentation The breakdown of food, usually by micro-organisms, in the absence of oxygen, to release energy.
Fission Division into parts.
Flagellum A whip-like projection from the surface of a *cell*; flagella enable simple *organisms* to move about.
Flora The plant population present at a particular time or place.
Fluoride A chemical salt containing the element fluorine, found naturally in food and water, which helps to prevent tooth decay in children.
Food-chain, -web *Organisms* linked by their dependence on one another for food; each eats the one preceding it and is itself eaten. A food-web is the total of food-chains in a community.
Fossil Remains or cast of an *organism* preserved in *sedimentary rock* deposits.

G

Galaxy The band of stars, including the Sun, called the Milky Way; any similar gigantic star system in space.
Gamete A reproductive or germ *cell*. The *ovum* is the female, the *spermatozoon* the male gamete in animals.
Gene One of the units of *heredity*.
Germination Beginning of growth of a plant embryo, *spore* or *pollen* grain.
Gill An *organ* for breathing under water; one of the radiating plates on the underside of a mushroom or toadstool.
Glacier A river of compressed ice.
Glycoside A vegetable compound containing a carbohydrate *molecule*.

H

Habitat The normal area inhabited by a plant or animal.
Half-life The time taken for the activity of a *radioactive* substance to fall to half its original value.
Haustorium An *organ* by which a *parasitic* plant absorbs food from its host.
Herbaceous Describes any plant which does not have a permanent woody stem.
Herbivorous Plant-eating.
Heredity Transmission of *characters* from one generation to the next.
Hermaphrodite An *organism* having both male and female reproductive *organs*.
Hibernation Winter sleep.
Holdfast Any *organ* other than a root that attaches a plant to its *substrate*.
Humidity The amount of water vapour present in the air per unit volume.
Humus Decomposing organic matter in the soil, providing food for plants.
Hybrid Animal or plant having parents of two different species or variety.
Hypha One of the fine threads growing from a fungus.

I

Igneous rock Rock formed from solidified molten rock on the Earth's surface.
Inflorescence The part of a plant which bears the flowers.
Inhibitor A substance that checks a chemical reaction or *enzyme* activity.
Instar The form of an insect between two successive *moults*.
Invertebrate Animal with no backbone.
Involucre A ring of *bracts*.

L

Laccolith A mass of *igneous rock* beneath the Earth's surface, forming a dome where *magma* has bulged upwards.
Larva The immature, active stage of some animals, differing from the adult.
Latex The milky juice of some plants such as the rubber tree.
Lava Volcanic rock material.
Leguminous Bearing pods.
Leprose Scaly.
Lophophore An aquatic creature with a ring of *tentacles* around the mouth.

M

Magma Molten rock beneath the Earth's crust, which solidifies as *plutonic rock*.
Mandible Biting mouth-part; the lower jaw of *vertebrates*.

Mantle (in Earth). The layer of the Earth immediately under the crust.
Mantle (in animals) A fold of skin which *secretes* the shell or *carapace*.
Marsupium The pouch in which the young of animals such as kangaroos live.
Meiosis *Cell* division in which *gametes* are formed, having half the number of *chromosomes* of the parent cell.
Membrane A thin film of *tissue*.
Metabolism All the chemical and physical processes occurring in an *organism*.
Metamorphic rock Rock re-formed from pre-existing rocks within the Earth.
Metamorphosis Change of structure or shape from *larval* to adult form.
Micaceous Containing the mineral mica.
Mitosis *Cell* division in which each daughter cell has the same number of *chromosomes* as the parent cell.
Molecule The smallest particle of any matter capable of independent existence, made up of the minimum number of atoms.
Monocotyledon A plant with one seed leaf in its *embryo*.
Monotreme Primitive egg-laying mammal such as the platypus or spiny ant-eater.
Moraine The trail of rock waste brought down by a *glacier*.
Moult To shed feathers or outgrown outer covering.
Mucilage A slimy fluid *secreted* by plants.
Mucus Slimy fluid *secreted* by animals such as slugs and snails.
Mutation A change in *gene* which persists in later generations.
Mutualism *Symbiosis* between two members of different species in which both partners benefit.

N

Nectar Sweet fluid *secreted* by a flower or leaf.
Nematocyst A sac containing the stinging mechanism of a jellyfish.
Nitrogen fixation Conversion of nitrogen in the air into nitrogen compounds in the soil by bacteria.
Nocturnal Active at night.
Notochord A skeletal rod along the back of some animals and replaced by the backbone in *vertebrates*.
Nucleus (cell) The chief *organelle* of the *cell*, containing its *chromosomes*.
Nymph An immature stage of mites, ticks and some insects.

O

Omnivorous Eating a diet of both animal and vegetable food.
Organ Any part of an *organism* that carries out a specific function.
Organelle Any part of a *cell* that carries out a specific function.
Organism A living animal or plant.
Ovary The female reproductive *organ* producing *ova* or *ovules*.
Oviparous Egg-laying.
Ovoviviparous Bearing live young which hatch from eggs inside the mother.
Ovule A female plant *gamete* that develops into an *embryo* after fertilisation.
Ovum A female animal *gamete* that develops into an *embryo* after fertilisation.

P

Parasite An *organism* which feeds on the body of another living organism and gives no benefits in return.
Parthenogenesis Development of an *ovum* without fertilisation by a male *gamete*.
Pectoral Of the chest.
Perianth The outer part of a flower consisting of *calyx* and *corolla*.
Petal The usually conspicuous, attractive part of a flower.
Petrifaction Turning of organic structures into stone.
Phloem The *vascular* layer that conducts synthetised food through a plant.
Photosynthesis The building up of carbohydrates from carbon dioxide and water by green plants, using sunlight.
Pigment Substance which gives colour to animal and plant *tissues*.
Placenta A spongy *organ* attached to the wall of the womb during pregnancy, through which the *embryo* is nourished.
Plankton Tiny floating *organisms* of lakes or sea, providing food for fish.
Plastids Small, dense bodies in plant *cells*, some of which are *chloroplasts*.
Plastron The lower shell of an animal such as a turtle, tortoise or crab.
Plutonic rocks *Igneous rocks* which have cooled down deep inside the Earth.
Pollen The fertilising powder produced by plants – the male *gamete*.
Pollination The transfer of *pollen* from *anther* to *stigma*.
Prehensile Adapted for grasping.
Proboscis A trunk; or long, flexible mouth-parts used for sucking.
Process A general term for a projection or extension.
Protein Complex organic compounds made up of *aminoacids*, essential to the living *cell*.
Protoplasm Substance within a *cell*, the material basis of living matter.
Pupa The inactive stage of development between *larva* and adult in insects.

R

Radioactivity Spontaneous disintegration of some elements, giving off alpha, beta or gamma rays.
Radula A horny membrane 'tongue' with which molluscs rasp their food.
Recessive Of a *character*, one which does not show itself in the presence of a corresponding *dominant* character.
Recycle To break down and process again materials that have already been used.
Respiration Taking in oxygen and giving off carbon dioxide; breathing.
Rhizoid An *organ* serving as a root in fungi, liverworts and mosses.
Rhizome A horizontal underground stem.
Rufous Reddish-brown.

S

Saprophyte An *organism* which feeds on decaying plant or animal *tissues*.
Savannah Tropical grassland.
Scales Thin, flat, horny plates covering creatures such as fishes and snakes; similar growths on plants.
Scavenger Animal that eats already dead meat rather than killing for itself.
Secretion Any substance produced by a gland, such as tears or *nectar*.
Sedentary Describes animals that remain in one place.
Sedimentary rock Rock formed from particles of existing rock laid down in layers by water; it may contain *fossils*.
Segment One of the repeated body sections of animals such as the worms.
Sepal A modified leaf outside a flower *petal*, forming part of the *calyx*.
Sessile Without a stalk; attached to the *substrate*.
Sex-linked Transmitted by a *gene* located on a sex (X or Y) *chromosome*.
Shale A fine-grained clay rock.
Sill A horizontal intrusion of volcanic rock through the Earth's crust.
Spawn A mass of eggs laid in water; the vegetative part of a fungus.
Spermatozoon The male *gamete* that forms an egg when it joins with an *ovum*.
Sporangium *Spore*-producing *organ*.
Spore Reproductive body of lower *organisms* such as fungi and bacteria.
Stamen Male reproductive part of a plant, producing *pollen*.
Steppes Mid-latitude grassland of Asia.
Sterile Unable to reproduce sexually.
Stigma The tip of the *style*, on which pollen alights and *germinates*.
Stimulus Any action or influence that produces a response in an *organism*.
Stipule One of a pair of leaf-like growths at the base of a leaf stalk.
Strain A group of *organisms* within a species having distinct *characters*.
Stratum A *cell* layer; a bed of rock.
Style The stalk connecting the *stigma* and *ovary* of a plant.
Substrate The solid basis beneath an *organism* or to which it is attached.
Symbiosis A partnership between two different types of *organism*, which may or may not be beneficial to them both.

T

Taiga Marshy *coniferous* forest land of northern Siberia and North America.
Taxonomy Classification of *organisms*.
Tectonic Relating to rock structures moulded by movement within the Earth.
Temperate Moderate in temperature.
Tentacle A slender *organ* used for feeling, grasping or moving.
Thorax The part of the body between the head and the *abdomen*.
Tissue A layer or group of similarly specialised *cells*.
Transpiration The loss of water vapour from a plant, mainly from the leaves.
Tundra The treeless Arctic plains.

U

Umbel An *inflorescence* in which numerous flower stalks arise from one point.
Umbilicus The navel.

V

Valve (in shellfish) One of the pieces making up the shell of shellfish.
Vascular Having vessels which conduct fluids, such as blood or sap.
Vector Any agent which carries disease.
Veld The elevated treeless grasslands of South Africa.
Vertebrate An animal with a backbone.
Viscera *Organs* in *thorax* and *abdomen*.
Viviparous Bearing live young which have been nourished through the *placenta*.

X

Xylem Wood. Plant *vascular* tissue that conducts water and mineral salts.

Index

A

Aardvark, 211
Aardwolf, 221
Aaron's rod (mullein), 105
Abies alba, 103
Abyssal zone, 58
Acari, 157
Accipiter nisus, 195
Accipitridae, 194, 195
Acetone, 87
Acer, 112
Acherontia atropos, 165
Acheulean deposits, 38
Acipenseriformes, 175
Aconite, 127
Aconitine, 126
Aconitum, 114, 115
Aconitum anglicum, 126
Acorn, 112
Actinothoë sphyrodeta, 137
Aculeata, 168
Adaptive radiation, 209, 214, 216
Addax, 229
Aegothelidae, 196
Aesculus 'conker', 112
Aestivation, 147
Aethusa cynapium, 117
Africa, 72, 73, 74, 104, 174, 177, 181, 188, 194, 197, 202, 205, 215, 221, 222, 226, 227, 229
Agamas, 182
Agami, 182
Agamidae, 182
Agar-agar, 91
Agarius hortensis, 98
Agouti, 216, 217
Agriotes lineatus, 166
Agropyron pungens, 130
Alaska, 10, 26
Alauda arvensis, 205
Alaudidae, 204
Albatross, 190, 191
Alcedinidae, 198
Alcedo atthis, 198
Alcidae, 191
Alder, 69, 113, 131
Aldrovanda vesiculosa, 125
Algae, 27, 70, 84, 86, 87, 88–91, 130, 135, 142, 146, 161
Alginate, 90, 91
Alisma plantago-aquatica, 109
Alkaloids, 118, 126, 127
Allergen, 126
Alligators, 181
Almond, 116
Alnus, 113
Alonella, 154
Alpaca, 227
Alphadon, 37
Alps, 15, 78, 79
Altai Mts., 46
Alticamelus, 37
Amanita phalloides, 99
Amaryllidaceae, 120–1
Amazon, 50, 167, 218
Amblypygids, 157
Ambrosia sp., 126
Ambrosia artemisiifolia, 119
America, Central, 104, 167, 196, 198, 199, 202, 204
– North, 37, 70, 72, 73, 75, 79, 103, 119, 123, 124, 125, 154, 156, 172, 175, 181, 196, 202, 221, 222, 223
– South, 37, 70, 71, 72, 73, 77, 104, 172, 174, 177, 181, 189, 192, 193, 196, 198, 199, 202, 205, 221, 223
Amiiformes, 175
Amino-acids, 24, 25
Ammonia, 24, 86
Ammonites, 27, 145
Ammophila, 109
Ammophila arenaria, 129, 130
Amoebae, 134
Amoebic dysentery, 135
Amphibians, 30, 31, 178–9
Amphioxus, 29
Amphitrite johnstoni, 140
Anabolia, 162
Anatidae, 192
Anchialina agiles, 154
Andes, Mts., 15, 78, 223
Andromeda Galaxy, 13
Anemone, wood, 70 (*and see* Sea anemone; Anemone, fish)
Angelica, 117
Anhimidae, 192
Angiosperms, 84, 104, 105, 110, 114, 119
Angler fish, 59
Angwantibo, 214
Animals with backbones, 170–71
Aniseed, 117
Annelida, 140–41
Annuals, 105
Anoa, 228
Anodorhynchis, 200
Anopheles (mosquito), 135
Anoplura, 161
Ansellia gigantea, 129
Anser anser, 192
Anseranas semipalmata, 192
Anser caerulescens, 192
Anser caerulescens caerulescens, 192
Anser cygnoides, 192
Anseriformes, 192
Ant, 26, 31, 35, 53, 65, 77, 164, 169
– wood, 65
– red, 68, 69
– tropical 169
– desert, 169
– driver, 169
Antarctic, 66, 188, 191, 219
Anteater, 207, 211
Antelope, 37, 72, 229
Antennae, 154, 159, 161, 164, 167
Anthozoans, 137
Anthrax, 87
Antibiotics, 87, 96, 97, 126
Antipatharians, 137
Antirrhinum, 118
Antlers, 170
Ant lion, 162
Ant pipit, 203
Ant-thrush, 203
Anumbius annumbi, 204
Anura, 179
Anurans, 179
Apatite, 171
Apes, 38, 215
Aphid, 43, 160, 161, 163, 169
Apis mellifera, 168
Aplacophora, 144
Aplite, 17
Aplysia, 60, 61
Apocrita, 168
Apoda, 178
Apodidae, 197, 202
Apodiformes, 197
Apollo butterfly, 79
Apple, 113, 116
Apricot, 116
Aptenodytes forsteri, 188
Apterygidae, 189
Apterygota, 158, 159
Apus apus, 197
Aquila chrysaetos, 195
Ara, 200
Arabia, 188
Arachnids, 156–7
Araneae, 157
Araucaria, 103
Archaeopteryx, 184, 201
Archegonia, 88
Archil, 95
Archosaurs, 32
Arctic, 66, 137, 147, 192, 194, 219, 222, 229
Ardeidae, 193
Arecaceae, 121
Argali, 228
Argyroneta, 156
– *aquatica*, 157
Argyroxiphium sandwicense, 83
Argyroxiphium virescens, 83
Aristotle (384–322 BC), 48
Arizona National Park, 26
Armadillo, 211
Armeria maritima, 129
Aromatic leaves and plants, 119
Arrowhead plant, 80, 109
Arsinotherium, 37
Arthropods, 60, 61, 152–3
Artiodactyla, 224, 226
Asbestos, 94
Ascaris, 139
Ascension Island, 190
Ascidiacea, 150, 151
Asco-lichens, 95
Ascomycete, 95, 97, 98
Ascus, 97, 98
Asexual reproduction, 134–5, 142, 151
Ash (tree), 112
Asia, 75, 79, 102, 103, 156, 181, 192, 193, 197, 205, 220, 221
Asparagus, 120
Asphalt, 18, 27
Asphodel, 120
Ass, wild, 75, 225 (*and see Equus*)
Aster, 119
– China, 119
Asteroidea, 148
Astrology, 49
Athena noctua, 195
Atoll, 63 (*and see* Coral reef)
Atrichornis clamosus, 203
Atrichornithidae, 203
Atropa belladonna, 126
Atropin, 127
Atropine, 126
Audubon, J. J., 237
Auk, 190, 191, 236
Auk, Great, 189
Auricularia auricula, 98
Auroch, 228, 233, 241
Australia, 36, 50, 70, 71, 72, 73, 77, 102, 103, 124, 137, 169, 174, 181, 188, 189, 192, 201, 203, 205, 208, 209, 216, 219, 223
Australopithecines, 38, 39
Australopithecus, 38, 39
Austria, 179
Auxin, 106
Avocado, 112
Avocet, 191
Axe, 38
Axolotl, 179
Aye-aye, 214
Azoic era, 23
Azobacter, 87

B

Babirusa, 226
Baboon, 214, 215
Backswimmer, 161
Bacteria, 42, 43, 65, 84, 86–7, 116, 126
– and fungi, 96–7
– and protozoa, 135
Badger, 56, 70, 71, 223
Bagum, Mt., 82
Bagworm, 165
Baikal seal, 219
Bailer shell, 63
Balanoglossus clavigerus and *gigas*, 150
Baleen, 218
Bamboo, 78, 104, 105, 123, 222, 223
Banana tree, 120
Barbados, 237
Barbet, 199
Bark, 106, 107
Barley, 123
Barnacle, 154, 155
Barometer, 141 (*and see* Leech)
Basalt, 16, 17, 20
Basidiolichens, 95
Basidiomycete, 95, 97, 98, 99
Bat, 37, 71, 77, 211–213
Bathypelagic zone, 59
Beach hopper, 153
Beachy Head (Sussex), 23
Beagle, 232
Beard lichen, 94
Bean, 105, 112, 116, 117, 160
Bear, 37, 69, 70, 71, 220, 222–223
Beaver, 68, 81, 216, 217, 236
Bed bug, 135
Bee, 111, 114, 158, 223, 232
Bee-eater, 198, 199
Beech, 71, 107, 131
Beefsteak fungus, 99
Beetle, 83, 166–7
Beggiatoa, 86
Belladonna, 126, 127
Bellbird, 203, 204
Belostoma, 161
Beluga, 219
Bent grass, 123
Benthos zone, 58
Berlin Zoo, 200, 238
Beyoars, 228
Bible, the, 22
Bichirs, 175
Biennials, 105
'Big Bang' theory, 12
Bighorn sheep, 79
Bilharziasis, 139
Binary fission, 134
Bindweed, 118, 128
Biotite, 17
Birch, 67, 68, 69, 99, 107
Birds: as pollinators, 111
– and their ways, 184–5
– wings, 184–5
– digestions, 184–5
– hearts, 185
– courtship displays, 186–7
– social life of, 186–7
– camouflage, 187, 193 (*and see* Camouflage)
– flightless, 188–9
– of the sea, 190–1
– wildfowl, 192–3
– nests, 192
– navigation, 196
– perching, 202–3, 204–5
– of Paradise, 205
– (*and see* Migration)
Bird's nest fungi, 99
Bird's nest orchid, 121
Birgus latro, 155
Bison, 37, 72, 73, 228, 241
Bistort, 104
Bitter cassava, 126
Bittern, 186
Bittersweet, 127
Bivalves, 60, 144, 145
Bivalvia, 60, 144, 145
Black ant, 169
Black Apple disease, 97
Black beetle, 167
Blackberry, 105, 113
Blackbird, 57
Blackbuck, 221, 229
Black bryony, 126
Black currant, 113, 117
Blackfly, 161
Black-tailed deer, 68
Blackthorn, 116, 117, 131
Black widow (spider), 157
Bladderwort, 124, 125
Bladderwrack, 91, 142
Blenny, 177
Blewit, 99
Blubber, 219
Bluebell, 70, 71
Bluebottle, 162
Blue gentian, 79
Blue gum tree (*see* Eucalyptus)
Boa, emerald, 183
Boa canina, 183
Bobcat, 221
Bog moss, 92
Boidae, 183
Boleti, 99
Boletus edulis, 99
Boletus toadstool, 65
Bombardier beetle, 167
Bone, 170–1
Booby, 190
Boomslang, 183
Bootlace worm, 139
Borage, 118
Boraginaceae, 118, 119
Borassus flabellifer, 121
Borneo, 215
Bos primigenius, 233
Botryllus schlosseri, 151
Botrytis, 97
Bovidae, 228
Bowfin, 174, 175
Bowhead (right whale), 219
Boxfish, 177
Box turtle, 181
Brachinus, 167
Brachinus crepitans, 167
Brachiopods, 26, 27, 29, 142
Bracken, 100
Brachiosaurus, 33, 34
Brain sizes, 38–9, 207, 214
Bramble, 105, 116, 128, 131
Branchiopoda, 154
Branchiostoma, 151
Branchiura, 155
Branta sandvicensis, 192
Brassica oleracea, 115
Bristletail, 159

Britain: lizards, 182
– birds, 194
British Columbia, 27
Brittle-stars, 148, 149
Broadbill, 203
Broadleafed forest, 70–71
Bromeliaceae, 120, 128
Bronze Age, 233
Broom, 129
Broom pod, 113
Broomrape, 118
Brown rot, 97
Brush turkey, 201
Bryce Canyon, 20
Bryophyta, 84, 92–3
Bryozoans, 142–3
Bubo bubo, 195
Bubonic plague, 87, 217
Bucconidae, 199
Buceros bicornis, 198
Bucerotidae, 198
Buckland, Dr. W., 35
Buckler fern, 100
Budgerigar, 72, 73, 200
Buffalo, 54, 228
Buffon, Georges Louis, Comte de (1707–1788), 48, 50
Bufo, 179
Bufonidae, 179
Bugs, 'true', 161
Bulbul, 205
Bullfrog, 45
Bulrush, 81, 104, 122, 130
Bunting, 202, 205
Burin, 38
Bur-marigold, 119
Burr-fish, 176
Bushbaby, 214
Bush pig, 226
Bustard, 73, 193
Butanol, 87
Butomaceae, 120
Buttercup, 97, 111, 114–5, 126
Butterfly, 47, 77, 111, 164–5, 199
– large blue, 53
Butterfly fish, 63, 174
Butterwort, 125

C

Cabbage, 114–5
Cabezon, 176
Cacomistle, 223
Cactus, 74
– water storage in, 128
Caddis fly, 162
Caecilians, 178–9
Caesalpinioideae, 116
Cakile maritima, 130
Calceolaria, 118
Calcite, 17
Calcium carbonate, 91
Caldera, 63
California, 90, 102
Calliactis parasitica, 53
Calliphora spp., 162
Callirhipis philiberti, 167
Caloplaca, 94
Calosoma, 167
Calosoma beetle, 71
Calosoma inquisitor, 167
Caltha palustris, 131
Calyptomene viridis, 203
Calystegia sp., 118
Calyx, 110, 119, 120
Camarhynchus pallidus, 205
Camberwell Beauty (butterfly), 164
Cambium, 106
Cambrian period, 23, 28, 30
Cambridge University, 22
Camouflage, 73, 165
– colours, 165
– mimicry, 165
– beetles, 167
– sharks, 173
– chameleon, 182
– birds, 187, 191, 193, 196, 233
Camel: Arabian, 74, 226, 227
– Bactrian, 74–5, 226, 227
Cameleopard, 235
Camel spiders, 156
Campodea staphyliniformis, 159
Canada, 209
Canidae, 222
Canoidea, 220
Cape gooseberry, 118
Cape hunting dog, 222
Capercaillie, 69
Capitonidae, 199
Caprimulgidae, 196
Caprimulgiformes, 196
Caprimulgus europaeus, 196
– *vociferus*, 196
– *carolinensis*, 196
Capsella, 105
Capsella bursapastoris, 115
Capuchin, 214
Capybara, 81, 217
Caracal, 221
Carapace, 180
Caraway, 117
Carbohydrates, 43
Carbon, 24
Carbonaceous rock, 18
Carbon dioxide, 43, 54, 84, 96, 97, 105
– and leaves, 108
– and protozoa, 135
– and moss animals, 142
Carboniferous period, 31, 33, 101, 175
Cardinal, 69
Caribbean Sea, 136, 154
Caribou, 66, 67, 227, 241
Carnation, 114–5
Carnivores, 37, 42, 52, 53, 70, 108
– in sea, 58, 145, 146, 173
– cats, 220–21
– dogs, 222–23
Carnivorous plants, 124–5 (*and see* Ant)
Carpel, 110, 111, 114, 116
Carpinus betulus, 131
Carrageenin, 91
Carrion crow, 202
Carrion fly, 99
Carrot, 117
Cartilage, 170, 171,172
Caryophyllaceae, 115
Caryopsis, 112
Caspian Sea, 241
Caspian seal, 219
Cassida viridis, 166
Cassowary, 188, 189
Castanea, 107, 112
Castor-oil plant, 112, 127
Casuariidae, 188
Casuariiformes, 188
Cat, 43, 220–21
– marbled, 221
– domestic, 232
Caterpillar, 69, 71, 162, 164
Caterpillar hunter, 167
Catfish, 177
Cathartidae, 195
Catkin, 110, 111
Cattle: Friesian, Hereford, Longhorn, 229
– Highland, 229, 233
– Jersey, 233
Cave paintings, 39
Cayman, 181
Cedar, 102, 103
Cedrus, 103
Celebes, 226
Celerio euphorbiae, 165
Celery, 117
Cell: animal, 42, 43
– plant, 42, 43, 84
– sea plant, 58
– freshwater plant, 81
Cellulose, 42, 53, 84, 86
Cenozoic era, 23, 36, 37
Centaur, 234
Centipede, 65, 152
Centropelma micropterum, 189
Cep, 99
Cephalocarida, 154
Cephalochordata, 150, 151
Cephalopoda, 144, 146, 147
Cephalopods, 27, 29, 145, 147
Ceratomella ulmi, 97
Ceratosaurus, 34
Certhiidae, 202
Cestodes, 138
Cestrum, 118
Cetacea, 218
Cetaceans, 218
– intelligence of, 207
Ceylon (see Sri Lanka)
Chaetopterus, 140
Chaffinch, 57
Chagas' disease, 135
Chalk, 18
Chamaecyparis, 103
Chamaeleonidae, 182
Chamaenerion angustifolium, 130
Chameleon, 182
Chamois, 79, 228
Chanterelle, 99
Charadriidae, 191, 200
Charadriiformes, 190
Charophytes, 91
Chatham Islands, 188
Cheddar caves, 21
Cheetah, 72, 220, 221
Cheilostome, 143
Chelicerae, 156, 157
Chelicerata, 156, 157
Chelonia, 180
Cherry, 113, 116
Chestnut, 107, 108, 112
Chevrotain, 227
Chickadee, 69, 205
Chicory, 119
Chile pine, 103
Chilopoda, 152
Chimaeras, 172
Chimpanzee, 38, 215
China, 102, 103, 115, 175, 203, 220, 223, 234, 235
Chinchilla, 79, 217
Chinese liver fluke, 138–9
Chipmunk, 207, 216
Chitons, 144, 145, 146
Chive, 121
Chlamydomonas, 88
Chlamydosaurus kingi, 32
Chlorella, 88, 94
Chlorophyll, 25, 42, 43, 108, 109, 121, 135
Chlorophyta, 88, 90
Chloroplast, 42, 88, 90, 108
Cholera, 87
Chordata, 170
Chordates, 150
Chordeilinae, 196
Chondropython viridis, 183
Chondrus crispus, 91
Chorda filum, 90
Chough, Alpine, 78
Chrisolina polita, 166
Chromatids, 45
Chromosome, 42, 44, 45
Chrysanthemum coccineum, 119
Chrysococcyx cupreus, 201
Chrysopela, 76
Chuckawalla, 74
Chuck-will's widow, 196
Cicada, 160
Cichlids, 177
Ciconiidae, 193
Ciconiiformes, 193
Cicuta virosa, 117
Cilia, 134, 135, 142, 145, 150, 151
Cinnabar moth, 165
Ciona intestinalis, 151
Cirripedia, 155
Citellus, 73
Citric acid, 96
Civet, 220, 221
Cladium mariscus, 122
Cladonia rangiferina, 67
Cladophora, 90, 91
Cladophora rupestris, 90
Clam, 63
– giant, 88
– burrowing, 147
Classification of plants and animals, 46–7 (*see* Taxonomy)
Claviceps purpurea, 97
Clay, 19, 20, 21, 28, 64
Clearwing, 164
Cleaver, 113
Clematis, 114, 115, 128
Clematis vitalba, 112, 128
Click-beetle, 167
– lined, 166
Climax community, 130, 131
Clostridium, 87
Clostridium botulinum, 87
Clostridium tetani, 87
Clouds, 15
Cloven-hoofed animals, 227 (*see* Ungulata)
Clover, 116, 117
Club fungi, 97
Club moss, 31, 101
Clubroot disease, 96
Coal, 10, 18, 26, 27, 31, 101
Coati, 223
Cocaine, 127
Coca shrub, 127
Cocci, 86
Coccinellia septempunctata, 166
Coccolith, 18
Coccolithophorids, 89
Cochlearia, 115
Cockchafer, 73, 166
Cockle, 144, 145, 191
Cocklebur, 119
Cock-o-the-rock, 77
Cockroach, 160
Cobra, 183
Coconut, 112, 113, 121, 155
Cod, 174, 177
Codeine, 114
Codium sp., 90
Coelacanth, 174, 175, 177
Coelenterates, 88, 136, 137
Colembola, 159
Coleoptera, 166–7
Collocalia, 197
Colobus, 215
Colonial star sea-squirt, 151
Colorado River, 18, 19
Colour blindness, 45
Colouring, of fish, 177
(*and see* Camouflage; Birds; Wasps)
Colubridae, 183
Colugo, 210
Columba livia, 200
Columbidae, 200
Columbiformes, 200
Columbine, 114, 115
Columbus, Christopher, 219
Comb-headed cardinal, 167
Comb-jellies, 137
Commensalism, 53
Common cord moss, 93
Common horsetail, 101
Common morel fungus, 98
Common polypody fern, 100
Comoro Islands, 174, 210
Compass plant, 129
Compositae, 83, 119
Conch, 63
Cone, 102–3 (*and see* Coniferales, Conifers)
Cone (mollusc), 147
Congo eel, 179
Conidia, 97
Conies, 224
Coniferales, 102–3
Conifers, 162
– forest, 68–9
Coniine, 126
Conium, 126
Conium maculatum, 117
Conophagidae, 203
Conservation, 238–9
– Organisations for, 238–9
– action needed for, 240–41
Continental drift, 14, 15
Continental shelf, 58, 59, 147, 173
Convolvulaceae, 118
Convolvulus arvensis, 118
Convolvulus major, 128
Coot, 80, 193
Copepod, 153, 155
Copepoda, 155
Copper, 16, 17
Copper butterfly, 164
Coracias candatus, 198
Coracias garrulus, 198
Coraciidae, 198
Coraciiformes, 198
Coral reefs, 27, 29, 62–3, 82, 147
– islands, 82
– polyps, 137
Coral reef cardinal fish, 177
Cordaits, 31
Coriander, 117
Coriscium, 95
Cork, 107
Cork oak, 107
Corm, 105
Cormorant, 188, 190
– flightless, 189
Corn-cockle, 126

Corolla, 110, 118, 119, 120
Corolliferae, 120
Corsica, 78, 228
Corundum, 17
Corvidae, 202, 205
Corvus corone, 202
Corylus avellana, 131
Corythosaurus, 34
Coscoroba coscoroba, 192
Coscoroba swan, 192
Cosmos, 119
Cotingidae, 203
Cotton-grass, 122, 131
Cotton spinner, 148
Cotyledon, 104, 108, 112
Couch grass, 123
Cougar, 221
Cow, 206
Cowbane, 117, 127
Cowfish, 177
Cowrie, 63
Coyote, 222
Coypu, 216, 217
Crab, 60, 61, 154, 155
Crab apple, 131
Cracticidae, 205
Crane, 192, 193, 202
Cranefly, 157, 163
Crania, 170
Crataegus sp., 131
Crayfish, 45, 71, 154, 155
Crepidula, 146
Cretaceous period, 23, 36
Cretaceous period, Upper, 18
Crick, Francis, (1916–), 49
Cricket, 160, 161
Crinoid, 26, 148
 – fossils, 149
Crinoidea, 149
Crocodile, 31, 33, 35, 180–81
Crocodilia, 180
Crocus, 105, 121
Cro-Magnon man, 39
Crops, 233
Crossbill, 69
Cross-breeding, 45
Cross-opterygian, 31
Crotalus cerastes, 75
Crow, 202, 205
'Crown of Thorns' (*see* Starfish)
Cruciferae, 115
Crustaceans, 58, 143, 147, 154–5
 (*and see* Crab, etc)
Crustose lichens, 94
Ctenida, 144
Ctenophores, 137
Cuba, 197
Cuckfield (Sussex), 35
Cuckoo, 201, 234–35
 – European, 55, 201
 – emerald, 200, 201
Cuckoo roller, 199
Cuculidae, 201
Cuculiformes, 201
Cuculus canorus, 200
Culpeper, Nicholas, 48
Cumaceans, 154
Cup fungi, 98
Cupressus, 103
Curare, 127
Curine, 127
Curassow, 201
Curlew, 191
Currant, flowering, 116
Cuscus, 77, 209
Cuscuta, 118
Cushion moss, 92
Cuttlefish, 144, 145, 146
Cycadales, 102
Cycads, 103
Cycas, 102
Cyclope, 81
Cyclops, 124, 155
Cyclostomes, 170–71
Cygnus atratus, 192
Cygnus melanocoryphus, 192
Cyperaceae, 122
Cyperus papyrus, 122
Cypress, 103
Cypsiurus parvus, 197
Cysts (protozoan), 134
Cytisine, 126
Cytisus laburnum, 126–7
Cytoplasm, 42

D

Dacelo novaeguinea, 198
Dachshund, 232
Dacoits, 127
Daddy-long-legs, 157
Daffodil, 105, 121
Dahlia, 105
Daisies, 119
Damping-off disease, 97
Damselfly, 161
Danaus plexippus, 164
Dandelion, 83, 119
Daphnia, 124, 155
Darters, 190
Darwin, Charles (1809–1882), 49, 50, 51, 205
Darwin, Erasmus, 50
Dassies, 224
Dasyatis pectinatis, 173
Datura stramonium, 126
DDT, 240
Dead-man's-fingers, 137
Dead-nettle, 111, 119
Death cap fungus, 99, 126
Death cap toadstool, 98
Death's head hawk moth, 166
Decapoda, 155
Deciduous forest, 70–71
Deer, 37, 71, 227
 – parasites of, 54
 – red, 226, 227
Deer mouse, 71
Deer Park, Nara, Japan, 239
Defoliation, 236
Delphinium, 114, 115
Deltas, 21
Dendrocolaptidae, 202, 203
Denmark, 232
Dentalium, 144
Derbyshire (caves and potholes), 21
Dermaptera, 160
Derris dust, 126
Desert: life in the, 74–75
 – plants of, 128
Desmid, 81
Destroying Angel fungus, 98
Devil's coach-horse, 167
Devonian period, 29, 30, 31
Dhole dog, 222
Diamond, 17
Diastema, 216, 217
Diatomite, 27, 89
Diatoms, 27, 53, 81, 88, 89, 142
Dik-dik, 229
Dicotyledon, 104, 107, 110, 114
Dictyoptera, 160
Digenea, 138
Digestion: and bacteria, 86–7
 – rabbits, 217
 – carnivores, 220
 – ruminants, 226
Digitalin, 127
Digitalis, 126, 127
Digitoxin, 127
Dill, 117
Dingo, 223
Dinoflagellates, 88, 89
Dinosaurs, 10, 32, 33, 34–5, 235
Diomedeidae, 190
Diomedea exulans, 190
Dionaea, 125
Diorite, 17
Diplodocus, 33
Diplopoda, 153
Diplura, 159
Dipper, 80
Diptera, 162
Display (birds), 194
 (*and see* Birds)
DNA, 49
Dock plant, 105
Dodder, 105, 118
Dodo, 236, 237
Dog, 220, 222–3, 232, 237
Dog-flea, 55
Dog lichen, 95
Dog rose, 131
Dog whelk, 60
Dolphin, 32, 58, 59, 218
Domestication of animals, 232–3
Donacia aquatica, 166
Donkey, 225
Dormouse, 71, 217
 – tree-dwelling, 216
Douc langur, 236
Douroucouli, 215
Dove, 200
Dragon, 234
Dragonfly, 80, 161
 – giant, 31
 – in Polar regions, 67
Dragon's teeth, 235
Dromedary, 227
Dromiceiidae, 188
Drone (bee), 168
Drone fly, 163
Drosera, 125
Drosophila, 163
Drought, 74
Drupe, 113, 117
Dryads, 235
Dryopithecus, 38
Dryopteris, 100
Dry rot fungus, 98
Dubautea plantaginea, 83
Duck, 192–93
 – Polar regions, 67
 – freshwater, 81
Duckweed, 104
Dugong, 219
Duiker, 228
Dung beetle, 73
Dutch elm disease, 97
Dykes, 17
Dynamite, 89
Dynastes hercules, 167
Dytiscus, 167
Dytiscus marginalis, 166

E

Eagle, 194, 195
Earth, 10, 12, 13, 14–15
 – structure, 14–15
 – dating age of, 22–23
 – origins of, 24–25
Earth stars, 99
Earthworms (*see* Worms)
Earwig, 160
Echidna, 208
Echinoderms, 29, 148–9, 170
Echinoidea, 149
Echinus esculentis, 149
Echo-location, 197, 219 (*and see* Bats; Birds; Swifts; Whales)
Ecological niche, 36, 80, 158
Ecology, 52–3, 236
Ectoparasite, 54, 138, 139
Ecuador, 197
Edelweiss, 79
Edentata, 210–11
Eel, 80
Eel-grass, 120
Eelworm, 65, 125 (*and see* Nematodes)
Eggs, fish, 176–7 (*and see* Fish)
 – turtle, 180
 – lizard, 182
 – bird, 185, 191, 192, 193, 194, 195, 201, 205
 – ostrich, 189
Egyptians, Ancient, 232, 234, 235
Eider duck, 238
Elapidae, 183
Elasmobranchiomorphi, 172
Elder tree, 98
Electra pilosa, 142
Electron microscope, 134
Elephant, 37
 – African, 224, 225
 – Asian, 224, 225
 – destruction of, 239
Elk, 68, 227
Elm tree, 112
Elymus arenarius, 130
Elytra, 166, 167
Emberizadae, 205
Embryo, 50, 51, 112
Emerald, 17
Emu, 188, 189
Endive, 119
Endoparasite, 54, 138, 139
Endopterygota, 158, 162
Endosperm, 112, 123
Endospore, 86, 87
England: erosion of coastline, 20
 – fossil remnants, 35
Enteromorpha, 91
Enteropneusta, 150
Entoprocta, 142–3
Environment, and survival, 57, 144, 147, 240 (*and see* Conservation)
Eocene epoch, 37
Eohippus, 36
Ephemeral plants, 105
Ephemerata, 161
Epiphragm, 147
Epiphyte, 121, 128, 129
Epiphytism, 128
Equator, 92
Equisetum arvense, 101
Equus: Asinus, 46
 – *caballus*, 46
 – *Przewalski*, 46
 – *zebra hartmannae*, 46
 (*and see* Ass; Horse)
Ergot fungus, 97, 98
Erica, 109
Eriophorum sp., 131
Eriphorum sp., 122
Erithacus rubecula, 186
Ermine, 223
Erosion, 10, 15, 20, 21, 64, 65
Escallonia, 117
Escharella immersa, 143
Eschscholzia california, 115
Estrildidae, 204
Ethyl alcohol, 96
Eucalyptus, 104, 209
Eudyptes crestatus, 188
Eudyptula minor, 188
Euglenoids, 89
Euphrasia, 118
Eurylaimi, 202, 203
Eurylaimidae, 203
Eusthenopteron, 175
Everest, Mt., 78
Everglades National Reserve, 239
Evolution, 50–51, 56
 – convergent, 197, 209
 – theory of, (*see* Darwin, Charles)
Exopterygota, 158, 160
Exoskeleton, 152
Extinct species, 236–7
Eye: insect, 158
 – beetle, 167
 – snake, 182
 – bird, 185
 – primate, 214
 – cat, 220
Eyebright, 118

F

Fagus, 107
 – *sylvatica*, 131
'Fairy rings', 99
Falconidae, 194
Falconiformes, 194, 195
Falcon, 194
Falco peregrinus, 194
Falkland Islands, 90, 91, 189
False fruits, 113
False scorpions, 156
Fan worm, 141
Farne Island, 238
Fayyum (Egypt), 37
Feather, 184, 185
Feather stars, 148, 149
Feldspar, 17, 19
Felidae, 220
Feloidea, 220
Fennel, 117
Ferns, 31, 78, 83, 100–101
Ferret, black-footed, 223
Fertilisation, 110–111
Fertilisers (seaweed), 91
Field-mouse, 65
Fig, 113
Figwort, 118
Fiji, 82
Filter feeders and feeding, 60, 147, 151
Fin (of fish), 175
Finch, 202, 205
 – Galapagos, 50, 51
Fire-bodies, 151
Fire brat, 159
Firefly, 167

Fire, forest, 130
Fireweed, 130
Firewood gatherer, 204
Fir tree, 103
Fish, 53, 170
– anemone, 176–7
– bony types, 174–5, 176–7
– life cycle, 176–7
Fisher (marten), 223
Fish louse, 153, 154, 155
Flagella, 86, 88, 92, 134, 135
Flamingo, 185, 193
Flask fungi, 98
Flatworm, 81, 88, 138, 143
Flat wrack, 61, 91
Flea, 55
Flies, biting, 67
Flight, birds, 185 (*and see* Birds)
Floret, 119
Flowering currant, 117
Flowering plants, 104–5
Flowers, 110–111, 115
– destruction of, 237
Fluke, 54
Flustra, 142
Fly, true, 162
– house, 158, 163
– Alder, 162
Fly agaric fungus, 99
– toadstool, 84
Fly-catcher, 43, 202, 203, 204
Flying fish, 58
Flying foxes (*see* Bats)
Foliose lichen, 95
Food chains, 52–3, 58, 89
Fool's parsley, 117, 127
Foraminifera, 134
Forewings (beetles), 166, 167
Forget-me-not (Borage), 118
Forget-me-not (Myosotis), 118
Formicariidae, 203
Formica rufa, 169
Fossa, 221
Fossils, 22, 26–7, 29, 30, 51
– collecting, 28
– of early Man, 39
– Crinoids, 149
Fox, 56, 70, 220
– Arctic, 57, 66, 67, 222
– kit, 74
– European red, 222
Fox-glove, 126, 127
France (cave paintings), 39
Fraxinus, 112
Freesia, 121
Fregata magnificens, 82
Fregatidae, 190
Fresh fly, 163
Freshwater life, 80–81
Frigate bird, 82, 190
Fringillidae, 202, 205
Fritillary, 120
Frog: life cycle, 178
– African clawed, 179
Frogmouths, 196
Fruit-fly, 45, 163
Fruticose lichens, 94, 95
Fruits and Seeds, 112–113
Fucoxanthin, 42, 90
Fucus spiralis, 61
Fucus vesiculosis, 91
Fungus, 43, 65, 84, 121, 131
– and algae, 87, 94
– smaller types, 96–7
– larger types, 98–9
Furnaria hygrometrica, 93
Furnaria rufus, 205
Furnariidae, 203
Furnarius, 204
Fur seal, 219

G

Gabbro, 17, 20
Gad-fly, 54
Galapagos Islands, 50, 51, 82, 180, 181, 205
– cormorants, 188, 189
Galaxies, 12
Galbulidae, 99
Galium aparine, 128
Galliformes, 201
Gallinaceous birds, 201
Gallinules, 193
Gall-wasp, 70
Game birds, 201
Game Parks, 238–9
Ganges, 218
Gannet, 186, 190
Garfish, 174
Garlic, 121
Garnet, 17
Garpikes, 175
Gasterosteus aculeatus, 177
Gathartes burrovianus, 194
Gastropoda, 144
Gastropods, 28–9, 143, 146
Gaur, 79, 228
Gazelle: Thompson's, 228, 229
– Grant's, 229
Gecko, 180, 182
Gekkonidae, 182
Gemsbok, 229
Gemstones, 17
Gene, 44, 45, 51
Genet, 221
Genetics, 44–5
Gentiana verna, 237
Genus (*see* Classification of Plants and Animals)
Geochronology, 22–3
Gerbil, 217
Gharial, 181
Gerenuk, 229
Giant's Causeway (Ulster), 16
Gibbon, 38, 215
Gibraltar, 215
Gigartina stellata, 91
Gila monster, 74, 182, 183
Gills, 51, 171, 172, 178 (*and see* Fish)
– of molluscs, 144–7
– crustaceans, 154
Gilpin, River, 21
Ginkgoales, 103
Ginkgo biloba, 103
Giraffe, 72, 227
Gir National Park, 239
Glaciers, 21
Gladioli, 121
Globe artichoke, 119
Globigerina, 134
Glochidia, 147
Gloiocapsa, 94
Glow-worm, 167
Glumes, 123
Glutton, 223
Glycosides, 126, 127
Glyptodon, 37
Goat, 228, 232
Goatsucker, 235
Goat willow, 112
Gobi Desert, 74, 227
Goby, 174, 177
Godwit, black-tailed, 191
Gold, 16, 17
Gomphocerippus rufus, 161
Goose, 192–3
– Polar regions, 67
– wild, 120
– Hawaiian or Ne-ne, 240–1
Goose barnacles, 235
Gooseberry, 113, 117
Goosegrass, 128
Gophers, pocket, 216
Gorgoman polyps, 137
Gorilla, 38, 214, 215
Gorse, 105, 112, 117, 130
Gracilaria sp., 91
Grain (for alcohol), 123
Gramineae, 104, 122
Grampian Mts., 30
Grand Canyon, 18, 19
Granite, 17, 19, 20
Grape, 113
Graptolites, 28
Grass parrakeet, 200
Grasses, 122–3
Grasshopper, 73, 160, 161
Grasslands, 72–3
Grass-snake, 183
Gravel, 64
Gravers, 38
Gravity, 13
Grazing animals, 72–3
Grebe, 81, 187
Greek mythology, 234, 235
Greenbottle, 163
Greenfly, 57, 161
Greenland, West, 22
Green tortoise beetle, 166
Grenadier (fish), 174
Greylag goose, 192
Grey seal, 219
Grey-top shell, 144
Gribble, 155
Grosbeaks, 69, 202
Ground-nut, 117
Grouse, 201
Gruiformes 193, 202
Guacharo, 196
Guanaco, 227
Guano, 213
Guillemot, 191
Guinea fowl, 201
Guinea pig, 217
Gull, 190, 191
Gulper eel, 59
Guppy, 174, 177
Gurney's pitta, 204
Gymnosperms, 84, 102, 104, 110
Gymnures, 210
Gyps fulvus, 194
Gypaëtus barbatus, 195
Gyrinus marinus, 166

H

Habitat, 52, 53, 54, 56, 95, 158, 195
– destruction of, 224, 237, 238, 240 (*and see* Conservation)
Haematococcus pluvialis, 88, 89
Haematopodidae, 191
Hagfish, 170, 171
Hair moss, 92
Half-chromosome, 45
Halimeda sp., 91
Halobates, 161
Halteres, 163
Hamster, 216, 217
Hannopterum harrisi, 188
Hare, 37, 216, 217, 232
– Nelson, 217
– varying, 217
Harlequin beetle, 77
Harpoons, 38
Harpy eagle, 77
Hart's tongue fern, 100
Harvestmen, 69, 156, 157
Harvey, William (1578–1657), 48
Harz Mts., 15
Hatchet fish, 59
Haustoria, 95, 119
Hathor, 235
Hawaii, 16, 82, 83, 219, 241 (*and see* Ne-ne goose)
Hawk, 194
Hawk moth caterpillar, 165
Hawthorn, 116, 131
Hay fever, 119, 126
Hazel hen, 69
Hazel (tree), 131
Heather, 109
Hedera, 109
Hedera helix, 127, 128, 131
Hedgehog, 210
Hedgehog skate, 172
Helleborus plants, 115
Hemichordates, 150
Hemiprocriidae, 197
Hemiptera, 161
Hemlock, 117, 126, 127
Herbal medicines, 48
Herbivores, 42, 52, 60, 71, 108
Hercules beetle, 167
Heredity, 44
Hermaphrodites, 138, 141, 143, 146, 151, 154
Hermit crab, 53, 154
Heron, 80, 192, 193
Herring, 59, 137, 174
Heterodontiformes, 172
Heteromerous lichens, 94
Hexanchiformes, 172
Hibernation, 147, 207, 212
Highland Wildlife Park (Scotland), 241
Himalayan blue poppy, 115
Himalayas, 203, 221, 225, 228
Himantarum gabrielis, 153
Hippopotamus, 81, 226, 235
Hirudinea, 141
Hirudineans, 141
Hirundinidae, 202
Hoatzin, 201
Hog, giant forest, 226
Holly, 109, 131
Holothurin, 149
Holothuroidea, 149
Hominids, 38
Homo: *erectus*, 38, 39
– *habilis*, 38, 39
– *sapiens*, 39
Homoiomerous lichens, 94
Homiothermia, 184
Honey bee, 168–9, 232 (*and see* Bee)
Honeycreepers, 82
Honeydew, 169
Honeyguide bird, 199, 223
Honeysuckle, 70, 105, 128, 131
Hookworms, 139
Hoopoe, 198, 199
Hoplia philanthus, 166
Hoplocarida, 155
Hops, 129
Hornbeam, 131
Hornbills, 198
Hornwort, 104
Hornwrack, 142
Horse, 36, 45, 46, 50, 224, 225, 232, 233
– wild European, 241
(*and see Equus*)
Horse chestnut (see Chestnut)
Horseshoe crab, 153, 157
Horseshoe shrimp, 154
Horsetails, 31
Hover fly, 163
Hummingbird, 77, 111, 196
Humus, 64, 65, 70
Hyacinth, 120
Hyaena, 72, 220, 221
Hyaenidae, 221
Hydra, 81, 136
Hydrangea, 117
Hydrobatidae, 190
Hydrogen, 24
Hydrogen sulphide, 86
Hydroids, 136, 143
Hydrophiidae, 183
Hydrophytes, 129
Hymenoptera, 168
Hypericum perforatum, 235
Hyphae, 94–5, 96, 97, 99, 103, 125
Hyracotherium, 36, 37
Hyrax, 224
Hystricomorpha, 217

I

Ibex, 78, 79, 228
Ibis, 193, 234
Ice Age, 205
Ice, as erosion agent, 21
Iceland moss, 92
Ichthyosaurs, 32, 33
Ichthyostegalians, 31
Iguana, 182
Iguanodon, 35
Iiwi, 82
Ilex aquilifolium, 109, 131
Impala, 229
Inarticulata, 29
'Inchworm', 71
India, 220, 227
Indian flycatcher, 82
Indian Ocean, 167, 173, 174, 176, 181, 219
Indians, American, 234
Indicatoridae, 199
Indonesia, 183
Indri, 214
Industrial Revolution, 138 (*and see* Pollution)
Inhibitors, 74
Ink-cap (lawyer's wig fungus), 65, 99
Ink-cloud (cephalopods), 145
Insectivores, 37, 210–11
Insects, 31, 56, 65, 69, 71, 83, 152–3, 158–9
– fossilized, 26
– parasites, 55
– and pollination, 110–111, 116, 117, 121, 128

– winged, 158–9
– aquatic, 161
– pupating, 162–3
– moulting, 160–1
Instar, 160, 161
Ipomoea batatas, 118
Ireland, 27, 97
Iridaceae, 121
Iris, 105, 121
Irish moss, 91, 92
Iron, 16, 26
Isatis tinctoria, 115
Isidium, 95
Islands, life on remote, 82–3
Isles of Scilly, 17, 143
Isoetes, 101
Isopoda, 155
Isoptera, 168, 169
Isotopes, 22
Isurus oxyrhynchus, 172
Italy, 19, 179
Iva xanthifolia, 119
Ivory, 224
Ivy, 70, 108, 109, 127, 128, 131
Ixias, 121

J

Jacamars, 199
Jacanas, 191
Jacanidae, 191
Jackals, 222
Jaguar, 220, 221
Jaguarund, 221
Jamoytius, 29
Japan, 70, 91, 154, 226
Java Man, 39
Jay, 69
Jellyfish, 136, 137, 181
Jerboa, 75, 217
Jerusalem artichoke, 119
Jewel-thrush, 204
Jew's ear fungus ('Judas's ear'), 98, 99
Joshua tree, 74
Judas-tree, 116
Jugoslavia, 179
Juniper, 103
Jupiter, 13
Jurassic shales, 27

K

Kagu, 189
Kakapo, 188, 189
Kangaroo, 72, 208, 209
Kangaroo rat, 74, 75, 216
Kangaroo tree, 77
Kelp, 90, 91
Keratin, 184
Kerry (Ireland), 95
Kiang, 225
Kilauea volcano (Hawaii), 16
King crab, 153
Kingbirds, 204
Kingfisher, 198
Kinixys, 181
Kinkajou, 223
Kiskadee, 204
Kiwi, 189
Klipspringer, 229
Koala, 209
Komodo dragon, 183
Kookaburra, 198
Krakatoa volcano, 17
Krill, 218
Kulan, 225
Kusimanse, 221

L

Labiatae, 119
Labidiaster sp., 148
Labrador duck, 241
Laburnum, 126, 127
Laccolith, 17
Lacertidae, 182
Lacertilia, 182
Lacewing fly, 43, 162, 163
– Hawaiian, 83
Lactrodectus, 157
Ladybird, 57, 152, 166, 167
Lady's slipper, 121
Lagomorpha, 217
Lakes, 23, 80–81, 130–31
– plants in, 101, 130–31
Lamarck, Chevalier de, 50
Lamellae (*see* Bone)
Lamellicorns, 167
Lamina, 109
Laminaria kelp, 91
Lamium sp., 119
Lammergeier, 195
Lampetra fluviatilis, 171
Lamprey, 170, 171
Lampshell (brachiopod), 142
Lancelets, 151
Landseer, Sir Edwin, 122
Langur, 215
Lantern fish, 59, 175
Larch, 103
Laridae, 191
Larix, 103
Lark, 204, 205
Larkspur, 114
Larus argentatus, 47
Larvacea, 151
Larvae: fly, 163
– mosquito, 163
– beetle, 166
Lasius flavus, 169
Lasius niger, 169
Laterite, 18
Latex, 115, 118
Lathyrus spp., 116
Latimeria, 175
Laughing jackass, 198
Lavender, 108, 119
Leaf, 108–9, 114, 121
– in soil decay, 65, 70
– in tropical forests, 77
– types of, 122
Leaf beetle, 166
Leaf-cutter ant, 169
Lechwe, 229
Leech, 140, 141
Leek, 120, 121
Leguminosae, 112, 116, 117
Lemming, 56, 57, 66, 67, 195
Lemna, 104
Lemon, 113
Lemon-scented balm, 119 (Melissa)
Lemur, 38, 210, 214
Lenticel, 107
Lentil, 117
Leopard, 72, 220, 221, 238
Leopard orchid, 129
Lepas anatifera, 155
Lepidoptera, 164
Lepisma saccharina, 159
Leprose lichen, 94
Leptophyes punctatissima, 161
Lesser reedmace, 81
Lettuce, 119
Leucobryum glaucum, 92
Leucrota, 235
Liana, 76, 128
Lice, 161
Lichen, 61, 64, 66, 67, 70, 78, 94–5, 130, 131
– and algae, 87, 88, 94–5
– Iceland moss, 92
– Beard, 94
Lichina, 94
Life, first signs on land, 30–31
Lightfoot, Dr. J., 22
Lightning, and trees, 107
Lignin, 86
Ligustrum vulgare, 127
Liliaceae, 120
Lily-of-the-valley, 119, 120, 126
Lilytrotters, 191
Lime, 26
– and seaweed, 91
Limenitis archippus, 165
Limestone, 18, 27, 28
– and coral reefs, 62, 63
Limnaea pereger, 138
Limnephilus, 162
Limnoria lignorum, 155
Limpet, 60, 144, 146
Lineus longissimus, 139
Lingula, 142
Linnaeus, Carl von (1707–1778), 46, 47, 48, 95
Linné (see Linnaeus)
Linsang, 221
Lion, 72, 220
Littoral zone, 147
Liver fluke worm, 138, 139
Liverwort, 88, 92–3, 131
Lizard, 75, 182–3
– Australian frilled, 32, 182
– horned, 74
– colour vision, 180
– European, 182
Llama, 227
Loam, 64
Lobaria pulmonaria, 94
Lobster, 154, 155
Lockjaw, 87
Locust, 56, 57, 73
– desert, 75
Locusta migratoria, 57
Lodicules, 123
Loganberry, 116
Longhorn beetle (*Monochammus titillator*), 68, 167
Longicorn, 77
Lonicera periclymenum, 128, 131
'Looper' caterpillar, 71, 165
Lophocoela heterophylla, 92
Lophonetta specularioides, 193
Lophophore, 142, 143, 150
Loris, 38, 214, 215
Louse, 54
Lousewort, 118
Love-in-a-mist, 114, 115
Lucerne (grass), 117
Lugworm, 61, 140
Lullula arborea, 205
Lulworth Cove (Dorset), 20
Lung: molluscs, 145
– birds, 185
(*and see* Oxygen; Mammals)
Lung-fish, 29, 174, 175
Lungworm, 54
Lunularia cruciata, 93
Lupin, 117
Lycaena sp., 164
Lycoperdon giganteum, 99
Lycopodium alpinum, 101
Lynx, 37, 221
Lyrebird, 203

M

Macaques, 215
Macaw, 77, 200
Mackerel, 59
Macrauchenia, 37
Macrocheira kaempferi, 154
Macrocystis pyrifera, 90
Madagascar, 182, 197, 210, 214, 219, 221
Madreporite, 148
Maggot, 162
Magma, 16
Magpie, bell, 205
Magpie goose, 192
Maidenhair tree, 102, 103
Maize (Corn), 105, 123, 233
Mako shark (see Shark)
Malachite, 17
Malacostraca, 155
Malaria, 135
Malaya, 124
Malay Archipelago, 50
Malaysia, 104, 122, 167, 203, 237
Mallard, 80, 192
Mallophaga, 161
Malus sp., 131
Mammals, 36–7, 206–7
– marsupial, 36
– placental, 36
– sea, 218–9
Mammoths, 26, 27, 37
Man, 230–1, 232, 233, 234, 235 (*and see Homo*)
Manakin, 203, 204
Manatee, 219
Manchuria, 220
Mandible, 207
Manihot esculenta, 126
Mangrove, 128, 147
Manila hemp, 120
Mannikins, 204
Manta, 172
Mantell, Dr. G., 35
Mantle (mollusc), 144, 145
– cavity, 146
Maoris, 172
Maranta leuconeura, 108
Marasmius oreades, 99
Marble, 19
Margay, 221
Marigold, 119
Markhor, 228
Marmoset, 214
Marmot, 78, 216
Marram grass, 109, 123, 129, 130
Mars, 13
Marshland, 130, 131
Marsh marigold, 131
Marsupials, 37, 71, 206–7, 209
– mice, 209
– moles, 209
Martens, 71, 223 (*and see* Pine marten)
Mauritius, 237
May apple, 126
Mayfly, 80, 161
Meadow fescue, 123
Meadowsweet, 97
Meconopsis, 115
Mecoptera, 162
Medawar, Sir Peter, (1915–), 49
Mediterranean Sea, 118, 136, 219
Medusae, 136
Meerkats, 221
Megachiroptera, 213
Megalosaurus, 35
Megapodes, 201
Megapodiidae, 201
Megatherium, 37
Meiosis, 45
Melissa, 119
Melittophagus bulocki, 199
Mellisuga helenae, 197
Melolontha melolontha, 166
Melopsittacus undulatus, 72
Mendel, Gregor (1822–1884), 44, 45, 49
Menurae, 202, 203
Menura novae hollandiae, 203
Menura superba, 203
Menuridae, 203
Merganser, 193
Meropidae, 198
Merostomata, 156
Merulius lachrymans, 98
Merychippus, 36
Mesophyll, 108
Mesophytes, 128
Mesozoic era, 23, 34, 37
Mesquite, 74
Metamorphic rock, 19
Metamorphosis, 160
– amphibians, 178
Meteorites, 25
Methane, 24
Metridium senile, 136
Mexican: burrowing toad, 179
– beaded lizard, 183
Mexico, 179, 183
Mica, 17, 19
Microchiroptera, 213
Micropyle, 112
Micro-whip scorpion, 156
Midwife toad, 178
Migration, 186, 187
– birds, 192, 196, 197, 203, 204, 240
– bats, 212
– whales, 219
Mildew, 97
Milkweed butterfly (Monarchs), 165
Miller, Dr. S., 24
Millipede, 65, 152, 153
Mimidae, 205
Mimosoideae, 116
Mimulus, 118
Mink, 68, 81, 223
Mint, 119
Miocene period, 38
Miohippus, 36
Mistle thrush, 105
Mistletoe, 70, 105, 235
Mite, 54, 64, 65, 152, 157
Mitosis, 44, 45
Moa, 189
Mockingbird, 205

Mock orange, 117
Moeris, Lake (now Birkit Qarun), 37
Moeritherium, 37
Mohs, Friedrich, 17
Mohs scale, 17
Mole, 56, 210
Mole rat, 216
Mollies, 177
Mollusc, 28, 29, 143, 144–5
 – life cycle, 146–47
Momotidae, 198
Momotus momota, 199
Monarch butterfly, 164, 165
Mongolia, 46, 225
Mongoose, 220, 221
Monitor, 182, 183
Monkey, 38, 77, 83, 214, 215, 236
Monkey puzzle tree, 103
Monkshood, 114, 115, 126
Monocotyledons, 104, 105, 107, 109, 110, 114, 120–21, 122
Monogenea, 138
Monoplacophora, 144
Monotremes, 37, 206, 208–209
Mont Pelée volcano, 16, 17
Moon, 12, 13
Moorhen, 193
Moose, 68, 69 (Elk in Europe)
Moraine, 21, 68
Morchella esculenta, 98
'Morepork', 196
Morgan, T. H. (1866–1945), 49
Morphine, 114, 115, 127
Moses sole, 176
Mosquito, 76, 135
Moss, 70, 78, 83, 92–3, 131
Moss animals, 142–43
Moths, 164–5
Mot-mots, 198, 199
Mouflon sheep, 78, 228
Mountain, zones of, 79
Mountain lion (cougar), 221
Mountains, 78–9
Mouse, 71, 82
 – jumping, 69
 – desert, 74
 – climbing, 77
 – house, 216
 – white, 216
Mucor, 96
Mud-puppy, 179
Mule-deer, 74
Musaceae, 120
Muscicapidae, 202, 205
Mushroom, 98–9
Musk-ox, 66, 67, 228–9
Muskrat, 81
Musophagidae, 201
Mussel, 61, 89, 145, 154, 191
 – freshwater, 147
Mustelidae, 223
Mutualism, 53
Mycelium, 96
Mycetozoa, 96
Myomorpha, 216–7
Myosotis sp., 118
Myrmeleotettix maculatus, 161
Myrmica ruginodis, 169
Mysid, 154
Mysidacea, 155
Mystacocarida, 154
Myxomycetes, 96

N

Nairobi Game Park, 238
Nannopterum harrisi, 189
Nansen jar, 58
Narcissus, 105
Narwhal, 219
Natantia, 155
Natterjack toad, 241
Natural selection, 50, 51
Nautilus, 145
Navigation, bird's, 187
Neanderthal Man, 39
Neanura, 159
Necklace shell, 60, 146
Nectar, 111, 114, 124, 165
Nekton zone, 58
Nematocysts, 136
Nematodes, 65, 138, 139, 143
Nemertea pelagonemertea, 138
Nemertines, 138
Nemesia, 118
Ne-ne goose (*see* Goose)
Neolithic Man, 233
Nesomicronus drepanoides, 83
Nest: birds', 187, 197, 203, 205
 – parasites', 199, 201
 (*and see* Cuckoo)
Neuroptera, 162
New Britain, 82
New Caledonia, 189
New Forest, 238
New Guinea, 77, 82, 183, 189, 192, 205
Newt, 178, 179
New Stone Age, 232
New Zealand, 71, 172, 188, 189, 192, 209
Ngorongoro Conservation Area, 239
Niagara Falls, 21
Nicotiana, 118
Nicotiana tobarum, 127
Nicotine, 127
Nigella damascena, 115
Nightjar, 196, 235 (*and see* Goatsucker)
Nightshade, 118
 – deadly, 126, 127
 – woody, 127
Nile river, 122
Nitrates, 87, 89
Nitrites, 87
Nitrogen, 24, 86, 87, 124
'Nitrogen-fixation', 86, 87, 95, 116
Nitro-glycerine, 89
Nitrous acid, 86
Nitrosomona, 86
Noctiluca, 88, 89
Norfolk, cliff erosion, 20
Norway spruce, 103
Nostoc (algae), 86, 87, 94
Notochord, 150, 151, 170, 171
Nucleus (of cell), 42, 43, 44
Numbat (banded anteater), 209
Nummulites, 134
Nyala, 132
Nyctibiidae, 196
Nymph, 160
Nymphalis antiopa, 164
Nymphalis io, 164

O

Oak, 56, 99, 106, 107, 109, 112, 131
 – as sacred tree, 235
 (*and see* Quercus)
Oarweed, 90, 91
Oats, 123
Obelia, 136
Obsidians, 17
Oceans, 24, 25, 58–9
Octopus, 60, 145, 146
Ocypus, 167
Ocypus olens, 167
Odonata, 161
Oenanthe sp., 117
Oil, 27
 – pipelines, 241
Oilbird, 196
Okapi, 227
Old man's beard, 112
Oligocene period, 37
Oligochaetes, 140
Olingo, 223
Olm, 179
Omnivores, 42
Onager, 225
Onion, 120, 121
Oniscus, 155
Onychophora, 152, 153
Opal, 17
Operculum, 142, 143
Ophidia, 183
Ophiuroidea, 149
Ophrys insectifera, 237
Opiliones, 157
Opisthobranchia, 145
Opisthocomidae, 201
Opisthocomus hoazin, 201
Opium poppy, 114, 115, 127
Opossum, 209
Opossum-shrimp, 154
Orange, 113
Orange-peel fungus, 98
Orang-utan, 38, 215
Orchid, 83, 121, 237
Orchidaceae, 121, 128
Orchil, 95
Ordovician period, 29
Orectolobus orhatus, 173
Organelles, 42, 86, 88
Oriole, 205
Oriolidae, 205
Ornithischians, 34
Orobanchaceae, 118
Orseille, 95
Orthoptera, 160
Oryx, 75, 229
 – Arabian, 241
Oscillatoria, 87
Oscines, 203, 204
Osprey, 194
Ossides, 207
Osteocytes, 171
Osteolepids, 29
Ostracod, 29
Ostracoda, 154
Ostrich, 73, 188, 189
Otididae, 193
Otter, 80, 81, 223
 – sea, 223
Otter civet, 221
Ounce, (leopard), 220, 221
Ovary, 110, 112, 118, 119, 122
Ovenbird, 203, 204, 205
Ovule, 103, 110, 112, 118, 119, 122
Owl, 57, 69, 70, 194, 195
 – snowy, 66, 67, 195
 – burrowing, 75
 – hearing, 195
 – sight, 195
Owlet, 196
Owl parrot, 188
Oxaletes, 126
Oxalis acetosella, 113
Oxfordshire, 35
Oxford University, 35
Oxpecker, 54
Oxygen, 16, 24, 30, 42, 43, 54, 62
 – in rivers, 80
 – and moss animals, 142
 – and amphibians, 178
 – and birds' lungs, 185
 – in breathing, 206, 207
Oyster, 145, 148, 149
Oystercatcher, 191

P

Pacific Ocean, 63, 82, 173, 176
Paddlefish, 175
Palaeocene epoch, 38
Palaeoecologist, 28
Palaeolithic age, 38
Palaeozoic era, 23, 29, 40, 145
Palm, 104, 121
Palmae, 121
Palmate leaf shape, 109, 117
Palm civet, 221
Palmella, 94
Palm swift, 197
Palmyra palm, 121
Palpigrades, 156
Pampas, 123
Pampas cat, 221
Panama, Isthmus of, 37
Pancake tortoise, 181
Panda, giant, 220, 222, 223
Pandion haliaëtus, 194
Pandionidae, 194
Pangolin, 211
Panther, 221
Papaver, 112
Papaveracaea, 115
Papaver rhoeas, 115
Papaver somniferum, 115
Papilio machaeon, 164
Papilionideae, 116
Papyrus grass, 81, 122, 235
Paradisaeidae, 205
Paradoxides, 28
Parakeet, 72, 73
Paramecium, 81, 135
Parapodia, 140
Parasites, 43, 54–5, 96, 163
Parasitism, 53, 54
Parasol mushroom, 99
Parchment worm, 140
Paridae, 205
Parmelia, 94
Parnassius apollo, 79
Parrot, 77, 200
 – Australian, 189
 – New Zealand, 189
Parrot fish, 63
Parsley, 117
Parsnip, 117
Parthenocissus tricuspidata, 128
Partridge, 201
Parulidae, 205
Pasang, 228
Passenger pigeon, 237
Passeriformes, 202–3
Pasteur, Louis (1822–1895), 49
Pastoral ant, 169
Pauropod, 153
Pea, 45, 111, 112, 117
Peach, 113, 116
Peacock butterflies, 164, 165
Peacock worm, 141
Pear, 116
Peat, 18, 27, 31, 93, 124
Peccary, 226
Pedicellariae, 149
Pedicularis sp., 118
Pedipalps, 156
Pegmatite, 17
Peking Man, 39
Pelagic zone, 58
Pelican, 190
Pelecanidae, 190
Pelecaniformes, 190
Pelecanoididae, 190
Peltigera canina, 95
Penguin, 66, 188, 189
Penicillium notatum, 97
Pentapora foliacea, 142
Penstemon, 118
Peony, wild, 240
Pepper, 118
Peppered moth, 50, 51
Peracarida, 155
Perch, 175
Perching birds, 204–5
Peregrine, 194
Perennation, 105
Perennials, 105, 118, 119
Perianth, 110
Pericarp, 112, 113
Peripatus, 153
Periwinkle, 61, 144, 147
Permian period, 15, 31, 32, 162
Perrisodactyla, 224
Perrisodactyls, 224
Persea, 112
Petiole, 109
Petrel, 190
Petunia, 118
Peziza aurantia, 98
Phaeophyta, 90, 91
Phaethon, 190
Phaethon aethereus, 82
Phalacrocoracidae, 190
Phalaenoptilus nuttallii, 196
Phalangers, 77, 209
Phalaropes, 187
Phalaropodidae, 187
Phanerozoic scale, 23
Phasmida, 160
Pheasant, 40, 71, 201
Philippines, 82, 203, 219
Phloem, 106, 107, 108, 109
Phoeniculidae, 198
Phoronids, 142
Phosphate, 26, 89
Photosynthesis, 42, 43, 54, 62, 88, 89, 90, 93, 95, 105, 108, 121, 129, 135
Phryganea, 162
Phycocyanin, 91
Phycoerythrin, 91
Phycomycetes, 97
Phyllitis scolopendrium, 100
Phyllobius urticae, 166
Phyllocarida, 155
Phyllotaxis, 109
Physalia, 137
Phytolaca, 126
Phytophthora infestans, 97
Phytoplankton, 89
Phytotoxin, 127
Picea, 103

Picea abies, 103
Picidae, 199, 202
Piciformes, 199
Picus viridis, 198
Piddock, 145
Pig, 226
– wild, 71, 226
Pigeon, 50, 200
Pika, 79, 217
Pike, 80, 81
Pill bug, 155
Pilot whale, 219
Pine, 99, 103
Pineapple, 113, 120
Pine hawk moth, 69
Pine marten, 68
Pinguicula, 125
Pink-headed duck, 236
Pin mould, 96
Pinnate leaf shape, 109
Pinus, 103
Pipefish, 174, 175, 177
Pipid toad, 179
Pipra mentalis, 204
Pipridae, 203, 204
Piranga olivacea, 203
Pisces, 174
Pitangus sulphuratus, 204
Pitcher plant, 124
Pitta, 203, 204
Pitta brachyura, 204
Pitta Gurneyi, 204
Pittidae, 203
Placenta, 206
Placentals, 206, 216
Placodonts, 32
Planarians, 139
Planctosphaeroidea, 150
Plane tree, 107
Plankton, 53, 58, 59, 62, 66, 88, 146, 151, 153, 155, 173
Plantain, 120
Plants, 84–5
– evolution of, 51
– and ecology, 52, 54
– with seed cones, 102–3
– parasites, 118
– poisonous, 126–7
– specialised, 128–9
– communities, 130–1
– and folklore, 234–5
– rare, 236–7
Plasma membrane, 42
Plasmodiophora brassicae, 96
Plasmodium, 135
Plastron, 180, 181
Plate, River, 218
Platies, 177
Platyhelminths, 138
Platypus, 208
Plecoptera, 161
Pleistocene epoch, 38, 39, 233
Plesiosaurus, 32, 33
Pleurococcus, 89
Pliny (AD 23–79), 48
Pliocene epoch, 38
Ploceidae, 186, 202, 205
Plott, Rev. R., 34–5
Plover, 191, 200
Plum, 113, 116
Plumule, 112
Plutonic rocks, 17
Pneumatophores, 128, 129
Podargidae, 196
Podargus, 196
Podophyllin, 126
Podophyllum peltatum, 126
Poisons: scorpions, 156
– spiders, 157
– butterflies and moths, 165
– fish, 176
– snakes, 182, 183
– lizards, 183
Poison ivy, 127
Poisonous plants, 126–7
Poison sumac, 127
Pokeweed, 126
Poland, 228, 233, 241
Polar bear, 66
Polar regions, 66–7, 92
Polecat, 70, 223
Polipodium vulgare, 100
Pollen, 110, 111, 119, 126
Pollination, 79, 103, 110, 111
– cross-pollination, 111
– self-pollination, 111
– by insects, 114, 163, 165
(*and see* Insects)
Pollinia, 121
Pollution, 50, 94, 240–41
Polychaetes, 53, 140, 143
Polyplacophora, 144
Polypodium ferns, 235
Polyps, 62, 63, 82, 88, 137
Polypteriformes, 175
Polystichum, 100
Polytrichum auranticum, 92
Polyzoans, 142
Pond-skaters, 161
Pondweed, 104, 131
Pony, Dartmoor, 46
Poor-will, 196
Poppy, 112, 113
– Arctic, 67
Population densities, 56–57
Porcupine, 217
Porcupine fish (*see* Burr-fish)
Porphyra sp., 91
Porpoise, 59, 218
Port Jackson shark, 173
Portuguese man-o-war (jellyfish), 59, 137
Possum, 77, 209
Potato, 45, 118–19, 126, 127
– blight, 97
Potentilla, 116
Poterium, 116
Potoos, 196
Potto, 214
Prairie dog, 73, 216
Prairie falcon, 74
Praunus flexuosus, 154
Prawn, 61
Praying mantis, 160
Pre-Cambrian period, 28
Pride system (lion pack), 220
Primaries (feathers), 204 (*and see* Birds)
Primates, 37, 38, 214–5
– intelligence of, 207
Primrose, 70, 111
Privet, 127
Proboscis (worm), 139, 140, 150
– insects, 164
– butterflies, 165
Proboscis monkey, 215
Proboscoidea, 224
Procellariidae, 190
Procellariiformes, 190
Proconsul, 38
Procyonidae, 223
Prokaryota, 84, 86–7, 88
Pronghorn, 72, 229
Prosobranchia, 14
Proteins, 24
Proterozoic era, 23
Prothallus, 101
Protochordates, 150
Protococcus, 94
Protoplasm, 25, 42, 96
Protozoa, 53, 81, 134–5, 142
– fossil, 134, 135
– parasitic, 134, 135
Protura, 159
Prunus spinosa, 131
Prussic acid, 126
Przewalski's horse, 46, 225
Psamma, 109
Psarisomus dalhpusiae, 203
Pseudocuma longicornis, 154
Pseudopodia, 134
Pseudoscorpion, 64, 65, 156
Psittacidae, 200
Psittaciformes, 200
Psychidae, 165
Ptarmigan, 201
Pteranodon, 32
Pteridium aquilinum, 100
Pteridophyta, 84
Pteridophytes, 100, 102
Pterobranchia, 150
Pterochidae, 200
Pterodactyl, 35
Pteropod, 58
Pterygota, 158
Pudu, 227
Puffball, 98, 99
Puffbird, 199
Puffer-fish, 176
Puffin, 190, 191
Pulmonata, 145
Puma, 69, 221
Pumice, 17
Pungitis pungitis, 177
Purple laver, 91
Pycnogonida, 156
Pycnonotidae, 205
Pygathrix nemaeus, 236
Pyrenees Mts., 79
– grottoes in, 21
Pyrenoid, 88
Pyrethrum, 119, 126
Pyrochroa serraticornis, 166
Pyrosoma sp., 151
Pythium sp., 97
Python, green, 183

Q

Quagga, 225
Quail, 201
Quartz, 17, 19
Quartzite, 19
Quercus (oak), 107, 112, 131
– *rubra* (red oak), 109
– *robur*, 109
– *suber* (cork oak), 107
Quiberon (Brittany), 20
Quillwort, 101

R

Rabbit, 37, 56, 216
– cottontail, 74
– and poison, 126
– varieties of, 217
Rabies, 77, 95, 213
Raccoon, 71, 220, 223
Radicle, 112
Radioactive dating method, 22
Ragweed, 119, 126
Ragworm, 140
Ragwort, 119
Raiätea (Polynesia), 62
Rails, 189, 193
Rainfall, 74, 76 (*and see* Desert)
Rain forests, 76, 104, 210, 215
Rajiformes, 172
Rallidae, 193
Ramalina, 94
Ramapithecus, 38
Ramphastidae, 199
Rana, 179
Rana temporaria, 179
Ranidae, 179
Ranunculaceae, 114
Ranunculus sp., 111, 126
Ranunculus aquatilis, 109
Raspberry, 116, 117
Rat, 82
– poison for, 127
– varieties of the, 216, 217
Ratel, 223
Ratfish, 172
Ratites, 188, 189
Rat-tail fishes, 59
Rattlesnake, 183
Ray, John (1627–1705), 46, 48
Rays, 172–3, 177
Ray-finned fishes, 29, 175
Rayless mayweed, 119
Razor shell, 61, 145
Reach (of rivers), 80
Red ant, 169
Red currant, 113, 117
Red deer, 71, 170
Red Indians, 234, 235
Red Sea, 176, 219
'Red tides', 89
Redwood, 84, 102
Reed-fish, 175
Reedmace, 104, 122
Reed warbler, 80
Refection (of food), 217
Reindeer, 67, 227
Remora, 53
Reptantia, 155
Reptiles, 31, 83, 180–81, 182–83
– brains of, 180
Requiem shark, 172
Respiration, 43
Reticularia lycoperdon, 96
Retriever, 232
Rhabopleura, 150
Rhacomitrium lanuginosum, 93
Rhagium bifasciatum, 166
Rhea, 73, 188
Rheidae, 188
Rhesus macaque, 215
Rhinanthus sp., 118
Rhinoceros, 37, 225, 236, 237
Rhizinae, 95
Rhizobium genus (bacteria), 87
Rhizoids, 92
Rhizomes, 100, 105, 120, 121
Rhizophora, 128
Rhodophyta, 90, 91
Rhodesia (ants), 169
Rhubarb leaf poison, 126
Rhus, 127
Rhynchocephalia, 180, 182
Rhynchopidae, 191
Rhynchops, 190
Rhynia, 30
Rhynochetos jubatus, 189
Rhyolite, 17
Ribbon-worm, 138, 139
Rice, 122, 123
Ricinin, 127
Ricinis communis, 127
Ricinulei, 157
Ricinuleids, 157
Rictal bristles, 196
Rivers, and erosion, 20–21
Roach, 80
Robin, 46, 57, 186, 187
Roccella, 95
Roccella tinctoria, 95
Rock dove, 200
Rock-hopper, 188
Rocky Mts., 15
Rocky Mountain goat, 79, 228
Rocks, 64
– igneous, 16–17
– Pre-Cambrian, 18, 22
– Metamorphic, 18, 19
– Secondary, 18–19
– Sedimentary, 18, 19, 20, 27
Rock salt, 18
Rodents, 27, 37, 56, 77, 78, 206, 207, 216–17
Roe deer, 68
Roller, 198
Roman mythology, 235
Roots: trees, 65
– desert plants, 74
– general, 106–7
– parasite plants of, 118
Rorqual, 219
Rosa canina, 131
Rosaceae, 116–17
Rose, 116, 117
Rosebay willowherb, 105
Rosemary, 119
Rotifer, 81, 142
Roundworm, 54, 139
Rove beetle, 167
Rubus, 116, 128
Rubus fruticosus, 131
Ruby, 17
Rudbeckia, 119
Ruminants, 226, 227, 228
Rush, flowering, 120
Rust disease, 97
Rye, 123

S

Sabella pavonina, 141
Sable, 223
Saccharum officinarum, 123
Saccoglossus Kowalevskii, 150
Sage, 119
Sagittaria sagittifolia, 109
Sagittaridae, 195
Sagittarius serpentarius, 195
Sahara Desert, 74
Saiga, 72, 229, 241
Sainfoin, 117
Saki, 214
Salad burnet, 116
Salamander, 178, 179
– species, 179

Salientia, 179
Salinity, 60
Salix Caprea, 112
Salp, 151
Salpa zonaria, 151
Salsify, 119
Salsola Kali, 128
Saltwort, 128
Sand, 64, 130
Sand-bank, 20
Sand-dunes, 130
Sand flea, 153
Sand-grouse, 75, 200
Sand hopper, 61
Sandpiper, 191
Sandstone, 18, 19
Sapphire, 17
Saprophytes, 96
Sarcophaga carnaria, 163
Sardinia, 78, 228
Sargasso Sea, 91
Sargassum nataus, 91
Sarothamnus scoparius, 129
Sauria, 182
Saurischians, 34
Savannah, 72 (*and see* Africa)
Sawbill, 193
Sawfly, 168
Saxifragacea, 117
Saxifraga cernua, 237
Saxifrage, drooping, 237
Saxifrages, 117
Scallop, 144, 145
Scampi, 155
Scaphopoda, 144
Scaphopod mollusc, 144, 145
Scavengers: seashore, 60, 61
 – insect, 152, 155, 159, 160, 162
 – beetle, 166, 222, 223
 – carnivorous, 221
 – and jackals, 222
Schizanthus, 118
Schizomida, 156–7
Schoenoplectus lacustris, 122
School (fish), 176
Scilly Isles, 17, 143
Scincidae, 182, 183
Sciuromorpha, 216
Sclerotina fructigena, 97
Scolopacidae, 191
Scorpion, 156, 157
Scorpiones, 156
Scorpion fly, 162
Scotland, 94, 239, 241
Scottish Highland Mts., 15
Scrophulariaceae, 118
Scrub-bird, 203
Scrupocellaria scruposa, 142
Scurvy, 115
Sea-anemone, 53, 60, 61, 63, 136, 137
Sea birds, 190–91
Sea couch grass, 130
Sea-cow, 218, 219
Sea cucumber, 59, 63, 148, 149
Sea, erosion by, 20
Sea fan, 63, 137
Sea gooseberry, 137
Seagull, 61
Sea horse, 175, 176, 177
Seal, 66, 83, 218, 219
 – varieties of, 219
Sea, life in the, 58–9
Sea lilies, 148, 149
Sealion, 219, 238
Sea lyme grass, 130
Sea mat, 142
Sea otter, 218
Sea pink, 128–9
Sea rocket, 130
Seashore, life on the, 60–61, 153
Sea slater, 61
Sea slug, 143, 144, 145, 146
Sea snail, 63, 144, 145, 146, 218
Sea-snake, 183
Sea spider, 143, 153
Sea squirt, 60, 150–51
Sea urchin, 29, 61, 63, 148, 149
'Sea-wasp', 137
Seaweed, 60–61, 88
Sea whip, 63
Secretary bird, 194, 195
Sedge, 122–3
Sedimentary rocks, 18, 19, 20, 27
 – dating, 23
Seed dispersal:
 – by animals, 113
 – by water, 113
 – by wind, 112, 113
Seed dormancy, 113
Self-heal plant, 119
Semionotiformes, 175
Senecio, 119
Sensitivity, of living things, 43, 88
Sepal, 110, 117, 118, 119 (*and see* Flowers)
Sequoia gigantea, 102
Sequoia sempervirens, 102
Serengeti National Park, 239
Serpentes, 183
Serpulids, 140
Serval, 221
Sewage-treatment, 135 (*and see* Bacteria)
Seychelles, 240
Seyouriamorphs, 31
Sexton beetle, 65
Shag, 190
Shale, 27
Shallot, 121
Shark, 53, 63, 172–73, 177
Sharpbill, 77
Shearwater, 190, 191
Sheep, 206, 228–9, 232
 – diseases of, 119, 138
Shelduck, 192
Sheld geese, 192–3
Shellfish, 88
Shepherd's purse, 105, 115
Shield fern, 100
Shingle banks, 20
Shipworm, 145
Shrew, 65, 69, 210, 211
Shrimp, 153, 154, 155
Siberia, 207
 – fossil remains, 26
Siberian tiger, 236
Sierra Nevada Mts., 15
Sifaka, 214
Silica, 17, 26, 88, 89, 101
Silicates, 19
Sills (rock formation), 17
Silphium laciniatum, 129
Silurian period, 29
Silver, 16, 17
Silverfish, 31, 159
Silverweed, 105
Siphonophores, 136–7
Sirens (urodela), 179
Siskin, 69
Sitatunga, 229
Skate, 173
Skeleton, 170, 171
 – reptile, 180
 – bird, 184–5
 – dog, man, 207
Skimmer, 190, 191
Skipjack, 167
Skua, 191
Slate, 19
Sleeping sickness, 135
Slime fungi, 131
Slime mould, 96
Slipper limpet, 146
Sloth, 77, 210, 211
Slug, 65, 144, 145, 146
Smilodon, 27, 37
Sminthurinus, 159
Smithornis capensis, 203
Smut, 97 (*and see* Fungus)
Snail, 65, 144, 145, 146, 147
Snake: 'sidewinding' type, 74, 75
 – flying, 76
 – skeleton of, 171
 – poisonous, 182, 183
Snake fly, 162
Snowdrop, 121
Snow leopard, 220
Socrates, 127
Social insects, 168–9
Soil: life in the, 64–5
 – and grasses, 72
 – types of, 130–1
 – and worm 'casts', 141
Solanaceae, 118–119
Solanum, 126
Solanum dulcamara, 127
Solanum tuberosum, 105
Solaster papposus, 148
Solifugae, 156
Sonneratia, 128
Soredria, 95
Sorghum, 123
'Soup', primeval, 25
South Africa, 90, 102, 141
Southern pine sawyer, 68
South Pole, 66 (*and see* Antarctic)
Sow thistle, 119
Soya bean, 117
Spade-foot toad, 179
Spain (cave paintings), 39
Spanish moss, 92, 120
Sparrow, 202
Sparrow-hawk, 195
Spearmint, 119
Species (*see* Classification of Plants and Animals)
Speckled bush cricket, 161
Speedwell, 118
Spermatophores, 179
Spermatophyta, 84
Sphaeridae, 147
Sphagnum moss, 92, 93, 131
Spheniscidae, 188
Sphenisciformes, 188
Spider, 31, 65, 69, 78, 83, 152, 156
Spindle tree, 160
Spinetail, 203
Spiraea, 116
Spirogyna, 90
Sponge, 60, 63, 88, 136
Spoonbill, 193
Sporangia, 30, 95, 96, 97, 100, 101, 102, 103, 110
Spore, 93, 97, 98
 – wind-borne, 93, 99, 101, 103
 – and ferns, 101
 – pollen grains, 110–111
Springbok, 229
Spring gentian, 237
Spring hare, 216
Springtail, 64, 65, 78, 159
Spruce, 103
Spruce grouse, 69
Spurge hawk moth caterpillar, 165
Spurge plants, 127
Squamata, 180, 182
Squamulose lichens, 95
Squid, 59, 144, 145, 146, 147, 173
Squilla mantis, 155
Squirrel, 37, 68, 71, 83, 216
 – flying, 69, 77, 216
 – ground, 73
 – antelope, 74
Sri Lanka (Ceylon), 104, 204
Stable fly, 163
Stag beetle, 70
Staghorn coral, 63 (*and see* Coral)
Stamens, 110, 111, 116, 117, 118, 119
 – in sedges, 122
St. Anthony's Fire (rye bread poisoning), 97
St. Anthony's Fire (erysipelas), 97
Starch, 109
Starfish, 60, 61, 63, 143, 148–9, 170
Starling, 202
St. Cuthbert (d.AD 687), 238
Steamer duck, 189
Steatornis carinensis, 196
Steatornithidae, 196
Stems, 106–7
Stenophylax, 162
Stentor, 134
Stentor coeruleus, 134
Stephanaetus coronatus, 194
Steppe, 123
Stercoratiidae, 191
Stick insects, 160
Stickleback, 177
Stenus bimaculatus, 166
Stigma, 110
Stilts, 191
Stinging nettle, 127
Sting-ray, 173
Stinkhorns, 99
St. John's wort, 235
St. Kilda, 232
Stoat, 56, 68, 70, 223
Stomate, 108
Stomatoids, 59
Stone fly, 80, 161
Stonewort, 91
Stork, 193
Strathclyde fossils, 29
Stratigraphy, 22–3
Straw, 123
Strawberry, 113, 116
Strigiformes, 194
Strigops habroptilus, 188, 189
Struthio camelus, 188
Struthiomidae, 188
Strychnine, 126, 127
Strychnos nux vomica, 126, 127
Strychnos toxifera, 127
Sturgeon, 174, 175
Sturnidae, 202
Sturnidoecus sturni, 160
Style, 110
Stylet (of worm), 139, 141
Sub-oscines, 202, 204
Suffolk, cliff erosion, 20
Sugar: in photosynthesis, 108–9
 – cane, 123
Sulidae, 186, 190
Sulphur, 16, 86
Sulphuric acid, 86
Sumatra, 215
Sunbird, 77
Sundews, 125
Sunflower oil, 119
Sun spiders, 156
Sunstars, 148
Surinam toad, 178
'Survival of the fittest' (*see* Evolution)
Sussex Downs, 230
Swallow, 187, 202
Swallowtail caterpillar, 164
Swamp, 81
Swamp cypress, 103, 129
Swan, 192
Sweet pea, 44, 116
Sweet potato, 118
Sweet rosemary, 119
Swift, 197, 202
Swimbladder, 174, 175
Sycamore, 108, 112
Syenite, 17
Sylviidae, 205
Symbionts, 96
Symbiosis, 53, 88, 94, 116, 121
Sympathetic magic, 234
Symphyla, 153, 168
Synallaxinae, 204
Syncarida, 155
Syriax, 204
Syrphus ribesii, 163
Systema Naturae (*see* Linnaeus)

T

Tabanidae, 163
Taboo, 234
Tachyeres, 189
Tadpole, 178, 179
Tahr, 79, 228
Taiga (*see* Tundra)
Taiwan, 82
Takir, 228
Talc, 17
Tapioca, 126
Tamandua, 211
Tanagers, 77, 202, 203, 205
Tanning (arthropods), 152
Tanzania meteorite, 25
Tapeworm, 54, 55, 138
Tapir, 224, 225
Taraxacum bicorne, latex from, 119
Tarpan, 46, 225
Tarsier, 214, 215
Tartarides, 156–7
Tasmania, 208
Tasmanian devil, 209
Tasmanian wolf, 73, 209
Tassel-fin, 174
Taueret, 235
Taxine, 126
Taxodium distichum, 129
Taxonomy, 46–7
 – zoologists' orders, 202
Taxus baccata, 126
Tayra, 223
Teeth:
 – mammals, 207
 – hamsters, 216, 217
 – rabbits and hares, 216, 217
 – carnivores, 220
Teleosts, 174, 175

Temperature, body, 206, 207
Tendrils, 109, 128
Tenebrionid beetle, 75
Tenrecs, 210
Termites, 53, 65, 169, 223
Tern, 191
Terrapin, 181
Territorial instincts, 57
Territory, birds', 186
Tersiphone paradisi, 82
Tertiary period, 37
Testa, 112
Testudinidae, 181
Tetanus, 87
Teton Range Mts., 15
Tetratoma fungorum beetle, 65
Thaliacea, 151
Thallophyta, 84
Thatching sedge, 122
Thecodonts, 32, 33
Thermobia domestica, 159
Thiobacillus, 86
Thistle, 119
Thoracica, 155
Thorn-apple, 126, 127
Thoth, 234
Thraupidae, 202, 205
Threskiormithidae, 193
Thrips, 161
Thrush, 57, 202, 205
'Thunder flies', 161
Thylacine (*see* Tasmanian wolf)
Thyme, 119
Thysanoptera, 161
Thysanura, 159
Tibet, 228
Ticks, 54, 152, 157
Tides, 13
Tiger, 220, 221
  – sabre-toothed, 37
  – Siberian, 68
Tillandsia usneoides, 120
Timothy grass, 123
Tin, 17
Titanium, 13
Titanus giganteus, 167
Titi, 214
Titmice, 69, 71, 205
Tits, 57, 205
Toad, spade-foot, 74
Toadstools, 99, 103
Tobacco, 118
  – plant, 127
Toddy cat, 221
Todidae, 198
Todies, 198, 199
Tomato, 118, 127
Tomarctus, 232
Toothcarp, 177
Tooth shell, 144, 145
Top shell, 146
Topaz, 17
Tortoise, 32, 83
  – desert, 74
  – Mediterranean, 181
  – giant Galapagos, 180, 181
Totem pole, 234
Toucan, 77, 199
Touraco, 201
Trachodon, 32
Transpiration (leaf), 106, 109
Trebouxia, 94
Tree, 31, 52
  – in mythology, 235
  (*and see* different species)
Tree creepers, 202
Tree frog, 179
Tree lungwort, 94
Tree toads, 179
Trematodes, 138
Trentepohlia, 94
Triassic period, 32
Triceratops, 35
Trichodesmium, 87
Trichoptera, 162
Trilobites, 27, 28, 29
Trionyx sp., 180
Tripod fish, 59
Triton shell, 63
Trochili, 197
Trochilidae, 197
Tropical forests, 76–7, 212
Tropic-bird, 190
Truffle, 98
Trumpet fish, 63
Trypanosoma, 135
Tsavo National Park, 239
Tsetse fly, 135
Tuatara, 180, 182
Tuber sp. (truffle), 98
Tuber (potato), 105, 118, 126
Tubifex worm, 81
Tuco-tuco, 217
Tulip, 120
Tundra, 66–7, 229
Tunicates, 150
Tunnels (for badgers and foxes), 241
Tunny fish, 58, 59
Turbellarians, 138
Turdidae, 202, 205
Turkey (bird), 201
Turtle, 32, 58, 83, 180–81
Tusk shell, 144, 145
Typhoid fever, 87
Typhus, 217
Tyrannosaurus Rex, 33, 35
Tyranni, 202, 203
Tyrannidae, 202, 203
Tyrannus, 204

U

Uintatherium, 36, 37
Ulex, 112, 130
Ulmus, 112
Ulva, 90
Ulva lactuca, 90
Umbelliferae, 117
Ungulates, 36, 37, 224–5, 228
Unio, 147
Upupa epops, 198, 199
Upupidae, 198
Uranium, 22, 238
Urial, 228
Urochordata, 150, 151
Urocystis anemones, 97
Urodela, 178–9
Uropygi, 156, 157
Uros, 233
Ursidae, 222
Urticaceae, 127
Urushiol, 127
Usnea, 94
Ussher, James (1581–1656), 22
USSR, 72, 123
Utricularia, 124–5

V

Vampire bat, 77 (*and see* Bat)
Van Leeuwenhoek, Anton (1632–1723), 48, 134
Varamidae, 183
Vascular cambium, 114
Vascular system (plants), 106
Veld, 72, 123, 229
Velamen, 128
Velvet worm, 153
Venom (*see* Poison entries)
Venus fly trap, 125
Veronica, 118
Verrucaria, 94
Vertebrae, 170–1
Vestiaria coccinea, 82
Vetch, 130
Viceroy butterfly, 165
Vicuña, 78, 227
Vietnam, 236
Viper, 183
Virginia creeper, 128
Viruses, 42, 43
Viscacha, 217
Viscum, 105
Viscum album, 235
Vitamin C, 115
Viverridae, 221
Volcano, 10, 15, 16, 17, 19
  – volcanic rocks, 17
  – and coral reefs, 62, 63, 82
Vole, 67, 216, 217
Volute, 146
Volvox, 88
Vorticella, 135
Vulture, 194, 195

W

Waders, 190, 191
Wading birds, 193
  – Polar regions, 67
Wallaby, 209
Wallace, A. R., 50, 51
Wall creeper birds, 78
Wallflowers, 110
Walnut, 108
Walrus, 219
Wapiti (elk), 227
Warbler, 71, 205
Warthog, 226, 227
Wasp, 158
  – social, 169
Water, and life process, 42, 43, 64, 74
  – and animals, 136–7
Water boatman, 161
Waterbuck, 229
Water crowfoot, 104, 109
Water dock, 81
Water dropwort, 117
Water flea, 81, 124, 136, 154, 155
Water forget-me-not, 80
Water lilies, 69, 80, 104, 129, 131
Water mint, 104
Water plantain, 109
Water-scorpion, 54
Water spider, 156, 157
Water storage pitchers, 128
Water tiger, 161
Watson, J. D. (1928–), 49
Weasel, 68, 70, 71, 222–3
Weaverbirds, 186, 202, 205
  – nests of, 205
Weaver finch, 204
Web (of spider), 156
Weevil, 167
Wegener, Alfred, 14, 15
Wellingtonia, 102
Western rock-skink, 74
West Indies, 167, 198, 219
Wet rot fungus, 98
Whale, 32, 37, 59, 66, 155, 218, 219
  – species of, 218–219
  – sperm, 59, 145, 219
Whalebone, 218
Wheat, 123, 233
Whelk, 144, 146
Whip-poor-will, 196
Whip scorpion, 156
Whirligig beetle, 166
Whitethroat, 54
Wild boar, 226, 227 (*and see* Pig)
Wild cat (European), 221
Wild dog (Asia), 222
Wildebeeste, 229
Wildfowl, 192–3
Wildfowl Trust, Slimbridge, Glos., 192, 240–41
Wild oats, 123
William the Conqueror, 238
Willow, 67, 131
Wind, 83
  – erosion by, 20
  – seed and spore dissemination, 95, 99
  – pollination by, 110, 111
  – pollination of grasses, 122
Wind scorpions, 156
Windscale Nuclear Plant, 241
Wings, 196, 197 (*and see* Birds)
Woad, 115
Wobbegong, 173
Wolf, 37, 67, 69, 72–3, 222
  – and man, 232
Wolff, Kaspar Friedrich (1733–1794), 48
Wolverine, 68, 223
Wombat, 208, 209
Wood anemone, 70
Wood ant, 169
Wood Buffalo National Park (Alberta), 239
Woodcreepers, 202, 203
Woodlark, 205
Woodlouse, 154, 155
Woodpecker, 69, 70, 71, 198, 199, 202
Wood sorrel, 113
Wood wasp, 168
Wood wasp, giant, 68, 69, 71
Worms, 138–9
  – earthworms, 56, 65, 140, 141, 152
  – seashore, 61
  – great African, 141
  – segmented, 140–41
  – acorn, 150
Wracks (*see* Seaweed, Algae)
Wrasse, 63
Wren, 71
  – New Zealand, 203

X

Xantheria lichen, 94
Xantheria varietina, 94
Xenicidae, 203
Xerophyte, 128, 129
Xylem, 106, 108, 109

Y

Yak, 79, 228
Yangtse River, 218
Yapok, 209
Yarrow, 119
Yeast, 97
Yellow cress, 105
Yellow flag plant, 81, 104
Yellow meadow ant, 169
Yellow rattles, 118
Yellowstone National Park, 238
Yellowstone River, 21
Yew, 103, 126, 127
Yugoslavia, 179

Z

Zebra, 45, 46, 72, 225, 229
Zebu, 229
Zinc, 17
Zinnia, 119
Zonation, 60
Zoological Gardens, 238, 240–41
Zosteraceae, 120
Zygote, 101

Acknowledgments

The publishers would like to thank the following individuals and organizations for their kind permission to reproduce the photographs in this book:

Heather Angel 10–11, 40–41, 55, 84–85, 90 above, 91, 92 above left, 92 below, 93 above, 93 below, 94 below, 94 above left and right, 95 above, 96 above and below, 97 below, 97 above right, 124, 131, 137, 139 below, 140, 141, 143, 149, 151 above, 171, 237 right; Ardea (L. R. Beames) 237 left, (M. D. England) 240–241 below, (K. W. Fink) 236 below, 238 left, (B. Gibbons) 110, (J. Gooders) 185, (S. Gooders) 54, 117, 234 above, (S. Gooders/ Linnaeus Society) 47, (P. J. Green) 189, (E. Lindgren) 82, (J. L. Mason) 92 right, 156, (E. Mickleburgh) 90 below, (P. Morris) 122, (V. Taylor) 62, 138, (A. Weaving) 129; Bio-Arts 160; Ron Boardman 53; By Courtesy of the Bodleian Library (Filmstrip 228. 9/8) 48 above, (227. 1/16) 48 below, (205 N/6) 49; Camera Press (Nasa/Pickerell) 15; Bruce Coleman 97 above left, (D. Bartlett) 45, (Jane Burton) 241 above right, (Bruce Coleman) 240 above, (N. Devore) 62 above, (G. Laycock) 236 above, (A. Power) 173, (H. Reinhard) 220, 236 centre; Gene Cox 87 above, 88–89, 90 centre; Gerald Cubitt 132–133; Douglas Dickens 17; Werner Forman Archive 234 below left, 234 below right, 235 above; Hale Observatories 13; Robert Harding Associates 230–231, (John G. Ross) 6–7; Eric Hosking 198; Alan Hutchison Library 8–9; Stephen Lowe 23; William McQuitty 4–5; Len Moore 29; Tony Morrison 76; Natural Science Photos (C. Banks) 183, (G. Montalverne) 142–143; NHPA 89, (A. Bannister) 75, (J. B. Blossom) 109, (D. Dickens) 226, (H. Lund) 87 below, (E. H. Rao) 225, (B. Wood) 151 below; Oxford Scientific Films 88 centre, 88 below, 134 above, 134 below, 135, 139 above, 142–143 below, 168; Picturepoint endpapers, 19, 175, 239 above; Bob Pope 159; Joyce Pope 71, 86, 143 right, 235 below; Spectrum 144, 155, 206, 238 right, 238–239; John Topham Picture Library (Christine Foord) 95 below; R. T. Way 20; Worldwide Butterflies (Robert Goodden) 165; ZEFA (Heydemann/Muller) 176, (E. Hummel) 27.

Illustrators

Mike Atkinson 60, 61, 63, 72, 73; John Barber 74, 75, 78, 79, 82, 83, 210, 211, 213, 216, 217, 218, 219, 220, 221, 222, 223, 232, 233; David Baxter 100, 101; Thelma Bissex 46, 47, 51, 66, 67; Wendy Bramall 124, 125, 130, 131, 170, 171, 208, 209; Giovanni Caselli 212, 224, 225, 226, 227; Lyn Cawley 16, 17, 50, 52, 53, 98, 99, 114, 115, 126, 127, 128, 129; Patrick Cox 106, 107, 120, 121; Andrew Farmer 12, 22, 23, 24, 25, 28, 29, 102, 103; Roger Gorringe 152, 153, 158, 159, 160, 161; Tim Hayward 111, 112, 113, 164, 165, 184, 185, 186, 187, 236; Ernest Hyde 228, 229; Frank Kennard 42, 43, 134, 135, 170; Richard Lewington 156, 157, 162, 163, 166, 167, 168, 169; Ken Lilly 196, 197, 198, 199, 253; Tom McArthur 14, 15, 18, 20, 21; Robert Morton 76, 77, 188, 189, 190, 191, 192, 193; Alex Murphy 148, 149; Colin Newman 136, 137, 138, 139, 140, 141, 150, 151, 154, 155, 172, 173, 174, 175; David Nockels 26, 32, 33, 34, 35, 36, 37, 38, 39, 54, 55, 56, 57, 64, 65, 80, 81, 206, 207; Thea Nockels 26, 27, 79; Gillian Platt 176, 177; Eric Robson 13, 43, 52, 68, 77, 144, 145, 146, 147, 214, 215; Basil Smith 108, 109; Kathleen Smith 116, 117, 118, 119; Charlotte Snooke 68, 69, 70; Ralph Stobart 33, 35, 37, 39, 49, 51, 58, 59, 86, 87; Rod Sutterby 27, 30, 31, 38, 44, 45; George Thompson 178, 179, 180, 181, 182, 183; Graeme Wilkins 108, 237; Ken Wood 194, 195, 200, 201, 202, 203, 204, 205; Elsie Wrigley 104, 105, 122, 123.